Rights-based Litigation, Urban Governance and Social Justice in South Africa

Rights-based Litigation, Urban Governance and Social Justice in South Africa considers the overlap between legal and everyday struggles for social and spatial justice in the particular context of Johannesburg, South Africa. Drawing from literature across disciplines of law, urban geography and urban planning, as well as from reported case-law concerning the invocation of constitutional rights in Johannesburg and other South African cities, the book critically examines whether, and to what extent, the invocation of legal rights before South African courts have contributed to the advancement of social justice in the city. It considers the impact of the legal assertion of different constituent aspects of the so-called 'right to the city' on the many people simultaneously performing the right, the governance structures responsible for enabling and facilitating its enjoyment and the physical place in which it is performed. Drawing broad conclusions on the utility of rights-based litigation for the achievement of social change and spatial justice, this book will be of interest to students and scholars of South Africa, constitutional law, human rights law, regulatory law, sociology of rights, studies of law and society, urban studies, urban geography, governance studies and development studies.

Marius Pieterse is Professor of Law at the University of the Witwatersrand, South Africa.

Routledge Contemporary South Africa

1 **#FeesMustFall and Youth Mobilisation in South Africa**
Reform or Revolution?
Musawenkosi W. Ndlovu

2 **Rights-based Litigation, Urban Governance and Social Justice in South Africa**
The Right to Joburg
Marius Pieterse

Rights-based Litigation, Urban Governance and Social Justice in South Africa

The Right to Joburg

Marius Pieterse

Routledge
Taylor & Francis Group
LONDON AND NEW YORK

First published 2017
by Routledge

2 Park Square, Milton Park, Abingdon, Oxfordshire OX14 4RN
52 Vanderbilt Avenue, New York, NY 10017

Routledge is an imprint of the Taylor & Francis Group, an informa business

First issued in paperback 2019

British Library Cataloguing in Publication Data
A catalogue record for this book is available from the British Library

Library of Congress Cataloging in Publication Data
A catalog record for this book has been requested

ISBN: 978-1-138-05928-3 (hbk)
ISBN: 978-0-367-88865-7 (pbk)

Typeset in Times New Roman
by Wearset Ltd, Boldon, Tyne and Wear

Contents

Preface and acknowledgements

I was probably 10 or 11 years old when, somewhere on the East Rand in the mid-1980s, I read about the sins, troubles and bright lights of Johannesburg in a salacious magazine article and solemnly promised myself that, come what may, I would one day live there. I am proud of having kept that promise and also of having written this book, an attempt to understand just some aspects of life in this endlessly fascinating city.

Thanks to the many colleagues, friends and family members who have provided support throughout the writing of this book. Neil Murray, Lea Bonthuys, Elsje Bonthuys, Amanda Spies and Thomas Coggin deserve special mention for their encouragement and moral support, for which I am extremely grateful.

The research in this book was enabled by a grant from the National Research Foundation of South Africa, for which I am very thankful. Thanks also to the many years of institutional support from the School of Law at the University of the Witwatersrand.

Marius Pieterse
Johannesburg
January 2017

1 Johannesburg as a site for rights

Introduction: on rights and place

Legal rights are sometimes criticised for being abstract, technically complex, contradictory and difficult to invoke, as well as for being fixated on procedure and being removed from the real experiences and needs of their beneficiaries.[1] This is also the case with so-called 'socio-economic rights', which are rights purporting to address the satisfaction of fundamental human needs, for instance, for housing, food, water and health care. The legal process, it is sometimes asserted, is not the ideal vehicle through which to obtain the satisfaction of such needs. This is due to its inaccessibility, its complexity, its tediousness and cost, its tendency to favour the interests of economically powerful sectors of society and to privilege the maintenance of the status quo, as well its contradictory powers to disrupt, reconfigure, valorise or ossify social relations.[2]

Yet, because of these very same powers, it is also often claimed that legal rights present some of the few effective political tools by means of which to confront the denial of human needs.[3] The legal process, moreover, holds the potential to enhance the participation of marginalised sectors of society in its affairs, and to insist that their interests be afforded due weight in decisions, policies and processes that impact on their lives and on the exercising of their rights.[4] Legal rights can therefore be empowering, equalising, constructive and transformative, while legal processes, regardless of their outcomes, can 'open up new possibilities for politics'.[5]

In evaluating the impact of legal rights on the lives of their beneficiaries, it is, however, necessary to understand rights as being much more than the legal iteration of individual entitlements. Indeed, their articulation and enforcement through the legal process is but one (albeit particularly high-profile) way in which rights are conceived and asserted. Much more commonly, rights are *lived*, performed through a range of human actions and interactions in an infinite array of everyday settings.[6] Far from being passive recipients of entitlements, goods and permissions from some benevolent authority, the bearers of rights are autonomous agents who, through their actions and relationships, assert their worldview, satisfy their needs and claim their space in society.[7]

Such a performative conception of human rights allows for a focus on the capabilities and agency of performers, the private as well as public nature of rights-performances and the relational nature of competing rights-claims. By looking at *where*, *how* and *with* or *through whom* people satisfy their needs and assert their capacities, against each other as well as against external sources of power, in the course of their everyday lives, we learn about the meaning of rights for their beneficiaries and develop an appreciation for the power of rights, their relationality, their interdependence, their contingency and their limits. Understood thus, the legal assertion of rights is but one way in which rights are performed, and the outcomes of legal processes aimed at vindicating rights are forces that structure the everyday performance of competing rights rather than to constitute the be-all and end-all of the rights themselves.[8]

Central to the performance of human rights is the *place* where they are acted out. People are shaped by their physical environments and, in turn, constitute and fashion these environments through their actions and interactions. Everyday life in a particular place is therefore constantly shaped and reshaped by myriad personal, environmental, social and political factors. Given that they are performed differently, by different people in a variety of physically situated contexts, the meaning of rights, as well as their impact on the lives of their beneficiaries, will differ depending on the place where they are performed.[9] Furthermore, the assertion of rights will have a bearing not only on their human subjects, but also on the physical environment in which these subjects find themselves.

This book aims to better understand the interaction between rights, people and place in relation to the city of Johannesburg (or Joburg, as it is often colloquially known and as it will regularly be referred to throughout this work). An immensely complex and contradictory place, which has been described as 'a heterogeneous assemblage of [radically different] mini-cities incongruously linked to form a contrived, illusory whole',[10] Johannesburg is South Africa's largest, richest, most diverse and (arguably) most fraught and contested urban centre. As the bedrock of the South African economy and home to the most representative cross-section of the South African population, Johannesburg has become a site and a symbol of South Africa's progress toward societal reconstruction and transformation in the aftermath of apartheid, much as it also very visibly continues to exemplify the hardships and inequalities occasioned by apartheid's injustices.[11]

The South African Constitution of 1996 envisages the wholesale transformation of South African society from its past of inequality, oppression and exclusion, into a future 'based on democratic values, social justice and fundamental human rights'.[12] Importantly, the Constitution regards fundamental human rights as the prime legal tools through which this transformation is to be achieved and to this end guarantees a large number of justiciable civil and political rights, as well as socio-economic rights, in its Bill of Rights. Since the Constitution's proclamation, the fundamental rights in the Bill of Rights have been invoked in a large variety of legal and physical contexts and have irrevocably altered South Africa's legal and political landscapes. In this book, I aim to better understand the impact of this invocation on Johannesburg's physical landscape, as well as on the way that the city is governed and on the ways in which its inhabitants perform rights in their everyday lives. This is apt because Johannesburg, and particularly its inner city, has itself been the actual site of a significant number of these legal rights struggles.

In a rapidly urbanising world, where cities are increasingly regarded as principal focus points for development and as prime engines of poverty alleviation, and where struggles over the use and control of urban space are increasingly articulated in rights-based terms, it is becoming increasingly necessary to study the manner in which legal, rights-based struggles and processes interact with and impact on urban development.[13] Given that Johannesburg embodies a vast array of contemporary urban developmental challenges and that it exists in a constitutional dispensation explicitly requiring a rights-based approach to development, it presents a particularly viable site for such study.

This book, therefore, presents a predominantly desk-based investigation into the interactions between the everyday performances and legal assertion of human rights in Johannesburg. It analyses the content of reported court decisions in matters concerning the invocation, balancing or limitation of a range of fundamental rights in an urban context, focusing on those cases that played off in Johannesburg, but also including landmark cases pertaining to urban rights assertion in other South African cities and towns. In doing so, it not only aims to present a full account of South Africa's burgeoning urban rights jurisprudence, but also to enable a pragmatic contemplation of the impact of the judgments studied, on their subjects, urban social movements, the city and various arms of the State.

Drawing from literature across disciplines of law, sociology, urban governance, urban geography and urban planning, and supplemented with insights from, first, press reports on the context and aftermath of particular court cases and, second, my own public realm observations in several of the locations of legal conflict across the city, this contemplation aims to contribute to the growing understanding of the potential and limits of rights-based litigation in effecting social change, as well as to the nascent literature on the bureaucratic impact of legal processes and the concomitant articulation between judicial rights-vindication and rights-based governance.

In the remainder of this introductory chapter, I aim to further theorise and contextualise the performance of rights in Johannesburg and to set the stage for the focused contemplations of particular incidences of rights-based struggle in the city that are to follow. I start by briefly expositing and explaining theory on the so-called 'right to the city', a concept rooted in socialist-leaning urban planning literature which, I argue, usefully contextualises the performance of rights in urban space and sheds light on the interactions between the various legal rights that are routinely implicated in urban settings. Significantly broader and more layered than conventional legal understandings of rights, the 'right to the city' represents the competing claims of all urban residents to the spoils of urban life and should accordingly be understood as underlying all performances of rights in Johannesburg. As such, it is at once enabled, configured and constrained by legal invocations of rights in the city.

Thereafter, I introduce what I regard as the three leading forces in legal struggles over rights to Johannesburg, over and above the people whose actions and interactions constitute the right to the city. Joburg itself is presented first, through a brief account of its history, its development, its issues and its people. At once the stage for, the object of, and a central player in the performance of rights to the city, Johannesburg is a microcosm of urban South African society and a test case for the achievement of the nation's constitutional vision.

Next in line is Joburg's government, the Johannesburg Metropolitan Council and its various subsidiaries (often referred to here as 'the City'), which is constitutionally charged with achieving this vision in and for the city. Representing citizens' primary encounter with State power in legal and everyday disputes over life in the city,[14] the City, through the workings of its bureaucracy and law enforcement, and the reactions of its various arms to the outcomes of rights-based legal processes, is obviously central to shaping, enabling and limiting the everyday performances of right to the city across the metropolis.

Finally, the Constitution, the rights it contains and the courts that are charged with enforcing these, are obviously crucial determining forces of the contours of the right to the city in Johannesburg. A brief overview of the rights in the Bill of Rights is provided, followed by a cursory discussion of the powers of courts in constitutional matters, which focuses mainly on the interpretative and remedial powers of the Constitutional Court, the highest court on constitutional matters in South Africa (which, not insignificantly, is physically located in central Johannesburg). The way in which the Court understands and enforces the various constitutional rights that are the legal constituents of the right to the city is an obvious indicator of the extent to which the right will find legal expression in urban South Africa, and is therefore a central focus of the inquiry in this book.

To conclude the chapter, I introduce and relate the thematic focus areas for the remainder of the book, and show how these contribute to the overall inquiry into the effects of rights-based litigation on the performance and continuous balancing of rights in the city.

The right to the city[15]

Originating at the time and in the political context of the 1968 French student riots and thereafter developed by left-leaning writers on city planning, architecture and urban design, the 'right to the city' was first articulated in the work of French philosopher Henri Lefebvre, who regarded it as a 'cry and a demand' by urban insurgents, marginalised masses and malcontents, to be accommodated in city life, to share in the spoils of the city and to participate in the making and remaking of the urban form.[16] The right is constantly performed through the actions of everyday life, and consists of elements of habitation (inhabiting the city through physical presence, ranging from simply being in the city to making a home and a living there) appropriation (using city space for the fulfilment of personal aspirations through a wide array of actions, ranging from accessing and using essential urban services to satisfy basic survival needs, to artistic expression, sexual activity and political protest) and participation (to participate in the making and remaking of the city, whether through formal legal and policy channels or through actions that themselves alter the city's shape, form or feel).[17]

While Lefebvre's conception of the right to the city was mainly focused on the performance of these actions by the urban poor and working classes (who, by exercising the right, at once draw attention to their concerns, demand the accommodation thereof and contribute to shaping authorities' response thereto), it can easily be construed more broadly, to also pertain to the actions and interactions of other marginal urban inhabitants (such as those who have been sidelined by mainstream society for reasons of their race, citizenship or sexual preferences)[18] and even of those urban residents who do possess power and resources.

The object of the right to the city is the physical form of the city itself, which is constantly constituted, altered and reconstituted by the performances of all who inhabit, appropriate or participate in it. Lefebvre described the city as an oeuvre, an ever-changing work in perpetual progress by an infinite number of different authors, all of whom have different intentions, priorities and views of what the city is or should be.[19] The city is thus at once the stage on which the right to the city is asserted, as well as its object, having come into being and forever continuing to evolve precisely through infinite enactments of the right. Importantly, as an eternal performance by multiple actors, the right to the city, much like its object, is not a stable concept and clashes over its content are multiple and regular. Indeed, conflict and struggle are central to the right, and its object is neither ever fully achieved nor ever fully defined.[20]

It is not only the city that is constituted through the multiple enactments of the right thereto – residents are also individually and collectively shaped through their multiple interactions in and with the city, so that an urban citizen and her personal identity emerges from interaction both with the physical form of the city and with all the other individual actions and identities that continuously shape it. This, what Lefebvre called 'individualization in socialization',[21] affirms the geographic specificity of individual rights performances and also explains the interaction between individual identity and communal city life, leading David Harvey to observe that 'the right to the city is far more than the individual liberty to access urban resources: It is a right to change ourselves by changing the city'.[22] Moreover, it calls to mind Iris Marion Young's notion of city life as a form of political community, arising from the city as a diverse melting pot of unassimilated difference, where people who have little in common with one another nevertheless form a community (albeit an often far from harmonious one) based on their sharing of urban space and their overlapping experiences of city life. In such a community, individuals are moulded, and ultimately enriched, through their contact and conflict with others who are (sometimes radically) different from them.[23]

Clearly extending far beyond the conventional legal understandings of what rights are and do, the right to the city challenges 'top-down' notions of urban planning and governance, emphasising instead that cities are ultimately constituted through myriad 'bottom-up' performances by a great variety of people, for whom a 'common good' is not easily ascertainable.[24] By vesting in people solely by virtue of their physical presence in the city (rather than, for instance, on the basis of their nationality or legal status), the right to the city transcends the insider/outsider distinctions inherent in conventional notions of legal standing, political community and constitutional citizenship. Indeed, given that it is exercised primarily outside of existing legal or political channels (such as the court system or electoral politics) through the performance of everyday human activities in the city, the right to the city relies on a far more fluid, and potentially more insurgent, notion of urban citizenship than prevailing legal and political notions,[25] and reminds us that people often experience legal and political structures and processes as secondary and incidental to the daily practices of their everyday lives.

But this does not mean that it is impossible to conceive of the right to the city in legal terms. As reflected by the recently proclaimed *World Charter on the Right to the City*, the right to the city may easily be understood as implicating a package of interrelated, mutually supportive and interdependent legal rights. These include the rights to equality, life (in the broad sense), freedom of movement, physical safety, freedom of assembly and association, freedom of trade and occupation, political freedom, as well as the right to a healthy environment (underpinned by the notion of sustainable development) and various socio-economic rights including rights of access to housing, food, water, health care services, social security, education, work, energy, sanitation, telecommunications and mobility. The uniqueness of the right to the city, however, lies in the manner in which it draws attention to the inter-linkages between these various legal rights (which are typically treated as discrete by legal institutions and processes) as well as to the fact that any number of these rights may be exercised in the conglomerate, often in a competing (or even irreconcilable) fashion.[26] The right to the city therefore requires us to transcend traditional conceptions of rights as discrete legal rules to be predictably invoked against public transgressions thereof, and instead requires of us to consider the context-specific and ongoing balancing of competing rights-claims.

Furthermore, not only does the right to the city demand that we transcend liberal understandings of the role of the State in public law by also recognising positive State obligations in the social and economic realms, it requires a rethink of what is meant by the very notion of 'State', and by concomitant understandings of public power and responsibility. In particular, the right to the city transcends the conventional preoccupation with national government as the primary source of State power and instead shifts the attention to local government as the embodiment of public power in the everyday urban realm. Additionally, the right to the city can as easily be invoked against private power (including, for instance, against actions by private developers, property owners and other urban inhabitants), to the extent that its exercise impacts on the form of the city and on the lived experiences of any of its inhabitants.[27]

Moreover, since the actions of those who impact on others' performance of the right to the city may themselves be viewed as competing performances of the right, the right to the city belies the notions of 'winners' and 'losers' inherent in much legal thinking and litigation, instead drawing attention to the continuous balancing, limitation and negotiation of competing rights (or, more accurately, competing aspects of the same right) in different places and contexts. Ultimately, the role of legal rules, rights and processes is to harness and channel the many competing performances of the right to the city in accordance with constitutional values, by facilitating and enforcing such a continuous balance between competing iterations of the right, with the goal of respecting and enabling as many simultaneous performances thereof as is feasible within a legal understanding of the common good.

This is necessarily a task that will be more easily achieved in some instances than in others. Accordingly, while this book treats the right to the city as something of a theoretical animating principle and seeks to understand and explain the legal conflicts that it discusses in light of the right, it does not necessarily view the individual achievement or advancement of the right as a realistic end goal of urban dispute resolution. I accept that the legal determination of a dispute, like any top-down imposition of State power, will inevitably limit or sacrifice some aspects of the right to the city in favour of others. Rather, I am interested in the terms, boundaries and repercussions of these limits and sacrifices and in the manner in and extent to which legal intervention alters the scope for, and the balances of power inherent in, individual performances of the right.

Struggling over the right to the city in Johannesburg: introducing the stage and the main institutional actors

Johannesburg

> So, in South African cities, spaces can change very quickly and also not at all.[28]

Johannesburg has always been a rough place. Established as a tented mining camp shortly after the discovery of gold on the Witwatersrand in 1886, in just under 10 years Johannesburg had become South Africa's largest city, bypassing Cape Town (almost 250 years its senior).[29] A booming city of immigrants and transients from the beginning, Joburg initially developed in sporadically planned fits and starts, in the area where the Central Business District (CBD) stands today.[30]

A male-dominated gold mining community for much of its early years, Joburg displayed a lawless, aggressively materialist edge from the very beginning.[31] Apart from mining, much of its early economy was built on liquor, gambling and prostitution, and violence was not at all uncommon on its streets. The city's relationship with the Zuid Afrikaansche Republiek (of which it then formed part) was a fraught one, with the Pretoria-based President Paul Kruger referring to it as a 'godless place' and begrudgingly granting it municipal autonomy only after prolonged struggle.[32]

Racial diversity and disharmony were among the city's defining characteristics from its inception. Apart from the white population (consisting of Englishmen, Afrikaners and many (predominantly eastern) European and American immigrants), the city was also called home by Indian traders from Natal, coloured workers from the Cape and large numbers of dodgily recruited African mine labourers from the early 1890s onwards. Joined by thousands of Chinese indented labourers after the Boer War, these population groups lived in roughly (though incompletely) racially segregated, often slum-like, areas on the (mostly western) edge of town and all enjoyed somewhat restricted freedom of movement and fewer rights of civic participation than the white residents.[33]

Always a place where big money has been made on the back of the labour of many but to the benefit of a few, Johannesburg's mining magnates and super-rich, after a brief foray into Doornfontein to the east, settled on the Parktown ridge to the north of the CBD from the mid-1890s onwards, starting a trend of northwards suburban settlement of wealth that continues to this day.[34] Meanwhile, white working class suburbs were laid out to the immediate east and west of the city centre (where, in the latter case, they coexisted uncomfortably with the 'non-white' settlements), as well as to the immediate south of the mining belt.[35]

When the global economy looked towards gold during the great depression of the early 1930s and South Africa abandoned the gold standard, foreign investment into Johannesburg skyrocketed and the materialist city wore its wealth on the outside. A building boom transformed the CBD into an Art Deco, skyscraper-filled 'African New York' (a title to which the city has continued to secretly aspire towards ever since), whereas a concomitant increase in residential housing demand led to the rise of dense 'flatlands' to the immediate north of the CBD, in Hillbrow, Joubert Park, Berea and, in a more up-market iteration, Killarney.[36] Meanwhile, slums spread to the west and south-west of the city and official intervention to keep these racially segregated intensified. These efforts included planned removals of Africans to Orlando to the far south west and Alexandra township to the far north, and of coloureds to Coronationville in the west, as well as the sponsored settlement of poor whites in the southern suburbs as well as inner working class areas such as Bertrams and Jan Hofmeyer.[37]

The political ascent of the Nationalist Party in 1948 ushered in the apartheid era, during which racial segregation in all South African cities would become a legal, administrative and spatial planning priority. Full access to cities was to become the preserve of white South Africans, with apartheid logic dictating a 'migrant labour'-model for urban residents of all other races, who were allowed to enter inner cities and surrounding areas for work, but were made to live in designated 'townships' on the far urban periphery.[38] In Johannesburg, the rise of apartheid coincided with the city abandoning its tram-based public transport system, which led it to become the exceedingly car-centric city it is today, while significantly contributing to the spatial marginalisation of township residents.[39]

Joburg's African townships were predominantly clustered around Orlando, in what would later come to be known as Soweto, white Joburg's black 'satellite city'. Over the coming decades, Africans from inner city areas were increasingly forced to move to Soweto, most famously from the inner-western suburb of Sophiatown (which was raised to the ground and subsequently rebuilt as the 'poor white' suburb of Triomf) in the mid-1950s. Indian and coloured residents were not spared either, and were respectively to be relocated, especially from the Vrededorp/Fordsburg/Pageview area, to Lenasia and Eldorado Park on Soweto's outskirts.[40] The only noteworthy spatial exceptions to this resettlement trend was the western coloured township (now Westbury), which remained across the road from Sophiatown, and Alexandra township, which was allowed to remain on the banks of the Jukskei river in the north of the city, where it was eventually separated from the wealthy suburbs' northward sprawl by the Marlboro/Wynberg industrial belt.[41]

In (white) commercial Joburg, the 1940s and 1950s saw the increased popularity and development of the inner flatlands and, after the construction of a number of new bridges spanning the railway line to the north of the CBD, the northward extension of the business district into the adjacent Braamfontein, which became a fashionable 'second city' from the 1950s onwards.[42]

The 1960s and 1970s saw almost unprecedented economic growth for Joburg (and for South Africa in general) and led to a second, skyscraper-heavy building boom in the CBD and surrounds, the zenith of which was the completion, in 1972, of the 52-floor Carlton Center, then the tallest building in the southern hemisphere and for many subsequent years the epitome of Joburg glitz and glamour.[43] The suburbs sprawled in all directions during the same time, spurred significantly by the completion of the circular highway system, which made the outskirts far more accessible, from the early 1960s.[44]

A major downside of this growth spurt was increasing traffic congestion and parking problems in the CBD.[45] Given the increased accessibility of the suburbs, the decentralisation of retail and the service sector appeared to be a logical solution. American-style suburban shopping malls went up rapidly from the 1960s onwards (with Killarney Mall going up in the mid-1960s, Sandton City and Rosebank Mall opening for business approximately a decade later and Eastgate being completed towards the end of the 1970s). A trickle of upmarket retailers from the CBD to the suburbs quickly developed into an outflow, which was followed by office workers, with decentralised office nodes developing in the wealthy northern suburbs from the early 1970s onwards – first in Parktown, and thereafter in Rosebank, Randburg and Sandton.[46]

The Soweto student uprising of 1976 was a watershed in South Africa's history, driving home both the cruelty and the ultimate unsustainability of apartheid, and doing long-term damage to investor confidence.[47] The uprising's effects would reverberate beyond the township – many of Joburg's white immigrant population, who were then based in Hillbrow, Berea and Yeoville, returned to Europe in its aftermath, leaving many empty apartments in their wake. In contravention of group areas legislation, these were filled not only by white tenants, but also by formerly displaced Indian and coloured Joburgers, desperate for accommodation closer to work and willing to pay the exorbitant rent that they, as a truly captive audience, were being charged.[48] Meanwhile, an increasing number of entertainment venues opened across the flatlands. As Hillbrow briefly became Joburg's most vibrant, diverse and cosmopolitan spot, the seeds for its subsequent decline were also being sown.[49]

As nationwide and international political pressure on the apartheid government mounted, it ineptly battled the racial diversification of the white-designated inner-city flatlands and surrounds. Its eviction practices in Hillbrow were resisted by an increasingly organised community of coloured and Indian residents. Forming 'ActStop' (the 'Action Committee to Stop Evictions') in 1979, the residents began to resort to the law in stepping up their resistance, subsequent to some 50 members of the Johannesburg Bar volunteering to defend evictees against the state, free of charge.[50] Perhaps surprisingly, given that the legal system at the time was not exactly sympathetic to the plight of non-white transgressors of apartheid laws, their campaign was ultimately successful. In the 1982 case of *S* v. *Govender*, an Indian resident of white-designated Mayfair on the other side of the city, assisted by ActStop, successfully resisted her eviction in court, with the Supreme Court holding that the State could not evict Joburg's non-white flouters of Group Areas legislation if it did not provide alternative, suitable housing to them.[51]

The *Govender* decision effectively brought an end to the enforcement of the Group Areas Act in Johannesburg and paved the way for the 'greying' of the inner-city flatlands, with increasing numbers of coloureds and Indians, and later Africans, moving into Hillbrow, Berea, Yeoville, as well as the 'inner ring' of working class suburbs (including Mayfair, Fordsburg, Troyeville and Bertrams).[52]

Much as this assertion of the right to the city was a victory for justice and diversity in Joburg, its effects in a city predominantly run by white capital amid political turmoil and the increasing failure of the State apparatus were not altogether positive. Wealthier (white) residents began to move out of the inner flatlands in droves, and banks soon started to 'redline' the areas (meaning that they would not grant loans to purchase property there). Stuck with unsellable apartments in a now less desirable area, many landlords quickly turned into slumlords, letting apartments to poorer people of all races (including to increasing numbers of poor Africans migrating into the city from the rural areas amidst the failing of South Africa's rural economy, and to African sex workers, as Hillbrow's increasingly seedy high streets became Joburg's unofficial red light district) and turning a blind eye to the overcrowding that resulted from flat-sharing arrangements aimed at being able to afford the rent.[53] Meanwhile, an equally destructive culture of 'flat-trashing' developed among (especially Hillbrow) tenants disgruntled with their living conditions and with their landlords' exploitative practices, whereas ActStop's resistance soon turned against landlords, in the form of organised tenant groups refusing to pay over rent and service charges.[54] The culmination of all of these factors meant that buildings rapidly deteriorated and, by the end of the 1980s, much of the inner-city flatlands and their surrounds were gradually transforming into an urban slum.

Elsewhere, the other major assertion of the right to the city, in 1980s Joburg, which was to deal as powerful a blow to the Apartheid State as ActStop, was the

Soweto Rates Boycott from 1984 onwards. The boycott, driven by the Soweto Civic Association and supported by national liberation movements, was a response to inferior service delivery in, and the separate administration of, Joburg's black townships, where the standard of municipal infrastructure and services, and the standard of living, was significantly lower than in white Joburg. The boycott, which involved the almost universal non-payment of rental and municipal service charges across the township, crippled municipal finance systems and forced the City Council to the negotiation table. In terms of the Soweto Accord of 1990, which was to exert some influence over national political negotiations of the early 1990s, arrear service charges in Soweto were written off and undertakings were made to establish non-racial, democratic and inclusive modes of metropolitan governance.[55]

The death of apartheid and the birth of South Africa's multiracial democracy in the 1990s ironically lent momentum to the physical decline of Johannesburg's CBD and surrounds. The pattern of 'white flight', slumlording and overcrowding in the inner-city flatlands intensified. Drug-related and other crimes, associated in the popular consciousness with an influx of Nigerian and Congolese migrants, spiralled in Hillbrow and neighbouring areas, which were soon regarded as 'no go zones' by the middle-classes.[56] Meanwhile, the decentralisation of inner city business, retail and entertainment venues to the northern suburbs became fuelled by 'crime and grime' concerns and accelerated into a proper exodus, leaving scores of empty, decayed and abandoned inner city office buildings in their wake. These were soon occupied by an influx of poor people from the outskirts of town (and, increasingly, also from beyond town, as South African urbanisation and concomitant rural depopulation blisteringly gained pace) and, indeed, from beyond national borders (since these, too, became significantly more porous after 1994).[57]

As if the abandonment by private capital was not enough, the administration of the newly formed Metropolitan Council (which eventually was to amalgamate not only Johannesburg and its southern and south-western townships, but also the northern municipalities of Sandton, Randburg and beyond, as well as Roodepoort to the west) was virtually paralysed by its momentous administrative responsibility and new developmental mandate. To make matters worse, a full-scale fiscal crisis in 1997 (spurred largely by a rates boycott in Sandton, where ratepayers were loath for their municipal revenue to cross-subsidise poorer areas in the amalgamated city)[58] meant that, in addition to a dearth of administrative capacity, the money for the Council to intervene in the rapidly declining inner city was simply not there.

Apart from a few corporate giants digging in, the inner city's physical and built environment crumbled and its formal economy went into free-fall, epitomised by the relocation of the Johannesburg Stock Exchange to Sandton by the end of the decade.[59] In formal businesses' place informality exploded, with the 'new', poor residents setting up makeshift stalls, from which they would sell small quantities of everyday essentials and snacks, on pavements and in public places all over the inner city.[60]

The northern suburbs, on the other hand, seemed to boom uncontrollably. Except for Parktown which, due to its proximity to downtown, fell out of fashion, the ostentatious office nodes of the north expanded beyond what was previously imaginable and Sandton became the city's new high-rise big business centre.[61] Social life, meanwhile, dispersed into the various 'high streets' of suburbs such as Melville, Greenside, Norwood and Parktown North, where decades ago tram stops had led to pockets of retail and higher density residential development. The northward boundaries sprawled unabashedly, with garish new nodes such as Midrand and Fourways developing in locations geographically not much further from the Pretoria CBD than from that of their own city, hence contributing to greater Joburg's administrative ungovernability.[62]

While the suburbs in all directions slowly became more racially integrated as black people began moving into areas that were previously forbidden to them (especially in the middle-class and upper working-class suburbs of the south, which became the neighbourhoods of choice for upwardly mobile former Sowetans),[63] they also became more socially isolated as violent crime, previously confined to townships and poor areas, increased across the city.[64] Arguably the greatest social scourge of post-apartheid Johannesburg, crime also fuelled suburban paranoia and led residents in upmarket suburbs to fortify themselves, first behind high walls and electric fences patrolled by private security companies and then also in cordoned off suburban enclaves and access-controlled residential 'security estates', which became the face of urban sprawl, especially to the north.[65] Violent crime also remained a major problem in poorer areas and townships, despite the more established among these (especially Alexandra and Soweto) being major benefactors of post-apartheid, State-led development and investment.[66]

The townships, meanwhile, became the major brunt-bearers of urbanisation, with the rural poor increasingly using them, as well as the inner-city flatlands, as ports of entry into the city. The resulting housing shortage has led not only to a proliferation of backyard shacks across the townships (to the point where several families ended up sharing stands initially designed to house one), but also to the mushrooming of informal settlements on their outskirts. A far cry from the northern suburbs, these settlements are, for the most part, places of acute poverty, environmental degradation, crime and illness.[67] In recent years, they have also increasingly been sites of urban unrest and discontent, with (often violent) so-called 'service delivery protests' becoming the order of the day.[68] Apart from the socio-economic, political and developmental challenges that they glaringly embody, the informal settlements draw attention to the fact that, much as significant efforts have been made, development in post-apartheid Johannesburg has not fully been able to address the socio-economic and spatial legacy of apartheid.[69]

Efforts to remedy this, as well as to contain sprawl and to halt and reverse the decay of the inner city, began in earnest at the end of the 1990s and gained momentum in the early 2000s. The Metropolitan Council of the City of Johannesburg led the way, with several innovative and committed policy and structural initiatives. These included the formation of the Johannesburg Development Agency (JDA) (which would be tasked with inner city regeneration as part of its broader development mandate) in 2000, the launch of the urban development zone tax incentive scheme (in terms of which businesses and developers would qualify for tax rebates in return for investing in the inner city) in 2004 and the proclamation of the Inner City Regeneration Charter in 2007.[70] As it emerged from the doldrums of its late 1990s bankruptcy, the City also put its money where its mouth was, investing millions into creating and upgrading public spaces and the public environment in and around the inner city, 'restoring order' amidst informality (through the construction of, for instance, linear markets for informal trade and taxi ranks), partnering with the private sector in upgrading and rejuvenating inner city buildings and districts, improving public transport provision and turning townships into more economically viable neighbourhoods.

Major city-driven inner-city developments in the early 2000s, such as the Newtown Cultural Precinct, Constitutional Hill and the Fashion Kapitol were only partly successful, but certainly began to galvanise the private sector, with a number of prominent developers buying and restoring office buildings all over the inner city and adjacent flatlands, with many of these being redeveloped into (predominantly working-class targeted) apartment complexes.[71] Inner city business, too, came to the party and, in addition to upgrading office stock, participated in the formation of so-called City Improvement Districts (CIDs), pockets of privately managed urban space, complete with public environment upgrades. The Main Street pedestrian 'mall', the most celebrated of these, remains a beacon of successful inner city regeneration to this day.[72]

Overall, while the inner city and environs certainly remain far from entirely 'regenerated', these early efforts appeared to have been successful in slowing down the business exodus to the north and in containing Joburg's outward sprawl,[73] while restoring a measure of investor and resident confidence and leading to a definite improvement in living conditions in the much of the inner city and the flatlands. Meanwhile, public transport developments (such as the high-profile and controversial Gautrain between Joburg, Pretoria and the OR Tambo International Airport, as well as initial phases of the City's 'Rea Vaya' rapid bus transit system) began, albeit imperfectly, to 're-stitch' the dispersed fabric of the apartheid City.[74] Efforts to contain sprawl were further boosted by the City winning control over its own spatial planning vision after a protracted court battle (the outcome of which vested the authority to grant permission for the proclamation of new neighbourhoods in the City, rather than in provincial development tribunals).[75] Since the mid-2000s, the 'inner ring' of greater Johannesburg ('fenced in' by highways on all sides) has significantly densified and continues to do so.[76]

Regeneration processes have, however, not been uncontroversial. Over and above some of the 'top-down' developmental initiatives being slow to take hold in a city that did not necessarily share in the official vision for the spaces that were being regenerated,[77] the (perhaps inevitable) displacement of the inner city's poor and homeless population as a result of regeneration and, in particular, the heartless and thoughtless manner in which evictions of poor occupiers of inner city buildings were initially handled, was much maligned and would lead to significant legal and popular opposition.[78]

Inner-city regeneration gained pace in the lead up to the 2010 Soccer World Cup (for which Joburg was a major host city, with both the opening ceremony and the final match taking place at Soccer City (now FNB Stadium) on the outskirts of Soweto),[79] but was dealt a significant blow by the global financial crisis of the late 2000s. While the World Cup and sound financial fundamentals buffered South African cities against the worst effects of the crisis, an estimated 90,000 jobs were nevertheless lost in Joburg and the Metropolitan Council's coffers rapidly ran dry once more,[80] negatively impacting its ability to manage and uplift the city.

Around the same time, Joburg reeled from a nationwide, but Joburg-centred, outburst of intense and brutal xenophobic violence against the large number of foreign African migrants who settled in the city after 1994. Given the intense competition for work, housing and social goods, xenophobic tensions had been simmering across the city for many years. In 2008, the pressure cooker exploded, with murderous violence targeted especially at foreigners occupying so-called 'RDP' ('Reconstruction and Development Programme') houses and/or operating small businesses in the townships.[81] The attacks also significantly affected the inner city, with large numbers of displaced and traumatised foreign nationals seeking refuge in and around the Central Methodist Church in Pritchard Street. The inner city's infrastructure, management and social networks took severe strain as a result.[82]

The regeneration of inner-city Joburg would gain momentum again as the City and the national economy slowly emerged from the after-effects of the global financial downturn. In 2011, the City published its *2040 Growth and Development Strategy*, an impressive document taking an overall view of development across the greater city region and aiming at economic growth, transport-led development and regeneration, densification, the eradication of poverty and the promotion of sustainable development, among other goals. This strategy informed the City's main post-2010 development policy initiatives, 2013's *Inner City Transformation Roadmap* (which replaced the *Inner City Regeneration Charter* and expressed commitment towards establishing and maintaining a well-governed, clean and safe, sustainable, productive and inclusive inner city)[83] and the 'Corridors of Freedom' policy (a transport driven vision of development, densification and sustainability),[84] both of which were generally positively received. On the downside, the City attracted increased criticism for its overblown, blitz-like approach to urban management, which often, as in the case of 2013's ill-fated 'Operation Clean Sweep', involved senseless and violent displays of authority from the Metropolitan Police Force against some of the more vulnerable inhabitants of the city.[85]

Private-sector driven inner city regeneration would also continue apace in the years since 2010. Over and above office and residential developments, the late 2000s would also see the rise of private capital-driven 'hipster enclaves' of gentrification, such as in the so-called 'Maboneng precinct' in the south-eastern corner of the inner city and in lower Braamfontein. While certainly adding zest and life to the areas in question, in addition to significantly upgrading previously neglected buildings and public infrastructure, these developments have often come under fire for their class-based exclusivity and for the trickle-down displacement that is feared to result from them.[86]

Given that regeneration in downtown Joburg has been piecemeal and focused on particular, diverse and spatially disparate nodes in the city, whilst different processes have transformed (sometimes for the better, sometimes for the worse) the places in between, the inner city today is often described as a patchwork of colliding worlds – 'an incongruous mosaic of disconnected pockets of revitalization surrounded by marginal, indeterminate zones of uncertainty, instability and possible danger'.[87] The sense of patchwork extends also to the suburbs, many of which are so vastly different in character that it is difficult to believe that they form part of the same city. In the north, Sandton and Rosebank have increasingly become upmarket, highly connected and technologically advanced mini-cities of their own,[88] whereas recent years have also seen the further development and further embedment of several, bustling and diverse 'mini-towns' around a great many suburban 'high streets' (in Parkhurst, Parktown North, Linden, Melville, Greenside, Norwood and more) as well as the rise of exclusive, upper-class, new-urbanism-style 'lifestyle theme park' developments such as Melrose Arch (which bring not only new glitzy expressions of cosmopolitanism but also their own problems of sustainability and exclusion).[89] More centrally, Fordsburg and Mayfair have transformed into a unique melting pot of Middle Eastern, Indian, Pakistani and Bangladeshi cultures, an inner city Ethiopian quarter and a Somali enclave in Mayfair thrive and are expanding daily, a long-settled orthodox Jewish community remains around Glenhazel, a bustling 'Chinatown' sprawled in Cyrildene to the east, the working class suburbs of the 'old south' have retained their Portuguese character whilst largely swopping their European Portuguese residents for ones from Mozambique and Angola, Jabulani in Soweto has become a cosmopolitan and cultural node, and Bedfordview to the east ostentatiously flaunts 'new money' tainted by whispers of organised crime.

The list of complex and diverse examples continues, making sure that today's Joburg is not a place that is easily, or at all, capable of being grasped or described. Martin Murray refers to Joburg as a 'city of extremes',

> as much an unregulated, sprawling, and polynucleated metropolis as it is a rooted historical city that still bears the imprint of earlier municipal planning efforts to segregate urban space along racial lines and to create, maintain and insulate privileged sites for the propertied urban elite,[90]

a place where trendy cosmopolitanism exists alongside squalor and desperation, and where radically different ways of life collide and interact in unpredictable, volatile and often violent ways.[91]

Johannesburg is physically and geographically huge, and is currently inhabited by approximately 4.5 million people, a number nearly double its inhabitants in the mid-1990s and which is expected to double again over the next 50 years.[92] It is a population that is incredibly diverse in race, nationality, culture, class and economic status.[93] Its economy is strong and continues to grow, but is far from large enough to fulfil the needs of all its inhabitants. It faces a broad array of social and developmental challenges, pertinently unemployment, crime, insufficient access to essential social services, energy shortages, environmental degradation (such as, notably, acid mine drainage) and poverty.[94] It is a brash, unsettled, hard-edged, materialist, violent, arrogant, nervous, fast-paced and ever-changing place, which at once evokes 'the epitome of urban chic and cosmopolitan sophistication' and 'a miasmic cesspool of abject misery and human degradation'.[95] Both in its physical form and in the conduct of its inhabitants, it has lost little of its insurgent spirit, its disregard for rules, laws and conventions.[96] Yet, it is also a beautiful place – green, vibrant and alive, a place of hope, opportunity and possibility, which has always lured people of all walks of life from far beyond national borders and continues to do so still:

> There is no question that Johannesburg is a city that, from the origins, has symbolized novelty, exuberance, adventurism and, to a large extent, the possibility of a kind of freedom.[97]

The Johannesburg Metropolitan Council

The birth of a unified management structure for Johannesburg, which coincided with the birth of multiracial democracy for South Africa, was not an easy one. A complex transitional local government framework was introduced nationally by the 1993 interim Constitution and the Local Government Transition Act, in terms of which the greater Johannesburg area (previously governed by a number of distinct municipalities) was gradually to be brought under a single management structure. Four transitional municipal substructures were created under the umbrella of the Greater Johannesburg Transitional Metropolitan Council. They were ultimately consolidated under a single council (governed by newly passed municipal systems and structures legislation) in late 2000.[98]

In accordance with the provisions of the Municipal Structures Act, the amalgamated Johannesburg Metropolitan Council (which functions as the city's policy-making body) is constituted equally by councillors elected to proportionally represent political parties voted for in local government elections ('proportional representation councillors'), and councillors directly elected by the residents of particular wards during the same elections ('ward councillors').[99] While proportional representation councillors tend to pursue an agenda determined by their political parties, the mandate of ward councillors is a more local one, and they tend to focus on issues specifically pertaining to their wards, as filtered through ward committees established in terms of the Structures Act. The ward committees, meanwhile, are envisaged as the city's main spaces for citizen participation in governance, with ward councillors responsible for channelling residents' concerns and civic suggestions upwards into the bureaucracy.[100]

Executively, the City is led by an executive mayor, presiding over an elected, ten-person, mayoral executive council. The City administration, which has been split into seven regions (each with separate, subordinate management structures) is led by a City Manager and a management team, which is also responsible for the implementation of the city's development plan.[101]

Overall, in terms of section 152 of the 1996 Constitution, local government bodies such as the Johannesburg Metropolitan Council are responsible

> to provide democratic and accountable government for local communities; to ensure the provision of services to communities in a sustainable manner; to promote social and economic development; to promote a safe and healthy environment; and to encourage the involvement of communities and community organisations in the matters of local government,

and must further 'structure and manage [their] administration and budgeting and planning processes to give priority to the basic needs of the community, and to promote the social and economic development of the community'.[102] The Constitution further vests local government bodies with the authority and primary responsibility to administer a range of service delivery- and urban management-related matters (such as, for example, municipal planning, public transport provision, public works, municipal health services, water and sanitation, refuse removal and the administration of public places),[103] while applicable housing legislation further tasks them with a range of responsibilities in relation to housing provision.[104] Given the prevailing inequality in, and the enormous developmental challenges faced by all South African cities, these are onerous responsibilities indeed, and carrying them out has proved challenging for all municipalities. This is so especially since the allocation of responsibilities has not always been matched by allocations of resources and decision-making power.[105]

In Joburg, the overwhelming proportions of this mandate in combination with somewhat overzealous spending in its pursuit, the complexity of the transitional governance arrangements and the severe negative financial consequences of a rates boycott by Sandton ratepayers (who objected to the cross-subsidisation of the southern and western municipal substructures by the rates income from the north and east),[106] caused a financial collapse in 1997, which necessitated intervention by the Gauteng Provincial Government.[107] Among the financial austerity measures adopted in an (ultimately successful) effort to emerge from this crisis, was the de-bundling and semi-corporatisation of several of the City's service delivery units. A number of utilities (Joburg Water, CityPower and Pikitup, responsible for delivery of water, electricity and refuse removal services respectively), agencies (the Johannesburg Development Agency and Johannesburg Roads Agency) and corporatised entities (including Metrobus, the Joburg Fresh Produce Market, City Parks and the Johannesburg Property Company) were established with the City Council as sole shareholder. The activities of these entities are typically monitored by both Contract Management Units responsible for looking after their service delivery performance in terms of constitutional and legislative mandates, as well as by Shareholder Units responsible for overseeing their financial performance and corporate governance.[108]

Together with the legislative, executive and other administrative arms of the Council, these bodies have all, to a greater or lesser extent, been tasked with service delivery, urban management, development and regeneration in greater Joburg. For most of them, the inner city has been a critical focus area since their establishment. This is partly because the legendary 'demise' of the CBD from the early 1990s onwards has come to symbolise much of what is popularly regarded as being 'wrong' with the city. Unfairly, given the diverse causes and long history of this decline and its definite roots in apartheid spatial planning and policing, it also tends to be popularly attributed to the failings of the post 1994, ANC-dominated government. The ANC-led Joburg Metropolitan Council has thus always regarded 'fixing' the inner city as a priority, not only for economic reasons, but also to restore citizen- and investor confidence in the city and thereby to boost the credibility of the ANC.[109]

According to its *2040 Growth and Development Strategy*, Johannesburg's Local Government aims to produce and maintain a greater Johannesburg urban environment that is well-governed, safe, resilient, sustainable, socially inclusive, liveable, economically robust, integrated and internationally competitive.[110] The latter goal, popularly associated with the City's slogan 'a world-class African city', is often criticised by social justice advocates for its neoliberal undertones and its preference for global notions of urban excellence over basic, localised social justice concerns.[111] This criticism notwithstanding, it has been observed that Joburg's governance has always been particularly developmental and regeneration oriented, especially when compared with other South African cities.[112]

On the delivery front, Joburg's overall performance of its vast and complex mandate has, perhaps predictably, been somewhat uneven. While the City has clearly made great strides in expanding and improving service delivery,[113] developing the economy, regenerating the inner city, overcoming the fragmentation of apartheid spatial planning and so forth, its performance in this regard has not always been commensurate with the amount of resources at its disposal.[114] Administratively, in particular, it has sometimes fallen short, as illustrated for instance by the 'billing crisis' of 2010 onwards, when revenue collection almost came to a halt following severe problems with incorrect and overinflated municipal service bills.[115] This said, financial and administrative management has continuously improved in the years subsequent to the 2011 Local Government elections, as attested for instance by consistent clean audits and continuous improvements in the City's ratings by international credit agencies (which, by 2016, outperformed the country's national ratings).[116]

However, overall achievement of Joburg's strategic goals has been somewhat retarded by conflicts within the City over how exactly they should be pursued. This has especially been the case in relation to housing delivery, urban regeneration and the city's main urban management bugbear – the 'ordering' of the inner city and the management of informality.[117] Not only has there been notable conflicts in urban development vision between the City and the Gauteng Provincial government (especially in relation to the location of housing projects, urban expansion and the manner in which housing delivery should take place), there has also been tension between the political agenda of proportional representation councillors on the one hand and the ward-specific developmental and urban management concerns of ward councillors on the other, between the short-term and election-focused priorities of councillors versus the more long-term, career-oriented goals of administrative officers, as well as between the more business-oriented concerns of the corporatised city management entities and the more altruistic motives of the council.[118]

More pervasively, in relation to urban management especially, there has been an observed clash in institutional culture between City-employees in agencies tasked with a more developmental role (such as the Johannesburg Development Agency, City Parks and the Johannesburg Social Housing Company) on the one hand, and those in the more delivery and management-oriented agencies, as well as those directly concerned with city management and law enforcement, on the other. Whereas the former group tends to be champions of urban inclusivity and to pursue visions of integration through place-making, urban design and community-oriented initiatives, the latter tends to be preoccupied with 'ordering' the city and with ensuring compliance with the law. It is the latter group that occupies more positions of direct executive power in the City, with the result that their more hardcore, managerial vision has tended to dominate.[119]

Unfortunately, this vision has coincided with a short-term, ad hoc, 'crisis-driven' 'quick-fix', 'blitz-focused' approach to urban management, involving high-profile, sudden clampdowns on informal activity in the city, regrettably associated with much brutishness on the part of the Metro Police.[120] This approach has arguably prevailed because it suits short-term political goals (to be seen to be taking decisive action and achieving measurable immediate results) as well as the performance management targets of individual employees and units, and because it is also capable of pursuit within prevailing resource constraints. However, it tends to address the symptoms of urban disorder rather than their causes and has often had devastating consequences for the livelihoods of poor inhabitants.[121] As such, the approach has exacerbated tensions between the different 'camps' within the City, and has also predictably attracted the wrath of human rights organisations. More significantly, it has served to pitch the interests of City managers against those of inhabitants and has brought the City face to face with the insurgency of its subjects:

> The municipality's impulse to fix, order and clean up the inner city, as though it could be scrubbed clean and polished bit by bit until it is all 'sorted out', has been frustrated by the myriad expressions of insurgent urbanism, quotidian survival tactics and strategies that collide in inner-city streets and buildings on a daily basis.[122]

Clearly, the City of Johannesburg is far from a monolithic entity with uniform goals, managed through a single, direct line of accountability. Indeed, there are so many different heads to the Joburg-beast that they are often accused of simultaneously pulling in different, sometimes opposing, directions. Yet, it is probably true that, within the City government,

> differences of professional identity and conflicts of interest are frequently transcended by a shared belief in the same strategic vision of Johannesburg after apartheid as a socially progressive, racially harmonious, aspirant world-class city with a postindustrial, high-tech future of cosmopolitan urbanity.[123]

It is the implementation of this vision, laudable and rights-infused as it may be, that often clashes with inhabitants' day-to-day enactments of their right to the city.

The Constitution, constitutional rights and the courts

The notion of enforceable individual rights was alien to South African legal culture prior to 1994. The 1993 interim Constitution (which came into operation on 27 April 1994), which contained a justiciable Bill of Rights, was thus a watershed moment also for the way law was practised in South Africa. The interim Constitution restored civil and political rights and freedoms to South Africans of all races whereas its successor, the 'final' 1996 Constitution, proceeded to also entrench a range of socio-economic rights, which hold the further promise of extending the more concrete benefits of social citizenship to all.[124]

An array of rights that may be understood as integral to the performance of the right to the city are enshrined in the Bill of Rights. These include the rights to equality, dignity, life, freedom and security of the person including the right to freedom from violence, freedom of expression, freedom of assembly and demonstration, freedom of association, freedom of movement, freedom of trade and occupation, a right to an environment that is not harmful to health or well-being, as well as rights of access to adequate housing, health care services, food water and social security, and education.[125]

Importantly, unlike in many other constitutional democracies, all the rights in the Bill of Rights, including the socio-economic rights (such as rights of access to water, food, health care services, education and housing) that it enshrines, are fully justiciable, meaning that citizens can enforce them against the State (and, in limited circumstances, also against private entities) in courts. The Constitution's permissive standing provision (in terms of which anyone whose rights are affected or threatened may approach a court for relief)[126] and the broad remedial powers that it grants to courts (who may grant any relief that is appropriate, just and equitable to remedy an infringement of any right in the Bill of Rights)[127] mean that South African citizens are significantly empowered to assert their rights before the courts, against abuses of public and private power. Inhabitants of Johannesburg have the further advantage that many NGOs and public interest organisations engaging in rights-based activism and litigation operate in the city (and are concentrated in the inner city and Braamfontein),[128] meaning that Joburg residents have significantly more access to the legal system and, therefore, opportunities to assert their rights 'officially', than their counterparts elsewhere.[129]

Johannesburg has a centrally located High Court, which will usually be the Court of first instance in constitutional matters. More significantly, South Africa's Constitutional Court, the highest court in constitutional matters, is located in Joburg, in a revamped former prison and fortress on 'Constitutional Hill' wedged between Braamfontein and Hillbrow, itself a major public urban regeneration project of the early 2000s. The innovative and vibrant design of the court building and the openness and accessibility of the public space at Constitutional Hill are said to symbolise not only a regenerated Johannesburg and a new South Africa, but also the increased accessibility and humanity of law and justice in both.[130]

The review powers of courts in constitutional matters, especially in matters involving the vindication of socio-economic rights, are controversial. All over the world, there are political tensions when unelected courts overturn, or otherwise interfere with, the legislative and/or policy decisions of the 'democratic' branches of government. This is typically viewed both as testing the boundaries of the public law doctrine of separation of powers (in terms of which legislative, executive and judicial power should be distinct and exercised separately, subject to checks and balances across functions), and as challenging societal commitment to principles of direct and representative democracy.[131] Moreover, courts are typically regarded as being somewhat ineffective when it comes to reforming socio-economic policy, seeing that they usually lack the technical and financial expertise necessary to decide highly specialist and intricate matters, and that they also do not have the institutional clout or manpower to ensure that their judgments are actually implemented by the legislative or executive branches.[132]

In this regard, it is often argued that rights-related matters, especially those involving socio-economic rights, are 'polycentric', meaning that they involve myriad interlinked, competing interests and that decisions which vindicate some of these over others tend to have a great number of unforeseen, and possibly undesirable, repercussions. Courts should be cautious when adjudicating polycentric matters and must exercise significant restraint in tailoring their orders in such cases.[133] The great many competing interests and simultaneous, co-dependent performances of the right to the city that are at stake in a space as diverse, multi-layered and heavily contested as the city of Johannesburg, are a powerful and very physical manifestation of polycentricity.

In interpreting and enforcing rights, there is further a danger that courts can limit the potential of rights through overly restrictive interpretations in particular contexts or, conversely, that overzealous and overbroad interpretation can unduly proscribe the regulatory possibilities open to government.[134] Judges are also often accused of being ignorant of or insensitive to the everyday realities of the lives of poor people and to the way in which rights are performed 'on the ground', meaning that their interpretations of rights may fail to account for such.[135] Similarly, the 'capture' of rights by well-resourced interest groups or powerful NGOs with particular political agendas, is also a real possibility.

Furthermore, the effect of judgments on bureaucracies and state agencies, who often do not understand precisely what rights mean or exactly what judgments require of them, is unpredictable.[136] This is significant because the manner and extent of the compliance of such bodies with legal judgments that impact on them are what ultimately determines the outcome of rights-based litigation for all of the people and embroiled interests concerned, and also effects the utility of legal rights assertion in the society more broadly (in that it will be of limited use to enforce rights through the legal process if the institutions or people against whom court orders are made do not comply therewith).[137]

But there are also many positive features of legal rights and the judicial process that make rights-based litigation a worthy pursuit. In line with the participatory elements of the right to the city, constitutional law scholars emphasise that, in a state committed to deliberative and participatory democracy, the determination of societal issues through dialogue between stakeholders, across the branches of the state as well as between the state and the citizenry, is preferable.[138] Provided that they are open and accessible, courts are good potential spaces for such dialogue, especially given that the rules of adjudication mean that the views of all parties to a legal matter are given equal weight, regardless of power imbalances that exist between them in the 'real world'.[139]

Judges, moreover, are experts at interpreting and applying the law and in solving disputes involving the balancing of competing interests. They are generally considered (and required) to be independent, impartial and even-handed, meaning that they are capable of ensuring a fair solution to complex (even polycentric) disputes.[140] Their significant power over the other branches of the state further means that they are good at vindicating rights by insisting on the removal of bureaucratic 'blockages' that impede their enjoyment, and at cutting through bureaucratic 'red tape'.[141] Importantly, the nature of judicial review, combined with the significant remedial flexibility that courts have under the 1996 Constitution, mean that courts can alter the manner in which they deal with different kinds of disputes, so as to exercise only so much, and such kind of, authority as is necessary to catalyse a rights-conducive outcome in any particular case.[142]

The ways in which judges decide rights-based challenges to public or private power is thus a significant object of study. Led by the Constitutional Court, South African courts have responded to the challenges posed by the justiciability of fundamental rights in the Bill of Rights, and especially socio-economic rights, with significant caution. The Constitutional Court has indicated that it understands its role in all rights-related matters to be to determine the content of the implicated rights, to evaluate whether challenged law or conduct falls short of the obligations inherent to the rights, to declare offending law or conduct unconstitutional and to award appropriate, just and equitable relief as is required by the nature and extent of the infringement.[143]

In socio-economic rights cases, the Court has chosen to give effect to these aspects of its role through a so-called 'reasonableness analysis', grounded in the constitutional requirement that the state must take reasonable legislative and other measures, to ensure the progressive realisation of the rights of access to housing, health care services, food, water and social security.[144] In its well-known judgment on the right to have access to adequate housing in *Government of the RSA* v. *Grootboom*, the Court held that the constitutional standard of reasonableness required of measures purporting to realise socio-economic rights be coherent, inclusive, comprehensive, balanced and flexible, and to emphasise the fulfilment of emergency needs in crisis situations as well as the urgent needs of the most vulnerable groups in society.[145]

While the Constitutional Court's reasonableness approach has attracted much criticism, mostly for failing to engage with the content of socio-economic rights and for being too lenient on the State,[146] it has also received some praise for its open-endedness, flexibility, context-boundness and the manner in which it balances the institutional tensions inherent to rights-based judicial review.[147] The Court has, for the most part, persisted with the approach notwithstanding the criticism that it has received, and the approach permeates many of the cases discussed in the this book.

A final, noteworthy, potentially problematic feature of higher court judgments (such as those handed down by the Constitutional Court) is that they are binding countrywide. While having the obvious and necessary benefits of legal uniformity and certainty, this means that the geographical context of rights struggles often falls by the wayside and that localised rights struggles are therefore often shaped by judgments emanating from matters originating in radically different places. However, Johannesburg has been fortunate that a significant number of the Constitutional Court's judgments pertaining to various features of urban social justice have originated from the city, meaning that the Court's jurisprudence, in theory at least, responds well to the Joburg context. This, it may be speculated, is even more so because the Court is itself Joburg-based, with the result that the everyday realities of this context overlap, at least in theory, with (at least some of) the experiences of the judges that are tasked with balancing the various tensions at play. On the other hand, all of this has meant that Joburg's context has had a somewhat disproportionate impact on shaping issues of urban social justice in other South African cities, which makes the Court's balancing of competing tensions in Joburg of even greater national significance.

Aims and focus of this book

The dawn of the constitutional rights-era in South African law and public life coincided with the culmination of much of Joburg's historical turmoil and, in particular, with the collapse of the former shape of its inner-city environment and economy and the subsequent struggle for their redefinition. Combined with Joburg's importance for South Africa generally, and with the fact that its population is largely a representative microcosm of all of South Africa's inhabitants, the city presents an ideal setting for an investigation into the spatial and social consequences of the legal assertion of human rights in the country.

This book, then, looks at various enactments of the right to the city in Johannesburg and at their coincidence and interaction with the legal assertion of certain aspects of the right before South African courts. It aims to better understand how such legal assertion draws from, but also inevitably shapes, structures and confines the extra-legal performance of the right to the city. In doing this, the book hopes to begin to fill a gap in knowledge over the effects of the interaction between law, rights and place, and over the manner in which this interaction shapes urban life, urban governance and urban development in South Africa.

In considering the impact of the legal assertion of rights to (various aspects of) the city on, first, the many people simultaneously performing those rights, second, the governance structures responsible for enabling and facilitating the enjoyment of the rights and, third, the place in which the rights are performed, the book also hopes to further our understanding of the manner and extent to which rights-based litigation can contribute to the achievement of social justice – individually, collectively and spatially. More specifically, the book attempts to make sense of courts' different adjudicatory approaches to matters concerning different elements of the right to the city, and thereby to contribute to the literature on appropriate judicial stances in polycentric and socio-economic rights disputes.

In the chapters that follow, I zoom in on different areas of rights-based struggle in Johannesburg and consider the way in which rights and the law have been used in the course of, or in response to these struggles. While attention is given both to legal and extra-legal expressions of the right to the city, the focus is mostly on the effects of instances where legal rights have been expressly invoked. More specifically, I engage in more detail with those instances where rights-based litigation has led to a judicially decided outcome, in the form of a reported judgment by one of the high courts or the Constitutional Court.

Spatially, the book focuses on Joburg and, especially, on its heavily contested inner city and immediate surrounds, although care is taken not to neglect the myriad performances of the right to the city in the townships and the suburbs. When it comes to legal cases and judgments, the emphasis is obviously on those arising from and decided in Johannesburg, although, given that judgments originating from struggles in other South African cities also shape the legal and political landscape within which rights are performed in Joburg, there is also engagement with some of these.

As for people and rights, the emphasis is, perhaps predictably, mainly on the socio-economic rights of Joburg's poorer inhabitants. However, the exercise of these rights cannot be understood separately from the simultaneous exercise of civil and political rights, nor from the various performances of rights by the working, middle and upper-classes, or from the perspective of those who are responsible for heeding rights. As Gustav Visser has argued, our understanding of cities must extend beyond analyses of urban poverty, not least because the activities and interests of better-off city dwellers tend to have as great (if not, in certain respects, greater) an impact on the physical urban environment and on the realities of everyday urban life.[148] Moreover, a large part of everyday city struggles is about freedom, so that ignoring the exercise of civil and political rights by various constituencies in the city will have a similar skewing effect. I therefore also pay attention to some of the rights-performances and legal challenges of groups other than the urban poor, as well as to the exercise of certain civil and political rights.

In Chapter 2, the focus is on what has arguably been the most hotly contested legal rights struggles in Johannesburg – assertions of the right of access to housing in the inner city and surrounding flatlands, on the one hand, and in informal settlements, on the other. The chapter first frames the habitation practices of Joburg's poorer residents as expressions of the right to the city and then considers the extent to which legal rights have served to protect the interests advanced through these practices in the face of displacement occasioned by inner-city regeneration and development. It further considers the impact of legal rights assertion on urban governance, with a focus on attempts to protect and improve the inner-city urban environment and to ensure its sustainability as an economic space.

Chapter 3 contemplates notions of urban citizenship and the role of the state in providing the necessities of urban life, by looking at the ways in which rights to receive and make use of essential urban services have been (legally and extralegally) performed across Johannesburg. It investigates the judicial balancing of urban inhabitants' needs for essential urban amenities, on the one hand, and City authorities' responsibilities to satisfy these in the context of environmental and resource constraints, on the other. In doing so, the chapter begins to uncover notions of urban citizenship, civic responsibility and civic participation underlying the courts' approach to urban rights disputes.

These concepts also permeate much of Chapter 4, which studies the performance and legal assertion of livelihood-related aspects of the right to the city by marginalised urban inhabitants in marginalised urban space. Focusing specifically on the rights of undocumented migrants, informal traders and persons involved in illegal livelihood practices across Johannesburg, the chapter is concerned with the operation of legal rights discourse in relation to actors and activities which are themselves uncomfortably situated in relation to the law. It accordingly evaluates judicial approaches to marginality, public presence and livelihood, in attempting to uncover the limits of legal protection of those whose lives significantly depart from some tacit tenets of courts' understanding of urban citizenship.

In Chapter 5, the focus moves outside of the inner city to the middle and upper-class suburbs to the north, and shifts from the place-making activities and rights struggles of the urban poor to those of the middle and upper classes, as well as to some of the related activities of formal business. Focusing specifically on spatial practices and legal strategies aimed at satisfying safety, environmental, property-related and economic concerns, the chapter interrogates the operation of courts' notion of civic responsibility in relation to better-off residents, and considers some of the challenges inherent in developing a broadly applicable rights jurisprudence via the prism of cases brought by an unrepresentative cross-section of the population. The cases discussed in the chapter further provide some of the most explicit examples of the ways in which courts attempt to balance competing assertions of the right to the city.

To illustrate that the right to the city encompasses not only class-based but also other identity-based appropriations of urban space, Chapter 6 considers the performance of rights pertaining to sexual liberty, identity and citizenship by Johannesburg residents in different spaces and across boundaries of race, gender and class. Zooming in on rights struggles pertaining to sex work and homosexuality, the chapter contemplates the effects of successful and unsuccessful legal invocations of rights to sexual difference, and comments on the ways in which these have shaped the everyday performance of sexual rights across the city. The chapter problematises the class-specific effects of narrowly framed litigation and again illustrates some of the limits inherent in judicial conceptions of urban citizenship.

Chapter 7 takes a step back and attempts to draw conclusions over the spatial consequences of rights-judgments, their bureaucratic impact and their interrelation with the right to the city. It first considers the directive principle effect of constitutional rights and the ways in which they have both shaped the urban regulatory environment and structured the relationships among urban inhabitants, before evaluating the judicial approaches to resolving the various tensions over the right to the city discussed in the book. Finally, the chapter considers the overall impact of rights-based litigation on urban governance in Johannesburg and elaborates on the legal notion of urban citizenship that has emanated from leading court decisions.

Notes

1 The best-known examples of such criticism are to be found in the work of the Critical Legal Studies movement of the 1980s. See, especially, Gabel (1984); Tushnet (1984). For a recasting of these arguments in relation to the invocation of socio-economic rights in South Africa, see Pieterse (2007: 800–801).

2 See Gloppen (2005); Harvey (2008); Liebenberg (2010); Pieterse (2007).

3 See McCann (1994: 48; 65); Williams (1987); Pieterse (2007: 801–804).

4 See Liebenberg (2010: 33, 37–38, 40–41).

5 Brown (2015: 147).

6 Malan (2008: 62–65); Malan (2009: 73); Pieterse (2009: 199–201).

7 Legal rights discourse is often criticised for its tendency to underplay individual agency. See Liebenberg (2010: 41–42); Pieterse (2007: 814).

8 Malan (2008: 59, 61); Malan (2009: 73–75, 77–79, 82–84); Pieterse (2009: 199–201).

9 See Connolly Carmalt (2007: 70–71); Parnell and Pieterse (2010: 148); Pieterse (2014a: 176); Pindell (2008: 69).

10 Murray (2011: 4).

11 See Beall *et al.* (2002: 7); Murray (2011: 1, 5).

12 Constitution of the RSA (1996): preamble. On the legal, moral and political significance of this constitutional aspiration, see Liebenberg (2010: 25–27).

13 Parnell and Pieterse (2010: 146, 148–149, 159); Pieterse (2014a: 176).

14 See Brown (2015: 49).

15 The discussion in this subsection draws heavily from, although extends significantly beyond, my exposition of the characteristics of the right to the city in two earlier works: Pieterse (2014a: 178–180) and Pieterse (2014b: 152–156).

16 Lefebvre (1996). See specifically 173–174.

17 Lefebvre (1996: 158–159; 173–174), as elaborated by, for instance, Coggin and Pieterse (2012: 259); Mitchell (2003: 18–20); Pindell (2006: 439–440); Purcell (2002: 102–103); Simone (2005: 323).
18 See Coggin and Pieterse (2012: 259–261, 271–272); Fernandes (2007: 208); Pindell (2008: 69); Purcell (2002: 106).
19 Lefebvre (1996: 101–103). See also Coggin and Pieterse (2012: 260); Frug (1996: 1051, 1077–1079); Jacobs (1961 [1993]: 72–73, 95); Mitchell (2003: 17–18); Pindell (2006: 438).
20 See Coggin (2016: 439) (likening the right to the city to the similarly contested and perpetually incomplete notion of transformative constitutionalism); Van Marle (2014: 172).
21 Lefebvre (1996: 173). See also Mitchell (2003: 18).
22 Harvey (2008: 23).
23 Young (1990: 226–256). See also Coggin and Pieterse (2012: 260–261); Frug (1996: 1051, 1077–1079); Jacobs (1961 [1993]: 72–73; 95); Mitchell (2003): 18; Pindell (2006: 438); Simone (2005: 323); Valentine (2008: 324–331); Van der Walt (2007: 223–227).
24 See Murray (2008: 23); Simone (2005: 323).
25 Purcell (2002: 102). See also Coggin and Pieterse (2012: 259–260); Holston (2009: 257).
26 See Coggin and Pieterse (2012: 261–263); Parnell and Pieterse (2010: 148).
27 Coggin and Pieterse (2012: 263); Holston (2009: 257); Parnell and Pieterse (2010: 158–159); Purcell (2002: 101–103).
28 Simone (2005: 325).
29 Beavon (2004: 6).
30 See Dinath (2014: 233–234); Tomlinson *et al.* (2003: 3).
31 See Czegledy (2003: 23); Dinath (2014: 234); Murray (2011: 1, 37).
32 Czegledy (2003: 23). See also Dinath (2014: 234); Van Onselen (1982: 6–8, 19–21). For detailed description and analysis of Joburg's early sex work and liquor industries see Van Onselen (1982: 47–164). On Joburg life and politics in the early years, see also Beavon (2004: 23–26); Murray (2011: 38–50).
33 See Beavon (2004: 8–10). On the 'incomplete and porous' racial segregation of early Johannesburg and other South African cities, see Davies (1981: 63–69).
34 See Beavon (2004: 61–62); Czegledy (2003: 29–31); Murray (2011: 43–44).
35 On the establishment and early history of the working class suburbs in the 'old South', see Harrison and Zack (2014: 272–273).
36 Beavon (2004: 93–94); Dinath (2014: 234–235); Murray (2011: 51–58); Tomlinson *et al.* (2003: 4).
37 See Harrison and Zack (2014: 274–275). On a macro level, see also Davies (1981: 64–69).
38 On apartheid planning logic and its legal and administrative pillars, see Davies (1981: 69–71); Emdon (2003: 217–218); Dinath (2014: 235); Tomlinson *et al.* (2003: 3, 5–6).
39 Beavon (2004: 161).
40 On these and other forced removals from the 1950s onwards, see Beavon (2004: 132); Tomlinson *et al.* (2003: 6). For detailed analysis of the making and early days of Soweto, see Beavon (2004: 121–145).
41 On early Alexandra, see Harrison *et al.* (2014b: 345–346).
42 Beavon (2004: 155–166); Murray (2011: 66–67, 139–140).
43 See Beavon (2004: 170–173); Murray (2011: 68–75); Tomlinson *et al.* (2003: 4–5).
44 Dinath (2014: 235).
45 Dinath (2014: 235); Murray (2011: 91).
46 See Beavon (2004: 173, 179–181, 205–206); Beavon and Larsen (2014: 378); Czegledy (2003: 27–28); Dinath (2014: 235); Murray (2011: 87–88).

47 Beavon (2004: 197–200); Tomlinson *et al.* (2003: 5, 8).
48 See Beavon (2004: 216–217); Morris (1999: 9–20); Murray (2011: 141); Winkler (2013: 312). The European outward migration coincided with the last influx of Europeans into Johannesburg, when large numbers of Portuguese expats relocated to Joburg from recently independent Mozambique and Angola, settling in the east and the 'old south'. Harrison and Zack (2014: 279).
49 Murray (2011: 140).
50 See Beavon (2004: 217); Morris (1999: 23–34).
51 See Beavon (2004: 218–219); Morris (1999: 37–39) as well as further discussion in Chapter 2.
52 See Beavon (2004: 219–220); Dinath (2014: 235); Morris (1999: 53–61); Rule (1989); Tomlinson *et al.* (2003: 5).
53 See Beavon (2004: 222–224); Dinath (2014: 236); Morris (1999: 57, 61–68); Murray (2011: 142); Tomlinson *et al.* (2003: 13); Winkler (2013: 312–314).
54 For detailed discussion of these practices, see Morris (1999: 129–140).
55 See Beall *et al.* (2002: 68, 71); Beavon (2004: 234–235); Tomlinson *et al.* (2003: 9); Van Donk and Pieterse (2006: 108–110). The boycott is discussed further in Chapter 3.
56 See Morris (1999: 195–218, 307–328); Murray (2011: 143–144).
57 See Dinath (2014: 236); Murray (2008: 66–70); Murray (2011: 142–147).
58 On the origins and extent of the 1997 fiscal crisis, see Beall *et al.* (2002: 88–90); Harrison *et al.* (2014a: 11); Tomlinson *et al.* (2003: 10).
59 See Harrison *et al.* (2014a: 15); Murray (2011: 88–90; 99, 114–115).
60 See Emdon (2003: 222–231); Murray (2008: 159); Murray (2011: 91, 103); Tomlinson *et al.* (2003: 16).
61 See Beavon and Larson (2014: 371, 379–383); Czegledy (2003: 25, 29–30); Murray (2011: 113–120); Murray (2014: 182–184).
62 On the extent of Joburg's sprawl during this period, see Beavon (2004: 6–7). On Fourways, Midrand and similar far-north 'new Joburg' areas, see Bremner (2004: 30–35); Murray (2011: 120–127).
63 See Harrison *et al.* (2014a: 10–11); Harrison and Zack (2014: 286–287); Tomlinson *et al.* (2003: 13).
64 See Benit-Gbaffou (2009: 55, 58); Murray (2011: 155). On the causes and aggravating factors of crime in Johannesburg, see Palmary *et al.* (2003).
65 See Benit-Gbaffou (2009: 55); Czegledy (2003: 32); Murray (2011: 18–22, 283–319) as well as discussion in Chapter 5.
66 Palmary *et al.* (2003: 106–107). On the scale and scope of post-apartheid investment and development in Soweto, see Harrison and Harrison (2014: 298–302). On Alexandra, see Harrison *et al.* (2014b).
67 See Ahmad and Pienaar (2014: 110–114); Huchzermeyer *et al.* (2014: 154–175); Murray (2008: 105–111); Vearey *et al.* (2010: 697–700). The City's responses to informal settlements will be discussed in Chapter 2.
68 While their multi-layered dynamics are generally beyond the scope of this book, service delivery protests will be discussed in more detail in Chapter 3.
69 Indeed, while spatial constraints have meant that state-sponsored developments aimed at housing the urban poor have mostly been on the southern and western edges of town, economic activity kept following business to the north, with the result that the city's poorer residents, and most of its newcomers, remain physically disconnected from the opportunities provided by the city. Tomlinson *et al.* (2003: 14). See also Murray (2011: 149–150).
70 See City of Johannesburg (2007); Rubin (2014: 216–217); Van der Walt (2007: 222).
71 On the successes of and challenges faced by early regeneration efforts, see Dinath (2014: 240–241); Murray (2008: 73–74, 81–82, 155); Murray (2011: 104).

72 On CIDs and their impact, see Dinath (2014: 239); Murray (2011: 256–265).
73 See Ahmad and Pienaar (2014: 105); Beavon and Larson (2014: 384).
74 City of Johannesburg (2011: 28; 68–69). See also Beavon and Larson (2014: 384); Coggin and Pieterse (2015); Murray (2011: 130–132).
75 *Johannesburg Metropolitan Municipality* v. *Gauteng Development Tribunal* (2010). For discussion, see Pieterse (2014b: 174).
76 See Harrison *et al.* (2014a: 8–9); Ahmad and Pienaar (2014: 103–104).
77 Dinath (2014: 241–242).
78 See Murray (2008: 31–34; 210–218). This will be discussed in Chapter 2.
79 See Harrison *et al.* (2014a: 11); Harrison and Harrison (2014: 302–303); Murray (2011: 132–133).
80 City of Johannesburg (2011: 17, 24, 51). See also Harrison *et al.* (2014a: 11–12).
81 See the various contributions in Hassim *et al.* (2008) as well as discussion in Chapter 4. Similar, though less widespread, violence would erupt against foreign (predominantly Somali) spaza shop owners in Soweto in 2015.
82 See Murray (2011: 165–168). The xenophobic violence and related legal conflicts are discussed in more detail in Chapters 4 and 5.
83 City of Johannesburg (2013a). See especially iv–v; 39–41.
84 City of Johannesburg (2013b). See Harrison *et al.* (2014a: 12).
85 See Dinath (2014: 245–246); Murray (2011: 227, 229, 233) as well as discussion in Chapter 4.
86 See Nevin (2014: 194–198); Walsh (2013); as well as discussion in Chapter 5.
87 Murray (2008: 158). See also Dinath (2014: 239); Murray (2011: 267).
88 See Beavon and Larson (2014) generally, also Mbembe and Nutall (2004: 363–364); Murray (2011: 113–120).
89 On Melrose Arch in this context, see Bremner (2004: 120–125); Murray (2011: 110–113).
90 Murray (2011: 5). See also Murray (2008: 1–2, 4, 16); Murray (2014: 179–180).
91 Mbembe and Nutall (2004: 356–357; 365–366); Murray (2008: 2, 28–29, 61); Murray (2011: 2–4, 30–31).
92 According to Statistics South Africa (n.d.), the Johannesburg metropole spans an area of 1645 square kilometres, and its 2011 population was estimated at 4,434,827. On the city's growth forecasts, see Harrison *et al.* (2014a: 7); City of Johannesburg (2011: 40).
93 On the diversity of Joburg people and characters, see Mbembe and Nuttall (2004: 365–366). According to Statistics South Africa (n.d.), Joburg's 2011 population consisted of 76.4 per cent black African people, 12.3 per cent European/white people, 5.6 per cent coloured people and 4.9 per cent Indian/Asian people. Twenty-five per cent of the 2,261,490 economically active inhabitants were unemployed, whereas average household incomes varied greatly, from some 16.8 per cent of households earning no income at all to an elite top percentage earning upwards of R2.5 million annually.
94 See City of Johannesburg (2011: 30, 52–62, 68).
95 Murray (2008: 2). See also Murray (2008: 1; 28–29; 75); Murray (2011: 2–4, 30–31, 37, 325–326).
96 See Dinath (2014: 234); Murray (2011: 37).
97 Mbembe and Nuttall (2004: 366).
98 For background on the transitional period and the amalgamation, see Beall *et al.* (2002: 76–80); Harrison *et al.* (2014a: 11); Tomlinson *et al.* (2003: 9–10).
99 Municipal Structures Act (1998: s 22). Both categories of councillors are elected for a five-year term. There are currently 260 councillors in Joburg, 130 of each of the two categories. For more information on the council, see the City's official website at www.joburg.org.za.

100 See Municipal Structures Act (1998: ss 72–78). The efficacy of ward committees is contested. See Brown (2015: 64–67) as well as discussion in Chapter 3. On formal channels for civic participation over and above ward committees, see Pernegger (2014: 68–69).

101 See www.joburg.org.za. The regions are: Region A: Diepsloot and Kya Sands; Region B: Randburg, Rosebank, Emmerentia, Greenside, Melville, Northcliff, Parktown and Parkton North; Region C: Roodepoort, Constantia Kloof and Northgate; Region D: Doornkop, Soweto, Dobsonville and Protea Glen; Region E: Alexandra, Wynberg and Sandton; Region F: The Inner City and Region G: Orange Farm, Ennerdale and Lenasia.

102 Constitution of the RSA (1996: s 153(a)). These provisions are further expounded by the provisions of the Municipal Systems Act (see specifically Municipal Systems Act, 2000: s 4(2)). For discussion, see Pieterse (2014b: 158–161) and authorities cited there.

103 Constitution of the RSA (1996: s 156(1) read with Parts B of Schedules 4 and 5). For elaboration and discussion, see Bronstein (2015: 642–646); Steytler (2004: 162–164); Pieterse (2014b: 159–160).

104 See the list of applicable legislation cited in Pieterse (2014b: at 160 n37). These responsibilities have further been elaborated by the courts, as will be discussed in Chapter 2.

105 See, for instance, Pieterse *et al.* (2008: 5); Smith and Morris (2008: 423); Steytler and De Visser (2008: 66).

106 On the causes and extent of the 1997 financial collapse see Harrison *et al.* (2014a: 11); Mabin (2006: 145); Tomlinson *et al.* (2003: 10). The Sandton ratepayers lost their legal challenge to the rates structure, effectively ending the boycott. See *Fedsure Life Assurance et al.* v. *Greater Johannesburg Transitional Metropolitan Council* (1999).

107 In terms of Constitution of the RSA (1996: s 139), Provincial Governments may intervene in the affairs of local municipalities when they fail to fulfil their executive obligations.

108 Smith and Morris (2008: 428–429). See also Morris (2008: 424–427); Harrison *et al.* (2014a: 11); Mabin (2006: 145–146); Murray (2008: 86–87).

109 See Dinath (2014: 236–237, 247); Emdon (2003: 229).

110 City of Johannesburg (2011: 9, 30–35, 92–101).

111 See Dinath (2014: 247); Murray (2008: 23–24, 84, 208–210); Rubin (2014); Schmidt (2008: 125).

112 Schmidt (2008: 125).

113 For instance, according to the City, 99.4 per cent of citizens had access to water and 94.5 per cent had access to sanitation at their homes by 2016. See City of Johannesburg (2016a: 14).

114 See Schmidt (2008: 125–127).

115 The billing crisis, which lingered as late as 2014, has been exhaustively covered in the popular press. See Cox (2011); Gifford (2014).

116 See for instance City of Johannesburg (2016a: 3, 19); City of Johannesburg (2016b).

117 On the ‘ordering’ of the city and the management of informality as a major headache for Joburg’s administration, see Dinath (2014: 242–244); Mabin (2006: 144); Murray (2008: 7, 16).

118 See Buccus and Hicks (2008: 528, 530); City of Johannesburg (2011: 83–84); Harrison *et al.* (2014a: 12); Pieterse (2014b: 171–175); Smith and Morris (2008: 441).

119 See Dinath (2014: 248–249).

120 See Dinath (2014: 245–246); Murray (2008: 227–229).

121 See Benit-Gbaffou (2006: 316); Dinath (2014: 247–249); Murray (2008: 227–230, 233).

122 Dinath (2014: 244). See also Dinath (2014: 249).

123 Murray (2008: 25).
124 Emdon (2003: 215; 219–220).
125 Constitution of the RSA (1996: ss 9–12, 16–18, 21–22, 23, 26–27, 29). On how these relate to the right to the city, see Coggin and Pieterse (2012: 262–263).
126 Constitution of the RSA (1996: s 38).
127 Constitution of the RSA (1996: ss 38, 172).
128 These include Lawyers for Human Rights (LHR); the Legal Resources Centre (LRC); the Centre for Applied Legal Studies (CALS); Section 27; the University of the Witwatersrand Law Clinic and the Socio-economic Rights Institute (SERI), all of which have offices in downtown or Braamfontein. SERI, in particular, is well-known for pursuing right-to-the-city-based claims.
129 On the significance of standing, remedial competence and access to courts for successful rights assertion, see Gloppen (2005: 158–160).
130 See Le Roux (2001); Le Roux (2004).
131 For discussion in the South African context see, for instance, Brand (2006: 225–226); Liebenberg (2010: 63–66); Mbazira (2009: 5–6, 27–32); McLean (2009: 108, 111–114); Pieterse (2004: 390–392).
132 See, for instance, Brand (2006: 225); Liebenberg (2010: 72).
133 In the South African context see, for instance, Liebenberg (2010: 72–75); McLean (2009: 114–115); Pieterse (2004: 392–395) and authorities cited there.
134 See Liebenberg (2010: 40); Steinberg (2006: 264, 268–269).
135 See Gloppen (2005: 160); Liebenberg (2012: 12); Pieterse (2008: 337); Wilson and Dugard (2011).
136 See Sunkin (2004: 52); also Coggin and Pieterse (2012: 274–275).
137 See Gloppen (2005: 162–163).
138 See Brand (2011: 623–624, 630–634); Dixon (2007); Liebenberg (2010: 66–7)1.
139 See Brown (2015: 139–140); Liebenberg (2010: 33, 46); Pieterse (2008: 336–337); Smith and Rubin (2015: 274).
140 For discussion of these advantages of the judicial process, see Liebenberg (2010: 45–46); Liebenberg (2015: 447–448); Pieterse (2004: 395); Smith and Rubin (2015: 274).
141 See Liebenberg (2010: 40–41, 74).
142 See Young (2010).
143 The Court articulated this understanding of its role most forcefully in *Minister of Health* v. *Treatment Action Campaign* (2002: paras 96–114). For discussion, see Brand (2006: 226–227); Liebenberg (2010: 45, 63–66); Pieterse (2004: 402–405).
144 Constitution of the RSA (1996: ss 26(2), 27(2)).
145 *Government of the RSA* v. *Grootboom* (2001: paras 39–44, 46, 66, 68, 82).
146 See, for instance, Bilchitz (2007: 144–145, 155–162); Brand (2003: 36–37, 46, 49–50, 55); Liebenberg (2010: 173–179); Liebenberg (2015: 457); McLean (2009: 187–189); Pieterse (2006: 486–488); Smith and Rubin (2015: 274–275).
147 See, for instance, Liebenberg (2008: 319–320); Steinberg (2006: 276, 284; Sunstein (2001: 131); Wesson (2004).
148 Visser (2013: 76, 86–88). See also Mbembe and Nuttall (2004: 356).

References

Ahmad, P. & Pienaar, H., 2014. 'Tracking changes in the urban built environment: An emerging perspective from the city of Johannesburg'. In: Harrison, P., Gotz, G., Todes, A., & Wray, C. (eds.), *Changing Space, Changing City: Johannesburg after Apartheid*, pp. 101–116. Johannesburg: Wits University Press.

Beall, J., Crankshaw, O. & Parnell, S., 2002. *Uniting a Divided City: Governance and Social Exclusion in Johannesburg*. London: Earthscan.

Beavon, K., 2004. *Johannesburg: The Making and Shaping of the City*. Pretoria: UNISA Press.

Beavon, K. & Larsen, P., 2014. 'Sandton Central, 1969–2013: From open veld to new CBD?' In: Harrison, P., Gotz, G., Todes, A., & Wray, C. (eds.), *Changing Space, Changing City: Johannesburg after Apartheid*, pp. 370–394. Johannesburg: Wits University Press.

Benit-Gbaffou, C., 2006. 'Police-community partnerships and responses to crime: Lessons from Yeoville and Observatory, Johannesburg'. *Urban Forum* 17(4), 301–326.

Benit-Gbaffou, C., 2009. 'Who control the streets? Crime, "communities" and the state in post-apartheid Johannesburg'. In: Locatelli, F. & Nugent, P. (eds.), *African Cities: Competing Claims on Urban Space*, pp. 55–79. Leiden/Boston: Brill.

Bilchitz, D., 2007. *Poverty and Fundamental Rights: The Justification and Enforcement of Socio-Economic Rights*. Oxford: Oxford University Press.

Brand, D., 2003. 'The proceduralisation of South African socio-economic rights jurisprudence, or "what are socio-economic rights for?"'. In Botha, H., Van der Walt, A. & Van der Walt, J. (eds.), *Rights and Democracy in a Transformative Constitution*, pp. 33–56. Stellenbosch: SUN Press.

Brand, D., 2006. 'Socio-economic rights and courts in South Africa: Justiciability on a sliding scale'. In: Coomans, F. (ed.) *Justiciability of Economic and Social Rights*, 207–236. Antwerpen: Intersentia.

Brand, D., 2011. 'Judicial deference and democracy in socio-economic rights cases in South Africa', *Stellenbosch Law Review* 22(3), 614–638.

Bremner, L., 2004. *Johannesburg: One City Colliding Worlds*. Johannesburg: STE Publishers.

Bronstein, V., 2015. 'Mapping legislative and executive powers over "municipal planning": Exploring the boundaries of local, provincial and national control', *South African Law Journal* 132(3), 639–663.

Brown, J., 2015. *South Africa's Insurgent Citizens: On Dissent and the Possibility of Politics*. Johannesburg: Jacana.

Buccus, I. & Hicks, J., 2008. 'Democratisation with inclusion: Revisiting the role of ward committees'. In: Van Donk, M., Swilling, M., Pieterse, E. & Parnell, S. (eds.), *Consolidating Developmental Local Government: Lessons from the South African Experience*, pp. 525–538. Cape Town: UCT Press.

City of Johannesburg website, www.joburg.org.za.

City of Johannesburg, 2007. *Inner City Regeneration Charter*.

City of Johannesburg, 2011. *Joburg Growth and Development Strategy 2040*.

City of Johannesburg, 2013a. *Inner City Transformation Roadmap*.

City of Johannesburg, 2013b. *Corridors of Freedom: Restitching our City to Create a New Future*.

City of Johannesburg, 2016a. *State of the City Address 2016 Delivered by the Executive Mayor, Cllr Mpho Parks Tau*.

City of Johannesburg, 2016b. 'Joburg moves four steps up the ladder in Moody's ratings', 12 May 2016, from www.joburg.org.za.

Coggin, T., 2016. 'Redressing spatial apartheid: The law of nuisance and the transformative role of social utility and the right to the city', *South African Law Journal* 133(2), 434–451.

Coggin, T. & Pieterse, M., 2012. 'Rights and the city: An exploration of the interaction between socio-economic rights and the city', *Urban Forum* 23(3), 257–278.

Coggin, T. & Pieterse, M., 2015. 'A right to transport? Moving towards a rights-based approach to mobility in the city' *South African Journal of Human Rights* 31(3), 294–314.

Connolly Carmalt, J., 2007. 'Rights and place: Using geography in human rights work', *Human Rights Quarterly* 29(1), 68–85.

Constitution of the Republic of South Africa, 1996 (Act 108 of 1996).

Cox, A., 2011. 'Joburg Billing Crisis Shock', *IOL News*, 4 February 2011, from www.iol.co.za/news.

Czegledy, A.P., 2003. 'Villas of the Highveld: A cultural perspective on Johannesburg and its "northern suburbs"'. In: Tomlinson, R., Beauregard, R.A., Bremner, L. & Mangcu, X. (eds.), *Emerging Johannesburg: Perspectives on the Postapartheid City*, pp. 21–42. New York, London: Routledge.

Davies, R.J., 1981. 'The spatial formation of the South African city' *GeoJournal* supp. 2, 59–72.

Dinath, Y., 2014. 'Between fixity and flux: Grappling with transcience and permanence in the inner city'. In: Harrison, P., Gotz, G., Todes, A., & Wray, C. (eds.), *Changing Space, Changing City: Johannesburg After Apartheid*, pp. 232–251. Johannesburg: Wits University Press.

Dixon, R., 2007. 'Creating dialogue about socio-economic rights: Strong-form versus weak-form judicial review revisited', *International Journal of Constitutional Law* 5(3), 391–418.

Emdon, E., 2003. 'The limits of law: Social rights and urban development'. In: Tomlinson, R., Beauregard, R.A., Bremner, L. & Mangcu, X. (eds.), *Emerging Johannesburg: Perspectives on the Postapartheid City*, pp. 215–230. New York, London: Routledge.

Fedsure Life Assurance et al. v. *Greater Johannesburg Transitional Metropolitan Council*, 1999. Decision of the South African Constitutional Court, reported as 1999 (1) SA 374 (CC).

Fernandes, E., 2007. 'Constructing the "right to the city" in Brazil', *Social & Legal Studies* 16(2), 201–219.

Frug, J., 1996. 'The geography of community', *Stanford Law Review* 48(5), 1047–1108.

Gabel, P., 1984. 'The phenomenology of rights-consciousness and the pact of the withdrawn selves', *Texas Law Review* 62(4), 1563–1599.

Gifford, G., 2014. 'Joburg billing chaos continues', *ENCA*, 20 August 2014, from www.enca.com.

Gloppen, S., 2005. 'Social rights litigation as transformation: South African perspectives'. In: Jones, P. & Stokke, K. (eds.), *Democratizing Development: The Politics of Socio-economic Rights in South Africa*, pp. 153–180. Leiden: Martinus Nijhoff.

Government of the RSA v. *Grootboom*, 2001. Decision of the South African Constitutional Court, reported as 2001 (1) SA 46 (CC).

Harrison, P. & Harrison, K., 2014. 'Soweto: A study in socio-spatial differentiation'. In: Harrison, P., Gotz, G., Todes, A., & Wray, C. (eds.), *Changing Space, Changing City: Johannesburg after Apartheid*, pp. 293–318. Johannesburg: Wits University Press.

Harrison, P. & Zack, T., 2014. 'The wrong side of the mining belt? Spatial transformations and identities in Johannesburg's southern suburbs'. In: Harrison, P., Gotz, G., Todes, A., & Wray, C. (eds.), *Changing Space, Changing City: Johannesburg after Apartheid*, pp. 269–292. Johannesburg: Wits University Press.

Harrison, P., Gotz, G., Todes, A. & Wray, C., 2014a. 'Materialities, subjectivities and spatial transformation in Johannesburg'. In: Harrison, P., Gotz, G., Todes, A., & Wray, C. (eds.), *Changing Space, Changing City: Johannesburg after Apartheid*, pp. 2–39. Johannesburg: Wits University Press.

Harrison, P., Masson, A. & Sinwell, L., 2014. 'Alexandra'. In: Harrison, P., Gotz, G., Todes, A., & Wray, C. (eds.), *Changing Space, Changing City: Johannesburg after Apartheid*, pp. 342–369. Johannesburg: Wits University Press.

Harvey, D., 2008. 'The right to the city', *New Left Review* 53, 23–40.

Hassim, S., Kupe, T. & Worby, E. (eds.), 2008. *Go Home or Die Here: Violence, Xenophobia and the Reinvention of Difference in South Africa*. Johannesburg: Wits University Press.

Holston, J., 2009. 'Insurgent citizenship in an era of global urban peripheries', *City & Society* 21(2), 245–267.

Huchzermeyer, M., Karam, A. & Maina, M., 2014. 'Informal settlements'. In: Harrison, P., Gotz, G., Todes, A., & Wray, C. (eds.), *Changing Space, Changing City: Johannesburg after Apartheid*, pp. 154–175. Johannesburg: Wits University Press.

Jacobs, J., 1961 [1993]. *The Death and Life of Great American Cities*, 3rd edn. New York: Modern Library.

Johannesburg Metropolitan Municipality v. *Gauteng Development Tribunal*, 2010, decision of the South African Constitutional Court, reported as 2010 (6) SA 182 (CC).

Lefebvre, H., 1996. *Writings on Cities* (trans., Kofman, E. & Lebas, E.). Oxford: Blackwell.

Le Roux, W., 2001. 'From acropolis to metropolis: The new Constitutional Court building and South African street democracy', *Southern African Public Law* 16(1), 139–168.

Le Roux, W., 2004. 'Bridges, clearings and labyrinths: The architectural framing of post-apartheid constitutionalism', *South African Public Law* 19(3), 629–664.

Liebenberg, S., 2008. 'Socio-economic rights: Revisiting the reasonableness review/minimum core debate'. In: Woolman, S. & Bishop, M. (eds.), *Constitutional Conversations*, pp. 303–329. Pretoria: PULP.

Liebenberg, S., 2010. *Socio-economic Rights Adjudication under a Transformative Constitution*. Cape Town: Juta.

Liebenberg, S., 2012. 'Engaging the paradoxes of the universal and particular in human rights adjudication: The possibilities and pitfalls of "meaningful engagement"', *African Human Rights Law Journal* 12(1), 1–29.

Liebenberg, S., 2015. 'Social rights and transformation in South Africa: Three frames', *South African Journal of Human Rights* 31(3), 446–471.

Local Government Transition Act 209 of 1993.

Mabin, A., 2006. 'Local government in South Africa's larger cities'. In: Pillay, U., Tomlinson, R. & Du Toit, J. (eds.), *Democracy and Delivery: Urban Policy in South Africa*, pp. 135–156. Cape Town: HSRC Press.

Malan, N., 2008. 'Rights, the public and the South African Constitution: Civil society and the performance of rights', *Anthropology Southern Africa* 31(1), 58–69.

Malan, N., 2009. 'The performance of the right to have access to social security', *Law, Democracy & Development* 13(1), 71–95.

Mbazira, C., 2009. *Litigating Socio-economic Rights in South Africa: A Choice between Corrective and Distributive Justice*. Pretoria: PULP.

Mbembe, A. & Nuttall, S., 2004. 'Writing the world from an African metropolis', *Public Culture* 16(3), 347–372.

McCann, M.W., 1994. *Rights at Work: Pay Equity Reform and the Politics of Legal Mobilization*. Chicago, London: University of Chicago Press.

McLean, K., 2009. *Constitutional Deference, Courts and Socio-Economic Rights in South Africa*. Pretoria: PULP.

Minister of Health v. *Treatment Action Campaign (No. 2)*, 2002. Decision of the South African Constitutional Court, reported as 2002 (5) SA 721 (CC).

Mitchell, D., 2003. *The Right to the City: Social Justice and the Fight for Public Space*. New York: Guilford Press.

Morris, A., 1999. *Bleakness & Light: Inner-city Transition in Hillbrow, Johannesburg*. Johannesburg: Wits University Press.

Municipal Structures Act, 117 of 1998.

Municipal Systems Act, 32 of 2000.

Murray, M.J., 2008. *Taming the Disorderly City: The Spatial Landscape of Johannesburg after Apartheid*. Ithaca, London: Cornell University Press.

Murray, M.J., 2011. *City of Extremes: The Spatial Politics of Johannesburg*. Durham, London: Duke University Press.

Murray, M.J., 2014. 'City of layers: The making and shaping of affluent Johannesburg after apartheid'. In: Haferburg, C. & Huchzermeyer, M. (eds.), *Urban Governance in Post-Apartheid Cities: Modes of Engagement in South Africa's Metropoles*, pp. 179–196. Pietermaritzburg: UKZN Press.

Nevin, A., 2014. 'Instant mutuality: The development of Maboneng in inner-city Johannesburg', *Anthropology Southern Africa* 37(3), 187–201.

Palmary, I., Rauch, J. & Simpson, G., 2003. 'Violent crime in Johannesburg'. In: Tomlinson, R., Beauregard, R.A., Bremner, L. & Mangcu, X. (eds.) *Emerging Johannesburg: Perspectives on the Postapartheid City*, pp. 101–122. New York, London: Routledge.

Parnell, S. & Pieterse, E., 2010. 'The "right to the city": Institutional imperatives of a developmental state' *International Journal of Urban & Regional Research* 34(1), 146–163.

Pernegger, L., 2014. 'The agonistic state: Metropolitan government responses to city strife post-1994'. In: Haferburg, C. & Huchzermeyer, M. (eds.), *Urban Governance in Post-Apartheid Cities: Modes of Engagement in South Africa's Metropoles*, pp. 61–78. Pietermaritzburg: UKZN Press.

Pieterse, M., 2004. 'Coming to terms with judicial enforcement of socio-economic rights', *South African Journal of Human Rights* 20(3), 383–417.

Pieterse, M., 2006. 'Resuscitating socio-economic rights: Constitutional entitlements to health care services', *South African Journal of Human Rights* 22(3), 473–502.

Pieterse, M., 2007. 'Eating socio-economic rights: The usefulness of rights talk in alleviating social hardship revisited', *Human Rights Quarterly* 29(3), 796–822.

Pieterse, M., 2008. 'On "dialogue", "translation" and "voice": A reply to Sandra Liebenberg'. In: Woolman, S. & Bishop, M. (eds.) *Constitutional Conversations*, pp. 331–347. Pretoria: PULP.

Pieterse, M., 2009. 'Relational socio-economic rights', *South African Journal of Human Rights* 25(2), 198–217.

Pieterse, M., 2014a. 'The right to the city and the urban environment: Re-imagining section 24 of the 1996 Constitution', *Southern African Public Law* 29(1), 175–193.

Pieterse, M., 2014b. 'Development, the right to the city and the legal and constitutional responsibilities of local government in South Africa', *South African Law Journal* 131(1), 149–177.

Pieterse, E., Parnell, S., Swilling, M. & Van Donk, M., 2008. 'Consolidating developmental local government'. In: Van Donk, M., Swilling, M., Pieterse, E. & Parnell, S. (eds.), *Consolidating Developmental Local Government: Lessons from the South African Experience*, pp. 1–24. Cape Town: UCT Press.

Pindell, N., 2006. 'Finding a right to the city: Exploring property and community in Brazil and in the United States', *Vanderbilt Journal of Transnational Law* 39(2), 435–480.

Pindell, N., 2008. 'The right to the city', *Harvard Blackletter Law Journal* 24(1), 69- 71.

Purcell, M., 2002. 'Excavating Lefebvre: The right to the city and its urban politics of the inhabitant', *GeoJournal* 58, 99–108.

Rubin, M., 2014. 'Johannesburg's Bad Buildings Programme: The World Class City hegemony at work?'. In: Haferburg, C. & Huchzermeyer, M. (eds.), *Urban Governance in Post-Apartheid Cities: Modes of Engagement in South Africa's Metropoles*, pp. 211–230. Pietermaritzburg: UKZN Press.

Rule, S.P., 1989. 'The emergence of a racially mixed residential suburb in Johannesburg: Demise of the Apartheid city?' *Geographical Journal* 155(2), 196–203.

S v. *Govender*, 1982. Decision of the Transvaal Supreme Court, reported as 1986 (3) SA 969 (T).

Schmidt, D., 2008. 'From spheres to tiers – Conceptions of local government in South Africa in the period 1994–2006'. In: Van Donk, M., Swilling, M., Pieterse, E. & Parnell, S. (eds.), *Consolidating Developmental Local Government: Lessons from the South African Experience*, pp. 109–129. Cape Town: UCT Press.

Simone, A., 2005. 'The right to the city', *Interventions* 7(3), 321–325.

Smith, L. & Morris, N., 2008. 'Municipal entities: A panacea for service delivery constraints?' In: Van Donk, M., Swilling, M., Pieterse, E. & Parnell, S. (eds.), *Consolidating Developmental Local Government: Lessons from the South African Experience*, pp. 423–444. Cape Town: UCT Press.

Smith, L. & Rubin, M., 2015. 'Beyond invented and invited spaces of participation: The Phiri and Olivia Road court cases and their outcome'. In: Benit-Gbaffou, C. (ed.), *Popular Politics in South African Cities: Unpacking Community Participation*, pp. 248–281. Cape Town: HSRC Press.

Statistics South Africa, n.d. 'City of Johannesburg', viewed 1 January 2017, from http://beta2.stassa.gov.za/?page_id=1021id=city-of-johannesburg-municipality.

Steinberg, C., 2006. 'Can reasonableness protect the poor? A review of South Africa's socio-economic rights jurisprudence', *South African Law Journal* 123(2), 264–284.

Steytler, N., 2004. 'Socio-economic rights and the process of privatizing basic municipal services', *Law, Democracy & Development* 8(1), 157–180.

Steytler, N. & De Visser, J., 2008. 'Local government'. In: Woolman, S., Bishop, M. & Brickhill, J. (eds.), *Constitutional Law of South Africa*, 2nd edn, ch. 22. Cape Town: Juta.

Sunkin, M., 2004. 'Conceptual issues in researching the impact of judicial review on government bureaucracies'. In: Hertogh, M. & Halliday, S. (eds.), *Judicial Review and Bureaucratic Impact: International and Interdisciplinary Perspectives*, pp. 43–75. Cambridge, UK: Cambridge University Press.

Sunstein, C.R., 2001. 'Social and economic rights? Lessons from South Africa', *Constitutional Forum* 11(4), 123–131.

Tomlinson, R., Beauregard, R.A., Bremner, L. & Mangcu, X., 2003. 'The postapartheid struggle for an integrated Johannesburg'. In: Tomlinson, R., Beauregard, R.A., Bremner, L. & Mangcu, X. (eds.), *Emerging Johannesburg: Perspectives on the Postapartheid City*, pp. 3–20. New York, London: Routledge.

Tushnet, M., 1984. 'An essay on rights', *Texas Law Review* 62(4), 1363–1403.

Valentine, G., 2008. 'Living with difference: Reflections on geographies of encounter', *Progress in Human Geography* 32(3), 323–337.

Van der Walt, J., 2007. 'Johannesburg: A tale of two cases'. In: Philippopoulos-Mihalopoulos, A. (ed.), *Law and the City*, pp. 221–236. Oxford, New York: Routledge.
Van Donk, M. & Pieterse, E., 2006. 'Reflections on the design of a post-apartheid system of (urban) local government'. In: Pillay, U., Tomlinson, R. & Du Toit, J. (eds.), *Democracy and Delivery: Urban Policy in South Africa*, pp. 107–134. Cape Town: HSRC Press.
Van Marle, K., 2014. 'Revisioning space, justice and belonging in the capital city of Pretoria/Tshwane', *De Jure* 47(2), 163–174.
Van Onselen, C., 1982. *New Babylon, New Nineveh: Everyday Life on the Witwatersrand 1886–1914*. Johannesburg, Cape Town: Jonathan Ball Publishers.
Vearey, J., Palmary, I., Thomas, L., Nunez, L. & Drimie, S., 2010. 'Urban health in Johannesburg: The importance of place in understanding intra-urban inequalities in the context of migration and HIV', *Health & Place* 16(4), 694–702.
Visser, G., 2013. 'Looking beyond the urban poor in South Africa: The new terra incognita for urban geography?' *Canadian Journal of African Studies* 47(1), 75–93.
Walsh, S., 2013. '"We won't move": The suburbs take back the center in urban Johannesburg', *City* 17(3), 400–408.
Wesson, M., 2004. '*Grootboom* and beyond: Reassessing the socio-economic jurisprudence of the South African Constitutional Court', *SAJHR* 20(2), 284–308.
Williams, P.J., 1987. 'Alchemical notes: Reconstructing ideals from deconstructed rights', *Harvard Civil Rights Civil Liberties Law Review* 22(2), 401–433.
Wilson, S. & Dugard, J., 2011. 'Taking poverty seriously: The South African Constitutional Court and socio-economic rights', *Stellenbosch Law Review* 22(3), 664–682.
Winkler, T., 2013. 'Why won't downtown Johannesburg "regenerate"? Reassessing Hillbrow as a case example', *Urban Forum* 24(3), 309–324.
World Charter on the Right to the City, 2005. Accessed 1 January 2017 from www.globalgovernancewatch.org/resources/world-charter-on-the-right-to-the-city.
Young, I.M., 1990. *Justice and the Politics of Difference*. Princeton: Princeton University Press.
Young, K.G., 2010. 'A typology of economic and social rights adjudication: Exploring the catalytic function of judicial review', *International Journal of Constitutional Law* 8(3), 385–420.

2 Inhabiting Johannesburg

Housing rights struggles

Introduction

The ways in which people make a home for themselves in the city are clear exercises of their right to the city, whereas the location of that home and the conditions prevailing there are clear indicators of the extent to which people enjoy the right.[1] Furthermore, housing practices are where performances of the right to the city most often clash with the rights of others, as well as with the efforts of the State to balance these competing exercises of the right in pursuit of the common good.

Struggles over living space have been central to Johannesburg politics since the city's early days. Being a city initially designed to keep black people out of the centre, and to restrict their movements to and within it, Johannesburg's post-apartheid reconstruction has predictably often involved conflicts over poor and black people's ways of inhabiting the city. The processes of the inner city's middle class and corporate abandonment, its appropriation by formerly excluded poor people as well as by opportunists eager to exploit them, and its contested reclamation by both public power and private capital in the name of urban regeneration, have interacted with broader processes of urbanisation that also play out on the city's outskirts, where informal settlements have intermittently mushroomed, languished and faced constant threats of eradication.

Notably, legal rights and adjudication have been central to housing struggles in Johannesburg since long before the formal legal entrenchment of housing rights. As alluded to in Chapter 1, the Transvaal Supreme Court effectively brought an end to the enforcement of the Group Areas Act and opened up the formerly 'white' inner city and surrounds for habitation by people of all races, by ruling in *S* v. *Govender* that it was unlawful to evict an 'illegal' Indian resident of Mayfair from her home, given the hardship that this would cause her in light of the lack of suitable alternative accommodation.[2]

Given the historical exclusion of the majority of South Africans from urban inhabitance, it was unsurprising that the democratic constitutional dispensation would uncompromisingly protect housing rights. Section 26(1) of the 1996 Constitution provides that 'everyone has the right to have access to adequate housing', with section 26(2) adding that 'the state must take reasonable legislative and other measures, within its available resources, to achieve the progressive realisation of this right'. Crucially, section 26(3) further stipulates that 'no one may be evicted from their home, or have their home demolished, without an order of court made after considering all the relevant circumstances' and that 'no legislation may permit arbitrary evictions'. Clearly grounded in the *Govender* court's finding that eviction orders should not be made 'without the fullest enquiry',[3] this latter provision ensured that courts would henceforth be pivotal to the resolution of struggles over urban inhabitance in South Africa.

An elaborate legislative framework was ushered in to give effect to the far-reaching provisions of section 26 of the Constitution.[4] The aims of the 1997 Housing Act, enacted solely for this purpose, include the promotion of 'the process of racial, social, economic and physical integration in urban and rural areas', as well as 'the establishment, development and maintenance of socially and economically viable communities and of safe and healthy living conditions to ensure the elimination and prevention of slums and slum conditions'.[5] The Act further requires all spheres of government to prioritise the housing needs of the poor and to meaningfully consult with individuals and communities affected by housing developments.[6]

While the Constitution envisages housing provision as a shared responsibility of national and provincial governments, the Housing Act introduced significant responsibilities for local government, especially in urban areas. For instance, section 9 of the Act requires that municipalities must 'take all reasonable and necessary steps', as part of their integrated development planning processes, to ensure that 'inhabitants ... have access to adequate housing on a progressive basis' and that 'conditions not conducive to the health and safety of the inhabitants ... are prevented or removed'. This mandate has proved burdensome, especially since its implementation has remained contingent upon national and provincial government's housing visions and upon their willingness to release sufficient resources for its realisation.[7]

Further integral to the realisation of section 26(3) of the Constitution has been the 1998 Prevention of Illegal Eviction from and Unlawful Occupation of Land Act (hereinafter 'the PIE Act'), which lays down procedural justice principles governing the process for evicting illegal land or building occupiers. The Act determines that courts may grant eviction orders only where this would be just and equitable in light of all relevant circumstances, including the special needs of vulnerable occupiers and, in the case of occupations exceeding 6 months in duration, the availability of alternative places for settlement.[8] These provisions would prove pivotal to the development of South Africa's housing rights jurisprudence and have, in practice, added significantly to local government's burden in carrying out its responsibilities in terms of the Housing Act.

As is apparent from the Housing Act, municipalities' housing-related obligations are narrowly intertwined with their constitutional responsibility (located in the section 24 environmental right) to ensure a sustainable, healthy and safe urban environment conducive to human flourishing.[9] In addition to the positive obligation to progressively cater for inhabitants' housing needs, municipalities must also ensure that housing conditions do not fall foul of minimum environmental and safety standards, and must protect the communal city living environment from degradation.[10] The clash between this obligation and occupiers' more immediate housing needs has significantly hampered municipalities' compliance with their broader developmental mandate, with cities and towns struggling to simultaneously satisfy urgent housing needs and maintain a sustainable living environment, within prevailing administrative and resource constraints.[11]

The City of Johannesburg has become the poster child of these difficulties. The prime urban magnet for impoverished rural South Africans in search of opportunity, Joburg has, both physically and administratively, simply been unable to cope with the extent of post-1994 urban housing demand. This has manifested itself in two housing-related policy pressure sores which have, between them, constituted the stage for most of the legal contestations to be discussed in this chapter. First, the unauthorised proliferation of informal settlements on Johannesburg's margins and on other pockets of empty land throughout the city[12] has squarely pitched the City's obligation to prevent the forming of slum conditions against informal settlers' need for *somewhere* to reside. Second, the (often illegal) residential occupation of abandoned inner city office and light-industrial buildings, together with overcrowding and neglect of nearby high-rise residential buildings, has led to large-scale environmental degradation, to the point where significant portions of the inner city and surrounding flatlands had, by the end of the 1990s, turned into the very slums that local government is legally obliged to prevent and eradicate.

On paper, the City's understanding of the habitation-related challenges that it faces and its policy vision for overcoming these have, over the years, become quite nuanced and impressive. Committed to overcoming the injustices resulting from Johannesburg's spatial fragmentation, the Metropolitan Council understands that exclusion from the opportunities provided by the city can be the result both of design (as with the historical situation of townships on the urban periphery, where people have been located far from opportunities) and of neglect (as with the deterioration and abandonment of the inner city and surrounds, which means that opportunities relocate away from people).[13] It also appreciates that, for various historical and developmental reasons, Johannesburg is a city of multiple nodes where it is not possible to pinpoint a single 'core' or 'periphery'.[14] As a result, the City's approach to habitation does not merely involve housing provision and enhancing access to a single social and economic centre, but is also tied up with drives to regenerate the inner city and surrounds, to develop economic opportunities across the city's sprawling geography (including in formerly marginalised townships), and to reform historically abysmal public transport networks so as to enhance mobility and access to opportunity within the city.[15]

As to the nature of habitation, the City follows national and provincial government in ascribing to a formal, ownership-centred notion of housing as at once providing a location within the city, a centre for family life and a locus for service delivery and consumption.[16] Ultimately nested within a conception of urban citizenship focused on individual self-responsibility and social upliftment through economic participation, this notion is also closely aligned to the idea of a housing/property 'ladder', in terms of which citizens progress from rental accommodation to ownership of homes of 'different levels of quality, cost, size and value' over time, as their economic prosperity increases.[17]

Of course, this understanding is idealistic, and is continuously thwarted by the day-to-day realities of the scores of Johannesburg inhabitants for whom such formal housing arrangements are either unaffordable or unpractical.[18] On the ground, the City's vision has in several respects failed to connect or respond to these realities and, as a result, the implementation of its policies has often fallen short of preventing or ameliorating slum conditions, both in the inner city and the outlying informal settlements.

In part, this has been because National and Provincial government-driven 'Reconstruction and Development Programme' ('RDP') housing delivery drives have, for the most part, directly frustrated the City's vision of a more connected and integrated urban environment. For a variety of practical and policy reasons, these drives (in terms of which qualifying low income families are given ownership over newly-constructed, state-subsidised houses, for which there are ever-growing waiting lists) have mostly involved the construction of matchbox-style, low-density housing developments on poorly located vacant land on the outskirts of the city, from where many housing beneficiaries have typically been unable to either meaningfully access the city or further ascend the 'property ladder'.[19]

Without the required legal authority or accompanying budget to launch and implement large-scale housing delivery projects of its own, the City has thus been relegated to realising its spatial vision primarily through measures associated with its responsibilities to prevent and eradicate slum conditions. In informal settlements, this has involved walking an uncomfortable tightrope between so-called 'in situ' upgrading schemes (in terms of which informal settlements are formalised and incorporated into the urban infrastructure) on the one hand, and the eradication and relocation of settlements deemed unfit for such upgrading on the other.[20] This has often involved hardship for the residents of informal settlements, who have resisted the City's efforts both through protest and defiance, and through the law.

In the inner city, the City has pursued its vision of a CBD that functions as 'a key residential node where a diverse range of people from different income groups and backgrounds can have their residential needs met', and which is neither 'a dormitory for the poor, nor an exclusive enclave of loft apartments, galleries and coffee shops',[21] mostly through targeting living arrangements that infringe on this vision. A prime policy vehicle for this has been different iterations of the so-called 'Bad Buildings Programme', conceptualised in terms of the City's *Inner City Regeneration Charter* and involving the identification and rehabilitation of 'slummified' buildings, logically preceded by the eviction of their residents.[22] However, the City's initial implementation efforts in terms of this policy neglected to address what, practically, was to happen to the scores of people evicted from 'bad' buildings.[23] The result was large-scale resistance and the mounting of a sustained legal challenge against the implementation of the policy.

It is these legal struggles and their effects, both on the people on whose behalf they have been waged and on the City, that form the focus of this chapter. Below, I first illustrate how the habitation practices of Johannesburg's poorest residents, in and of themselves, amount to rights assertion, while at the same time sometimes posing a threat to the realisation of other right-serving objectives. Thereafter, I consider the legal invocation and vindication of the constitutional right of access to adequate housing and its accompanying guarantee against arbitrary eviction, canvassing both the Constitutional Court's initial, ground-laying jurisprudence in this regard and the turn of this jurisprudence towards urban housing struggles, with a focus on cases involving Johannesburg.

Housing practices of Johannesburg's urban poor

That affordable, well located and decent housing options are scarce in Johannesburg is no understatement. Across the city's vast geography, a great many people are not formally housed. Often, this is because they cannot afford to be – there is a widely-reported lack of housing options at the lower rungs of the so-called 'housing ladder', especially for newcomers to the city, unemployed persons and low-wage earners. This is not to say that there are no low-income housing options across wider Johannesburg – there are plenty, with both state-sponsored social housing and privately developed 'affordable housing' rental supply constantly increasing. But it is safe to say that demand for such accommodation significantly outstrips supply, especially in areas that are well located in terms of opportunities for low-skilled and informal work, such as the inner city and immediate surrounds, Alexandra and Soweto.[24]

Moreover, especially among poor and informally employed persons, motivations for habitation practices and their intersection with livelihood-generating strategies are complex and multi-layered, and find expression in complicated, transient and volatile housing arrangements that belie simple categorisation in terms of affordability and location. For instance, an increasingly observed and ostensibly baffling Johannesburg phenomenon is that not insignificant numbers of informally housed or seemingly homeless people are, in fact, the owners of state-provided RDP houses (often, but not always, located at the outskirts of the city), but nevertheless opt for informal living arrangements. Their many reasons for this include the (often) poor location of state-provided housing, the financial and other burdens associated with home ownership and the choice to rather use homes to generate capital (by selling them or renting them out to others).[25]

While it is therefore so that a great many of Johannesburg's poorer residents are housed formally (in homes or apartments that they either own or rent), many others seek out (temporary or more permanent) accommodation in the city's burgeoning informal market. In the inner city and surrounding flatlands, for instance, there is an elaborate and high-demand rental market for single rooms or other spaces (ranging from cordoned off portions of rooms and enclosed balconies to part-time bed sharing deals) in shared apartments.[26] Across the upmarket northern suburbs, meanwhile, backyard rooms and domestic workers' quarters are rented or otherwise occupied by poorer families (often linked to some employment relationship between the occupier and the owner of the property), while there are tens of thousands of rented rooms or so-called 'backyard shacks' across established townships like Alexandra, Diepsloot and Soweto.[27]

What all of these forms of accommodation have in common are their often temporary and highly flexible nature which, while associated with low security of tenure, often leads occupiers to opt for them rather than more formal housing arrangements, even where these are strictly affordable to them.[28] Moreover, while the market for such housing operates almost entirely outside of that envisaged by prevailing legal frameworks (sometimes to the point where living conditions fall significantly short of applicable health and safety laws), it is an intricate, organised and lively one, often perceived by tenants as being more in touch with their needs (such as the need for a temporary base – rather than a home – during the working week, or the need for flexible and impermanent accommodation to enhance mobility in pursuit of economic opportunity), and as ultimately operating more fairly, more flexibly and less exploitatively towards them than its formal, 'legal', counterpart.[29]

While the City does not approve of these informal arrangements (remaining wedded, as it does, to a notion of urban citizenship that is more stable, law-abiding and settled) it largely leaves them be, perhaps mindful of the crucial purpose that they serve and of the limited number of realistic formal alternatives.[30] However, there are close connections and interactions between these informal living practices and those that the City does regard as problematic.

The first of these is occasioned by the fact that the inner city informal rental market often spills over into abandoned or otherwise empty industrial and commercial buildings, or sets poorly managed residential buildings on a downward path of physical decline, with an accompanying reduction in living conditions. A particularly pernicious subspecies of this has been so-called 'building hijacking', where buildings fall into the hands of criminal 'landlords' who, while themselves lacking any legal entitlement to buildings, 'take over' their 'management' and charge rent to occupiers while doing nothing to ensure suitable living conditions. Hijacking, alongside similarly abhorrent practices of 'shack farming' (where legal owners or illegal 'landlords' of industrial buildings allow for the erection of countless shacks within, in return for rental), more conventional neglect by absentee landlords and more straightforward building 'invasions' (where empty buildings are illegally occupied on occupiers' own initiative), have contributed to a situation where scores of people live in severely unhealthy, unhygienic and dangerous conditions (with the destruction of buildings by fire and collapse, often with resulting fatalities or serious injuries for occupiers, a regular occurrence).[31]

Second, the City has always shared national and provincial government's disapproval of informal settlements, of which a great many have over the years developed across Johannesburg – often, but not always, on the periphery.

In many instances, these have come into being incrementally and with varying degrees of acquiescence from authorities, while at other times they have been the result of highly organised and intricately planned 'land invasions' organised by rent-charging 'planners' who bear more than a passing similarity to the building hijackers of the inner city.[32] Informal settlements typically consist a variety of building structures of varying degrees of permanence and, over time, come to resemble densely populated suburbs. Perhaps the most concrete example of urban place-making 'from below', national housing policy allows for informal settlements to become permanent under certain conditions, in which case they are 'formalised' and subsumed into the urban fabric. However, the associated official processes are fraught with complexities, contradictions and conflict. Much as official policy acknowledges their inevitable place in the urban fabric and expresses a commitment to their 'in situ' upgrading, informal settlements have remained sites of struggle, with demolitions, evictions and forced relocations from Joburg's informal settlements routinely making headlines.[33]

Overall, while there are often elements of illegality (and, in the case of both informal settlements and inner city building occupation, outright criminality) in informal habitation practices, and while the unhealthy, unsustainable and often dangerous environmental conditions associated with many of them should not be left unaddressed, it must be remembered that those who live informally are simply ordinary people, struggling to make ends meet in an urban environment that tends to be hostile to their needs.[34] Their practices should be viewed as a direct enactment of the right to the city, an appropriation of the urban environment to serve not only their needs of habitation, but also of livelihood, family life and other needs integral to human dignity.[35]

At the same time, while the geographic and economic limitations on their choices are real, the fact of their conscious enactment of the right to the city warns against viewing informally housed urban inhabitants as agency-less victims with nowhere to go and at the perpetual mercy of others. As Marie Huchzermeyer has observed in relation to informal settlements:

> While the real lack of options must be acknowledged, informal settlements would not exist without the will or resolve of thousands of households or individual men and women, who assess their situation and decide actively to connect their lives to the city or its fringes through a particular informal settlement, and by consciously navigating among (and at times resisting or defying) players whom they know exploit their existence.[36]

Not all housing practices by the poor are desperate attempts at survival. In many instances, they are practical, strategic and adaptable actions taken by autonomous individuals after having considered several alternative options and having taken account of a legion of factors. As such, they need neither be immune from nor at the mercy of State attempts to refashion the urban environment in the common interest.

While it is clearly necessary for authorities to adopt a flexible and accommodating approach to informal habitation practices,[37] many competing interests equally inherent to the right to the city are advanced by attempts to maintain a safe and sustainable urban environment and to resist further fragmentation and exclusion, both by way of peripheralisation and of neglect. There are a great many intricate balances to be struck, and it is to the legal struggles over these balances that I now turn.

Urban habitation struggles in the courts

Of all the socio-economic rights entrenched in the 1996 Constitution, the right of access to housing and its accompanying guarantee against arbitrary eviction has arguably had the most profound influence on the state of South African law where, prior to 1994, private property rights reigned supreme and trumped all competing rights, not to mention habitation practices that did not conform to the associated property regime.[38] In the discussion that follows, I pay only cursory attention to the general development of the South African common law of property in the face of constitutional values, focusing instead only on those aspects of this development that impact urban habitation. Moreover, the discussion below is predominantly (though not exclusively) focused on impermanent and informal forms of urban habitation. Accordingly, it does not deal with those strands of housing rights jurisprudence that have enhanced safeguards for poor people's rights of home-ownership.[39] Nor is it concerned with jurisprudence pertaining to informal habitation in more rural areas,[40] except insofar as this jurisprudence overlaps directly with that on informal settlements.

The focus, then, is on the two 'pressure sores' of the implementation of housing and urban management policies in Johannesburg: informal settlements and inner city building occupation. The latter takes up the bulk of the discussion, not least because a greater proportion of the relevant case-law originated specifically from Johannesburg.

Setting the stage in informal settlements: Grootboom, PE Municipality *and* Modderklip

The Constitutional Court's initial housing rights jurisprudence was developed in the context of cases originating from struggles over land invasion and the formation of urban informal settlements elsewhere in South Africa. Of these cases, the most significant has been *Government of the RSA* v. *Grootboom*, where the Constitutional Court declared that the national and provincial housing policy frameworks in the Western Cape, and the actions of the City of Cape Town in terms thereof, were unconstitutional.

Originating from fallout over the eviction and demolition of an informal settlement near Wallacedene on the Cape Flats, the *Grootboom* case turned on the demand by evicted community members that they be provided with adequate shelter. Rejecting the argument that the right of access to adequate housing in section 26(1) of the Constitution embodied an immediately enforceable minimum core obligation upon the State to provide everybody with rudimentary shelter,[41] the Court instead decided the claim by evaluating the reasonableness of the challenged housing policies, in terms of section 26(2). It found that the policies were unreasonable and therefore unconstitutional, primarily because they did not cater for the emergency needs of the most vulnerable members of the community.[42] Cautioning that its judgment should not be read as condoning land invasions (especially not where this was a strategy to jump the queue for state-allocated permanent housing), the Court also spoke out against the manner in which the eviction took place and emphasised that occupiers of informal settlements should be treated humanely and with procedural fairness, in accordance with the constitutional obligation to respect the right of access to housing.[43]

Grootboom remains the only case in which the Constitutional Court elaborated on the meaning of the phrase 'access to adequate housing' in section 26(1) of the Constitution. It held that the notion of 'access' entailed that housing amounted to 'more than bricks and mortar', and that the right encompassed prerequisites of available land, a constructed dwelling and associated service provision.[44] Clearly reflecting the government's understanding of housing provision as ultimately requiring delivery of ownership over formal, permanent self-standing units, the Court further acknowledged that the 'adequacy' of housing would depend on context which, in urban areas, would include factors such as location, mobility and access to other urban services.[45]

The Court viewed the State's role in relation to housing provision as predominantly being an enabling one. For those who could afford housing themselves, the Court held that the State's responsibilities were limited to 'unlocking the system, providing access to housing stock and a legislative framework to facilitate self-built houses through planning laws and access to finance'.[46] However, there were more direct obligations in relation to those who could not afford their own housing, where the state's obligations were held to be linked to its developmental responsibilities and to its constitutional obligation to provide adequate social assistance to those who are unable to care for themselves.[47]

The 'reasonableness' inquiry conducted in *Grootboom* to ascertain whether the challenged housing policies complied with the right of access to adequate housing, has been the subject of extensive academic debate, as elaborated in Chapter 1. It is worth reiterating here that much of the criticism of the inquiry as yardstick for constitutional compliance has centred on its procedural nature and conceptual emptiness, in that the inquiry arguably fails to set substantive standards to which challenged policies should adhere. On the other hand, the Court's approach has often been praised for being context-sensitive and for embodying an iterative and dialogic model of policy development, which is said to reflect an appropriate institutional balance between the powers of courts and those of the 'democratic' branches of State.

Policy development wise, the reasonableness yardstick has proved useful, with government departments in various fields reportedly taking care to ensure that their policies comply with the requirements laid down in *Grootboom*.[48] The most significant of these requirements for present purposes is that reasonable government policy ought to consider the needs of the most vulnerable members of society, and should especially respond to their immediate, emergency needs.[49] Given that the housing policy challenged in *Grootboom* was found to be unconstitutional precisely for not complying with this aspect of reasonableness, the judgment sparked a policy response that culminated in the inclusion of emergency housing provisions in the National Housing Code.[50] More importantly, it is this part of the reasonableness analysis that would subsequently inform the Constitutional Court's urban eviction jurisprudence.

While the *Grootboom* judgment was initially criticised for seemingly failing to provide concrete relief for the Wallacedene community (over and above temporary measures agreed upon between the occupiers and the Oostenberg Municipality during the hearing),[51] its policy effect on similarly situated communities was therefore significant. Indeed, the Wallacedene community was one of the first beneficiaries of permanent housing delivered in terms of the housing policy developed in the judgment's wake. It is also reported that the community became better organised and more involved in the housing provision process in the wake of the judgment, and that the judgment thereby enhanced the participatory elements of the right to the city.[52]

These participatory elements would find explicit expression in the next housing rights case to reach the Constitutional Court. *Port Elizabeth Municipality* v. *Various Occupiers* presented the first case in which the Court was explicitly required to consider the guarantee against arbitrary eviction in section 26(3) of the Constitution, as operationalised by the provisions of the PIE Act. The case originated from resistance against attempts by the Port Elizabeth Municipality to evict and relocate inhabitants of an informal settlement on private land within the municipal area. The landowner was not a party to the proceedings and was ostensibly unconcerned with the occupation. The inhabitants were, in principle, willing to vacate the settlement, on the condition that they then be allowed to settle elsewhere in the municipal area, without the threat of further eviction. This condition became the crux of the dispute, with the Municipality indicating that the occupiers should move to Walmer township, but not pinpointing land there on which shacks could be erected. This was not acceptable to the occupiers, who were concerned with the lack of tenure security inherent in this 'solution', as well as with the general conditions in the township, which they regarded as 'crime-ridden and unsavoury, as well as overcrowded'.[53]

The Constitutional Court emphasised that section 26(3) of the Constitution required 'concrete and case-specific' solutions to disputes such as these[54] and that, together with the PIE Act's requirement that evictions only be authorised where this would be 'just and equitable', it required of Courts to strike a careful and principled balance between competing rights of ownership and inhabitance, a balance needed ultimately to promote 'the constitutional vision of a caring society based on good neighbourliness and concern'.[55] While concerned with the bigger picture of spatial justice in Port Elizabeth, the Court felt that

> it cannot be presupposed that the greatest good for the many can be achieved at the cost of intolerable hardship for the few, particularly if, by a reasonable application of judicial and administrative statecraft, such human distress could be avoided[56]

and emphasised that

> it is not only the dignity of the poor that is assailed when homeless people are driven from pillar to post in a desperate quest for a place where they and their families can rest their heads. Our society as a whole is demeaned when State action intensifies, rather than mitigates, their marginalisation.[57]

The Court's insistence on a balance between ownership rights and public objectives on the one hand, and habitation rights on the other, clearly indicated a departure from the previous legal approach to land occupation disputes, in terms of which ownership rights inevitably trumped competing considerations.[58] In proceeding to strike the balance, the Court further signalled that it would seldom regard large-scale evictions as just and equitable where they would render inhabitants homeless and destitute.[59] While taking care to point out that there was 'no unqualified constitutional duty on local authorities to ensure that in no circumstances should a home be destroyed unless alternative accommodation or land is made available',[60] the Court nevertheless felt that eviction orders should only reluctantly be granted against settled occupiers in circumstances where reasonable alternative accommodation was not available.[61]

Importantly, the Court was further of the opinion that opposing rights in eviction matters could potentially be reconciled in a 'dignified and effective' manner if parties were encouraged (and perhaps even required) to 'engage with each other in a proactive and honest endeavour to find mutually acceptable solutions'.[62] It proceeded to provide a broad outline of how mediation between parties could enable them to 'relate to each other in pragmatic and sensible ways'[63] in seeking to reach a compromise between their clashing objectives. As to the nature of 'mutually acceptable solutions', the Court was at pains to point out that, while authorities should guard against viewing and treating occupiers as 'faceless and anonymous squatters automatically to be expelled as social nuisances',[64] this did not mean that occupiers could not also be expected to contribute to a compromise. It stated:

> At the same time, those who find themselves compelled by poverty and landlessness to live in shacks on the land of others, should be discouraged from regarding themselves as helpless victims, lacking the possibilities of personal moral agency. The tenacity and ingenuity they show in making homes out of discarded material, in finding work and sending their children to school, are a tribute to their capacity for survival and adaptation. Justice and equity oblige them to rely on this same resourcefulness in seeking a solution to their plight and to explore all reasonable possibilities of securing suitable alternative accommodation or land.[65]

Proceeding to find that the question of whether mediation between parties had been attempted should be taken into account when deciding whether a proposed eviction would be 'just and equitable' (with a negative answer mitigating against the granting of an eviction order), the Court was nevertheless of the opinion that, in the present dispute, 'too much water has flowed under the bridge to make it appropriate that mediation be attempted now'.[66] It then proceeded to weigh the various competing interests in the dispute against each other and concluded that, all things considered, the granting of an eviction order would not be just and equitable.[67] However, in conclusion it added that its decision 'in no way precludes further efforts to find a solution to a situation that is manifestly unsatisfactory to all concerned'.[68]

Clearly introducing a new chapter in South African property law, *PE Municipality* has been lauded for emphasising the need for inhabitants of urban informal settlements to participate in processes that impacted on their habitation in the city.[69] This not only amplified their voice in eviction disputes but, through emphasising their agency, also acknowledged that the right to the city is ultimately dependent on the actions of its beneficiaries.

The next housing rights case to reach the Constitutional Court, *President of the Republic of South Africa* v. *Modderklip Boerdery*, more directly pitched housing rights against private property ownership. The owner of agricultural land on the outskirts of Benoni sued the State for failing to assist him to execute an eviction order against a community of informal settlers, who had 'spilled over' onto the farm from the adjacent Daveyton township. Acknowledging that large-scale urban homelessness was a direct consequence of exclusionary apartheid urban planning policies, the Constitutional Court found that, while failing to prevent and eradicate the informal settlement amounted to an infringement of the land owner's property rights, it would cause 'unimaginable social chaos and misery and untold disruption' to insist on the occupiers' eviction, for the simple reason that they appeared to have nowhere else to go.[70] Like the Supreme Court of Appeal before it, the Constitutional Court understood the *Grootboom* requirement that emergency housing needs of vulnerable people must be taken into account as implying that large-scale evictions would not be constitutionally permissible in circumstances where there were no other reasonable housing alternatives,[71] hence laying the foundation for future claims of alternative accommodation in urban eviction cases.[72]

In the event, the Constitutional Court held that the State's conduct effectively infringed both the landowner's right to property and the occupiers' right of access to adequate housing, and decided that the occupiers could remain on the land until alternative land had been provided to them, while the State had to pay compensation to the landowner for the infringement of its property rights.[73] This was complied with, and several community members were subsequently accommodated in a nearby State-sponsored housing development, although there have been further instances of conflict, evictions and demolitions in the informal settlement in the years since, with further litigation at one stage appearing inevitable.[74]

Subsequent application of the legal framework created by *Grootboom*, *PE Municipality* and *Modderklip* by courts in urban eviction cases confirmed the case-by-case and context specific nature of the balancing exercise inherent in section 26(3) of the Constitution, as well as its links to the requirement of reasonableness for the implementation of housing policy. For example, in *City of Cape Town* v. *Rudolph*, the Cape High Court refused to grant an eviction order against a group of informal occupiers of a Cape Town park, finding instead that, by failing to provide for their emergency housing needs, the City of Cape Town was in breach of its constitutional obligations towards the occupiers. The Court accordingly ordered the City to report to it on the steps it had taken to remedy the situation.[75] Then, in *Tswelopele Non-profit Organisation* v. *City of Tshwane Metropolitan Municipality*, the Supreme Court of Appeal found that the unauthorised eviction and demolition of an informal settlement in Garstfontein, Pretoria, was unconstitutional. The Court ordered the City of Tshwane to reconstruct the shelters it had demolished and thus to return possession of the land to the occupiers, pending the outcome of a 'proper' eviction application in terms of the PIE Act.[76]

The aftermath of two eviction disputes in Johannesburg, however, illustrates that the balance of competing interests was not always to favour occupiers, especially not in the short- to medium-term. First, human rights lawyers opposed the Metropolitan Council's decision to eradicate the informal settlement of Mandelaville in the centre of Diepkloof, Soweto and to relocate all occupiers who could not find their own alternative accommodation to the (at the time poorly connected and underdeveloped) Sol Plaatje development at the outskirts of the city. It was argued that the relocation would remove Mandelaville residents from the work opportunities provided by their central Soweto location as well as from essential amenities such as schools and shops, and that it would cause them various forms of hardship.

The court, however, sided with the City, which justified Mandelaville's eradication because of the significant crime and social problems that it brought to Diepkloof. The City further showed that the Sol Plaatje relocation site was in fact within reach of schools and facilities and was better serviced than Mandelaville, and indicated that it would be upgraded for formal housing within a year. The eviction order was granted and the relocation proceeded. Relocated residents complained of a significant escalation in living costs, severe daily inconvenience and various other hardships, whereas commentators bemoaned the ease with which the court accepted the City's version of dispute over that of the residents. On the upside, the City did eventually make good of its promise to develop and upgrade the Sol Plaatje settlement, and conditions there improved significantly.[77]

Similarly, residents of two abandoned warehouses in Wynberg (a light industrial area wedged between Sandton and Alexandra) were ultimately unsuccessful in relying on *PE Municipality* to resist their displacement by the development of a shopping mall aligned to the City's Alexandra Renewal Project. Turning to the courts only after prolonged negotiation with developers and the City ended in deadlock, the occupiers were initially victorious, with the High Court finding that, while conditions in the warehouses were abysmal to the point of rendering them near uninhabitable, the occupiers were constitutionally entitled to 'dignified and individualised treatment with special consideration for the most vulnerable',[78] and ultimately insisting that the City come up with plans for their alternative accommodation. An agreement was then reached to temporarily accommodate the occupiers at a 'transit camp' outside of Alexandra, until they could be allocated housing in a new development extension to the township. The warehouses were duly demolished after this relocation, and the shopping mall project went ahead, but the erstwhile warehouse residents remained at the temporary location for several years, with negative consequences for their day-to-day lives and livelihoods.[79]

While thus generally credited for injecting humanity into cities' response to homelessness, for balancing the various competing interests at stake in eviction disputes and for ensuring that evictees are typically provided with temporary emergency shelter, the courts' initial application of the *Grootboom* reasonableness yardstick in eviction disputes seemed to fall somewhat short of providing more lasting housing solutions.[80] Moreover, the extent of deference to the State's vision for housing delivery and spatial justice inherent to the standard[81] appeared to signal that, as long as occupiers were treated with dignity and their circumstances were seriously considered in the course of eviction disputes, courts were not prepared to interfere with cities' decisions on the location and implications of housing provision and urban development.

Olivia Road and meaningful engagement

Perhaps inevitably, it was the Johannesburg inner city that would provide the context for the most significant development in South African urban evictions law. As discussed above, scores of buildings in the CBD and surrounding flatlands had degenerated into vertical slums by the late 1990s, to the point where they posed a major health and safety risk, and threatened the sustainability of the inner city as a social and economic environment.

In the first of a series of attempts aimed at stemming and reversing this tide, City authorities launched an inner city regeneration strategy in 1999, aiming mainly to improve the public environment so as to lure private sector investment back into the CBD. A central pillar of this strategy was what would come to be known as the 'Bad Buildings Programme', in terms of which buildings that had degenerated into slums would be acquired by the City, cleared of occupiers in terms of health and safety legislation and regulations, and transferred to private developers for refurbishment as commercial or residential stock.[82] Evidently preferring the interests of business or (admittedly lower) middle class residential tenants over those of the bad buildings' 'illegal' (and desperately poor) inhabitants, the implementation of the policy boiled down to simply evicting 'illegal' occupants onto the streets, from where they would typically scramble for shelter in remaining 'bad buildings'.[83]

As evictions gained momentum, an inner-city residents' association, the Inner City Forum/Resource Centre, formed and mobilised in opposition to the implementation of the Bad Buildings Programme. When its public protests fell on deaf ears,[84] the Forum turned to the Law Clinic at the University of the Witwatersrand, and subsequently to the Centre for Applied Legal Studies (CALS), for legal assistance in opposing court applications for eviction orders.[85] This opposition would eventually culminate in a constitutional challenge.

The matter of *City of Johannesburg* v. *Rand Properties* involved resistance to evictions from several properties in the inner city and immediate surrounds, including a dilapidated high-rise apartment block on Olivia road in Berea. Brought by CALS on behalf of the inhabitants, the crux of the legal challenge was that it was unconstitutional to evict inner city building occupiers, without providing them with alternative accommodation within proximity of their economic livelihoods. The challenge succeeded in the Johannesburg High Court, which declared the City's housing policy unconstitutional and interdicted it from evicting the occupiers without first providing alternative accommodation.[86]

The City and inner city property owners reacted negatively to the judgment, which they accused of derailing the Inner City Regeneration Strategy.[87] The City appealed to the Supreme Court of Appeal (SCA), with significant success. While acknowledging that the City lacked a coherent plan on what to do with people that it evicted from inner city buildings and ultimately ordering it to provide those residents who would be rendered homeless by these evictions with temporary accommodation, the SCA regarded the buildings in question as uninhabitable and held that the eviction process undertaken by the City in terms of the National Building Regulations and Building Standards Act was not unconstitutional.[88] The Court's reasons for this finding included that the right of access to adequate housing did not extend an entitlement to remain indefinitely housed in unsafe and dangerous conditions, and that the City had a duty to ensure that such housing conditions did not persist.[89] The Court further asserted that the Constitutional Court's housing jurisprudence did not give evictees an absolute entitlement to receive alternative accommodation, other than temporary, emergency accommodation.[90] Significantly, while holding that the availability and location of alternative accommodation had to be taken into account when deciding whether an eviction was just and equitable, the Court asserted that 'the Constitution does not give a person a right to housing at State expense at a locality of that person's choice (in this case the inner city)',[91] and regarded the occupiers' insistence on 'nothing short of permanent accommodation in the inner city' as unhelpful and unconstructive.[92]

CALS appealed the SCA decision to the Constitutional Court, whose judgment in the matter was reported as *Occupiers of 51 Olivia Road Berea Township* v. *City of Johannesburg* (hereinafter '*Olivia Road*'). CALS called upon to the Court to decide on the constitutionality of the City's housing plan and on that of the relevant provisions of the National Building Regulations and Building Standards Act, as well as on the extent of the City's obligation to provide evictees with alternative accommodation (including the location of such alternative accommodation) and on the question of whether the PIE Act applied to inner city evictions.

The Constitutional Court surprised all parties by making an interim order that required them to

> engage with each other meaningfully and as soon as it is possible for them to do so, in an effort to resolve the differences and difficulties aired in this application in light of the values of the Constitution, the constitutional and statutory duties of the municipality and the rights and duties of the citizens concerned,

while the City in the meantime had to 'alleviate the plight of the applicants who live in the two buildings concerned in this application by making the buildings as safe and conducive to health as is reasonably practicable'.[93] The Court's subsequent judgment then mainly consisted of reasons for this interim order.

Building on its finding in *PE Municipality* that mediation and engagement should ordinarily precede an eviction, and apparently viewing such engagement as constituting the procedural link between the guarantee against eviction in section 26(3) of the Constitution, the City's developmental responsibilities in terms of section 152 and the requirement in *Grootboom* (derived from subsections 26(1) and (2)) that the implementation of housing policy must be 'reasonable', the Constitutional Court found that 'a municipality that ejects people from their homes without first meaningfully engaging with them acts in a manner that is broadly at odds with the spirit and purpose of [its] constitutional obligations'.[94] An obligation to (individually and collectively) engage with occupiers would accordingly arise in every instance where homelessness was a real, foreseeable consequence of an eviction.[95]

The Court proceeded to hold that the objectives of an engagement process preceding an eviction included determining the consequences of an eviction and the extent to which the City could help to alleviate them, the possibility of rendering buildings habitable in the interim, as well as the extent of the City's obligations towards the occupiers and the manner and time at which it could fulfil these.[96] It emphasised that both the City and the occupiers had to display good faith in the engagement process meaning that, on the one hand, the City had to make every reasonable effort to engage meaningfully and could abandon the process only if these efforts were all to fail whereas, on the other hand, occupiers could not 'content themselves with an intransigent attitude or nullify the engagement process by making non-negotiable, unreasonable demands'.[97] Like in *PE Municipality*, the Court affirmed the agency of occupiers, stressing that 'people in need of housing are not, and must not be regarded as a disempowered mass' and adding that they, as well as the civil society organisations that represent them, should act proactively, and not merely defensively, in working towards a solution with the City.[98]

The Court thus justified its interim engagement order by saying that an eviction in the present case would have been unreasonable and inappropriate unless it had been preceded by meaningful engagement.[99] It proceeded to evaluate the settlement agreement reached between parties as a result of the interim engagement order.[100]

As it happened, the settlement agreement presented a major victory for the occupiers, with the City, probably anticipating an adverse finding by the Court, capitulating to almost all their pre-hearing demands. It tendered alternative accommodation in two especially refurbished buildings in the inner city, against payment of very low (indeed, nearly entirely subsidised) rental. It was agreed that the occupiers could remain in this temporary accommodation either until they chose to move elsewhere, or until the City could offer them more permanent, realistic housing solutions. Occupiers were further afforded input into the individual aspects of their relocation, and could inspect their new buildings before relocation and make some (albeit limited) preferences known. Finally, it was agreed that the relocation from Olivia Road would not be implemented by the City's go-to security company (whose employees had collectively become known as the 'Red Ants' and were widely derided for their brutality in effecting inner city evictions).[101] The Court commended the City for having softened its stance towards the occupiers during the litigation, found that the City's response to the engagement order was 'reasonable', and endorsed the settlement.[102]

Having thus solved the immediate issue of what was to happen to the occupants, the Constitutional Court proceeded to briefly consider the remaining substantive points in dispute. It found that the challenged provisions of the National Building Regulations and Building Standards Act were constitutionally problematic only insofar as they did not explicitly require that evictions proceed only after court orders authorising them had been obtained. Emphasising that 'it is appropriate to encourage to leave unsafe or unhealthy buildings in compliance with [a] court order for their eviction',[103] it held that the punitive provisions of the Act (in terms of which someone could be arrested for resisting a health and safety-motivated eviction) applied only when occupiers ignored a duly issued eviction (court) order.[104]

Apart from this finding, the Court essentially declined to decide any of the further points of contention. It found that, in light of the solution reached, it was unnecessary to decide whether the PIE Act applied to the dispute.[105] As to the reasonableness and constitutionality of the City's housing plan and its policy approach to permanent housing provision in and around the inner city, the Court was unwilling to act as court of first instance, but indicated that, in light of the settlement reached, it was satisfied by the City's undertaking to refine its approach over time, in consultation with building occupiers.[106] Finally, the Court did not regard it necessary to decide on the reach and applicability of sections 26(1), (2) and (3) of the Constitution in relation to the City's practices in eviction matters,[107] which pertinently left the question of the location of alternative accommodation undecided.

These (non)findings have been lambasted in the literature, especially by those in favour of an interpretation of section 26 of the Constitution that embodies an entitlement to alternative accommodation close to the location from which people have been evicted. These scholars have bemoaned that the Constitutional Court's silence on the location issue means that the SCA decision in *Rand Properties* (which, it will be recalled, emphatically denied the existence of such an entitlement) remains the authoritative judicial pronouncement on this issue.[108] Similarly, scholars have been disappointed by the Court's strategic deflection of the issue of the overall constitutionality of the City's approach to the inner city housing question, with the effect that it has effectively been allowed to continue with evictions while the extent of occupiers' housing rights have been rendered contingent on the outcome of engagement processes and litigation, on a case by case basis.[109]

Indeed, the Court's relegation of the substantive issues in this case to the 'meaningful engagement' process has been decried as an extreme instance of the 'proceduralisation' of its socio-economic rights jurisprudence, in that it has provided a procedural solution to a substantive housing dispute without laying down any normative parameters to which engagement processes must adhere, or providing any indication of what, at a minimum, building occupiers can expect from the city in future disputes of this kind.[110] The effect of this, it has been argued, is that the extent and enforceability of occupiers' housing entitlements in future disputes have been rendered contingent on the features and dynamics of the engagement process in every individual case, and that meaningful engagement accordingly amounts to little more than a procedural entitlement of occupiers to have their views heard in matters pertaining to their future urban habitation.[111] This, in turn, raises concerns over inequalities in bargaining power in engagement processes, especially in cases where occupants lack legal representation, and perhaps unwisely places a lot of faith in the bona fides of City officials.[112]

This said, most commentators agreed that the 'meaningful engagement' remedy was one with much progressive potential, and that it provided a useful space for inner city inhabitants' voice to be heard in habitation disputes that concern them.[113] Indeed, several scholars have praised the Court for the extent to which it has enhanced principles of deliberative and participatory democracy through the manner that it has crafted and implemented the remedy in *Olivia Road*.[114] In particular, by emphasising case-by-case, context-bound solutions to everyday habitation disputes through the active participation of those at their centre, the Court has indicated a preference for iterative, open, dialogic and dynamic solutions to urban housing disputes, thereby enhancing the participatory elements of the right to the city, the agency of urban inhabitants and the significance of everyday practices of habitation.[115]

Certainly, the effects of the *Olivia Road* judgment on its immediate subjects have been concrete and significant – the occupants were afforded well-located, secure alternative accommodation in the inner city, of a better quality than that from which they had been evicted. While the years since the judgment have seen a souring of the relationship between them and the City, particularly in relation to the maintenance of the buildings to which they have been relocated and the City's continued reluctance to devise more permanent housing solutions for them, few can argue that their individual plights have been significantly improved by the judgment and the City's compliance.[116]

Policy wise, *Olivia Road* made it clear that the inner city regeneration drive had to take the needs of the city's current poor inhabitants seriously, and in all but name established an entitlement to suitable alternative accommodation as a precondition for a successful eviction.[117] The City explicitly took some elements of the judgment on board, with its 2007 Inner City Regeneration Charter and later Inner City Transformation Roadmap acknowledging that its approach to the upliftment of the inner city had to include addressing the systemic inner city housing shortage, and that it had to look into alternative accommodation for those evicted in the course of its operations (although it maintained that it would not always be possible for it to provide such accommodation in the inner city).[118] Indeed, the judgment effectively brought an end to implementation of the Bad Buildings Programme (at least in the form that it took until then) and brought about a definite decrease in the number of City-led evictions from buildings in the CBD.[119]

But there was also a downside to this. Still belaboured with the environmental obligation to improve the inner-city environment, which remains severely threatened by 'bad buildings',[120] City officials have bemoaned the *Olivia Road* judgment, which has significantly tied their hands in carrying out these obligations and appeared initially to have derailed progress on the City's overall inner city regeneration drive. This despondence has seemingly spilled over into the City's public interactions over inner city housing issues. In particular, the relationship between the City and the local NGO sector (notably with SERI, into which the unit in CALS that brought the *Olivia Road* case had morphed) has become extremely strained.[121] There are also several reports of the City now treating inner city building occupiers with hostility and circumspection, and of it behaving cynically in the course of meaningful engagement processes, where it has proved unwilling to accommodate the concerns of occupiers beyond the terms expressly laid down in the *Olivia Road* judgment.[122]

From Olivia Road *to* Blue Moonlight

Informal settlements

That orders of meaningful engagement would not always assist vulnerable persons in makeshift accommodation was illustrated shortly after *Olivia Road* when, in the aftermath of the 2008 xenophobic violence, the Constitutional Court was urgently approached on behalf of displaced persons attempting to resist the closure of temporary refugee camps on the East Rand. The Court issued an engagement order similar to that in *Olivia Road*,[123] but this was either misinterpreted or ignored by the Gauteng Provincial government, which went ahead and closed the camps anyway. The case was subsequently dismissed as moot, so that the non-compliance with the engagement order was never addressed.[124]

But it was in a Cape Town informal settlement where the remedial potential of meaningful engagement would be most strenuously tested. Resistance to the peripheral relocation of thousands of residents from the Joe Slovo informal settlement on Cape Town's outskirts, to make place for the N2 Gateway Project, a large-scale, mixed income housing development (which was also intended to benefit residents of the settlement), made it to the Constitutional Court in mid-2009. With help from the Legal Resources Centre, residents concerned over the extent to which they would be accommodated in the new development, challenged their relocation on a wide array of grounds and insisted that the settlement be upgraded in situ. Much of the challenge related to inadequacies in the consultation process which preceded government's implementation of the relocation plan, which was argued to fall short of meaningful engagement.

Emphasising that meaningful engagement did not mean that there had to be consensus on all aspects of an eviction and relocation, the Constitutional Court in *Residents of Joe Slovo Community, Western Cape* v. *Thubelisha Homes* held that the engagement process, while flawed in several respects, was nevertheless reasonable in the circumstances, and that the shortcomings in the engagement process were thus not so fundamental as to delegitimise the relocation.[125] Many commentators decried this finding, viewing it as a significant retreat from *Olivia Road*'s more substantive conception of meaningful engagement and as accordingly watering down its remedial potential.[126]

The Court attached significant weight to the fact that the ultimate policy goal underlying the relocation was to improve conditions in Joe Slovo, which it regarded as unacceptable and unsustainable.[127] While acknowledging that the relocation would cause hardship to many residents, the Court felt that this was counterbalanced by the greater long-term community benefit to be derived from the Gateway Project, with Yacoob J going as far as to state that 'there are circumstances in which there is no choice but to undergo traumatic experiences so that we can be better of later'.[128] The judgment thereby accepted the government's policy vision for Joe Slovo, even as this vision conflicted with residents' own preferences. Accordingly, much of the judgment appeared to be concerned primarily with ensuring that the government implemented its policy in a manner that causes as little hardship as possible.[129]

The Constitutional Court was further swayed by the temporary nature of the relocation, as well as by the fact that the City undertook to provide transport for relocated residents to their places of work, schools and so forth. This the Court regarded as significantly alleviating the disruption occasioned by the relocation. The Court thus signalled that, rather than fixating on the location of accommodation, it viewed habitation rights as being linked to mobility and to the notion of access to the city.[130] Indeed, there are several indications in the judgment that the Court agrees with the views of the SCA in *Rand Properties* on the question of the location of alternative accommodation, with Ngcobo J going so far as to state that, while regard must be had to the links between the location of alternative accommodation and access to places of livelihood, 'the Constitution does not guarantee a person a right to housing at government expense at the locality of his or her choice'.[131]

Accordingly, finding that the relocation could go ahead, the Court then issued a very detailed order in which it effectively insisted that the City deliver on all its undertakings towards relocated residents (including undertakings pertaining to the features of the houses to which they would be relocated, their access to services and their transportation to workplaces, schools and clinics). It further ordered that all relocated residents had to be meaningfully engaged on all of these issues, thereby handing residents a significant degree of control over the circumstances of their relocation.[132] Furthermore, the Court retained jurisdiction over the matter and allowed parties that were unhappy with the implementation of the order to approach it for a variation thereof.[133] This order stands out as one of the only instances in which the Court has ever exercised a degree of supervisory jurisdiction, and has been welcomed for operationalising the judgment's commitment to ensuring a dialogic and participatory relocation process.[134]

The order proved too much for the City of Cape Town to implement. No doubt influenced by a change in political leadership in the Western Cape (with the DA, which at the time already controlled the City of Cape Town and had from the outset had reservations over the implementation costs of the Gateway project, also taking over the provincial government from the ANC), which meant that there was no longer political will to proceed with the Gateway Project, the City re-evaluated its responsibilities in terms of the *Joe Slovo* order, and decided that it would rather upgrade the settlement in situ. In accordance with the supervisory aspects of the order, the residents re-approached the Constitutional Court to set aside the original relocation order. The Court noted the changes in circumstances since its previous order and, since there seemed to be no prospect of the ordered relocation going ahead, it rescinded that order in its entirety.[135] Despite effectively 'losing' the original legal challenge to their relocation, the effect of *Joe Slovo* was thus that the residents got what they initially demanded, and that their tenure in the redeveloped settlement was now more secure than it had been before.[136]

The Constitutional Court handed down two further judgments pertaining to informal settlements around the same time as the initial *Joe Slovo* judgment. In the first, *Abahlali baseMjondolo Movement SA* v. *Premier, KwaZulu Natal*, it upheld a challenge by Abahlali baseMjondolo, a Durban-based shack-dwellers movement opposed to the eviction of residents from informal settlements, against a KwaZulu Natal provincial Act aimed at eradicating slum conditions, in terms of which owners of land upon which slums had developed would be obliged to institute eviction proceedings.[137] Essentially finding that the Act compelled the circumvention of the PIE Act and allowed for arbitrary evictions without meaningful engagement, the majority of the Constitutional Court declared the relevant provisions of the Act unconstitutional.[138] The judgment notably strengthened the Abahlali movement and was also a significant victory for residents of informal settlements more broadly, since its message was that evictions from informal settlements, rather than in situ upgrading, could only be pursued as a matter of last resort.[139]

However, hopes that the housing right could be used to compel in situ upgrading were dashed by the Constitutional Court's subsequent judgment in *Nokotyana* v. *Ekhurheleni Metropolitan Municipality*, which dismissed a claim by inhabitants of an informal settlement on the East Rand for the provision of interim services pending a provincial government decision on whether to upgrade the settlement. The Court was not prepared to ground a right to in situ upgrading directly in section 26 of the Constitution, and found that the relevant chapter of the Housing Code could only be invoked once the government had in fact taken a decision to upgrade a settlement.[140] While thus again signalling that it would generally defer to local government's spatial planning vision, the Court regarded the government's delay in deciding whether or not to upgrade the settlement as unacceptable, and ordered that a decision be taken within 14 months.[141]

Read together, and in light of *Olivia Road*, these judgments appear to indicate that, while the Constitutional Court is serious about securing the participation of residents in decisions pertaining to their housing conditions, it will not let individual housing claims override broader policy processes. Rather than providing an entitlement to have individual housing preferences accommodated, the Court's meaningful engagement jurisprudence appears to be an attempt to democratise urban planning and management processes and to sensitise decision makers to the many interests at stake.

The inner city

Olivia Road was, predictably, a game-changer for evictions from 'bad' buildings in inner city Johannesburg. The City pursued notably fewer evictions in the judgment's wake,[142] and put in place onerous administrative mechanisms in an attempt to institutionalise meaningful engagement. The majority of eviction cases to reach Gauteng courts after *Olivia Road* thus concerned evictions at the behest of private owners or developers, who were increasingly involved in inner city regeneration.

From the resolution of these disputes, it appeared that courts were taking the intertwined notions of engagement and mediation seriously and also that, while it was not an absolute requirement for the granting of an eviction order, the availability of well-situated alternative accommodation had become a central consideration in determining whether an eviction was just and equitable.[143] On more than one occasion, courts refused or overturned eviction orders where it appeared that the residents of a building would be rendered homeless if an order was granted, and where the engagement/mediation process prior to the eviction was deficient, or where alternative accommodation was unavailable or inadequate.[144]

While commentators generally welcomed these developments, the emerging evictions case law posed an increasing headache to the City and to the private developers who counted on it to enable and assist them to redevelop inner city buildings. Even a Johannesburg High Court judge added his voice to the growing murmurs of discontent. In *Emfuleni Local Municipality* v. *Builders Advancement Services*, Willis J postponed the hearing of an eviction matter and declined to be involved in its adjudication. Declaring himself the wrong person to decide the matter, the judge despondently lashed out against the manner in which courts were applying section 26 of the Constitution. To him, the effect of the prevailing judicial approach to inner city evictions was that hijacked buildings remained hijacked, something he regarded as economically disastrous, as making unwarranted demands on the City's resources and as ultimately dashing all hopes of effective inner city regeneration.[145]

But at least part of the blame for this frustration lay with the manner in which the City internalised, or failed to fully internalise, the *Olivia Road* judgment. While conforming with *Olivia Road* in relation to its own pursuit of regeneration objectives, the City insisted that the ruling did not apply to eviction proceedings instituted by building owners. Accordingly, while it put pressure on owners to institute eviction proceedings in terms of health and safety laws, it declined to assist evicted residents in finding alternative accommodation, insisting that private evictions were beyond its control and beyond the purview of the *Olivia Road* ruling.[146] The effect of this somewhat cynical buck-passing was either that occupiers could not be evicted, which frustrated ownership rights, development plans and regeneration initiatives (as bemoaned in *Emfuleni*), or that they were evicted onto the streets, which made a mockery of the protection of habitation rights under *Olivia Road* and the PIE Act.

Attempting to transcend this impasse, the Joburg High Court began to require that the City be joined in eviction matters brought by private landlords or developers. Holding that the duty to ensure that occupiers are not rendered homeless through an eviction did not rest on private owners, the Court in *Lingwood* v. *The Unlawful Occupiers of Erf 9 Highlands* and in *Sailing Queen Investments* v. *Occupants La Colleen Court* required the joinder of the City, since it regarded the City's constitutional obligations as being triggered by any eviction in the city.[147] These judgments, which were generally praised for their innovative bridging of the divide between private and public law,[148] set the stage for the battle over the extent of the City's obligations in matters of this nature.

This battle was to come to a head in *City of Johannesburg Metropolitan Municipality* v. *Blue Moonlight Properties*. The case concerned the eviction of some 86 people who were unlawfully occupying a disused industrial building in Doornfontein (adjacent to the Johannesburg CBD) by a private developer, who had acquired the building in full knowledge of its occupation, with some of the occupiers having lived on the site, with permission from past owners, for more than a decade. The Constitutional Court summarised the competing interests at stake as follows:

> The practical questions to be answered in this case are whether the Occupiers must be evicted to allow the owner to fully exercise its right regarding its property and, if so, whether their eviction must be linked to an order that the City provide them with alternative accommodation. The City's position is that it is neither obliged nor able to provide accommodation in these circumstances. The owner wishes to exercise its right to develop its property and wants no part in the dispute about the City's responsibilities or the plight of the Occupiers. And the Occupiers do not want to end up homeless on the street.[149]

The Court found that the competing rights and responsibilities in the case had to be balanced against each other in the context of the developmental responsibilities of local government, and of municipalities' statutory and constitutional obligations in relation to housing provision.[150] It held that it was irrational and unreasonable to distinguish between the housing situation of persons who were rendered homeless as a result of an eviction pursued by the City, and those who were similarly evicted from their homes by private property owners. In both instances, the Court found, the eviction could lead to an emergency, triggering *Grootboom*'s obligation upon the City to provide temporary emergency relief. It was therefore unreasonable of the City to deny such relief to certain occupiers, just because of who happened to be behind their eviction.[151]

The Court affirmed that building owners could not be expected to indefinitely provide free housing to unlawful occupiers of their properties and that they were not responsible to ensure that occupants secured alternative accommodation. However, it held that the constitutional housing right required of owners to exercise a degree of patience, and to accept that their rights to develop their properties could temporarily be restricted, whilst the City fulfils its public law responsibilities towards occupiers.[152]

The City's assertion that it lacked the resources to take responsibility for the emergency housing needs of 'private' evictees (in that it did not budget for the eventuality that it would be responsible for their plight and that its request to the Gauteng Provincial Government for financial assistance in the lead-up to the litigation was denied) was dismissed, with the Court sternly determining that:

> [t]his Court's determination of the reasonableness of measures within available resources cannot be restricted by budgetary and other decisions that may well have resulted from a mistaken understanding of constitutional or statutory obligations. In other words, it is not good enough for the City to state that it has not budgeted for something, if it should indeed have planned and budgeted for it in the fulfillment of its obligations.[153]

Regardless of the fact that the Constitution only envisages a supporting role for Local Government in housing provision, the Court thus regarded the City as being constitutionally responsible for financing its own emergency housing scheme and required that the needs of all inner city evictees, regardless of whether their evictions resulted from an exercise of public power or of private ownership rights, had to be catered for by such a scheme.[154] As in *Olivia Road*, however, the Court was at pains to emphasise that its judgment was concerned only with the provision of temporary emergency accommodation, and did not pertain to long-term housing solutions in the inner city.[155]

Blue Moonlight was generally welcomed for illustrating that private property rights no longer reigned supreme in disputes over property development, for extending *Grootboom* and *Olivia Road*'s protection (especially in relation to temporary alternative accommodation) also to cases where inner-city evictions were driven by private or commercial interests, and for reflecting a right-to-the-city-based conception of the City's responsibilities towards those threatened by homelessness.[156] However, the burdens placed by the judgment upon both the City (which now had also to take responsibility for the housing plight of potentially thousands of additional inner city residents for which it, rightly or wrongly, did not plan)[157] and upon private owners (whose duty to show patience while the City fulfils its responsibilities towards unlawful occupiers in practice boiled down to development processes being stalled for up to several years, with often severe accompanying losses)[158] were certainly significant.

In particular, while the Court's reasoning on the City's budgetary arguments cannot be faulted, the effect of its rejection of the seemingly genuine plea that the City could not afford to implement the judgment was to place the City, which had already been walking a precarious tightrope of having to fulfil significant housing-related obligations with limited financial and other support from provincial and national government, in a near paralysing bind.[159] It thus came as no surprise that the City reacted to the judgment with much despondence, whereas even the National Minister of Human Settlements expressed his dismay with the Court's seeming endorsement of illegal building occupations.[160] Practically, the City's inability or unwillingness to come to terms with the obligations imposed upon it by *Blue Moonlight* would impact significantly on further regeneration efforts in the inner city.

After Blue Moonlight

Informal settlements

A week after *Blue Moonlight*, the Constitutional Court handed down three short judgments pertaining to evictions from peri-urban land. In the first, *Pheko* v. *Ekurhuleni Metropolitan Municipality*, it affirmed that the procedural provisions of the PIE Act, together with the principles laid down in its own jurisprudence, also pertained to emergency health and safety evictions in terms of the 2000 Disaster Management Act. The Ekurhuleni Metropolitan Council's demolition of an informal settlement on geologically unstable land near Bapsfontein on Ekurhuleni's rural outskirts was found to be unconstitutional, because the Municipality proceeded with the demolition and accompanying evictions without first seeking a court order.[161] Since, on the facts, the evictions were not actually urgent, the Court found that the provisions of the Disaster Management had to be applied in conformance with the constitutional rule that no evictions may take place without judicial oversight. It ordered that the evicted community be accommodated on land in the immediate vicinity of their previous location, while the municipality had to report to the court on steps it had taken to resettle them more permanently.[162]

Then, in both *Occupiers of Portion R25 of the Farm Mooiplaats 355 JR* v. *Golden Thread* and *Occupiers of Skurweplaas 353 JR* v. *PPC Aggregate Quarries*, the Court declined to grant eviction orders against inhabitants of informal settlements from peri-urban land in Gauteng, because there was no alternative accommodation lined up for them.[163] The findings in both cases were influenced by the fact that the landowners had no immediate plans for the gainful use of the property, so that there was no pressing reason to go ahead with the evictions.[164] An application of this principle in inner cities may well have far-reaching implications for property developers that buy derelict buildings, evict their residents and brick the buildings up against occupation, without any immediate plans to develop them.

While this trio of judgments concludes the Constitutional Court's informal settlement jurisprudence to date, two recent decisions by the Joburg High Court have further applied the principles crystallising from its housing rights case-law to disputes concerning residents of informal settlements. In *Mbatha* v. *City of Johannesburg Metropolitan Municipality*, the Court found that the City was obliged to provide emergency assistance to residents of an informal settlement on Kliptown Square in Soweto, which was flooded after heavy rains. In some ways the flipside of the *Pheko* decision, the judgment emphasised that people could not be left to live in unhealthy and dangerous conditions, dismissed the City's contention that the situation of the applicants was not urgent, and required it to relocate the residents from the flooded are to a safe and dry site nearby.[165]

Finally, in the recent *Melani* v. *City of Johannesburg*, residents of the Slovo Park informal settlement near Eldorado Park and Soweto successfully resisted an attempt by the City to relocate them to a new housing development some 11 kilometres from their current location. The Johannesburg High Court found that the residents, some of whom had resided in Slovo Park for up to 20 years, had a legitimate expectation that the City would upgrade the settlement in situ, partly because the City had, through the years, taken several steps towards such an upgrade. The Court found that it was unreasonable under section 26(2) of the Constitution and in terms of the national legislative and policy framework for the City to (seemingly without reason) abandon the possibility of in situ upgrading and to instead persist with relocation, while ignoring the hardship and disruption that this would cause.[166]

An appeal in *Melani* is likely. While seemingly consistent with *Mooiplaats* and *Skurweplaas*, in that the Court was not prepared to authorise a relocation where there seems to have been no compelling interest served by doing so, it is unclear how the judgment squares with the Constitutional Court's findings in cases like *Joe Slovo* and *Nokotyana*, which seem somewhat more deferent to the developmental vision of local government. While both *Mbatha* and *Melani* represent important victories for vulnerable urban inhabitants, the judgments do point to continued tension between the City's sense of what is required to address the poor environmental conditions in informal settlements, on the one hand, and residents' own preferred solutions, on the other.

The inner city

After *Blue Moonlight*, the Constitutional Court's judgments pertaining to inner city habitation and displacement, while vindicating the rights of occupiers, did so in a manner that indicated a slight swing of the pendulum away from *Blue Moonlight*'s unwavering stance towards the City and developers, towards a position somewhat more sensitive to both the public and private sector interests embroiled in inner-city regeneration.

Maphango v. *Aengus Lifestyle Properties* was notable for being the Court's first judgment pertaining to the application of the 1999 Rental Housing Act, and to the habitation rights of a slightly more economically secure class of occupiers. The applicants were tenants in an apartment block in Braamfontein, who approached the Court after their new landlord cancelled their leases and would renew them only if they would agree to payment of higher rental. The landlord was a property company actively involved in Braamfontein's partial gentrification, purchasing and renovating residential buildings before putting them back on the market as more upmarket, and more expensive, rental accommodation. In resisting the termination of their leases as a way to force them to either agree to higher rental or move out, the tenants laid a complaint with the Rental Housing Tribunal (which mediates rental disputes in terms of the Rental Housing Act). However, they abandoned this complaint in the months that followed, during which time the landlord instituted eviction proceedings against them.[167]

In declining to decide the merits of the complaint, a majority of the Constitutional Court found that the eviction proceedings were premature, and that the Rental Housing Tribunal ought to have adjudicated the complaint to determine whether the cancellation of the leases was fair. It ordered a stay in the eviction process to enable the complaint to be re-lodged with the Tribunal, holding that the evictions could go ahead if the tenants were to fail to re-lodge the complaint within 15 days of the judgment.[168]

While finding that a determination of the fairness of the landlord's actions by the Rental Housing Tribunal had to pay heed to the constitutional right of access to adequate housing (which the Court found also placed an obligation on private landlords not to inhibit or impair such access),[169] the Court also emphasised that the tribunal would have to balance the rights and interests of the tenants against the landlord's concerns over 'the unsustainability of the building and of its business model at present rents, and the failure of lustre of its investment in [the building]'.[170] A strongly worded minority judgment went as far as to side fully with the landlord, holding that section 26 of the Constitution was not limited by the lease terminations in and of themselves. It also emphasised that the tenants had voluntarily entered into their lease agreements (which contained a termination clause allowing the landlord to cancel them) and were free to reject the proposed higher rental and move out, and that the landlord could not be forced to 'continue with the leases as they stood, no matter how much the losses it was suffering and would continue to suffer if the rent was not drastically increased', especially seeing that the tenants opted not to pursue their complaint at the Rental Housing Tribunal.[171]

After the order, the tenants proceeded to re-lodge their complaint with the Rental Housing Tribunal but, again, failed to follow through with it. As a result, the complaint was never adjudicated and it appears that the tenants all ended up either accepting the increased rental, or moving out of the building.[172] While the *Maphango* judgment thus affirmed tenants' right to adequate housing and emphasised that evictions and related practices by landlords had to comply with relevant legal processes,[173] the case ultimately presents a failed reliance on the Constitution in an effort to resist the market forces associated with inner-city gentrification.

Somewhat more successful were the low-income tenants in the roughly contemporaneous *Schubart Park Residents' Association* v. *City of Tshwane Metropolitan Municipality*, who were summarily evicted from their high-rise apartment block in central Pretoria after a fire broke out in the building during violent protests over the discontinuation of services to the building. The protests, fire and evictions were the culmination of a long and drawn out battle between the tenants and the City (who owned the building and leased the apartments to the tenants as a form of low-cost housing provision) with both parties accusing each other of allowing the building to deteriorate into a near uninhabitable slum. The fire was the last straw for the City, which planned to demolish the building and redevelop the property. Evicted residents scrambled for a roof over their heads, with the High Court eventually ordering that they be provided with emergency accommodation elsewhere in the city.[174]

While the Constitutional Court, like the High Court before it, found that the Tshwane Municipality was justified in evicting the applicants during the fire[175] (a finding for which it has endured some criticism, specifically because it appears to accept the City's version of events, and its assessment of the state of the building, over the competing versions put forward by the tenants[176]), it faulted the High Court for not specifying that they were entitled to eventually return to their apartments after the damage from the fire had been repaired.[177] It lamented the City's treatment of the tenants as 'obnoxious social nuisances' as well as its 'top-down' approach to determining 'when, for how long, and ultimately whether at all, the applicants may return to Schubart Park',[178] and ordered it to engage with the tenants over the repair of the building and their eventual reoccupation thereof.[179] The order led the City to reconsider its plans for the building and to eventually commit to its refurbishment.[180]

Apart from *Maphango* and *Schubart Park*, much of inner city housing litigation subsequent to *Blue Moonlight* continued to revolve around the fate of the applicants in that case, who had become poster children for the City's seemingly unproductive response to both the *Olivia Road* and *Blue Moonlight* decisions.

As alluded to above, it appeared that the City had become increasingly loath to evict occupants of 'bad buildings' after the *Olivia Road* judgment. Instead, it attempted to transfer the burden of eviction to building owners, by issuing them with notices requiring compliance with health and safety bylaws. One dispute over the extent of the City's obligations in such matters, arising from attempted compliance with such a notice by the owners of a 'hijacked' light-industrial inner city building which had been turned into a 'shack farm', ended up before the Supreme Court of Appeal. In a judgment mostly concerned with the process that should be followed in order for evictions to comply with *Olivia Road* and *Blue Moonlight*, the SCA in *City of Johannesburg* v. *Changing Tides 74* found that the City's new, indirect approach to 'bad buildings' was 'less than satisfactory'.[181] The Court emphasised that occupants of buildings where living conditions had deteriorated to the point of constituting a health and safety risk had to be 'moved away from that situation as soon as possible'.[182] The City, proceeded the Court, needed to be 'actively engaged' in urgently addressing the situation in such buildings and, while it did not bear an absolute obligation to provide alternative long-term accommodation to occupiers in every case, it had to ensure that they were catered for in temporary emergency accommodation while assessing their eligibility for more long-term housing.[183]

Meanwhile, the occupiers of Blue Moonlight's property had little joy in negotiating with the City about the kind of alternative accommodation that would be provided to them after their eviction. While they were holding out for temporary housing like that provided to the occupiers in *Olivia Road*, the City instead tendered accommodation in an 'emergency shelter' jointly run by a religious charity. This entailed that occupiers would have to stay in dorm-like conditions, where they would be subjected to strict house rules (including rules requiring them to leave the shelter during daytime on working days and rules requiring that men and women stay separately, which meant that families could not share rooms). With negotiations reaching deadlock and the date for the eviction fast approaching, SERI urgently approached the Constitutional Court for an order that would postpone the eviction for two months and require the City to engage meaningfully with the occupants over the nature, conditions and location of their temporary accommodation.[184]

In a brief judgment reported as *Occupiers of Saratoga Avenue* v. *City of Johannesburg Metropolitan Municipality*, the Constitutional Court refused this application. Of the view that the City still had time to comply with the order in *Blue Moonlight*, and emphasising that that order was (unlike the order in *Joe Slovo*, for instance) not of a supervisory nature, the Court declined to hear the matter as court of first instance.[185] In doing so, it expressly left open the question of whether the obligation of meaningful engagement entailed also an obligation to engage on the quality of temporary accommodation, although it seemed to suggest that it likely did not, as the effect of providing temporary accommodation with which occupiers was dissatisfied would not be to render them homeless.[186]

The eviction of the *Blue Moonlight* occupiers eventually took place, with those who could afford to pay for social housing being accommodated in a new inner city building managed by the Johannesburg Social Housing Company, others being moved to the very Ethuthuleni homeless shelter to which they objected, and others still refusing to do so and resorting to finding their own shelter in other 'bad buildings' in and around the inner city.[187]

Assisted by SERI, those occupiers relocated to the homeless shelter immediately instituted legal proceedings challenging the constitutionality of the conditions there. They were initially victorious, with the Joburg High Court finding in *Dladla* v. *City of Johannesburg Metropolitan Municipality* that the shelter's daytime lockout rule and its insistence on gender segregated dormitories infringed the constitutional rights to dignity, privacy and freedom and security of the person.[188] However, the Supreme Court of Appeal overturned this judgment, emphasising that the shelter was only a temporary solution to the occupiers' housing needs, meaning that occupiers' rights were only being temporarily restricted by conditions there, which accordingly could not be expected to be of the same standard as conditions in permanent housing.[189] It noted that shelter management had allowed ample exceptions to its rules for the occupiers, including permitting them to stay in the shelter during lock-out hours and allowing the only married couple among them to occupy a room ordinarily intended for more people, and also pointed out that the conditions at the shelter were far superior to the buildings in Doornfontein from which the occupants had been evicted.[190] Given the shortage in the City's temporary housing stock and the short-term and emergency nature of the accommodation, the Court concluded that the rules were not unreasonable.[191] This judgment is currently on appeal before the Constitutional Court.

Meanwhile, several of the occupiers who had themselves relocated to other bad buildings were soon again embroiled in eviction proceedings. These were resolved along now predictable lines, with building owners being granted eviction orders, but these being suspended until the City could provide occupiers with alternative accommodation. Just as predictably, the implementation of these orders has often been marred by the City either failing to provide alternative accommodation, or offering rooms in homeless shelters and having these rejected by occupiers.

In one case pertaining to such a deadlock, the Johannesburg High Court indicated that it had had enough of the City's apparent failure to internalise the *Blue Moonlight* judgment. In *Hlope* v. *City of Johannesburg*, the Court declared that Joburg's mayor, municipal manager and housing director were constitutionally and statutorily obliged to ensure that orders for temporary shelter are complied with. It further required them to personally provide a signed list of answers to a range of questions, relating to the steps the City had taken to comply with *Blue Moonlight* both at a policy and administrative level.[192] The court was scathing of the City's perceived foot-dragging, stating that

> this obligation to shelter the occupiers has not been suddenly sprung upon the City of Johannesburg. Nothing has leapt out of the blue. There has been a gradual process of enlightenment. There has been opportunity to absorb both the general and specific import of court decisions. There has been opportunity to understand and appreciate the role which the city is required to play in sheltering these occupiers. There has been opportunity to prepare the appropriate response to the obligations which the Constitution and our courts have placed upon the city.[193]

and that

> the City of Johannesburg cannot sit back and throw up its hands in horror each time a group of persons is to be evicted as unlawful occupiers, about to

> become homeless, and the city is therefore required to provide temporary accommodation. The city must act in a constitutional and professional manner and this has not been done to date in this litigation.[194]

In addition to answering the questions, the officials were personally directed to 'take all the administrative and other steps necessary' to ensure that the occupiers in question be provided with temporary accommodation as stipulated in their original eviction order, at the risk of contempt proceedings and constitutional damages for non-compliance.[195]

The City appealed to the SCA, which confirmed the appropriateness of the mandatory order to ensure that the occupiers be provided with temporary accommodation.[196] However, the SCA overturned the reporting order (including the requirement to answer the court's questions), since this order transgressed the separation of powers by covering issues far beyond what was actually before the High Court, as well as by applying regardless of whether alternative accommodation was provided to the applicants and by effectively prescribing to the City how it should heed its constitutional obligations.[197]

While it is perhaps too early to speculate, the SCA's judgments in *Dladla* and *Hlope*, as well as the Constitutional Court's judgment in *Saratoga Avenue*, do suggest that, much as there is legitimate frustration with the City's perceived foot-dragging and partial compliance with eviction judgments, there is increased judicial sensitivity to the severe difficulties that the City faces in carrying out its constitutional obligations, especially in a micro-political environment which has arguably become unproductively hostile and litigious.[198]

Indeed, while there may be some truth to accusations that the City has cynically been exploiting ambiguities in the evictions jurisprudence to intimidate, disregard and displace illegal building occupiers,[199] the picture emerging from the above discussion is of a local government reeling, caught between a hefty constitutional mandate, limited resources and limited political autonomy, while consistently faced with a barrage of litigation from but one of the competing interest groups that it is constitutionally obliged to accommodate.

To illustrate the extent of this bind, a recent report by the Public Protector also lambasted the City for poor compliance with the legal framework laid down in *Blue Moonlight*, but from the perspective of property owners rather than occupiers. The report details the case of two entrepreneurs who had lost their business and capital, and were at risk of also losing their house to foreclosure, after they had been unable to secure the City's cooperation in evicting occupiers from a light-industrial building in Doornfontein, which they had intended to convert into a shoe factory. The occupiers of the building had also consumed a vast amount of unpaid electricity services at the site, for which the owners were billed despite several pleas to the City to disconnect the electricity supply and to prevent illegal connections. The result of the massive service arrears was that the building could not be sold.[200]

Affirming that the City had a constitutional responsibility to deal with illegal occupiers and to assist with effecting evictions, in terms of the right to property in section 25 of the Constitution read with the *Blue Moonlight* judgment, the Public Protector found that the City's maladministration caused the owners to suffer severe financial, emotional and psychological damage. It ordered the City to purchase the buildings from the owners, to apologise to them, to 'ensure that an urgent investigation is conducted in respect of all privately owned buildings that are illegally occupied' and to ensure that occupiers of such buildings be moved to temporary alternative accommodation.[201]

Over and above illustrating the extent of the City's predicament, the Public Protector's Report reminds us that the interests of illegal building occupiers are not the only ones at stake in disputes over urban habitation. Property owners are often far from the capitalist moguls that they tend to be portrayed as, whereas illegal occupiers share the CBD not only with middleclass suburbanites, businesspeople and hipsters intent on displacing them through regeneration, but also with a great many other poor and working class people whose living conditions and livelihoods depend on the city remaining a sustainable economic organism. In this regard, it has been pointed out that legal victory for one group of residents has often entailed that equally valid and urgent competing needs have, directly or indirectly, been jettisoned in attempts to give effect to court orders.[202]

Reflections

There can be no doubt that the constitutional entrenchment of a right of access to adequate housing has dramatically altered the South African urban property landscape. Section 26 of the Constitution has directly spawned a progressive, pro-poor legislative framework and a progressive, pro-poor line of case law that, between them, have served to overthrow South African property law's prior absolute preference for individual property rights over competing habitation interests.[203] Moreover, this jurisprudence and legislative framework have served to disrupt the State's monopoly over the shape and form of urban areas and have directly inserted the needs and voices of poor urban residents into the discourse over the development and redevelopment of their cities.[204] As such, it is not far-fetched to suggest that section 26 has inserted important elements of the right to the city into South African law.[205]

Rights-based opposition and litigation in the interests of both inner city building occupiers and the inhabitants of informal settlements, and the culmination of these legal challenges in the various court judgments discussed here, have clearly played an integral role in this process. Through their judgments, the courts have established and fleshed out, first, an entitlement not to be arbitrarily evicted from a place of habitation and, second, an entitlement to be (at least) temporarily accommodated in dignified conditions, when rendered homeless through an eviction.[206] Importantly, the jurisprudence has further required that inhabitants be consulted and heard, and that their specific needs be viewed sympathetically and taken seriously, in processes pertaining to their eviction and relocation.[207]

At the same time, the courts have been careful to emphasise the importance of protecting living environments, and the city as a whole, against degradation and slummification, and have shown awareness of the range of local government's other constitutional responsibilities towards all urban citizens, including property owners and developers and other poor and not-so-poor residents who share the urban living environment. Courts have further emphasised the agency of all inner-city inhabitants, including the poor, and have indicated that the interests of these inhabitants, too, will sometimes have to yield to the collective pursuit of a better and more sustainable city for all.

A central feature of the inner-city housing jurisprudence discussed here has been the Constitutional Court's ostensible commitment to participatory and dialogic solutions to habitation disputes. This is evident, for instance, from the way that the Court conceived of the requirement of meaningful engagement in cases such as *Olivia Road* and *Joe Slovo*, as well as from its referral of the *Maphango* matter for resolution by a statutory dispute resolution body. This commitment has been heralded for strengthening participatory democracy and affirming the needs of residents, while at the same time preserving for the City a margin of discretion that enables it to pursue its democratic mandate and its urban policy objectives.[208] On the other hand, its pursuit has led to accusations that the Court has deliberately avoided deciding issues such as the constitutionality of the City's housing policy more broadly, the location of alternative accommodation, the need for permanent inner city housing solutions and the parameters and minimum requirements for meaningful engagement. This, it has been argued, reflects undue deference to the City's developmental vision and to its own understanding of how it should carry out its constitutional obligations, and often amounts to turning a deaf ear to the articulation of several crucial habitation-related needs.[209]

This latter criticism notwithstanding, the discussion here has shown that heeding the court orders handed down against it has not been a walk in the park for the City. Proportionately the largest per capita spender on social housing in the country, and having upgraded some 30,000 homes in informal settlements in situ since 2011,[210] the City nevertheless remains severely stretched by the intertwined demands of urbanisation, poverty and the spatial legacy of apartheid. There can be no doubt that the housing jurisprudence discussed here has significantly added to this burden. This said, perhaps the jurisprudence's greatest accomplishment has been ensuring that the City remains focused on solving Johannesburg's housing problems, while not losing sight of inhabitants' needs and rights in the process.

Notes

1 See Coggin and Pieterse (2012: 261, 264); Huchzermeyer (2011: 26); Pieterse (2014a: 153–154).

2 *S* v. *Govender* (1983: 969F-971I, 972D). See Rule 1989: 196–200 as well as discussion in Chapter 1.

3 *S* v. *Govender* (1983: 969F).

4 On the extent to which this framework gives effect to s 26, see Strauss and Liebenberg (2014: 432–434).
5 Housing Act (1997: ss 2(1)(e)(iii)–(iv)). In operationalising these provisions, the Act is supplemented by two important policy documents: The National Housing Code (2009) (which, importantly, contain chapters on the upgrading of informal settlements and the provision of emergency housing assistance) and the Comprehensive Housing Plan for the Development of Integrated Sustainable Human Settlements (2004), which 'aims to address urban poverty and the continued segregation of informal settlements by eradicating informal settlements through in situ upgrading in desired locations or the relocation of households where in situ development is not possible' – Strauss and Liebenberg (2014: 432).
6 Housing Act (1997: ss 2(1)(a)–(b)).
7 For assessment of local government's constitutional and statutory responsibilities in relation to urban development, in light of its limited powers and resources, see Pieterse (2014a: 156–162).
8 PIE Act (1998: ss 4(6)–(7)). For assessment of the PIE Act in light of s 26 of the Constitution, see Van der Walt (2009: 147–153).
9 On the implications of the environmental right for urban management see Pieterse (2014b: 180–187).
10 See City of Johannesburg (2007: 12); Muller (2015: 618–620); Pieterse (2014b: 182–183, 189–190). In heeding these obligations, cities rely on provisions of urban environmental legislation such as the National Building Regulations and Building Standards Act 1977 and the Disaster Management Act 2002.
11 See Murray (2008: 99, 220).
12 There are an estimated 200 informal settlements throughout the Johannesburg Metropolitan area, although this figure is contested. See Huchzermeyer *et al.* (2014: 154).
13 City of Johannesburg (2011: 76).
14 See Charlton (2014a: 179).
15 See City of Johannesburg (2007; 2011: 76; 2013a); Charlton (2010: 2–3, 8; 2014a: 186); Coggin and Pieterse (2015: 304–306, 308–311).
16 See Charlton (2010: 4; 2014a: 177–179); Maas (2011: 762).
17 Charlton (2010: 5–6). See also Tissington (2014: 12–13).
18 See Charlton (2010: 15–16); Maas (2011: 763); Poulsen (2010: 23); Tissington (2014: 14, 33, 69–72).
19 See City of Johannesburg (2011: 76); Centre on Housing Rights and Evictions, COHRE (2005: 7–8, 33); Charlton (2010: 7–8; 2014a: 179, 181–182, 187–188); Langford (2014: 190); Murray (2008: 100–101); Poulsen (2010: 22); Strauss and Liebenberg (2014: 433–434). There have been some better integrated developments, such as in Cosmo City to the north-west and Pennyville to the south of the inner city, and in Alexandra. There have also been social housing developments in the inner city and surrounds, especially to the south. See Charlton (2014a: 185); City of Johannesburg (2016: 6–7).
20 On the dynamics at play in this context, see (COHRE 2005: 76–93); Charlton (2014a: 188); Huchzermeyer (2011: 112–138); Huchzermeyer *et al.* (2014: 154–159); Langford (2014: 191); Murray (2008: 101–111).
21 City of Johannesburg (2007: 4–5).
22 See City of Johannesburg (2007: 12–13, 43–46); COHRE (2005: 68) as well as discussion below.
23 See COHRE (2005: 42); Murray (2008: 220–223); Wilson (2011a: 275); Wilson *et al.* (2015: 482).
24 For critical analysis of this undersupply in the inner city see Tissington (2014: 50–64) (although this analysis fails to consider the interplays between the inner-city housing market and that in surrounding areas). The inner-city undersupply is

acknowledged by the Metropolitan Council – see City of Johannesburg (2007: 43–44; 2013a: 12–13). More broadly, see Charlton (2010: 14–15; 2014a: 184–185); COHRE (2005: 7–8, 35, 69–70); Dickinson (2011: 487–488); Poulsen (2010: 23); Wilson (2014: 280–281); Wilson *et al.* (2015: 473–474).

25 See Charlton (2014a: 187–190; 2014b: 541); Murray (2008: 168); Poulsen (2010: 25).

26 For a detailed case study and analysis of this informal residential market, see Mayson and Charlton (2015). See also Poulsen (2010: 26–27); Tissington (2014: 64–66); Wilson (2014: 281).

27 For an in-depth case study of backyard rooms and shacks in Alexandra, see Shapurjee and Charlton (2013). See also City of Johannesburg (2016: 7); Murray (2008: 175, 178–188); Poulsen (2010: 27–32); Wilson *et al.* (2015: 473).

28 See Mayson and Charlton (2015: 353–355).

29 See Charlton (2010: 11–12, 15–16); Mayson and Charlton (2015: 345, 351–367); Poulsen (2010: 23); Shapurjee and Charlton (2013: 658–664).

30 See Charlton (2010: 16); Mayson and Charlton (2015: 344–345, 367); Shapurjee and Charlton (2013: 664).

31 See, for instance, COHRE (2005: 8, 42, 48, 50); City of Johannesburg (2007: 12; 2013a: 52); Murray (2008: 118, 168–174); Sinwell (2010: 156–157); Strydom and Viljoen (2014: 1222, 1238); Wilson (2011b: 133–135).

32 On land invasion and associated settlement practices see Murray (2008: 111–118).

33 See COHRE (2005: 19–20, 76–93); Huchzermeyer *et al.* (2014: 155–159); Murray (2008: 101–111).

34 See COHRE (2005: 42); Murray (2008: 171, 220–223).

35 See Huchzermeyer (2011: 26).

36 Huchzermeyer (2011: 26).

37 See Charlton (2010: 2–3, 15–18); Huchzermeyer *et al.* (2014: 155); Mayson and Charlton (2015: 367–368).

38 See Van der Walt (2009: 29–31, 53–60); Wilson (2009: 270–271).

39 Two judgments of the Constitutional Court have provided protection for perilous ownership rights. The first was *Jaftha* v. *Schoeman* (2005), where the Court found that legislation which permitted for sales of homes in execution of minor debts, without judicial oversight, was in unjustifiable breach of s 26(3) of the Constitution. On *Jaftha*'s impact and implications see Liebenberg (2010: 215–220). Rules of the High Court allowing for home sales in execution at behest of High Court registrars were similarly declared unconstitutional in *Gundwana* v. *Steko Development* (2011).

40 See *Hattingh* v. *Juta* (2013), where the Constitutional Court struck a balance between the property rights of a farm owner and the tenure rights of the family members of a former farm worker, under the Extension of Security of Tenure Act, 1997.

41 *Government of the RSA* v. *Grootboom* (2001, paras 27–33).

42 Ibid., paras 44, 66, 69, 99.

43 Ibid., paras 88, 92.

44 Ibid., para 35.

45 Ibid., para 37. For discussion, see Coggin and Pieterse (2015: 304); McLean (2009: 140–141).

46 *Government of the RSA* v. *Grootboom* (2001, para 36).

47 Ibid., referring to Constitution of the RSA (1996: ss 27(1)(c), 152).

48 Langford (2014: 203–204).

49 *Government of the RSA* v. *Grootboom* (2001: paras 44, 66, 69, 99).

50 See Langford (2014: 199–200); Wilson (2009: 275–276); Wilson *et al.* (2015: 478–479).

51 See Langford (2014: 195–198); Pillay (2002: 256–257, 262–265). As Langford (2014: 196) points out, however, permanent housing was never claimed in the case.

52 See Langford (2014: 197–199); Pillay (2002: 273).

53 *Port Elizabeth Municipality* v. *Various Occupiers* (2005: para 2).
54 Ibid., para 22.
55 Ibid., para 37. See also paras 12–16, 23.
56 Ibid., para 29.
57 Ibid., para 18.
58 See Liebenberg (2010: 274–275, 278–279); Strauss and Liebenberg (2014: 435); Van der Walt (2009: 154–155); Wilson (2009: 282).
59 See Wilson (2009: 280–281, 289; 2011a: 266, 269–271).
60 *Port Elizabeth Municipality* v. *Various Occupiers* (2005: para 28).
61 Ibid.
62 Ibid., para 39.
63 Ibid., para 43.
64 Ibid., para 41.
65 Ibid.
66 Ibid., para 47. See also paras 45, 61.
67 Ibid., paras 48–60.
68 Ibid., para 61.
69 See Liebenberg (2010: 276–277).
70 *President of the Republic of South Africa* v. *Modderklip Boerdery* (2005: para 47). See also para 36.
71 Ibid. See also *Modder East Squatters* v. *Modderklip Boerdery; President of the RSA* v. *Modderklip Boerdery* (2004: paras 22; 26).
72 See Liebenberg (2010: 285–286); Wilson (2009: 277–279; 2011a: 269–271).
73 *President of the Republic of South Africa* v. *Modderklip Boerdery* (2005: para 68); *Modder East Squatters* v. *Modderklip Boerdery; President of the RSA* v. *Modderklip Boerdery* (2004: paras 28, 41).
74 See Langford (2014: 214–215); Tissington (2011).
75 *City of Cape Town* v. *Rudolph* (2003).
76 *Tswelopele Non-profit Organisation* v. *City of Tshwane Metropolitan Municipality* (2007). For criticism of *Tswelopele*'s depiction of the interests of residents of informal settlements, see Brand (2014).
77 For detailed critique of the Mandelaville judgment and relocation by a member of the occupiers' legal team, see Wilson (2006). See also COHRE (2005: 78–82); Langford (2014: 212–213); Murray (2008: 104–105).
78 *Ritama Investments* v. *Unlawful Occupiers of Erf 62 Wynberg* (2006: para 13).
79 The story, effects and implications of the Marlboro evictions are discussed by Sinwell (2010). See also Murray (2008: 118–119).
80 See Liebenberg (2015: 454–455); Wilson *et al.* (2015: 477, 480).
81 See Woolman (2013: 269–270, 320).
82 For critical discussion, see COHRE (2005: 20, 60–63); Rubin (2014: 211–214, 220–224); Wilson (2011b: 134–135); Wilson *et al.* (2015: 482).
83 An estimated 10,000 people were evicted from inner-city buildings between 2002 and 2006. Wilson (2011b: 127, 135–137). See also COHRE (2005 6, 64–65, 68); Murray (2008: 212–223); Rubin (2014: 214).
84 See Pernegger (2014: 68–69).
85 For a detailed account of these and other events in building the initial legal resistance to inner city evictions, see Wilson (2011b: 137–144).
86 *City of Johannesburg* v. *Rand Properties* (2007a). For discussion, see COHRE (2005: 70–71), Wilson (2011b: 144–146).
87 See Wilson (2011b: 146).
88 *City of Johannesburg* v. *Rand Properties* (2007b: paras 2, 8, 10, 51–56, 67, 73, 77–78). The finding has been criticised for favouring the City's version of the living conditions in the buildings over those of their residents – see Coggin and Pieterse (2012: 266); Wilson (2011b: 146).

89 *City of Johannesburg* v. *Rand Properties* (2007b: para 67). See also para 46, where the Court stated that 'the contention that to deprive a person of unsafe housing denies him or her access to adequate housing is not correct. The corollary would be that to deny someone poisonous food is to deny that person food'.
90 Ibid., paras 5, 48–49, 68.
91 Ibid., para 44. See also paras 5, 75–77.
92 Ibid., para 77.
93 *Occupiers of 51 Olivia Road Berea Township* v. *City of Johannesburg* (2008: para 5).
94 Ibid., para 16. See also paras 10–15, 17–20. On the constitutional and jurisprudential foundations of meaningful engagement, see Chenwi (2009: 379–380); Chenwi and Liebenberg (2013: 14); Liebenberg (2010: 296–299); Pieterse (2014a: 169–170); Van der Walt (2009: 156).
95 *Occupiers of 51 Olivia Road Berea Township* v. *City of Johannesburg* (2008: para 13).
96 Ibid., para 14.
97 Ibid., paras 15, 20.
98 Ibid. On occupiers' obligations in meaningful engagement see also Woolman (2013: 271).
99 *Occupiers of 51 Olivia Road Berea Township* v. *City of Johannesburg* (2008: para 22).
100 Ibid., paras 24–30.
101 Ibid., para 26. On the settlement process and agreement, see Chenwi (2009: 378); Chenwi and Liebenberg (2013: 13); Liebenberg (2012: 15); Smith and Rubin (2015: 253–254); Wilson (2011a: 276–279; 2011b: 147–148).
102 *Occupiers of 51 Olivia Road Berea Township* v. *City of Johannesburg* (2008: paras 27–29).
103 Ibid., para 50.
104 Ibid., paras 47–51. For criticism of this finding see Chenwi (2009: 376–377); Muller (2015: 627–629); Strauss and Liebenberg (2014: 437).
105 *Occupiers of 51 Olivia Road Berea Township* v. *City of Johannesburg* (2008: para 38). For criticism, see Chenwi and Liebenberg (2013: 16); Muller (2015: 637).
106 *Occupiers of 51 Olivia Road Berea Township* v. *City of Johannesburg* (2008: paras 32–36).
107 Ibid., para 37.
108 See Chenwi (2009: 387–388); Dugard (2008: 237–238); Liebenberg (2015: 456); Murray (2008: 222); Strauss and Liebenberg (2014: 443–444).
109 See Chenwi (2009: 389–390); Coggin and Pieterse (2012: 267); Dugard (2008: 237–238); Liebenberg (2012: 19); McLean (2009: 150–151; 2010: 238–239); Ray (2014: 186); Strauss and Liebenberg (2014: 438, 442–443).
110 See Chenwi (2009: 384–385); Liebenberg (2012: 19–20, 27); Liebenberg (2014: 328–329); Ray (2011: 109); Van der Berg (2013: 387–388); Wilson and Dugard (2014: 46–47); Woolman (2013: 329–330).
111 See Liebenberg (2015: 469); McLean (2010: 239–240); Pieterse (2012: 363); Wilson and Dugard (2014: 46).
112 See Chenwi (2009: 384); Liebenberg (2010: 302; 2012: 19; 2014: 328–329; 2015: 468–470); Muller (2011: 753); Wilson and Dugard (2014: 46–47).
113 See McLean (2009: 150); Liebenberg (2010: 301–302); Pieterse (2014a: 170); Ray (2014: 185); Wilson and Dugard (2014: 46).
114 See Chenwi (2009: 373, 381–382, 392); Liebenberg (2012: 17–18, 26; 2014: 327); Muller (2011: 753, 755, 757); Ray (2011: 109, 113–114); Strauss and Liebenberg (2014: 437); Van der Berg (2013: 385–386, 396–397); Woolman (2013: 326–327, 440–441).

115 See Coggin and Pieterse (2012: 267); Pieterse (2014a: 170–171); Smith and Rubin (2015: 270); Woolman (2013: 271).

116 See Chenwi (2009: 388); Langford (2014: 217–218); Smith and Rubin (2015: 254); Wilson (2011a: 279–280); Van der Walt (2009: 69); Woolman (2013: 441–442).

117 See Van der Walt (2009: 69); Wilson (2011b: 148–149).

118 City of Johannesburg (2007: 43–48; 2013a: vii–viii). See also Smith and Rubin (2015: 269–270); Wilson (2011b: 149).

119 See Rubin (2014: 226); Smith and Rubin (2015: 270, 274); Wilson *et al.* (2015: 484).

120 According to City of Johannesburg (2013a), bad buildings remain the biggest urban management challenge in the CBD.

121 See Charlton (2014a: 189); Smith and Rubin (2015: 269–270); Wilson (2011a: 280); Woolman (2013: 328–329).

122 See Ray (2011: 122); Smith and Rubin (2015: 272–274); Wilson (2011b: 150).

123 *Mamba* v. *Minister of Social Development* (2008).

124 For discussion of *Mamba* as a failure of meaningful engagement as remedy, see Chenwi (2009: 385–386); Ray (2011: 111–112, 122–123); Van der Berg (2013: 384–385).

125 See *Residents of Joe Slovo Community, Western Cape* v. *Thubelisha Homes* (2010: 113, 117, 238, 244.

126 See Chenwi (2009: 382); Liebenberg (2010: 309–310; 2012: 22–23, 25); McLean (2009: 159; 2010: 237); Ray (2011: 112, 123); Strauss and Liebenberg (2014: 440–443); Van der Berg (2013: 385); Wilson *et al.* (2015: 501).

127 *Residents of Joe Slovo Community, Western Cape* v. *Thubelisha Homes* (2010: paras 24, 234–235, 321, 363). See also Pieterse (2014b: 189–190).

128 *Residents of Joe Slovo Community, Western Cape* v. *Thubelisha Homes* (2010: para 107). See also paras 108, 229, 259, 303, 321 as well as discussion in Pieterse (2014b: 190).

129 For criticism of this, see Wilson and Dugard (2011: 678–679; 2014: 50); Wilson et al (2015: 501).

130 See *Residents of Joe Slovo Community, Western Cape* v. *Thubelisha Homes* (2010: paras 7.11.4.7, 107, 254–255, 321–322). For discussion, see Coggin and Pieterse (2015: 305).

131 *Residents of Joe Slovo Community, Western Cape* v. *Thubelisha Homes* (2010: para 254). See also para 256.

132 Ibid., paras 710–7.11. For discussion, see Liebenberg (2012: 24); Ray (2011: 111–112, 124).

133 *Residents of Joe Slovo Community, Western Cape* v. *Thubelisha Homes* (2010: para 7.21).

134 See Liebenberg (2012: 26); McLean (2010: 237); Woolman (2013: 462).

135 See *Residents of Joe Slovo Community, Western Cape* v. *Thubelisha Homes* (2011: paras 4–7, 11–12, 37).

136 On the *Joe Slovo* aftermath and the rescission judgment, see Huchzermeyer (2011: 154, 165); Langford (2014: 212); McLean (2010: 231–232); Ray (2011: 109, 112–113); Strauss and Liebenberg (2014: 441); Wilson and Dugard (2014: 48).

137 On Abahlali's emergence, its initial activities and the history of its opposition to the KZN Slums Act, see Huchzermeyer (2011: 202–212).

138 See *Abahlali baseMjondolo Movement SA* v. *Premier, KwaZulu Natal Abahlali* (2010: paras 104–122). A dissenting judgment by Yacoob J emphasised the importance of eradicating inhabitable slum conditions. Ibid., paras 32, 36–37, 46, 48, 52–54.

139 See Huchzermeyer (2011: 221); Wilson and Dugard (2014: 54).

140 *Nokotyana* v. *Ekhurheleni Metropolitan Municipality* (2010: paras 38–44, 48–49). For criticism, see Huchzermeyer (2011: 227–240).

141 *Nokotyana* v. *Ekhurheleni Metropolitan Municipality* (2010: paras 55–57). Other aspects of the case are discussed in Chapter 3.

142 See Langford (2014: 220); Wilson *et al.* (2015: 484).

143 See Liebenberg (2010: 315); Wilson (2009: 289; 2011a: 269).

144 See *Lingwood* v. *The Unlawful Occupiers of Erf 9 Highlands* (2008); *Machele* v. *Mailula* (2010); *Occupiers, Shulana Court, 11 Hendon Road, Yeoville, Johannesburg* v. *Steele* (2010).

145 *Emfuleni Local Municipality* v. *Builders Advancement Services* (2010: paras 12, 14–16, 19, 25, 28). See further Woolman (2013: 328–329).

146 See Wilson *et al.* (2015: 484).

147 *Lingwood* v. *The Unlawful Occupiers of Erf 9 Highlands* (2008: paras 26, 37); *Sailing Queen Investments* v. *Occupants La Colleen Court* (2008: paras 6, 9, 10, 19). See also *Shorts Retreat* v. *Daisy Dear Investments* (2010: paras 11–14).

148 See Liebenberg (2010: 313); Pieterse (2014a: 171); Wilson (2009: 283–285); Wilson (2011a: 271–272). For in-depth contemplation of the joinder strategy, see Muller and Liebenberg (2013).

149 *City of Johannesburg Metropolitan Municipality* v. *Blue Moonlight Properties* (2012: para 3). The facts of the matter are further exposited at ibid., paras 6–14, 39, 78–80. See also Dickinson (2011: 488–489); Tissington and Wilson (2011).

150 *City of Johannesburg Metropolitan Municipality* v. *Blue Moonlight Properties* (2012: paras 22–26).

151 Ibid., paras 90–97, 101, 104.

152 Ibid., para 40. See Strydom and Viljoen (2014: 1222–1223).

153 *City of Johannesburg Metropolitan Municipality* v. *Blue Moonlight Properties* (2012: para 74). See also paras 73, 96.

154 Ibid. See also paras 46–47, 52, 67.

155 Ibid., paras 93–94, 98.

156 See for instance Kruuse (2011: 620–632); Pieterse (2014a: 172); Ray (2014: 214, 217, 219); Tissington and Wilson (2011: 3–6); Wilson and Dugard (2014: 61); Wilson *et al.* (2015: 487).

157 See Dickinson (2011: 488–489, 495); Pieterse (2014a: 173).

158 See Dickinson (2011: 492); Kruger (2014: 329, 334–335, 339–340, 348–352); Kruuse (2011: 623). Indeed, it took approximately 6 years from the institution of proceedings for the occupiers to eventually vacate the premises. Kruger (2014: 335).

159 See Kruuse (2011: 626–629); Pieterse (2014a: 173–174).

160 See Dickinson (2011: 494); Tissington and Wilson (2011: 6).

161 See the Court's exposition of the facts in *Pheko* v. *Ekurhuleni Metropolitan Municipality* (2012: paras 5–11).

162 Ibid., paras 36–41, 44–45, 50, 53. See also Wilson *et al.* (2015: 499); Muller (2015: 619–620, 631–633).

163 *Occupiers of Portion R25 of the Farm Mooiplaats 355 JR* v. *Golden Thread* (2012: paras 11–12); *Occupiers of Skurweplaas 353 JR* v. *PPC Aggregate Quarries Skurweplaas* (2012: paras 13–14). For discussion, see Ray (2014: 226–230).

164 *Occupiers of Portion R25 of the Farm Mooiplaats 355 JR* v. *Golden Thread* (2012: para 19); *Occupiers of Skurweplaas 353 JR* v. *PPC Aggregate Quarries Skurweplaas* (2012: para 12). For commentary, see Wilson *et al.* (2015: 486).

165 *Mbatha* v. *City of Johannesburg Metropolitan Municipality* (2015: paras 7–18, 30–35, 37).

166 *Melani* v. *City of Johannesburg* (2016: paras 3–7, 41–50).

167 The facts are set out in *Maphango* v. *Aengus Lifestyle Properties* (2012: paras 2–4, 11, 14) and discussed in more depth by De Villiers (2014a: 2178–2181).

168 *Maphango* v. *Aengus Lifestyle Properties* (2012: paras 48, 67–70). The Court has endured some criticism for 'avoiding' the issue. See Ray (2014: 207, 210).

169 *Maphango* v. *Aengus Lifestyle Properties* (2012: paras 34–35).

170 Ibid., para 60.
171 Ibid., paras 120, 126–129, 132, 146. For criticism, see De Villiers (2014a: 2185).
172 See De Villiers (2014a: 2186).
173 See Ray (2014: 201, 203, 210); Wilson *et al.* (2015: 491).
174 See *Schubart Park Residents' Association* v. *City of Tshwane Metropolitan Municipality* (2013: paras 1–10, 13). For details of the build-up to the events, see Van Marle and De Villiers (2013: 136–142).
175 Ibid., paras 35; 38.
176 See Brand (2014: 196–200); De Villiers (2014b: 213–214); Van Marle and De Villiers (2013: 132, 136–137, 141–142).
177 *Schubart Park Residents' Association* v. *City of Tshwane Metropolitan Municipality* (2013: paras 40–41).
178 Ibid., para 50.
179 Ibid., paras 51–53.
180 See De Villiers (2014b: 204–206).
181 *City of Johannesburg* v. *Changing Tides 74* (2012: para 54).
182 Ibid. See also paras 51–52. Notably, the Court also regarded the occupiers' lawyers' stance (which was to resist eviction until each occupier had been duly assessed and placed in alternative accommodation) as 'overlook[ing] the fact that the court is dealing with a situation in which people are living in a "death trap"', from which they had to be removed as soon as possible. Ibid.
183 Ibid., paras 15, 53–54. See also para 56.
184 See Dugard (2014: 269–270); Ray (2014: 220–221); Wilson (2014: 283–284, 288–289, 292–295).
185 *Occupiers of Saratoga Avenue* v. *City of Johannesburg Metropolitan Municipality* (2012: paras 1–2, 5, 12, 15–16).
186 Ibid., paras 16–18. For criticism see Dugard (2014: 270–271); Ray (2014: 220–221).
187 See Dugard (2014: 271); Wilson (2014: 290).
188 *Dladla* v. *City of Johannesburg Metropolitan Municipality* (2014: paras 31–43). For discussion, see Wilson (2014: 291–294, 296).
189 *City of Johannesburg* v. *Dladla* (2016: paras 8, 14, 19–20, 22).
190 Ibid., paras 8, 11–15.
191 Ibid., paras 15, 23–25.
192 *Hlope* v. *City of Johannesburg* (2013: paras 27–31); as well as the order of the Court at 222B-224D. For discussion, see Dugard (2014: 277–278).
193 *Hlope* v. *City of Johannesburg* (2013: para 10).
194 Ibid., para 26.
195 Ibid., 224C-E.
196 *City of Johannesburg Metropolitan Municipality* v. *Hlope* (2015: paras 21–6).
197 Ibid., paras 27–28.
198 See Charlton (2014a: 189).
199 See Dugard (2014: 274, 279); Tissington (2014: 33); Wilson (2014: 293).
200 Public Protector of South Africa (2014: 4–6).
201 Public Protector of South Africa (2014: 13, 50, 54–56).
202 See Sinwell (2010: 154, 166–167).
203 See Van der Walt (2009: 69–70); Wilson (2009: 271–272; 281–289); Wilson *et al.* (2015: 503).
204 See Langford (2014: 222); Ray (2014: 175–176).
205 Also argued by Goebel (2015: 184–185).
206 See Liebenberg (2015: 455–456); Wilson *et al.* (2015: 487).
207 See also *Ekurhuleni Metropolitan Municipality* v. *Various Occupiers, Eden Park Extension 5* (2014); *All Building and Cleaning Services* v. *Matlaila* (2015). In both these judgments, the unique experiences and needs of occupiers led the courts to find that evicting them would not be just and equitable.

208 See Ray (2014: 177–179); Van der Berg (2013: 385–386); Woolman (2013: 270, 326–327, 440–441); Young (2014: 236, 239, 243).

209 See Brand (2014: 196–198); Dugard (2014: 273); Muller (2014); Tissington (2014: 12); Van Marle and De Villiers (2013: 144); Wilson (2006: 559–561; 2011b: 128–130; 2014: 284, 292–293, 296); Wilson *et al.* (2015: 477, 500, 502). This criticism relates to broader displeasure with the conceptual sparsity of, and the lack of meaningful normative parameters and concrete entitlements embodied in, the Constitutional Court's socio-economic rights jurisprudence. See McLean (2009: 175); Ray (2014: 174–175); Wilson and Dugard (2011: 665, 669–673).

210 City of Johannesburg (2016: 2).

References

Abahlali baseMjondolo Movement SA v. *Premier, KwaZulu Natal*, 2010. Decision of the South African Constitutional Court, reported as 2010 (2) BCLR 99 (CC).

All Building and Cleaning Services v. *Matlaila*, 2015. Decision of the Gauteng High Court, reported as [2015] ZAGPJHC 2.

Brand, D., 2014. 'Law and the city: Keeping the poor on the margins', *De Jure* 47(2), 189–201.

Centre on Housing Rights and Evictions (COHRE), 2005. *Any Room for the Poor? Forced Evictions in Johannesburg, South Africa*. COHRE.

Charlton, S., 2010. 'Inclusion through housing: Limitations and alternatives in Johannesburg', *Urban Forum* 21(1), 1–20.

Charlton, S., 2014a. 'Public housing in Johannesburg'. In: Harrison, P., Gotz, G., Todes, A., & Wray, C. (eds.), *Changing Space, Changing City: Johannesburg After Apartheid*, pp. 176–193. Johannesburg: Wits University Press.

Charlton, S., 2014b. 'Waste pickers/informal recyclers'. In Harrison, P., Gotz, G., Todes, A., & Wray, C. (eds.), *Changing Space, Changing City: Johannesburg After Apartheid*, pp. 539–545. Johannesburg: Wits University Press.

Chenwi, L., 2009. 'A new approach to remedies in socio-economic rights adjudication: *Occupiers of 541 Olivia Road and Others* v. *City of Johannesburg and Others*', *Constitutional Court Review* 2, 371–393.

Chenwi, L. & Liebenberg, S., 2013. 'The constitutional protection of those facing eviction from "bad buildings" ', *ESR Review* 9(1), 12–17.

City of Cape Town v. *Rudolph*, 2003. Decision of the Cape High Court, reported as 2003 (11) BCLR 1236 (C).

City of Johannesburg, 2007. *Inner City Regeneration Charter*.

City of Johannesburg, 2011. *Joburg Growth and Development Strategy 2040*.

City of Johannesburg, 2013a. *Inner City Transformation Roadmap*.

City of Johannesburg, 2013b. *Corridors of Freedom: Restitching our City to Create a New Future*.

City of Johannesburg, 2016. *State of the City Address 2016 Delivered by the Executive Mayor, Cllr Mpho Parks Tau*.

City of Johannesburg v. *Changing Tides 74*, 2012. Decision by the Supreme Court of Appeal, reported as 2012 (6) SA 294 (SCA).

City of Johannesburg v. *Dladla*, 2016. Decision by the Supreme Court of Appeal, reported as [2016] ZASCA 66.

City of Johannesburg v. *Rand Properties*, 2007a. Decision by the Witwatersrand High Court, reported as 2007 (1) SA 78 (W).

City of Johannesburg v. *Rand Properties*, 2007b. Decision by the Supreme Court of Appeal, reported as 2007 (6) SA 417 (SCA).

City of Johannesburg Metropolitan Municipality v. *Blue Moonlight Properties*, 2012. Decision by the South African Constitutional Court, reported as 2012 (2) SA 104 (CC).

City of Johannesburg Metropolitan Municipality v. *Hlope*, 2015. Decision by the Supreme Court of Appeal, reported as [2015] 2 All SA 251 (SCA).

Coggin, T. & Pieterse, M., 2012. 'Rights and the city: An exploration of the interaction between socio-economic rights and the city', *Urban Forum* 23(3), 257–278.

Coggin, T. & Pieterse, M., 2015. 'A right to transport? Moving towards a rights-based approach to mobility in the city', *South African Journal of Human Rights* 31(3), 294–314.

Constitution of the Republic of South Africa, 1996 (Act 108 of 1996).

Department of Human Settlements, 2004. *Comprehensive Housing Plan for the Development of Integrated Sustainable Human Settlements.*

Department of Human Settlements, 2009. *National Housing Code.*

De Villiers, I., 2014a. 'Spatial practices in Lowliebenhof: The case of *Maphango* v. *Aengus Lifestyle Properties*', *Potchefstroom Electronic Law Journal* 17(5), 2165–2193.

De Villiers, I., 2014b. 'Tshwane 2055 and the (im)possibility of spatial justice', *De Jure* 47(2), 202–217.

Dickinson, G.S., 2011. 'Blue Moonlight rising: Evictions, alternative accommodation and a comparative perspective on affordable housing solutions in Johannesburg', *South African Journal of Human Rights* 27(3), 466–495.

Disaster Management Act, 57 of 2002.

Dladla v. *City of Johannesburg Metropolitan Municipality*, 2014. Decision of the South Gauteng High Court, reported as [2014] 4 All SA 51 (GJ).

Dugard, J., 2008. 'Courts and the poor in South Africa: A critique of systemic judicial failures to advance transformative justice', *South African Journal of Human Rights* 21(2), 214–238.

Dugard, J., 2014. 'Beyond *Blue Moonlight*: The implications of judicial avoidance in relation to the provision of alternative housing', *Constitutional Court Review* 5, 265–279.

Ekurhuleni Metropolitan Municipality v. *Various Occupiers, Eden Park Extension 5*, 2014. Decision of the Supreme Court of Appeal, reported as 2014 (3) SA 23 (SCA).

Emfuleni Local Municipality v. *Builders Advancement Services*, 2010. Decision by the South Gauteng High Court, reported as 2010 (4) SA 133 (GSJ).

Extension of Security of Tenure Act, 62 of 1997.

Goebel, A., 2015. *On Their Own: Women, Urbanization and the Right to the City in South Africa.* Montreal: McGill-Queens University Press.

Government of the RSA v. *Grootboom*, 2001. Decision by the South African Constitutional Court, reported as 2001 (1) SA 46 (CC).

Group Areas Act, 36 of 1966.

Gundwana v. *Steko Development*, 2011. Decision by the South African Constitutional Court, reported as 2011 (3) SA 608 (CC).

Hatting v. *Juta*, 2013. Decision by the South African Constitutional Court, reported as 2013 (3) SA 275 (CC).

Hlope v. *City of Johannesburg*. Decision by the South Gauteng High Court, reported as 2013 (4) SA 212 (GSJ).

Housing Act, 107 of 1997.

Huchzermeyer, M., 2011. *Cities With "Slums": From Informal Settlement Eradication to a Right to the City in Africa*. Cape Town: UCT Press.

Huchzermeyer, M., Karam, A. & Maina, M., 2014. 'Informal settlements'. In: Harrison, P., Gotz, G., Todes, A., & Wray, C. (eds.), *Changing Space, Changing City: Johannesburg After Apartheid*, pp. 154–175. Johannesburg: Wits University Press.

Jaftha v. *Schoeman; Van Rooyen* v. *Stolz*, 2005. Decision of the South African Constitutional Court, reported as 2005 (2) SA 140 (CC).

Kruger, M., 2014. 'Arbitrary deprivations of property: An argument for the payment of compensation by the State in certain cases of unlawful occupation', *South African Law Journal* 131(2), 328–364.

Kruuse, H., 2011. '"The art of the possible" in realising socio-economic rights: The SCA decision in *City of Johannesburg Metropolitan Municipality* v. *Blue Moonlight Properties 39 (Pty)Ltd*'. *South African Law Journal* 128(4), 620–632.

Langford, M., 2014. 'Housing rights litigation: *Grootboom* and beyond'. In: Langford, M., Cousins, B., Dugard, J. & Madlingozi, T. (eds.), *Socio-economic Rights in South Africa: Symbols or Substance?*, pp. 187–225. Cambridge, UK: Cambridge University Press.

Liebenberg, S., 2010. *Socio-economic Rights Adjudication under a Transformative Constitution*. Cape Town: Juta.

Liebenberg, S., 2012. 'Engaging the paradoxes of the universal and particular in human rights adjudication: The possibilities and pitfalls of "meaningful engagement" ', *African Human Rights Law Journal* 12(1), 1–29.

Liebenberg, S., 2014. 'Participatory approaches to socio-economic rights adjudication: Tentative lessons from South African evictions law', *Nordic Journal of Human Rights* 32(4), 312–330.

Liebenberg, S., 2015. 'Social rights and transformation in South Africa: Three frames', *South African Journal of Human Rights* 31(3), 446–471.

Lingwood v. *The Unlawful Occupiers of Erf 9 Highlands*, 2008. Decision of the Witwatersrand High Court, reported as 2008 (3) BCLR 325 (W).

Maas, S., 2011. 'Rental housing as adequate housing', *Stellenbosch Law Review* 22(3), 759–774.

Machele v. *Mailula*, 2010. Decision of the South African Constitutional Court, reported as 2010 (2) SA 257 (CC).

Mamba v. *Minister of Social Development*, 2008. Unreported decision of the South African Constitutional Court, case number CCT 65/08.

Maphango v. *Aengus Lifestyle Properties*, 2012. Decision of the South African Constitutional Court, reported as 2012 (5) BCLR 449 (CC).

Mayson, S.S. & Charlton, S., 2015. 'Accommodation and tenuous livelihoods in Johannesburg's inner city: The "rooms" and "spaces" typologies', *Urban Forum* 26(3), 343–372.

Mbatha v. *City of Johannesburg Metropolitan Municipality*, 2015. Decision of the South Gauteng High Court, reported as [2015] 1 All SA 575 (GJ).

McLean, K., 2009. *Constitutional Deference, Courts and Socio-Economic Rights in South Africa*. Pretoria: PULP.

McLean, K., 2010. 'Meaningful engagement: One step forward or two back? Some thoughts on *Joe Slovo*', *Constitutional Court Review* 3, 223–242.

Melani v. *City of Johannesburg*. Decision of the South Gauteng High Court, reported as [2016] ZAGPJHC 55.

Modder East Squatters v. *Modderklip Boerdery; President of the RSA* v. *Modderklip Boerdery*, 2004. Decision of the Supreme Court of Appeal, reported as 2004 (8) BCLR 821 (SCA).

Muller, G., 2011. 'Conceptualising "meaningful engagement" as a deliberative democratic partnership', *Stellenbosch Law Review* 22(3), 742–758.

Muller, G., 2014. 'On considering alternative accommodation and the rights and needs of vulnerable people', *South African Journal of Human Rights* 30(1), 41–62.

Muller, G., 2015. 'Evicting unlawful occupiers for health and safety reasons in post-apartheid South Africa', *South African Law Journal* 132(3), 616–638.

Muller, G. & Liebenberg, S., 2013. 'Developing the law of joinder in the context of evictions of people from their homes', *South African Journal of Human Rights* 29(3), 554–570.

Murray, M.J., 2008. *Taming the Disorderly City: The Spatial Landscape of Johannesburg after Apartheid*. Ithaca, London: Cornell University Press.

National Building Regulations and Building Standards Act, 103 of 1977.

Nokotyana v. *Ekurhuleni Metropolitan Municipality*, 2010. Decision of the South African Constitutional Court, reported as 2010 (4) BCLR 312 (CC).

Occupiers of 51 Olivia Road, Berea Township v. *City of Johannesburg*, 2008. Decision of the South African Constitutional Court, reported as 2008 (3) SA 208 (CC).

Occupiers of Portion R25 of the Farm Mooiplaats 355 JR v. *Golden Thread*, 2012. Decision of the South African Constitutional Court, reported as 2012 (4) BCLR 372 (CC).

Occupiers of Saratoga Avenue v. *City of Johannesburg Metropolitan Municipality*, 2012. Decision of the South African Constitutional Court, reported as 2012 (9) BCLR 951 (CC).

Occupiers of Skurweplaas 353 JR v. *PPC Aggregate Quarries*, 2012. Decision of the South African Constitutional Court, reported as 2012 (4) BCLR 382 (CC).

Occupiers, Shulana Court, 11 Hendon Road, Yeoville, Johannesburg v. *Steele*, 2010. Decision of the Supreme Court of Appeal, reported as 2010 (9) BCLR 911 (SCA).

Pernegger, L., 2014. 'The agonistic state: Metropolitan government responses to city strife post-1994'. In: Haferburg, C. & Huchzermeyer, M. (eds.), *Urban Governance in Post-Apartheid Cities: Modes of Engagement in South Africa's Metropoles*, pp. 61–78. Pietermaritzburg: UKZN Press.

Pheko v. *Ekurhuleni Metropolitan Municipality*. Decision of the South African Constitutional Court, reported as 2012 (4) BCLR 388 (CC).

Pieterse, M., 2012. 'Procedural relief, constitutional citizenship and socio-economic rights as legitimate expectations', *South African Journal of Human Rights* 28(3), 359–379.

Pieterse, M., 2014a. 'Development, the right to the city and the legal and constitutional responsibilities of local government in South Africa', *South African Law Journal* 131(1), 149–177.

Pieterse, M., 2014b. 'The right to the city and the urban environment: Re-imagining section 24 of the 1996 Constitution', *South African Public Law* 29(1), 175–193.

Pillay, K., 2002. 'Implementation of *Grootboom*: Implications for the enforcement of socio-economic rights', *Law, Democracy & Development* 6(2), 255–277.

Port Elizabeth Municipality v. *Various Occupiers*, 2005. Decision of the South African Constitutional Court, reported as 2005 (1) SA 217 (CC).

Poulsen, L., 2010. 'A room in the city: Strategies for accessing affordable accommodation', *Urban Forum* 21(1), 21–36.

President of the Republic of South Africa v. *Modderklip Boerdery*, 2005. Decision of the South African Constitutional Court, reported as 2005 (5) SA 3 (CC).

Prevention of Illegal Eviction from and Unlawful Occupation of Land Act, 19 of 1998.

Public Protector of South Africa, 2014. *Broken Promises: A Report on an Investigation into Alleged Maladministration by the City of Johannesburg relating to the City's Failure to Comply with its By-laws and the Constitution regarding Hijacked Buildings*, Report 11 of 2014/2015.

Ray, B., 2011. 'Proceduralisation's triumph and engagement's promise in socio-economic rights litigation', *South African Journal of Human Rights* 27(1), 107–126.

Ray, B., 2014. 'Evictions, aspirations and avoidance', *Constitutional Court Review* 5, 173–232.

Rental Housing Act, 50 of 1999.

Residents of Joe Slovo Community, Western Cape v. *Thubelisha Homes*, 2010. Decision of the South African Constitutional Court, reported as 2010 (3) SA 454 (CC).

Residents of Joe Slovo Community, Western Cape v. *Thubelisha Homes*, 2011. Decision of the South African Constitutional Court, reported as 2011 (7) BCLR 723 (CC).

Ritama Investments v. *Unlawful Occupiers of Erf 62 Wynberg*, 2006. Decision of the South Gauteng High Court, reported as [2006] ZAGPHC 6.

Rubin, M., 2014. 'Johannesburg's Bad Buildings Programme: The World Class City hegemony at work?' In: Haferburg, C. & Huchzermeyer, M. (eds.), *Urban Governance in Post-Apartheid Cities: Modes of Engagement in South Africa's Metropoles*, pp. 211–230. Pietermaritzburg: UKZN Press.

Rule, S.P., 1989. 'The emergence of a racially mixed residential suburb in Johannesburg: Demise of the Apartheid city?', *Geographical Journal* 155(2), 196–203.

S v. *Govender*, 1982. Decision of the Transvaal Supreme Court, reported as 1986 (3) SA 969 (T).

Sailing Queen Investments v. *Occupants La Colleen Court*, 2008. Decision of the Witwatersrand High Court, reported as 2008 (6) BCLR 666 (W).

Schubart Park Residents' Association v. *City of Tshwane Metropolitan Municipality*, 2013. Decision of the South African Constitutional Court, reported as 2013 (1) SA 323 (CC).

Shapurjee, Y. & Charlton, S., 2013. 'Transforming South Africa's low-income housing projects through backyard dwellings: Intersections with households and the state in Alexandra, Johannesburg', *Journal of Housing & the Built Environment* 28(4), 653–666.

Shorts Retreat v. *Daisy Dear Investments*, 2010. Decision of the Supreme Court of Appeal, reported as 2010 (4) BCLR 354 (SCA).

Sinwell, L., 2010. 'The Wynberg concerned residents' disempowering court victory', *Urban Forum* 21(2), 153–169.

Smith, L. & Rubin, M., 2015. 'Beyond invented and invited spaces of participation: The Phiri and Olivia Road court cases and their outcome'. In: Benit-Gbaffou, C. (ed.), *Popular Politics in South African Cities: Unpacking Community Participation*, pp. 248–281. Cape Town: HSRC Press.

Strauss, M. & Liebenberg, S., 2014. 'Contested spaces: Housing rights and evictions law in post-apartheid South Africa', *Planning Theory* 13(3), 428–448.

Strydom, J. & Viljoen, S., 2014. 'Unlawful occupation of inner-city buildings: A constitutional analysis of the rights and obligations involved', *Potchefstroom Electronic Law Journal* 17(4), 1207–1261.

Tissington, K., 2011. 'Demolishing development at Gabon informal settlement: Public interest litigation beyond Modderklip?', *South African Journal of Human Rights* 27(1), 192–205.

Tissington, K., 2014. *Minding the Gap: An Analysis of the Supply of Low-Income Rental Accommodation in Inner-City Johannesburg.* SERI Research Report, Johannesburg.

Tissington, K. & Wilson, S., 2011. 'SCA upholds rights of urban poor in Blue Moonlight judgment', *ESR Review* 12(1), 3–6.

Tswelopele Non-profit Organisation v. *City of Tshwane Metropolitan Municipality*, 2007. Decision by the Supreme Court of Appeal, reported as 2007 (6) SA 511 (SCA).

Van der Berg, S., 2013. 'Meaningful engagement: Proceduralising socio-economic rights further or infusing administrative law with substance?', *South African Journal of Human Rights* 29(2), 376–398.

Van der Walt, A.J., 2009. *Property in the Margins.* Oxford, Portland: Hart.

Van Marle, K. & De Villiers, I., 2013. 'Law and resistance in the city of Pretoria: Space, history and the everyday', *Australian Feminist Law Journal* 38(1), 129–145.

Wilson, S., 2006. 'Judicial enforcement of the right to protection from arbitrary eviction: Lessons from Mandelaville', *South African Journal of Human Rights* 2(4), 535–562.

Wilson, S., 2009. 'Breaking the tie: Evictions from private land, homelessness and a new normality', *South African Law Journal* 126(2), 270–290.

Wilson, S., 2011a. 'Planning for inclusion in South Africa: The State's duty to prevent homelessness and the potential of "meaningful engagement"', *Urban Forum* 22(3), 265–282.

Wilson, S., 2011b. 'Litigating housing rights in Johannesburg's inner city: 2004–2008', *South African Journal of Human Rights* 27(1), 127–151.

Wilson, S., 2014. 'Curing the Poor: State housing policy in Johannesburg after *Blue Moonlight*', *Constitutional Court Review* 5, 280–296.

Wilson, S. & Dugard, J., 2011. 'Taking poverty seriously: The South African Constitutional Court and socio-economic rights', *Stellenbosch Law Review* 22(3), 664–682.

Wilson, S. & Dugard, J., 2014. 'Constitutional jurisprudence: The first and second waves'. In: Langford, M., Cousins, B., Dugard, J. & Madlingozi, T. (eds.), *Socio-economic Rights in South Africa: Symbols or Substance?*, pp. 35–62. Cambridge, UK: Cambridge University Press.

Wilson, S., Dugard, J. & Clark, M., 2015. 'Conflict management in an era of urbanisation: 20 years of housing rights jurisprudence in the South African Constitutional Court', *South African Journal of Human Rights* 31(3), 472–503.

Woolman, S., 2013. *The Selfless Constitution: Experimentalism and Flourishing as Foundations of South Africa's Basic Law.* Cape Town: Juta.

Young, K.G., 2014. 'The avoidance of substance in constitutional rights', *Constitutional Court Review* 5, 233–243.

3 Struggles over essential services

Introduction

The ways in which people access and consume the goods and services that are essential for everyday urban survival and flourishing, are important expressions of the right to the city.[1] Since the provision, delivery and distribution of such goods and services to and between urban inhabitants are among the most essential functions of local government, issues pertaining to service delivery and consumption typically feature centrally in interactions between city dwellers and the State. As such, the ways in which essential services are accessed, as well as the interactions and conflicts between and among urban inhabitants and the State over such access, are important indicators and determinants of the benefits, obligations and dynamics of urban citizenship.

As elsewhere, many facets of essential service delivery in South Africa are legally and constitutionally regulated. Section 152(1)(b) of the 1996 Constitution determines that 'the provision of services to communities in a sustainable manner' is a central objective of local government, while municipalities must, in terms of section 153(a), 'structure and manage [their] administration and budgeting and planning processes to give priority to the basic needs of the community, and to promote the social and economic development of the community'. Section 156(1) read with parts B of Schedules 4 and 5 of the Constitution then proceeds to award local government executive authority over, and the right to administer, the delivery of a range of essential services, including the provision of water, sanitation, electricity, street lighting, waste removal, municipal health services and public transport.

While local government is thus granted a fairly wide discretion as to the manner in which essential services are delivered, municipalities are bound by the values and principles governing public administration, listed in section 195 of the Constitution. These include that public administration must be transparent, accountable and development orientated, that services must be provided fairly, impartially, equitably and without bias, that public administration and service provision must be responsive to the needs of the people, that service provision should be accessible as well as environmentally and financially sustainable, and that public participation in relevant policy-making processes should be encouraged. In addition, section 4(2) of the Municipal Systems Act of 2000 determines that municipal services must be provided in a 'financially and environmentally sustainable manner', that community members must have equitable access to services and that they ought to be consulted over the 'level, quality, range and impact of municipal services' as well as over 'available options for [the manner of] service delivery'.[2]

Citizens' expectations of essential service delivery are further coloured by the fact that section 27 of the Constitution awards them an explicit, justiciable right to have access to sufficient water and to health care services (which the State must realise progressively, within its available resources, through taking reasonable legislative and other measures), whereas section 39 determines that the values underlying an open and democratic society based on dignity, equality and freedom, as well as the spirit, purport and objects of the Bill of Rights, must inform the interpretation of all other constitutional and statutory provisions (such as those governing the responsibility of local government to provide essential services). Moreover, the manner of essential service delivery is impacted by the environmental right in section 24 of the Constitution, which requires economic and social development to be sustainable, with due regard to the needs of both present and future generations.[3]

The constitutional ensconcement of justiciable rights to have access to certain essential services has enabled urban inhabitants to supplement everyday struggles over service delivery with litigation, challenging 'both the mode of delivery of essential urban services and the manner in which such service provision has structured the relationship between them and the City'.[4] In this chapter, I examine the manner and extent to which such rights-based litigation has shaped, supplemented and impacted upon everyday assertions of service-related aspects of the right to the city, as well as on the manner in which local government (and, in particular, the City of Johannesburg) conceives of and conducts itself in the provision of essential urban services.

Both water and electricity provision in Johannesburg relate to the distribution of scarce resources. South Africa is an arid country that has to import significant amounts of water from its neighbours, and limitations in its electricity generating capacity have led to a widely publicised and much maligned energy crisis in recent years.[5] Whereas inhabitants of Johannesburg on average have greater and better quality access to these (and other) essential services than elsewhere in South Africa (especially when compared with rural areas),[6] historical discrepancies in access linger, and several features of the delivery systems of both resources render them ultimately unsustainable and in need of reform.[7] Everyday access to these resources in Johannesburg is therefore far from uncomplicated, whereas the City has to balance a number of competing considerations in conceiving and implementing relevant service delivery policies and mechanisms.

This chapter proceeds to provide a historical overview of access to services in the city as well as an overview of the City government's approach to service delivery after 1994. I then consider the various ways in which citizens have, through the years, themselves attempted to shape their access to essential urban services, by zooming in on insurgent practices of access to services, the formation and activities of service-related social movements across the city, as well as the widely publicised 'service delivery protests' occurring across several Joburg townships in recent years. Thereafter, the focus shifts to attempts to assert rights to receive essential urban services through litigation, and I discuss and critique Constitutional Court and High Court decisions pertaining to access to services in South African cities.

Access to, contestation over and delivery of essential services in Johannesburg

Discrepancies in service provision between white and black residential areas was a central feature of apartheid cities, and Johannesburg was no exception. Residents in white suburbs typically received world class, in-house water, electricity and sanitation services provided on a consumption credit basis, whereas black townships were initially not electrified, and received only pit sanitation and standpipe water services, for which they tended to be charged at a flat rate.[8]

Township service provision became acutely politicised after the 1976 Soweto riots, after which Joburg's townships were electrified for the first time.[9] In post-uprising Soweto, opposition to apartheid combined with dissatisfaction with the mechanics and quality of service delivery, to culminate in the Soweto rates boycott (which, because of its severe financial consequences for the City Council, is widely credited for having driven home the unsustainability of the apartheid state at local government level) from 1984 until 1990. The boycott involved a near absolute embargo on payment of rent and service charges across Soweto (and other Joburg townships), to the point where the City Council would give up on credit control efforts and ceased reading meters and sending service bills in the township by mid-1988. While 1990's so-called 'Soweto Accord' (in terms of which some 516.2 million rand of unpaid service debt was written off by the Council) included an undertaking by boycott-organisers that payment for services would resume, the boycott entrenched a widespread and tenacious culture of non-payment for water and electricity in the township, which has persisted and remains a major headache for the Joburg Metropolitan Council.[10]

As democracy dawned, Joburg's newly established transitional metropolitan council faced the massive task of beginning to correct for the apartheid-era discrepancies in service provision, and immediately stepped up service infrastructure and logistics in all areas where these were formerly neglected. It did this under significant nationally imposed financial constraints, and in a context of extra costs and losses occasioned by city-wide crumbling of existing service-related infrastructure (which, in many parts, were now about a century old).[11]

With its budget for service provision largely dependent on its own ability to collect payment for services rendered,[12] the Council was especially hard hit by the inherited after-effects of the Soweto boycott. A mid-1990s campaign to foster a sense of civic responsibility and a culture of payment for services in the township (the so-called 'Mashakane' campaign) was a resounding failure, and service arrears mounted anew.[13] Added to this were the complications imposed on credit control processes by the constitutional entrenchment of a right to have access to water (with the 1997 Water Services Act introducing a burdensome credit control process, in terms of which it was no longer permissible for the Council to disconnect water services for non-payment where this would lead to the denial of a basic water supply to indigent persons),[14] as well as the devastating financial effects of an additional rates boycott – this time by wealthy residents of the former Sandton municipality, who objected to their rates payments being used to cross-subsidise service provision in poorer areas.[15]

The result – perhaps predictably – was a full-scale financial crisis, with the young Council effectively going bankrupt, and being subjected to a nationally imposed financial restructuring plan, in 1997.[16] On a policy level, the City responded by formulating *iGoli 2002*, a three-year 'transformation plan' commencing in 1999 and resulting in the City corporatising all of its service delivery functions by forming three service orientated 'public utilities' responsible for service delivery: Joburg Water for water delivery, City Power for electricity and Pikitup for waste collection and disposal.[17] These utilities all adopted a 'corporatised' approach to service delivery, emphasising cost recovery and payment for services[18] (much as the City's billing department would develop and retain a reputation for decidedly un-corporate inaccuracy and inefficiency). Joburg Water signed a controversial management agreement with French water company Suez in 2000, and increasingly resorted to water disconnections in cases of non-payment.[19] Electricity supply was managed similarly, with City Power further increasingly installing prepaid electricity meters (in terms of which electricity supply automatically ceases when credit runs out), especially (though not exclusively) in former township areas.[20]

Many citizens did not take kindly to these developments, especially in townships, where residents felt unduly targeted by the City's sudden turn towards cost recovery and its increasing insistence on prepaid services.[21] Despite the City's insistence that *iGoli 2002* was aimed primarily at improving service delivery, the South African Municipal Services Workers Union ('SAMWU') declared a dispute with the City over the degree of privatisation implied by the policy and over the lack of consultation in its inception. Supported by the South African Communist Party ('SACP'), the Union eventually took to the streets to protest the policy's introduction. The City remained resolute, however, and *iGoli 2002* was implemented as planned, notwithstanding that relations between the Council and the Union would remain strained.[22]

Two, closely related, social movements arose in response to *iGoli 2002*. The first, the Anti-Privatisation Forum ('APF'), was formed in mid-2000 after an Urban Futures conference held at Wits University, in opposition not only to *iGoli 2002*, but also to the mooted privatisation and outsourcing of some support services at the university. A heterogeneous umbrella organisation initially consisting of SAMWU, other trade unions, community groups, the SACP and academics, the APF would generally oppose the State's perceived neoliberal agenda, including the privatisation of essential service delivery, over the years to come. While its agenda would become more diffuse and its membership would dwindle significantly after both *iGoli 2002* and the Wits restructuring went ahead notwithstanding its opposition, factions of the APF remained active, periodically engaging in various marches, pickets, demonstrations and awareness campaigns across Gauteng.[23]

One of the APF's most active affiliates, the Soweto Electricity Crisis Committee ('SECC') was formed at around the same time, mainly in response to the Metropolitan Council's disconnection of Soweto households' electricity in cases of non-payment. While often publicly fronted by elderly ladies from Soweto (whose pension money is typically used to pay for services in the township's more impoverished households), the SECC is a very amorphous and unstructured (some would say somewhat anarchic) organisation, linked to various 'gangs' of young men who go about illegally reconnecting disconnected electricity supplies across the township.[24] In addition to these reconnections, SECC members also regularly partook in APF-led marches and demonstrations, and would also sometimes stage boycotts and protests of their own, most notably in early 2002, when a group of SECC members were arrested outside the Kensington home of Joburg's then-mayor, Amos Masondo, for trying to disconnect his electricity supply.[25] Like the APF, the SECC has been negatively regarded by both the City and national government (as well as by the press, the middle-classes and the less radical, 'law-abiding' poor who do pay for services, also in Soweto) with its actions often being publicly derided and its members being (perhaps disproportionately) targeted by police.[26]

Over and above public protests and electricity reconnections associated with the APF and the SECC, everyday activities in the face of the city's attempts to install a 'customer-centred' culture of payment for services across Joburg, have included illegal electricity connections and reconnections, barricades and physical resistance to prevent officials from disconnecting water and electricity supplies, and the vandalising or ripping out of prepaid electricity meters (with these often being dumped in front of the offices of the Metropolitan Council or ESKOM).[27] Most notably, the Council's increased credit control efforts appeared to make little difference to non-payment for services in the townships, with over 80 per cent of Soweto's service bills remaining unpaid in the early 2000s.[28]

This said, inhabitants were by no means undivided in their opposition to the council. Many households across different classes continued to pay for their services as required, and there has for instance been notable community resistance to the 'lawlessness' of the SECC.[29] Similarly, many residents (in townships and elsewhere) prefer to receive basic services through pre-paid (rather than conventional credit) meters, especially since the installation of prepaid meters tended to be accompanied by the City writing off arrear debts, and given residents' general distrust of the Council and ESKOM's billing practices.[30]

Meanwhile, important changes in the national legislative framework and policy environment, during the time of implementation of *iGoli 2002*, would significantly change the face of service delivery in Johannesburg. First, the Metropolitan Council became 'institutionalised' following the 2000 Local Government elections and the concomitant coming into operation of new legislation governing local government. Both the Municipal Services Act and Municipal Structures Act of 2000 envisaged rights-based service delivery and participatory local governance, with the latter inter alia establishing a Ward Committee system through which inhabitants could enter into dialogue with municipal councils over a range of issues, including service delivery.

Unfortunately, this system has proved somewhat dysfunctional. Much as ward councillors have been perpetually occupied with attempting to solve citizens' billing and other service-related concerns, ward councils tend to be bogged down in technocratic and bureaucratic slog, and are often accused of being toothless talkshops or unrepresentative handmaidens of the ANC, with little genuine engagement over modes and effectiveness of service delivery systems.[31] While the Johannesburg Metropolitan Council has spent significant institutional energy on overcoming these weaknesses, and has supplemented ward councils with a range of participatory structures (such as a petitions management system, a service ombudsman, mayoral roadshows and outreach programmes around the implementation of the City's Integrated Development Plan),[32] it is felt that these have not contributed much in the way of real dialogue over service delivery in the city (with the Council often accused of taking a rigid, technocratic and 'top-down' approach to service delivery that is insensitive to the peculiar circumstances of individual households).[33]

A far more significant consequence of the new legislative and policy framework was the extent to which it operationalised constitutional entitlements to receive essential services. The lead-up to the 2000 Local Government elections saw the ANC promising free basic services to low-income households, an undertaking which the government decided to follow through – spurred by a cholera epidemic in KwaZulu Natal in late 2000.[34] National regulations first formulated in 2001 determined that all South African households should receive at least six kilolitres of free basic water per household per month (translating into roughly 25 litres per person per day for an average-sized household of eight people). An additional four kilolitres per month for sanitation was added to this amount in 2008. As to electricity, regulations allowing for a free basic electricity allocation of 50 kilowatt hours per household per month were gazetted in 2003.[35] While often dismissed as being too low, especially for large households,[36] these entitlements (a rarity, worldwide) have provided much relief across the country. Johannesburg has been quick to roll out the free basic services and has commendably tended to exceed the national minimum benchmarks. While the City has tended towards prepaid meters as the prime vehicle for delivering free basic services to low income areas,[37] and has continuously stepped up its credit control efforts in other areas, its good performance in terms of rolling out free basic services has ensured that it has been able to fulfil the most basic needs of most residents.[38]

The City's efforts have not always been uncontroversial, however. In Soweto, its rollout of free basic water was tied to the maligned Operation Gcin'amanzi ('to save water'), which was aimed at addressing the unsustainable 'flat rate' consumption system inherited from apartheid and at reducing unaccounted and unpaid for water, in yet another effort to break the prevailing culture of non-payment in the township. The project was to be piloted in the suburb of Phiri, one of Soweto's poorer areas. In addition to significant water infrastructure improvements, Operation Gcin'amanzi involved giving households a choice between receiving unlimited water through a yard standpipe or to be provided with in-house, piped access, but through a pre-paid meter which would dispense the monthly amount of free basic water and would thereafter discontinue the supply, unless and until further credits were purchased.[39]

Its sound aims notwithstanding, Operation Gcin'amanzi was initially predictably met with opposition from residents who, given the Council's inability to effectively enforce the flat rate consumption system against them, had 'illegally' been accessing unlimited amounts of water, free of charge, for years. It also raised the ire of the APF. While a major official education campaign over the aims of Operation Gcin'amanzi and an undertaking by the City to write off all arrear water charges in return for compliance therewith led to most residents reconciling themselves with the project,[40] the APF mobilised the remainder in a series of high-profile protest actions. These actions included a 2004 march to Council offices in Braamfontein (during which several prepaid meters that had been ripped out were dumped on the Council building's steps), digging out and destroying prepaid meters as soon as they were installed, and preventing their installation through erecting barricades and through acts of physical intimidation against municipal workers.[41]

When the City persisted with the operation, backed by police and going as far as to obtain a court interdict against APF members to prevent them from disrupting its implementation, the APF also resorted to litigation.[42] Their (ultimately unsuccessful) constitutional challenge to Operation Gcin'amanzi (which will be discussed below) took years to progress through the court system, during which the operation was effectively halted. During the same time (and in response both to the litigation and to a national indigency policy requiring special attention to be paid to the service-related needs of poor households), the City altered its free basic water policy to also provide for additional free water for indigent households.[43]

While the litigation tied the City's hands for many years, and while it did not follow through on its court victory for some time thereafter (ostensibly because the issue had been heavily politicised and it feared further acts of resistance), the ultimate vindication of its position has led it to resume installing prepaid meters across Soweto and other similar neighbourhoods (albeit with some important modifications spurred by the litigation). In the years subsequent to the APF litigation, it has pretty much been business as usual for the City – it has remained focused on improving service delivery infrastructure and on devising and implementing more ecologically and financially sustainable modes of service delivery. Its efforts in this regard remain complicated by the tenacious culture of non-payment in townships, as well as by continued 'illegal' electricity connections, vandalism of infrastructure, theft of electricity cables and by the capacity of its billing and credit control systems.[44]

More pertinently, a major structural challenge over recent years has been the marked growth in the informal settlements on Joburg's edges, as well as the significant informal densification of established township neighbourhoods (through the erection of backyard shacks). Sustainably delivering services to households, which are by their nature tenuous, often temporary and unconnected to existing infrastructure, poses a planning and logistical conundrum to which current modes of planning and delivery have not successfully responded.[45] 'Informal' residents, as a result, have been forced by circumstance to access services 'illegally', with all the associated dangers and sustainability challenges implied by this, while informal settlements are increasingly the sites for service-related protest and conflict between city officials and residents.[46]

In fact, so-called 'service delivery protests' in townships and informal settlements have become a regular feature of South African public life over recent years. While a nationwide phenomenon, a disproportionate number of these protests, which are typically violent and destructive, have taken place in Gauteng and, specifically, on the outskirts of Joburg.[47] Often wrongly ascribed solely to dissatisfaction with the quality of housing and service delivery, the causes of these protests are clearly more nuanced, not least because they appear to be more numerous in areas that are comparatively well serviced by national standards.[48] Research indicates that a significant number of the protests may more accurately be ascribed to a breakdown in communication over service delivery, with community members finding that they can draw the attention of both City officials and national politicians to service-related and other local governance issues in their specific areas far more effectively and immediately through acts of civil disobedience than by attempting to engage authorities through the conventional municipal engagement/participation structures, which are more cumbersome and less responsive.[49] As such, the protests are about the participatory dimensions of the right to the city rather than purely about the physical objects of daily struggles for survival.

Indeed, it appears that many of the conflicts over service delivery in Joburg through the years have, at their core, been conflicts about the nature and entitlements of urban citizenship. For example, Soweto residents' insurgency in relation to service consumption is historically rooted in resistance to being treated as second class citizens by the apartheid state, and remains as much about redressing the lingering after-effects of that disavowal as about resisting the commercialisation of the necessities of life. By contrast, the City's efforts in the township has, on the one hand, been about inculcating a more docile, 'responsible' form of urban citizenship rooted in frugality and consumerism,[50] while, on the other hand, it has been about securing buy-in into a common citizenship with shared developmental aspirations.

Service delivery and citizenship disputes in the courts

The frame: Walker, *equality and spatial justice*

The first service delivery matter to be decided by South African courts in the constitutional era concerned local government's burden of addressing apartheid's legacy of spatial inequality. Framed by the right to equality in the interim Constitution, the judgment of the Constitutional Court in *Pretoria City Council* v. *Walker* is best known for its careful balancing of the rights of formerly advantaged, white urban residents against the local government obligation to improve the provision of municipal services in former black townships.

As in Joburg, residents in nearby Pretoria's two most prominent 'black' townships, Mamelodi and Atteridgeville, received municipal services that were vastly inferior to those enjoyed by residents of the city's 'white' suburbs. As in Joburg, they were also charged differently for such services, with the established 'white' areas typically receiving in-dwelling water, electricity and sanitation billed on a consumption credit basis, whereas township residents were provided with either communal, on-premises or (limited) in-house services, charged at a flat rate. Moreover, as in Joburg, a township culture of non-payment for services developed towards the end of apartheid, in response to the inequalities in apartheid-era urban citizenship as manifested by the discrepancies in service quality. The challenges faced by the Pretoria City Council at the dawn of the democratic dispensation were therefore similar to those prevailing in Johannesburg.

Mr Walker was a resident of Sunnyside in what the Constitutional Court referred to as 'old' (white) Pretoria, who, together with other members of a residents' association, refused to pay arrear service charges. His argument was that the practices of the City Council, first, to effectively charge residents of old Pretoria more for services than it charged those living in Mamelodi and Atteridgeville (given that the township flat rate was lower than individual rates charged in the suburbs) and, second, to only institute credit control proceedings against defaulters in 'old Pretoria' and not against those in townships, amounted to unfair racial discrimination.

The Constitutional Court found that, given how apartheid laws and policies required people of different races to reside in distinct areas in South African cities, it was indeed possible for differentiation based on place of residence to amount to indirect racial discrimination.[51] It thus proceeded to consider whether the distinction between the mode of levying service charges in Mamelodi and Atteridgeville on the one hand, and in the suburbs of 'old Pretoria' on the other, amounted to unfair discrimination. In finding that it did not, the Court expressed appreciation for the enormity of the task of correcting for the historical inequalities in service provision across the city, and for the fact that, until the Council had installed credit meters and upgraded service infrastructure and quality in the townships, it was not feasible for it to adopt uniform billing practices across the city.[52]

While remarking that the Council should have more effectively and openly communicated with residents over the measures it had taken and the difficulties it faced in implementing them (particularly in relation to the installation of credit consumption meters in Mamelodi and Atteridgeville), the Court held that the different service delivery and billing practices in different parts of the city, in the course of correcting for the inequalities of the past, were not unfair. This was particularly because the Court felt that the Council was entitled to be paid for the services that it rendered, and because it did not expect white residents to pay anything more than what they duly (and admittedly) owed for the high-quality services they had received.[53]

However, the Court was less impressed with the Council's selective credit control practices in relation to amounts duly owed by residents of different areas. It regarded the decision not to act against defaulters in Mamelodi and Atteridgeville as arbitrary and un-transparent, since it was not grounded in a rational and coherent policy aimed at improving the quality of service provision or at addressing the culture of non-payment in those areas. The Court therefore held that singling out defaulters in the formerly white areas of Pretoria for prosecution for non-payment did amount to unfair discrimination, and was therefore unconstitutional.[54]

The *Walker* judgment was generally welcomed, subject to some reservations over how the Court interpreted and applied the right to equality.[55] Little attention was paid to the Court's findings on the way essential services had been delivered, possibly because the interim Constitution neither contained a right to receive services, nor an explicit duty on local government to provide them. In retrospect, it is instructive to note how the Court viewed the public obligation to provide services as being intertwined with citizens' obligation to pay for them. While the Court was prepared to accept that services could be delivered, and charged for, in different ways in different parts of the city, particularly where this was necessary to overcome historical inequalities and inadequacies, it appeared resolute that residents who had duly been billed for services rendered, regardless of the mode of delivery, were all equally obliged to pay what they owed.

Coming to terms with a rights-based approach to service delivery: water disconnections and the High Courts

Walker's equality frame for deciding service delivery disputes was soon supplemented by the explicit right to have access to water, and the express obligations upon local government to sustainably deliver essential services in accordance with the values of the Bill of Rights, in the 1996 Constitution. These more direct rights to enjoy essential urban services were soon strengthened by legislation and policy, with the 1997 Water Services Act making it clear that water disconnections for non-payment would be impermissible where they deprived people of access to 'basic water', and subsequent national policy requiring municipalities to provide for access to free basic water, electricity and sanitation.

Just as the free basic water policy began to be implemented across the country in 2001, two high court disputes tested the extent to which this new rights-based framework could assist residents in resisting the termination of their water services for non-payment. In the first, *Manqele* v. *Durban Transitional Metropolitan Council*, the Durban High Court dismissed a challenge against the discontinuation of water services to the applicant, who had been provided with a monthly amount of six kilolitres of free water, but used more than this allocation without paying for the excess. The Court felt that the City complied with its obligation not to deny indigent residents access to basic water services, by delivering the required amount of free basic water. It thus held that the City was justified to cut off Ms Manqele's water supply if she chose to use additional water without payment, provided it followed the procedures prescribed by its bylaws and by the Water Services Act.[56]

In the second case, the Joburg High Court proved to be somewhat more sensitive to the plight of residents. In *Residents of Bon Vista Mansions* v. *Southern Metropolitan Local Council*, the inhabitants of a Hillbrow apartment block, who alleged that their water supply had been disconnected unlawfully, but were unable to engage the Council or to obtain relief through the manager of the premises, approached the Court for an interim interdict to restore the water to the building. The Court found that the discontinuation of water services to a residential building constituted an infringement of the obligation to respect the constitutional right of access to water, and that such infringement would only be permissible in circumstances where the Council could justify its actions in terms of the Constitution's general limitation clause. While the Court felt that compliance with the relevant provisions of the Water Services Act would likely satisfy the limitation clause's requirements (hence appearing to agree with the judgment in *Manqele*), the City did not provide any evidence of having complied with the Act at this interim stage of the proceedings. The Court accordingly granted the interdict.[57]

While the *Bon Vista Mansions* judgment's vindication of the obligation to respect the right to have access to water has been welcomed,[58] it must be noted that the relief ordered was only temporary and subject to final determination of whether the Council acted within its rights in terms of the Water Services Act to disconnect the water. The judgment therefore did not really go any further than *Manqele* in asserting a constitutional entitlement to receive water services over and above the basic minimum allocation in terms of the Water Services Act.

Procedural rights for responsible citizens: **Mkontwana** *and* **Joseph**

In 2004, the Constitutional Court handed down its first judgment pertaining to municipal service charges under the 1996 Constitution. *Mkontwana* v. *Nelson Mandela Metropolitan Municipality* involved a challenge by property owners in Port Elizabeth against the provisions of section 118(1) of the Municipal Systems Act, in terms of which the transfer of property was not permitted without a certificate issued by the local municipality, which confirmed that all arrear service charges incurred on the property had been paid. The applicants, who could not transfer their properties to new owners after tenants had racked up significant unpaid service arrears on their properties without their knowledge, claimed that the provision constituted an unacceptable limitation the right to property in section 25 of the Constitution, since it restricted their right to alienate their properties.

A majority of the Constitutional Court found that the restriction did not amount to an arbitrary deprivation of property and was therefore constitutionally permissible.[59] In reaching this finding, the Court emphasised that municipalities had a 'public duty' to provide essential services in a sustainable manner, which included obligations to 'send out regular accounts, develop a culture of payment, disconnect the supply of electricity and water in appropriate circumstances, and take appropriate steps for the collection of amounts due' as well as to 'take reasonable steps to secure timeous payment' of due amounts.[60] The Court found that the challenged provision served an 'important' and 'laudable' purpose, in that it had 'the potential to encourage regular payments of consumption charges and thereby to contribute to the effective discharge by municipalities of their constitutionally mandated functions'.[61]

Given that enjoyment of municipal services, in the view of the Court, enhanced use and enjoyment of property (and therefore increased the amount of rent payable), it found that property owners shared in the responsibility to ensure that service charges incurred by tenants were paid.[62] Indeed, part of the challenged provision's desirability was found to lie precisely in its 'potential to encourage owners of property to discharge their civic responsibility by doing what they can to ensure that money payable to a government organ for the delivery of service is timeously paid'.[63] While acknowledging that it may be unfairly burdensome on owners to delay the sale of their properties in relation to charges incurred by tenants without their knowledge, the Court found that municipalities' responsibilities in this regard consisted simply of ensuring accurate and transparent billing systems, so that owners could be kept abreast of the service charges incurred on their properties.[64]

Criticised for being unfairly harsh on property owners,[65] the *Mkontwana* judgment makes it clear that the inclusion of service-related rights and governmental obligations in the 1996 Constitution did not shift the Constitutional Court's view of rights to receive municipal services being closely intertwined with obligations to pay for them. Indeed, the *Mkontwana* Court appears to view the relationship between local government and its subjects as resting on a notion of 'responsible' urban citizenship, where citizens enable and assist local government to perform its constitutional obligations, by not only paying for the services that they consume themselves, but also by ensuring that others (such as tenants) do the same.[66]

The Constitutional Court would pay closer attention to government's obligations in terms of this relationship in the subsequent *Joseph* v. *City of Johannesburg*, where residents of an apartment block to the south of the Joburg CBD challenged the City's disconnection of the power supply to their building. While they had been making monthly electricity payments to their landlord it transpired that, without their knowledge, he had never paid these over to the City. When arrears became unacceptably high, the City terminated the power supply without notice to the tenants. By the time the case reached the Constitutional Court, there had been no electricity in the building for approximately a year. Arguing that the right to adequate housing in section 26 of the Constitution encompassed a right to receive electricity services, the Centre for Applied Legal Studies (CALS) submitted on behalf of the applicants that the disconnection of electricity without notice or opportunity to make representations was unconstitutional, and breached relevant provisions of the Promotion of Administrative Justice Act. The City opposed, claiming that it had no obligations towards the tenants, since its contract for service provision had been with their landlord, who was evidently in breach of its obligations.[67]

Declining to decide whether there was a right to receive electricity latent to the constitutional right of access to adequate housing,[68] the Constitutional Court turned instead to assessing the developmental responsibilities of local government. It held that there indeed existed a public-law obligation upon local government to deliver essential services, flowing from the '"special cluster of relationships" that exist between a municipality and citizens, which is fundamentally cemented by the public responsibilities that a municipality bears in terms of the Constitution and legislation in respect of the persons living in its jurisdiction'.[69] As a logical flipside to this obligation, citizens had a correlative public-law right to receive services such as electricity from their municipalities.[70] While the exact content of this 'public-law right' was not expounded, it was held to be animated by the right to administrative justice in section 33 and the principles governing public administration in section 195 of the Constitution which, taken together, were held to require of government to 'act in a manner that is responsive, respectful, and fair' when fulfilling its public law obligations.[71]

As a result, it was found that City Power had an obligation of procedural fairness towards the applicants and others in their position.[72] In determining what this obligation entailed, the Court reiterated its position in *Mkontwana* that debt collection formed an important part of municipalities' service-related obligations and again affirmed that citizens' rights to receive services entailed responsibilities, including a responsibility to pay for them.[73] The Court further declined to pronounce on the general acceptability of electricity cut-offs as a debt control mechanism.[74] However, it felt that the City's approach to debt collection in relation to the applicants was illogical,[75] and should at least have entailed pre-termination notice. To the extent that Joburg's bylaws allowed for disconnections without such notice, they were held to be unconstitutional.[76]

In order to be adequate, the Court held, pre-termination notice of an electricity disconnection had to contain all relevant information (including the date and time of the proposed disconnection, the reason for it and a place where the residents could challenge its basis) and had to allow sufficient time to enable residents to 'make any necessary enquiries and investigations, to seek legal advice and to organise themselves collectively if they so wish'.[77] While accepting that it would be too administratively onerous to expect City Power to allow for representations from all tenants affected by proposed electricity disconnections, the Court found that those tenants who approached City Power within the notice period and raised valid challenges to a proposed disconnection ought to be heard, and to be dealt with in good faith. It accordingly commended City Power for undertaking, during the course of the litigation, to engage with the applicants.[78]

The *Joseph* Court's elaboration of a public-law right to receive municipal services has generally been welcomed by commentators, who regard it as a progressive platform upon which to base future claims to receive municipal services.[79] While the entitlement to procedural fairness inherent to this right did not, in fact, assist the applicants in the case (since, by the time the judgment had been handed down, their building had been stripped of its electrical wiring, which made reconnecting the electricity supply impossible), it appears to have had a positive influence on city officials' actions in similar matters, while NGOs have since successfully relied upon it to resist electricity disconnections in inner-city suburbs as well as in Soweto.[80] Yet, some have pointed out the limited nature of the relief inherent in this 'public-law right' (which, in essence, amounts to a right to receive notice of impending disconnections and not much more) and have lamented that the Court conceived of the matter only as an issue of procedural justice, neglecting to conduct a more context-sensitive rights-based inquiry and to acknowledge or remedy the (often dire) impact of electricity disconnections on the daily lives of poor people.[81]

It is further clear that, in step with its earlier judgments on municipal service delivery, the Constitutional Court in *Joseph* conceived of the public-law right to receive services as being largely reliant upon compliance with a correlative obligation to pay for them. Indeed, as in *Mkontwana*, the *Joseph* Court quite explicitly held forth a conception of constitutional citizenship that requires citizens to conduct themselves as responsible, paying consumers of urban services.[82]

Accountability rather than entitlement: Mazibuko

Arguably, the Constitutional Court's most significant judgment on service delivery, *Mazibuko* v. *City of Johannesburg* (decided mere weeks after *Joseph*) concerned the APF-led challenge against the implementation of Operation Gcin'amanzi in Soweto's Phiri suburb. The APF and a newly formed affiliate, the Coalition Against Water Privatisation (CAWP), instituted legal action against the Joburg Metropolitan Council when its protest action against the installation of prepaid water meters in Phiri appeared to be fruitless, and as ground-level resistance against Operation Gcin'amanzi began to wane (with most households in Phiri having capitulated into accepting either a prepaid water meter or a standpipe, in accordance with the policy, by mid 2004).[83] Assisted by CALS, the APF's legal challenge was fronted by five impoverished Phiri residents, all of whom lived in households where, for different reasons (but often because of the number of people living on a single stand), the amount of free basic water per household allocated by the City and dispensed by means of prepaid water meters was insufficient, and where paying for additional water or instead accessing water through a standpipe was not a feasible or desirable alternative.[84]

A great number of legal and constitutional challenges were mounted against the City's implementation of Operation Gcin'amanzi. First, it was contended that the allocation of six kilolitres of free water per household per month was constitutionally unreasonable for various reasons, but especially because the amount of water was too little (in this regard, it was argued that the constitutional right of access to sufficient water required provision of at least 50 litres of free water per person per day).[85] Operation Gcin'Amanzi was further argued to amount to an unreasonable retrogressive measure, in that it effectively required people to pay for water which they had in the past received for free, since many residents (albeit illegally) did not pay for the water they received under the discontinued flat rate system.[86] Moreover, the prepaid meters' automatic disconnection of water supply after the free basic allocation had run out, without notice or opportunity for engagement, was argued to infringe the constitutional obligation to respect existing enjoyment of the right of access to water, as well as several provisions of the Promotion of Administrative Justice Act.[87] Finally, the fact that prepaid meters were (at the time) only installed in Phiri, a poor suburb with predominantly black residents, and not in Joburg's richer northern suburbs, where residents could access unlimited amounts of water on credit (provided that they did eventually pay for it), was argued to amount to unfair racial discrimination, in line with the *Walker* decision.[88]

The Johannesburg High Court agreed with several of these arguments and found that Operation Gcin'amanzi was unconstitutional. It held that the prepaid meters unreasonably denied access to water and ordered the City to devise a system in terms of which residents of Phiri would be provided with at least 50 litres of free water per person per day.[89] This victory significantly emboldened the APF and CAWP who, contrary to their former circumspect attitude towards legal processes, loudly celebrated the judgment as a triumph for social justice.[90] Less law-abidingly, they encouraged Phiri residents to rip out and destroy their 'unconstitutional' prepaid water meters, which many did, much as the legal team, keen to present 'respectable' applicants in an anticipated appeal hearing, advised against this.[91]

The City appealed the judgment to the Supreme Court of Appeal (SCA), which essentially upheld the High Court's finding although, for various reasons, it lowered the amount of water that the City was required to provide to residents to 42 litres per person per day.[92] Once again, the City appealed, this time to the Constitutional Court, while the applicants cross-appealed the lowering of the amount of water to which residents were entitled. As before the lower courts, the City's main retort to the applicants' claims was that its constitutional obligation to progressively realise the right of access to water did not require of it to provide any specific amount of water to individuals. Rather, the City argued that it was only obliged to provide residents with the amount of free basic water stipulated by the Water Services Act – which, under Operation Gcin'amanzi, it did. The City also pointed to its indigency policy, implemented from early 2007 onwards and revised on several occasions throughout the litigation, in terms of which households who satisfied a means test and registered on an 'indigency register' qualified for an additional monthly allowance of four kilolitres of water as well as for a further annual once-off 'emergency' allocation upon application.[93]

In a unanimous judgment, the Constitutional Court sided with the City in all respects and overturned the judgments of the High Court and the SCA. Holding that the case needed 'to be understood in the context of the challenges facing Johannesburg as a City'[94] and that the right of access to water had further to be understood in light of the need to carefully manage water as a scarce resource,[95] the Court emphasised throughout its judgment that the previous (flat-rate based) system of water delivery in Soweto (complete with the adjacent problem of non-payment) was unsustainable and in dire need of reform.[96] Operation Gcin'amanzi was regarded as being effective in addressing the problems it was devised to combat, and the Court also noted that the majority of Phiri residents accepted and abided by the policy, and were satisfied with its implementation.[97]

Emphasising that the right of access to water did not require of the State to immediately provide sufficient water to everyone, but rather to take reasonable steps within its available resources to realise the right progressively,[98] the Court rejected the argument that it should give effect to the right by quantifying an appropriate amount of water sufficient for dignified life. It found that such a determination would be out of step with the proper institutional role of the judiciary in a constitutional democracy, as articulated in its previous socio-economic rights jurisprudence, and accordingly that the High Court and SCA were wrong to quantify the content of the right.[99] This meant that the City was right to argue that its only quantifiable obligation towards the people of Phiri was to provide at least the nationally legislated amount of free basic water.[100]

Turning to assess the reasonableness of the City's Free Basic Water policy, the Court emphasised at the outset that the applicants did not challenge the national free basic water policy as being unreasonable, which meant that it would be difficult for them to prove that a local government policy that complied with the national policy fell short of the reasonableness standard.[101] The Court nevertheless proceeded to evaluate the applicants' various challenges against the City's policy. It dismissed them all, in effect holding that a policy in terms of which a nationally prescribed amount of free basic water was provided to all households, calculated on a per-household rather than per-person basis and based on an assumed average household size, was reasonable, not least because alternative measures (such as providing free water only to specific households, or on a per-person basis, or taking into account the actual size of each individual household) would be so administratively burdensome as to be unworkable.[102] As to the argument that the policy unreasonably provided too little free water to large or needy households, the Court found that the amount of free water would more than satisfy the needs of most average households, and that to increase the amount would therefore unfairly advantage smaller households.[103]

The existence of the indigency policy was taken as evidence that the City also catered for the special needs of those for whom the basic allocation was not sufficient and who could not afford to purchase further water, while its constant refinement over the years further attested to the policy's flexibility. As such, the indigency policy was central to the Court's finding that the City's overall policy was reasonable.[104] While the Court acknowledged that the means test inherent to the indigency policy in some respects rendered it under-inclusive and that some residents might find it demeaning to be subjected to a means test, the laudable objectives of the means test and the absence of any workable alternative meant that it, too, was found not to be unreasonable.[105]

In relation to the argument that the introduction of prepaid water meters in an area where residents previously had free access to water amounted to a retrogressive measure that failed to respect existing access to water, the Court was adamant that

> the fact that residents did not pay for water in the past in breach of their obligations cannot mean that a new system that provides them with free water for the first time is an infringement of their right of access to water.[106]

It found that, in light of the free basic water allocation under Operation Gcin'amanzi, which did not exist previously, water in Phiri was in fact more affordable under the new policy than had previously been the case. The policy was therefore found to be a progressive rather than a retrogressive measure.[107]

The Court also dismissed all arguments pertaining to the illegality and unconstitutionality of the way that prepaid water meters cut off water supply once the free basic allocation had run out, finding that this amounted to a suspension rather than a discontinuation of water, since the water supply could be reinstated simply by purchasing extra credit, or would otherwise be reinstated automatically when a new basic water allocation was made in the following month. It therefore made no sense to apply the onerous notice requirements in the Water Services Act in relation to the temporary suspensions of water services.[108] In any event, the Court found that the suspension of a water supply in terms of the policy did not deprive residents of a basic water supply, since it would only occur after such supply (i.e. the free basic water allocation) had already been dispensed.[109]

The argument that offering Phiri residents the limited choice of a prepaid water meter or a standpipe was unlawful because it forced citizens to either accept one of these options (rather than a credit meter, for instance) or no water at all, was also dismissed, with the Court firmly stating that 'any resident of the City who wishes the City to provide them with a water service is limited to the options that the City offers' and indicating that, as long as such options were in and of themselves lawful, residents had no choice but to accept them.[110] The overarching policy decision to install either prepaid meters or standpipes in Phiri was further held to amount to executive rather than administrative action, which meant that the procedural protections in the Promotion of Administrative Justice Act did not apply,[111] whereas the Court further regarded the consultation processes preceding Operation Gcin'amanzi as exhaustive and fair, meaning that allegations of procedural unfairness in terms of the Municipal Systems Act also did not hold water.[112]

Finally, the Court also rejected the contention that the installation of prepaid meters in a poor suburb with predominantly black residents amounted to indirect racial discrimination, noting that the City not only did not apply the policy to richer areas with a predominantly white population, but also did not do so in other areas, such as Alexandra or Orange Farm, where mostly poor and black people lived.[113] In line with *Walker*, the Court held that it would sometimes be necessary for the City to adopt different approaches to water delivery and credit control in different parts of Johannesburg, especially where, as in this case, this was necessitated by problems arising from the unequal provision of services in the past.[114] It further pointed out that water over and above the free basic allocation was cheaper in terms of a prepaid meter system than under a credit meter system, while the prepaid meter system also did not come with any of the negative credit control measures (such as credit blacklisting and permanent discontinuation of service) associated with the credit meter system.[115] For the Court, therefore, any differentiation between the manner in which the City chose to deliver water and collect arrears in different areas worked to the advantage of residents of Phiri, meaning that it could not be held to constitute unfair discrimination against them.[116]

Understandably a massive blow to the APF and CAWP,[117] *Mazibuko* also received a rather hostile reception from commentators. Socio-economic rights scholars have bemoaned the bluntness of the Court's refusal to quantify an amount of water inherent to the right to have access to sufficient water, its restrictive understanding of its own institutional competence in socio-economic rights matters and the formalism of its reasonableness analysis.[118] In particular, several scholars have lamented that the reasonableness analysis in *Mazibuko* paid virtually no heed to the lived experiences and needs of the applicants or to Operation Gcin'amanzi's impact on their lives, but rather used the City's urban management challenges as its point of departure.[119] Accordingly, it has been argued, the Court accepted the City's view of the 'problem' of water delivery in Soweto as given, and unquestioningly accepted its motives, its calculations, its reliance on average household size in determining the adequacy of free water allowances and, ultimately, its view of the reasonableness of its own response.[120]

The Court's application of the right to equality has been similarly decried, with commentators bemoaning the Court's lack of appreciation of the impact of Operation Gcin'amanzi on the residents of Phiri and its failure to grapple with the discrepancies between the City's treatment of Phiri as a 'problem area', on the one hand, and its more lenient, trusting and engaging approach to consumers in other suburbs, on the other.[121] Furthermore, the Court's finding that it amounts to a suspension rather than a discontinuation of water supply when a prepaid water meter shuts down until further credit has been purchased, has been sharply criticised for being overly formalist and for effectively shutting down all avenues of engagement between the City and residents over water cutoffs.[122]

Salient as these criticisms may be, they do overlook or underplay the extent to which the findings in *Mazibuko* are consistent with the Constitutional Court's previous jurisprudence in all the related areas. The Court's conception of its institutional competence, its aversion to awarding claimable entitlements and its 'proceduralist' approach to reasonableness in socio-economic rights matters is very much in line with its earlier judgments pertaining to access to housing, health care and social security, which have all endured similar criticism. Its dismissal of the equality challenge appears perfectly consistent with *Walker* which, it will be recalled, also held that differentiated billing practices aimed at correcting for apartheid discrepancies in service delivery and at addressing attending cultures of non-payment in townships are legitimate, and that township residents must be required to pay their service-related debts. Furthermore, its findings of procedural fairness and the legitimacy of the City's chosen cost recovery measures reverberate with both *Mkontwana* and *Joseph*, as well as with the Durban High Court's judgment in *Manqele*.

Indeed, what is most striking about *Mazibuko* is the Court's unwavering stance on the principle that rights to receive essential services are tied to citizens' obligations to conduct themselves responsibly by paying their dues, notwithstanding that, unlike in the case of the claims to electricity as were in issue in *Joseph* and *Mkontwana*, access to water is explicitly guaranteed in the Bill of Rights.[123] In addition, the *Mazibuko* Court is adamant that it is the State, rather than citizens, who has the final say on the manner in which services are delivered, as long as its chosen methods are in and of themselves legitimate.[124] At most, the Court views the right to water as an accountability mechanism which ensures that these methods take account of, and are responsive to, residents' divergent needs and interests.[125]

The City's response to the *Mazibuko* litigation (both during its course and in its aftermath) certainly appears to bear out this accountability-enhancing function of the right to water. It formulated and adapted the indigency policy largely in response to the litigation and, subsequent to the case, has increased the amount of free basic water available to the poorest of the poor, to the point where it is currently providing an amount similar to that demanded by the applicants.[126] Moreover, when it eventually resumed installing prepaid meters across Soweto, these now came with 'trickler devices' ensuring that water supply slowed down significantly, rather than shut down completely, when prepaid allowances ran out, likely in response to the applicants' challenges against the manner in which meters shut off the water supply. The City further undertook not to prosecute any Phiri residents who ripped out their water meters subsequent to their short-lived High Court victory.[127]

On the other side of the 'public law relationship', the litigation was further reported to have had positive effects on morale in Phiri, where residents felt heard and affirmed.[128] Perhaps counterintuitively, the struggle over water meters, both inside and outside the courtroom, appeared not to have politically alienated Phiri residents from the Council, with 2011 local government election results showing undiminished support for the ANC in the township.[129] Despite initially also appearing to energise the APF and CAPW in their struggles against the commodification of basic services across Johannesburg,[130] however, the blow of the courtroom loss proved too much for both, and has been pinpointed as a significant contributing factor in their ultimate deflation and demise, with the APF officially disbanding in 2010.[131]

Rights, obligations and urban citizenship after **Mazibuko**

A handful of judgments handed down after *Mazibuko* have further cemented the judiciary's stance on service delivery matters. First, in *Nokotyana* v. *Ekurhuleni Metropolitan Municipality*, the Constitutional Court dismissed a demand by residents of the Harry Gwala informal settlement in Ekurhuleni to be provided with sanitation and high mast lighting, since it held that they would be entitled to receive such services only once the Ekurhuleni Metropolitan Council had committed to upgrading the settlement in situ. As in *Joseph*, the Court was unwilling to consider whether the right of access to adequate housing included a right to receive municipal services.[132] While not prepared to decide on the extent of entitlements to service provision in Harry Gwala until such time as the decision on in situ upgrading had been taken, the Court lamented the Council's delay in reaching this decision and ordered it to do so within 14 months of the judgment.[133] An undertaking by the Council to provide temporary refuse removal services to the settlement in the interim was incorporated in the Court's order.[134] The Council also proceeded to install a number of toilets as well as high mast lighting in the settlement in the wake of the judgment, despite not being ordered to do so.[135]

Like *Mazibuko*, *Nokotyana* has been criticised for its reluctance to award content to the implicated constitutional rights and for not affording sufficient weight to the needs and living conditions of the applicants.[136] The decision further signalled the Court's continuing endorsement of government's spatial vision for cities over the place-making practices of their residents, as it regarded rights to service provision as vesting only in those who reside in areas that 'officially' form part of the city. In right-to-the-city terms, the Court thus rendered entitlements to the spoils of the city subject to the outcome of official processes over whether a settlement is recognised as forming part of the city in the first place.

But in settlements that *were* officially recognised, a Cape High Court judgment indicated that the content of the 'public law obligation' to provide essential services was not similarly left entirely to the discretion of cities. *Beja* v. *Premier of the Western Cape* concerned a challenge against the manner in which the City of Cape Town rolled out sanitation services in informal settlements in and around Khayelitsha. Following community resistance to the construction of communal toilet facilities, the City devised a scheme in terms of which some 1316 individual yard toilets would be installed across Khayelitsha but, in an effort to minimise costs and promote community 'ownership' of the project, these needed to be enclosed by residents themselves. Residents proceeded to enclose all but 55 of the toilets although, in some cases, enclosures were predictably rather ramshackle.[137]

The matter of the unenclosed toilets became politicised, with a local branch of the ANC Youth League (ANCYL) filing a complaint with the South African Human Rights Commission (which would, eventually, find against the City). As the City attempted to enclose toilets following the Commission's investigation, ANCYL members prevented them from doing so, and demolished various enclosures across the township.[138] Meanwhile, a number of community members were assisted by a local NGO to challenge the provision of unenclosed toilets before the Western Cape High Court. During the hearing and following an in loco inspection, the judge made a temporary order requiring the immediate enclosure of toilets, but the City's efforts to comply were stymied by the ANCYL and community members. Upon learning of this, the Court amended its order to the effect that the police were required to investigate and prosecute the vandalism of toilets.[139]

As to the content and implementation of the policy, the Court emphasised that local government is required to heed the rights in the Bill of Rights when carrying out its service delivery-related obligations.[140] It found that the policy and pursuant community agreement to provide unenclosed toilets infringed the rights to dignity, freedom and security of the person and privacy, as well as the right to housing, the right to health and the right to an environment not harmful to individual wellbeing.[141] The City was accordingly ordered to enclose all toilets forming part of the project,[142] and promptly complied with the order.

The *Beja* judgment is significant for being the first in which a court explicitly engages with the manner in which local government delivers essential services. Its finding that residents' basic rights must be respected in the course of devising and implementing service delivery policies, is consistent with an earlier finding of the Constitutional Court in the case of *Rail Commuters Action Group* v. *Transnet t/a Metrorail*, that Metrorail had to respect the rights in the Bill of Rights in the course of providing passenger rail services, and that it was accordingly under a legal obligation to ensure the physical safety of passengers on commuter trains.[143] *Beja*'s concretisation of this principle in the context of essential service delivery has been praised by commentators, who have further lauded the judgment's elevation of the complainants lived experiences over the City's urban management objectives.[144]

Beja was also the first judgment to explicitly address insurgent practices of community opposition to service delivery projects. In this respect, its interim order that the police intervene to stop and prosecute illegal demolition of toilets signals that courts will not lightly tolerate extra-legal forms of community resistance (such as, to use the example of previous cases, the ripping out of water or electricity meters). This affirms, once again, that courts understand rights to receive essential services as being contiguous to 'responsible', law-abiding constitutional citizenship.

A similar balance between obligations of service providers on the one hand and of the recipients of services on the other was evident from the Pretoria High Court's judgment in *Federation for Sustainable Environment* v. *Minister of Water Affairs*. The Court ordered a district municipality in Mpumalanga to urgently rehabilitate and restore water supply to townships outside of Carolina, where water was unavailable due to being polluted through acid mine drainage. While finding that its constitutional obligations required the municipality to resolve the water crisis 'speedily', through 'a progressive plan' and whilst engaging the community throughout,[145] the Court declined to also declare that the Council's failure to effectively provide potable drinking water in the interim was unlawful. This was because the Council's efforts in this regard were bedevilled by community members, who went so far as to burn two water tankers. The Court thus regarded them as being partly to blame for the situation.[146]

Then, in *Rademan* v. *Moqhaka Local Municipality*, the Constitutional Court remained unwavering in relation to residents' obligation to pay for municipal services. Ms Rademan and fellow members of a Kroonstad ratepayers association withheld municipal rates payments in protest against what they regarded as substandard service delivery. In accordance with its bylaws, the municipality terminated Ms Rademan's electricity supply when she failed to heed notices requiring her to settle the arrears on her account. She challenged the legality of this action, averring that her water and electricity account was fully paid up and that the council was not entitled to terminate her electricity supply due to her refusal to pay rates and taxes. Upon rejecting her challenge, the Constitutional Court emphasised local government's obligations to deliver services sustainably and to collect due service charges, as well as residents' concomitant obligations to comply with bylaws and to promptly pay for the services that they received.[147]

Noting that the bylaws allowed for consolidated municipal accounts which did not distinguish between various constituent components, and that residents did not have a choice to only pay part of their bills, the Court concluded that Ms Rademan was in breach of her obligations towards the municipality and that it was therefore entitled to terminate her electricity supply.[148] While finding that the obligation to pay for services did not extend to services that had for some or other reason not been rendered, the Court felt that non-payment was not a legitimate manner in which to address billing and service quality disputes, which had to be resolved either within the dispute resolution mechanisms provided for in the bylaws or, otherwise, through the courts.[149]

Finally, at a more overarching level, the Constitutional Court's treatment of a cluster of challenges to the Gauteng Province's controversial 'E-tolling' policy (in terms of which the costs of improving a number of highways in the province, including the highways into Johannesburg, was to be borne by motorists through tolls levied electronically by 'gates' spanning the highways) is instructive for the way in which it positions its understanding of 'responsible' constitutional citizenship in relation to the separation of powers. The E-tolling policy was duly legislatively authorised and was lawfully conceived and implemented, including in compliance with prevailing requirements pertaining to public involvement in legislative and policy processes. It became controversial only upon implementation, when motorists realised its implications for their daily lives and, spurred by opposition political parties and COSATU, revolted. Amid mass demonstrations and threats of boycott, the hastily-formed 'Opposition to Urban Tolling Alliance' obtained an interdict against the implementation of the tolls from the Pretoria High Court.

Upon appeal, the Constitutional Court overturned the interdict, lambasting the High Court for not heeding the boundaries of the separation of powers. The Court characterised the policy as being about 'determining how public resources are to be drawn upon and reordered' and as accordingly lying 'in the heartland of executive-government function and domain'.[150] Unswayed by arguments that the tolls were unreasonable and that enforcing them would be unworkable because of a wide-scale boycott by motorists, the Court affirmed that, however unpopular the policy may be, it was perfectly legitimate of government to expect motorists to pay for road improvements from which they benefited, and that the method of securing such payment was solely up to government. It did not regard any rights in the Bill of Rights as being implicated by Executive's decision to recoup the costs through imposing E-tolls.[151]

Reflections

The constitutional ensconcement of a justiciable Bill of Rights has predictably lent a new and unpredictable dimension to disputes over the nature and form of urban service delivery, and has turned courts into alternative fora for disputes over the content of urban citizenship.

It is clear from the judgments discussed in this chapter that courts are prepared to enforce the service-related developmental responsibilities of cities, albeit with significant sensitivity to city managers' autonomy over how these responsibilities are heeded. Having gone as far as articulating a 'public law right' to receive essential services in accordance with local government's developmental responsibilities in *Joseph*, the Constitutional Court is clearly prepared to hold the State to account over its compliance with its developmental mandate, even beyond the overlap between this mandate and rights in the Bill of Rights. However, the Court has been rather sparse in articulating substantive standards against which the State's conduct will be measured in this regard. Thus far, judgments have affirmed that services must be delivered sustainably (both in an environmental and in an economic sense)[152] and that they must be delivered in a manner that is both procedurally fair and that respects citizens' basic rights (to, for instance, dignity and security of the person).

However, as long as these requirements are met, the courts have made it clear that they are not prepared to second-guess the manner in which government has decided to deliver services to residents, or to recover the costs that it incurs in doing so. While courts are prepared to insist that cities engage citizens in formulating and implementing policy, the ultimate decisions over how services are delivered rest with cities. Dissatisfied residents should accordingly resort to democratic channels rather than judicial review in attempts to influence or alter these decisions.[153]

Moreover, courts understand the public-law right to receive essential services as being nested within a notion of citizenship in terms of which residents assist local government in carrying out its obligations and conduct themselves responsibly and within the boundaries of the law. The courts have made it clear that the obligations of citizenship in this context include requirements to pay for services rendered and to accept the manner of service delivery. Notably, courts are not prepared to endorse insurgent practices of accessing services, or to tolerate illegal or destructive ways of protesting against the mode of service delivery.

But this is not to say that service-delivery-related adjudication has not significantly empowered citizens vis-à-vis municipalities. As the Constitutional Court emphasised in *Mazibuko*, rights-based litigation presents an important way in which to hold the City to account for the manner in which it complies with its constitutional obligations.[154] Successful invocation of the 'public-law right' to receive services in a manner that is procedurally fair and accords with the rights in the Bill of Rights has, more than once, meant that cities (including the City of Johannesburg) have had to modify their service delivery practices in ways that have ultimately made these practices more sensitive and responsive to the needs of residents. In this respect, rights-based litigation has shown itself capable of cutting through bureaucratic inertia and red tape, of sparking more progressive policy responses and of softening the impact of existing policy.[155]

Notes

1 See Coggin and Pieterse (2012: 261); Pieterse (2014a: 153–154).
2 See also Municipal Systems Act (2000: ss 51, 73), which echo s 195 of the Constitution. On how the provisions elaborated here structure essential service delivery by municipalities, see Mbazira (2013: 263); Pieterse (2014a: 157–162); Steytler (2004: 160–167).
3 On the importance of the standard of sustainable development for essential urban service delivery in South Africa see Kotze (2010: 137–140, 158); Pieterse (2014b: 183–186); Stewart and Horsten (2009: 488–492, 498, 503).
4 Coggin and Pieterse (2012: 268).
5 On the energy supply crisis, see Pickering (2008: 445–447).
6 See Beall *et al.* (2002: 151, 156–158). According to 2011 census data, 90.8 per cent of Johannesburg households have access to electricity, whereas only 1.4 per cent do not have access to piped water at their place of residence, with 64.4 per cent having access to in-dwelling piped water and 26.4 per cent with piped water on the outside premises. Only 0.8 per cent of inhabitants have no access to toilet facilities, whereas more than 95 per cent of residents have their refuse removed by relevant city agencies. Statistics South Africa (n.d.: 11–15).
7 See Kotze (2010: 139–140); City of Johannesburg (2011: 26–28, 54–58, 60–62).
8 See Beall *et al.* (2002: 152); Dugard (2008: 603); Narsiah (2011: 150).
9 Beall *et al.* (2002: 159).
10 On the boycott and its after-effects, see Beall *et al.* (2002: 91–92, 153); Beavon (2004: 234–235, 268); Von Schnitzler (2008: 909–910).
11 See Beall *et al.* (2002: 87–89, 153); Narsiah (2011: 150); Von Schnitzler (2008: 905).
12 See Mbazira (2013: 264).
13 See Beall *et al.* 2002: 91–92; Von Schnitzler 2008: 906–907.
14 See Water Services Act 1997: s 4(3). For discussion, see Kidd 2004: 122, 129–130, 133–134.

15 See Beall *et al.* (2002: 89–90) as well as discussion in Chapter 5.
16 For detailed analysis of the causes and extent of the 1997 financial crisis, see Beall *et al.* (2002: 87–94).
17 See Beall *et al.* (2002: 95); Dugard (2008: 602–603); Smith and Morris (2008: 428–429) as well as discussion in Chapter 1.
18 See Beall *et al.* (2002: 87); Bond (2013: 130); Dugard (2008: 604; 2014: 426).
19 See Beall *et al.* (2002: 103–104); Bond and Dugard (2008: 5–6, 17); Ruiters (2006: 294); Smith and Morris (2008: 425).
20 See Ruiters (2006: 301); Von Schnitzler (2008: 904, 910).
21 See Ruiters (2006: 302).
22 For detailed discussion of the dispute, fallout and protest, see Beall *et al.* (2002: 99–105).
23 See Buhlungu (2006: 69–75); Goebel (2015: 155–156); Smith and Rubin (2015: 262).
24 See Bond (2013: 133); Egan and Wafer (2006: 45–57); Goebel (2015: 161); Madlingozi (2014: 110–111); Von Schnitzler (2008: 907).
25 See Egan and Wafer (2006: 53–54).
26 Egan and Wafer (2006: 54–55); Madlingozi (2014: 110–111).
27 See Madlingozi (2014: 106); Ruiters (2006: 294, 302); Van Zyl (2003: 36–38).
28 See Bond (2013: 37–38); Netswera (2008: 512); Von Schnitzler (2008: 906).
29 Egan and Wafer (2006: 54–55).
30 Beall *et al.* (2002: 160–161); Von Schnitzler (2008: 904–905).
31 See Brown (2015: 64, 67); Glaser (2015: 149).
32 See Pernegger (2014: 68–71).
33 See, for instance Benit-Gbaffou (2012: 180–182, 187); Booysen (2007: 23–25); Goebel (2015: 156–157, 180–181); Madlingozi (2014: 108–109); Mbazira (2013: 264); Netswera (2008: 511, 515–519); Oldfield (2008: 488–492); Smith and Morris (2008: 432–433).
34 See Bond and Dugard (2008: 6); Dugard (2008: 600–601); Ruiters (2006: 294).
35 See Dugard (2008: 600–601; 2014: 278–280); Williams (2010: 166).
36 Dugard (2008: 601, 606; 2014: 278–281); Fuo (2014: 197–198, 200); Ruiters (2006: 298–299); Smith and Morris (2008: 431).
37 See Fuo (2014: 202); Ruiters (2006: 295).
38 See City of Johannesburg (2016: 7; 14–15); also Beall *et al.* (2002: 105, 156–157); Pernegger (2014: 68); Ruiters (2006: 291); Smith and Morris (2008: 431–432).
39 See Dugard (2008: 604–605); Kotze (2010: 150); Narsiah (2011: 150); Von Schnitzler (2008: 900–901, 905–906); Williams (2010: 166).
40 See Bond and Dugard (2008: 10); Smith and Rubin (2015: 261); Von Schnitzler (2008: 904, 913–914).
41 See Bond and Dugard (2008: 9); Dugard (2008: 595–596, 606–608); Von Schnitzler (2008: 899, 903).
42 See Dugard (2008: 594–596, 607–608); Dugard and Langford (2011: 43); Narsiah (2011: 152); Smith and Rubin (2015: 263–265); Von Schnitzler (2008: 903).
43 See Narsiah (2011: 154); Williams (2010: 167).
44 See City of Johannesburg (2011: 61–62; 2016: 13). On the dynamics of, and challenges posed by, electricity cable theft, see Pretorius and Prinsloo (2014).
45 See Beal *et al.* (2002: 153, 160–161, 167–169).
46 A high-profile example has been the protests in Thembelihle adjacent to Lenasia, much of which has centred on the City's reluctance to extend 'official' water and electricity services to the informal settlement which, being located on dolomite land, the City regards as unsustainable and in need of relocation. See Brown (2015: 87–89, 98–102); Clark (2014: 11–31).
47 See Jain (2010: 8–11, 17–23); Pernegger (2014: 63).
48 See Alexander (2010: 32); Goebel (2015: 150–153); Mbazira (2013: 265–267).

49 See Brown (2015: 16–19, 74–75); Benit-Gbaffou (2008: 5–6, 9–13, 18–20); Bilchitz (2015: 86–93); Booysen (2007: 24–25); Dugard (2014: 287–288); Goebel (2015: 156–157); Jain (2010: 29–31); Matlala and Benit-Gbaffou (2015: 45–46); Mbazira (2013: 266–268); Pernegger (2014: 65). There are also fascinating internal (ANC) party-political dimensions to the protests, which are beyond the scope of this discussion. See Alexander (2010: 31–33); Booysen (2007: 25–31).
50 See Von Schnitzler (2008: 906, 910–916).
51 *Pretoria City Council* v. *Walker* (1998: para 32) (per Langa DP for the majority).
52 Ibid., paras 52–53.
53 Ibid., paras 47, 49, 52–53, 56, 62–63, 65 (per Langa DP for the majority); 103, 105, 107, 123, 127 (per Sachs J, partially dissenting).
54 Ibid., paras 70–81 (per Langa DP for the majority). Sachs J dissented on this point, holding that, as with the levying of different charges, the selective credit control did not adversely impact on residents of old Pretoria, who were the beneficiaries of unfair past discrimination in service provision and were still simply required to pay for the services they received. Ibid., paras 112, 119, 123, 127.
55 See for instance Albertyn and Goldblatt (1998: 259–260, 268).
56 *Manqele* v. *Durban Transitional Metropolitan Council* (2002: 429F-I, 430B-E). The Court did not regard itself as competent, within the boundaries of the separation of powers, to pronounce on the exact amount of basic water to which a person should be entitled (ibid., 427E) and would not consider whether the Council's actions infringed s 27 of the Constitution, since this was not argued on the papers (ibid., 427H-I). For critical discussion of the judgment, see Kidd (2004: 131–132).
57 *Residents of Bon Vista Mansions* v. *Southern Metropolitan Local Council* (2002: paras 20, 30, 33–34). Section 36(1) of the Constitution determines that rights in the Bill of Rights may be limited, but only 'in terms of law of general application to the extent that the limitation is reasonable and justifiable in an open and democratic society based on human dignity, equality and freedom and taking into account all relevant factors…'.
58 See Kidd (2004: 126–129); Pieterse (2003: 41–48).
59 *Mkontwana* v. *Nelson Mandela Metropolitan Municipality* (2005: paras 59–60) (per Yacoob J for the majority). Section 25(1) of the Constitution contains a rather restrictive formulation of the right to property, determining that 'no one may be deprived of property except in terms of law of general application, and no law may permit arbitrary deprivation of property'.
60 *Mkontwana* v. *Nelson Mandela Metropolitan Municipality* (2005: paras 47, 49). See also paras 1, 38.
61 Ibid., para 38. See also para 52.
62 Ibid., paras 40, 42, 53, 73.
63 Ibid., para 38.
64 Ibid., paras 66–67, 73.
65 See Bilchitz (2010a: 73–75).
66 See Bilchitz (2010a: 74); Pieterse (2012: 376).
67 *Joseph* v. *City of Johannesburg* (2010: paras 1–2, 7–9, 15, 31).
68 Ibid., paras 31–32. For criticism, see Bilchitz (2010a: 51–52, 54); Brand *et al.* (2013: 288–289); Murcott (2013: 489–490); Wilson and Dugard (2014: 53).
69 *Joseph* v. *City of Johannesburg* (2010: para 24). See also paras 23, 33, 39, 46. The Court sourced this duty in ss 152–53 of the Constitution, ss 4(2) and 73 of the Municipal Systems 2000 and s 9(9) of the Housing Act 1997. Ibid., paras 36–39.
70 *Joseph* v. *City of Johannesburg* (2010: para 39).
71 Ibid., para 45. See also paras 42–44.
72 Ibid., para 46. This obligation was regulated by s 3 of the Promotion of Administrative Justice Act (2000), since infringement of the public law 'right' to receive services was held to trigger the Act's application. Ibid., para 32.

73 Ibid., paras 50–51. The Court stated: 'Citizens who can, must take responsibility for paying for services provided to them in fulfilment of government's statutory and constitutional obligations. Government is entitled to require this of citizens'.
74 Ibid., para 54.
75 Ibid., para 52.
76 Ibid., para 70.
77 Ibid., para 60. In the present circumstances, the Court felt that a notice period of 14 days would have been sufficient. Ibid.
78 Ibid., paras 62–63. See also para 28, where the Court emphasised the importance of administrative efficiency in local governance and held that, to avoid administrative paralysis, courts must 'remain vigilant not to impose unduly onerous administrative burdens on the state bureaucracy'.
79 See Bilchitz (2010a: 56–59, 62, 67, 77–78); Dugard and Langford (2011: 46); Murcott (2013: 486); Van der Berg (2013: 390); Wilson and Dugard (2014: 53).
80 See Dugard (2014: 298); Dugard and Langford (2011: 46, 60).
81 See Bilchitz (2010a: 54); Brand *et al.* (2013: 288–290); Murcott (2013: 488, 490, 493).
82 See Bilchitz (2010a: 56–59); Brand *et al.* (2013: 291); Coggin and Pieterse (2012: 271); Dugard and Langford (2011: 51–52); Murcott (2013: 488–489); Pieterse (2012: 375–376; 2014a: 167).
83 *Mazibuko* v. *City of Johannesburg* (2010: paras 15, 17); Dugard (2008: 606–607); Madlingozi (2014: 111).
84 See *Mazibuko* v. *City of Johannesburg* (2010: para 4); Dugard (2008: 594); Narsiah (2011: 151–152).
85 Other arguments of unreasonableness included that the amount was based on a misconception on the part of the City that it was not under a constitutional obligation to provide people with free water; that the policy was inflexible by not providing for circumstances in which households could access free water over and above the basic allocation; that it unreasonably allocated water per stand rather than per person and that it allocated an equal amount of free basic water to all Johannesburg residents, regardless of their financial means or other circumstances. See *Mazibuko* v. *City of Johannesburg* (2010: paras 44, 83–86, 90).
86 See *Mazibuko* v. *City of Johannesburg* (2010: paras 138–139).
87 Ibid., paras105–106, 115, 117, 125–127.
88 Ibid., para 148.
89 *Mazibuko* v. *City of Johannesburg* (2008). For discussion, see Dugard (2008: 593–595); Liebenberg (2010: 467–468); Williams (2010: 171–173).
90 See Dugard (2008: 596, 608–610).
91 See Dugard (2014: 301); Dugard and Langford (2011: 58); Madlingozi (2014: 112); Roithmayr (2010: 327).
92 *City of Johannesburg* v. *Mazibuko* (2009). For discussion, see Liebenberg (2010: 468); Williams (2010: 173–174).
93 See *Mazibuko* v. *City of Johannesburg* (2010: paras 91–96). For more detail on the means test, see Williams (2010: 167–168).
94 *Mazibuko* v. *City of Johannesburg* (2010: para 7).
95 Ibid., para 3. On the importance of this framing, see Kotze (2010: 156–157).
96 *Mazibuko* v. *City of Johannesburg* (2010: paras 11–12, 166).
97 Ibid., paras 13–15, 149, 166–167.
98 Ibid., paras 48–50, 57.
99 Ibid., paras 52–68. The Court has held on several occasions that it was not appropriate for courts to determine 'minimum core content' of socio-economic rights or to prescribe the exact content of socio-economic policies to the legislature or executive, and that, when it comes to the positive obligations engendered by socio-economic

rights, courts should confine themselves to assessing the reasonableness of measures aimed at progressively realising the rights.

100 Ibid., paras 69–76, 85.

101 Ibid., para 76.

102 Ibid., paras 83–85, 89.

103 Ibid., paras 88–89. On the extent to which the analysis zoomed in on households of average size, see Pillay and Wesson (2014: 350); Williams (2010: 179, 194).

104 *Mazibuko* v. *City of Johannesburg* (2010: paras 90–97, 143). See also Liebenberg (2010: 471).

105 *Mazibuko* v. *City of Johannesburg* (2010: paras 98–102). For critical discussion of the Court's finding in relation to means testing see Fuo (2014: 203); Liebenberg (2010: 472; 2015a: 457–458); Pillay and Wesson (2014: 351).

106 *Mazibuko* v. *City of Johannesburg* (2010: para 137).

107 Ibid., paras 136–142.

108 Ibid., paras 120–124. For the Court, payment was all that stood in the way of a continued water supply in these circumstances. Pieterse (2012: 376).

109 *Mazibuko* v. *City of Johannesburg* (2010: para 121). In this regard, the judgment is consistent with that of the Durban High Court in *Manqele*.

110 *Mazibuko* v. *City of Johannesburg* (2010: para 126). See also paras 155–156, where one of the reasons that the Court finds there not to be discrimination inherent in the fact that Phiri residents were not offered the option of a credit meter was that residents of the northern suburbs were not offered the option of a prepaid meter either.

111 Ibid., para 131. Liebenberg (2010: 475) laments this finding, arguing that it narrows the scope for public participation in socio-economic rights cases.

112 *Mazibuko* v. *City of Johannesburg* (2010: paras 132–134).

113 Ibid., para 149.

114 Ibid., paras 150–151, 156.

115 Ibid., paras 152–154.

116 Ibid., paras 154; 157.

117 See Bond (2013: 135); Brown (2015: 133–134); Smith and Rubin (2015: 274).

118 See Liebenberg (2010: 467–470, 480; 2015a: 455); Murcott (2015: 879, 896–901); Roithmayr (2010: 323–324); Williams (2010: 176–177); Wilson and Dugard (2014: 55–56).

119 See Brand *et al.* (2013: 288–290, 292); Liebenberg (2010: 468; Liebenberg 2015b: 430–433); Wilson and Dugard (2011: 665, 672–675).

120 See Pillay and Wesson (2014: 352); Williams (2010: 146–147, 189–195); Wilson and Dugard (2011: 675–677).

121 See Liebenberg (2010: 478–479; 2015a: 463; 2015b: 431–433); Pillay and Wesson (2014: 351); Williams (2010: 168).

122 See Liebenberg (2010: 473–474); Wilson and Dugard (2014: 57).

123 See Brown (2015: 135); Coggin and Pieterse (2012: 270–271); Dugard and Langford (2011: 51–52); Murcott (2015: 879, 896, 902–903); Narsiah (2011: 154); Liebenberg (2015a: 469); Pieterse (2012: 376–377; 2014a: 165, 168); Roithmayr (2010: 317, 319, 322–324).

124 See Coggin and Pieterse (2012: 275); Pieterse (2014a: 165).

125 See *Mazibuko* v. *City of Johannesburg* (2010: paras 159–165); Pieterse (2012: 370–371); Williams (2010: 178).

126 See Dugard (2014: 301–302); Dugard and Langford (2011: 58); Narsiah (2011: 154); Pillay and Wesson (2014: 353); Smith and Rubin (2015: 267–269).

127 See Dugard (2014: 301–302); Dugard and Langford (2011: 58); Smith and Rubin (2015: 268–269).

128 See Dugard (2014: 301–302); Dugard and Langford (2011: 57–58).

129 See Matlala and Benit-Gbaffou (2015: 50–54).

130 See Dugard and Langford (2011: 57–58); Madlingozi (2014: 112).

131 See Brown (2015: 119, 135); Smith and Rubin (2015: 273–274).
132 *Nokotyana* v. *Ekurhuleni Metropolitan Municipality* (2010: para 47).
133 Ibid., paras 39, 42, 47–49, 55, 57. For criticism, see Bilchitz (2010b: 594–597); Wilson and Dugard (2014: 51).
134 *Nokotyana* v. *Ekurhuleni Metropolitan Municipality* (2010: paras 2–3, 8–9, 11).
135 See Dugard (2014: 304–305).
136 See Bilchitz (2010a: 51–52, 54; 2010b: 597, 601); Wilson and Dugard (2011: 680–681). David Bilchitz has further remarked upon the curious absence of the 'public law right' to service delivery established in *Joseph*, from *Nokotyana* which was handed down mere weeks later; Bilchitz (2010a: 71; 2010b: 597).
137 *Beja* v. *Premier of the Western Cape* (2011: paras 13–20, 29–30, 78–84).
138 Ibid., paras 21, 24–25.
139 Ibid., paras 32–35.
140 Ibid., paras 141–144.
141 Ibid., paras 98–101, 146, 150.
142 Ibid., para 192.
143 *Rail Commuters Action Group* v. *Transnet t/a Metrorail* (2005 paras 78, 82–84, 86, 88, 109, 111). For discussion, see Coggin and Pieterse (2012: 269; 2015: 301–302).
144 See Wilson and Dugard (2011: 680–681).
145 *Federation for Sustainable Environment* v. *Minister of Water Affairs* (2012: para 24). These findings are welcomed by Murcott (2015: 907–908).
146 *Federation for Sustainable Environment* v. *Minister of Water Affairs* (2012: para 22).
147 *Rademan* v. *Moqhaka Local Municipality* (2013: paras10, 16–20, 28).
148 Ibid., paras 25–35, 39, 46.
149 Ibid., paras 40–45.
150 *National Treasury* v. *Opposition to Urban Tolling Alliance* (2012: paras 67–68).
151 Ibid., paras 3–5, 38, 47, 53, 56, 62–68, 70–72. For criticism, see Swart and Coggin (2013: 357–360) (arguing that the tolls impact on the enjoyment of several socio-economic rights as well as the right to freedom of movement).
152 For critical discussion of the extent to which sustainability concerns have been articulated and accommodated in the Court's service delivery-related jurisprudence, see Kotze (2010: 158–160); Pieterse (2014b: 191–192); Stewart and Horsten (2009: 488–489, 496).
153 See Bilchitz (2015: 92–93). See in this respect also *Merafong Demarcation Forum* v. *President of the Republic of South Africa* (2008: paras 50–51, 58–60), where the Constitutional Court held that citizens ultimately hold government accountable through elections rather than judicial review and that the constitutional obligation to facilitate citizens' participation in the legislative process therefore neither meant that citizens had to be satisfied with the decisions that government ultimately takes, nor that government had to keep engaging citizens until it secured buy-in into all legislative or policy initiatives.
154 See *Mazibuko* v. *City of Johannesburg* (2010: paras 159–165).
155 See Bilchitz (2015: 105–108); Coggin and Pieterse (2012: 270); Pieterse (2012: 363, 370–371.

References

Albertyn, C. & Goldblatt, B., 1998. 'Facing the challenge of transformation: Difficulties in the development of an indigenous jurisprudence of equality', *South African Journal of Human Rights* 14(2), 248–276.

Alexander, P., 2010. 'Rebellion of the poor: South Africa's service delivery protests – a preliminary analysis', *Review of African Political Economy* 37(1), 25–40.

Beall, J., Crankshaw, O. & Parnell, S., 2002. *Uniting a Divided City: Governance and Social Exclusion in Johannesburg*. London: Earthscan.
Benit-Gbaffou, C., 2008. 'Are practices of local participation sidelining the institutional participatory channels? Reflections from Johannesburg', *Transformation: Critical Perspectives on Southern Africa* 66(1), 1–33.
Benit-Gbaffou, C., 2012. 'Party politics, civil society and local democracy – reflections from Johannesburg', *Geoforum* 43(2), 178–189.
Beavon, K., 2004. *Johannesburg: The Making and Shaping of the City*. Pretoria: UNISA Press.
Beja v. *Premier of the Western Cape*, 2011. Decision by the Western Cape High Court, reported as 2011 (10) BCLR 1077 (WCC).
Bilchitz, D., 2010a. 'Citizenship and community: Exploring the right to receive basic municipal services in *Joseph*', *Constitutional Court Review* 3, 45–78.
Bilchitz, D., 2010b. 'Is the Constitutional Court wasting away the rights of the poor? *Nokotyana* v. *Ekurhuleni Metropolitan Municipality*', *South African Law Journal* 127(4), 591–605.
Bilchitz, D., 2015. 'Are socio-economic rights a form of political rights?' *South African Journal of Human Rights* 31(1), 86–111.
Bond, P., 2013. 'Water rights, commons and advocacy narratives', *South African Journal of Human Rights* 29(1), 125–143.
Bond, P. & Dugard, J., 2008. 'The case of Johannesburg water: What really happened at the pre-paid "parish pump" ', *Law, Democracy & Development* 12(1), 1–28.
Booysen, S., 2007. 'With the ballot and the brick: The politics of attaining service delivery', *Progress in Development Studies* 7(1), 21–32.
Brand, D., De Beer, S., De Villiers, I. & Van Marle, K., 2013. 'Poverty as injustice', *Law, Democracy & Development* 17, 273–297.
Brown, J., 2015. *South Africa's Insurgent Citizens: On Dissent and the Possibility of Politics*. Johannesburg: Jacana.
Buhlungu, S., 2006. 'Upstarts or bearers of tradition? The Anti-Privatisation Forum of Gauteng'. In Ballard, R., Habib, A. & Valodia, I. (eds.), *Voices of Protest: Social Movements in Post-Apartheid South Africa*, pp. 67–87. Pietermaritzburg: UKZN Press.
City of Johannesburg, 2011. *Joburg Growth and Development Strategy 2040*.
City of Johannesburg, 2016. *State of the City Address 2016 Delivered by the Executive Mayor, Cllr Mpho Parks Tau*.
City of Johannesburg v. *Mazibuko*, 2009. Decision of the Supreme Court of Appeal, reported as 2009 (3) SA 592 (SCA).
Clark, M., 2014. *An Anatomy of Dissent & Repression: The Criminal Justice System and the 2011 Thembelihle Protest*. SERI Research Report, Johannesburg.
Coggin, T. & Pieterse, M., 2012. 'Rights and the city: An exploration of the interaction between socio-economic rights and the city', *Urban Forum* 23(3), 257–278.
Coggin, T. & Pieterse, M., 2015. 'A right to transport? Moving towards a rights-based approach to mobility in the city', *South African Journal of Human Rights* 31(3), 294–314.
Constitution of the Republic of South Africa, 1996 (Act 108 of 1996).
Dugard, J., 2008. 'Rights, regulation and resistance: The Phiri water campaign', *South African Journal of Human Rights* 24(3), 593–611.
Dugard, J., 2014. 'Urban basic services: Rights, reality and resistance'. In Langford, M., Cousins, B., Dugard, J. & Madlingozi, T. (eds.), *Socio-economic Rights in South Africa: Symbols or Substance?* pp. 275–309. Cambridge, UK: Cambridge University Press.

Dugard, J. & Langford, M., 2011. 'Art or science? Synthesising lessons from public interest litigation and the dangers of legal determinism', *South African Journal of Human Rights* 27(1), 39–64.

Egan, A. & Wafer, A., 2006. 'Dynamics of a "mini-mass movement": Origins, identity and ideological pluralism in the Soweto Electricity Crisis Committee'. In Ballard, R., Habib, A. & Valodia, I. (eds.), *Voices of Protest: Social Movements in Post-Apartheid South Africa*, pp. 45–65. Pietermaritzburg: UKZN Press.

Federation for Sustainable Environment v. *Minister of Water Affairs*, 2012. Decision of the North Gauteng High Court, reported as [2012] ZAGPPHC 128.

Fuo, O., 2014. 'Local government indigent policies in the pursuit of social justice in South African through the lenses of Fraser', *Stellenbosch Law Review* 25(1), 187–208.

Glaser, D., 2015. 'Uncooperative masses as a problem for substantive and participatory theories of democracy: The cases of "people's power" (1984–6) and the "xenophobia" (2008) in South Africa'. In Benit-Gbaffou, C. (ed.), *Popular Politics in South African Cities: Unpacking Community Participation*, pp. 139–170. Cape Town: HSRC Press.

Goebel, A., 2015. *On Their Own: Women, Urbanization and the Right to the City in South Africa*. Montreal: McGill-Queens University Press.

Housing Act, 107 of 1997.

Jain, H., 2010. *Community Protests in South Africa: Trends, Analysis and Explanations*. Community Law Centre Local Government Working Paper No 1, UWC Community Law Centre, Cape Town.

Joseph v. *City of Johannesburg*, 2010. Decision of the South African Constitutional Court, reported as 2010 (4) SA 55 (CC).

Kidd, M., 2004. 'Not a drop to drink: Disconnection of water services for non-payment and the right of access to water', *South African Journal of Human Rights* 20(1), 119–137.

Kotze, L.J., 2010. 'Phiri, the plight of the poor and the perils of climate change: Time to rethink environmental and socio-economic rights in South Africa?' *Journal of Human Rights & Environment* 1(2), 135–160.

Liebenberg, S., 2010. *Socio-economic Rights Adjudication under a Transformative Constitution*. Cape Town: Juta.

Liebenberg, S., 2015a. 'Social rights and transformation in South Africa: Three frames', *South African Journal of Human Rights* 31(3), 446–471.

Liebenberg, S., 2015b. 'Toward an equality-promoting interpretation of socio-economic rights in South Africa: Insights from the egalitarian liberal tradition', *South African Law Journal* 132(2), 411–437.

Madlingozi, T., 2014. 'Post-apartheid social movements and legal mobilisation'. In Langford, M., Cousins, B., Dugard, J. & Madlingozi, T. (eds.), *Socio-economic Rights in South Africa: Symbols or Substance?*, pp. 92–130. Cambridge, UK: Cambridge University Press.

Manqele v. *Durban Transitional Metropolitan Council*, 2002. Decision of the Durban High Court, reported as 2002 (6) SA 423 (D).

Matlala, B. & Benit-Gbaffou, C., 2015. 'Against ourselves – local activists and the management of contradictory political loyalties: The case of Phiri, Johannesburg'. In Benit-Gbaffou, C. (ed.), *Popular Politics in South African Cities: Unpacking Community Participation*, pp. 42–69. Cape Town: HSRC Press.

Mazibuko v. *City of Johannesburg*, 2008. Decision of the Witwatersrand High Court, reported as [2008] 4 All SA 471 (W).

Mazibuko v. *City of Johannesburg*, 2010. Decision of the South African Constitutional Court, reported as 2010 (4) SA 1 (CC).

Mbazira, C., 2013. 'Service delivery protests, struggle for rights and the failure of local democracy in South Africa and Uganda: Parallels and divergences', *South African Journal of Human Rights* 29(2), 251–275.

Merafong Demarcation Forum v. *President of the Republic of South Africa*, 2008. Decision of the South African Constitutional Court, reported as 2008 (5) SA 171 (CC).

Mkontwana v. *Nelson Mandela Metropolitan Municipality*, 2005. Decision of the South African Constitutional Court, reported as 2005 (1) SA 530 (CC).

Municipal Structures Act 117, of 1998.

Municipal Systems Act 32 of 2000.

Murcott, M., 2013. 'The role of administrative law in enforcing socio-economic rights: Revisiting *Joseph*', *South African Journal of Human Rights* 29(3), 481–495.

Murcott, M., 2015. 'The role of environmental justice in socio-economic rights litigation', *South African Law Journal.* 132(4), 875–908.

Narsiah, S., 2011. 'Urban pulse – the struggle for water, life and dignity in South African cities: The case of Johannesburg', 32 *Urban Geography* 32(1), 149–155.

National Treasury v. *Opposition to Urban Tolling Alliance*, 2012. Decision of the South African Constitutional Court, reported as 2012 (6) SA 223 (CC).

Netswera, F.G., 2008. 'A case study of community participation in governance and service delivery in the city of Johannesburg'. In: Van Donk, M., Swilling, M., Pieterse, E. & Parnell, S. (eds.), *Consolidating Developmental Local Government: Lessons from the South African Experience*, pp. 511–523. Cape Town: UCT Press.

Nokotyana v. *Ekurhuleni Metropolitan Municipality*, 2010. Decision of the South African Constitutional Court, reported as 2010 (4) BCLR 312 (CC).

Oldfield, S., 2008. 'Participatory mechanisms and community politics: Building consensus and conflict'. In Van Donk, M., Swilling, M., Pieterse, E. & Parnell, S. (eds.), *Consolidating Developmental Local Government: Lessons from the South African Experience*, pp. 487–500. Cape Town: UCT Press.

Pernegger, L., 2014. 'The agonistic state: Metropolitan government responses to city strife post-1994'. In Haferburg, C. & Huchzermeyer, M. (eds.), *Urban Governance in Post-Apartheid Cities: Modes of Engagement in South Africa's Metropoles*, pp. 61–78. Pietermaritzburg: UKZN Press.

Pickering, M., 2008. 'The distribution of power: Local government and electricity distribution industry reforms'. In Van Donk, M., Swilling, M., Pieterse, E. & Parnell, S. (eds.), *Consolidating Developmental Local Government: Lessons from the South African Experience*, pp. 445–461. Cape Town: UCT Press.

Pieterse, M., 2003. 'Towards a useful role for section 36 of the Constitution in social rights cases? *Residents of Bon Vista Mansions* v. *Southern Metropolitan Local Council*', *South African Law Journal* 120(1), 41–48.

Pieterse, M., 2012. 'Procedural relief, constitutional citizenship and socio-economic rights as legitimate expectations', *South African Journal of Human Rights*, 28(3), 359–379.

Pieterse, M., 2014a. 'Development, the right to the city and the legal and constitutional responsibilities of local government in South Africa', *South African Law Journal* 131(1), 149–177.

Pieterse, M., 2014b. 'The right to the city and the urban environment: Re-imagining section 24 of the 1996 Constitution', *Southern African Public Law* 29(1), 175–193.

Pillay, A. & Wesson, M., 2014. 'Recession, recovery and service delivery: Political and judicial responses to the financial and economic crisis in South Africa'. In Nolan A. (ed.), *Economic and Social Rights after the Global Financial Crisis*, pp. 335–365. Cambridge, UK: Cambridge University Press.

Pretoria City Council v. *Walker*, 1998. Decision of the South African Constitutional Court, reported as 1998 (2) SA 363 (CC).

Pretorius, L. & Prinsloo, J., 2014. 'The extent and impact of copper cable theft in Gauteng, South Africa', *Acta Criminologica* Special Edition, 101–113.

Promotion of Administrative Justice Act, 3 of 2000.

Rademan v. *Moqhaka Local Municipality*, 2013. Decision of the South African Constitutional Court, reported as 2013 (4) SA 225 (CC).

Rail Commuters Action Group v. *Transnet t/a Metrorail*, 2005. Decision of the South African Constitutional Court, reported as 2005 (2) SA 359 (CC).

Residents of Bon Vista Mansions v. *Southern Metropolitan Local Council*, 2002. Decision of the Witwatersrand High Court, reported as 2002 (6) BCLR 625 (W).

Roithmayr, D., 2010. 'Lessons from *Mazibuko*: Persistent inequality and the commons', *Constitutional Court Review* 3, 317–346.

Ruiters, G., 2006. 'Social control and social welfare under neoliberalism in South African cities: Contradictions in free basic water services'. In: Murray, M.J. & Myers, G.A. (eds.), *Cities in Contemporary Africa*, pp. 289–308. New York: Palgrave Macmillan.

Smith, L. & Morris, N., 2008. 'Municipal entities: A panacea for service delivery constraints?' In: Van Donk, M., Swilling, M., Pieterse, E. & Parnell, S. (eds.), *Consolidating Developmental Local Government: Lessons from the South African Experience*, pp. 423–444. Cape Town: UCT Press.

Smith, L. & Rubin, M., 2015. 'Beyond invented and invited spaces of participation: The Phiri and Olivia Road court cases and their outcome'. In: Benit-Gbaffou, C. (ed.), *Popular Politics in South African Cities: Unpacking Community Participation*, pp. 248–281. Cape Town: HSRC Press.

Statistics South Africa, n.d. 'City of Johannesburg', viewed 1 January 2017, from http://beta2.stassa.gov.za/?page_id=1021id=city-of-johannesburg-municipality.

Stewart, L. & Horsten, D., 2009. 'The role of sustainability in the adjudication of the right to access to adequate water', *Southern African Public Law* 24(2), 486–505.

Steytler, N., 2004. 'Socio-economic rights and the process of privatizing basic municipal services', *Law, Democracy & Development* 8(1), 157–180.

Swart, M. & Coggin, T., 2013. 'The road not taken: Separation of powers, interim interdicts, rationality review and E-tolling in *National Treasury* v. *Opposition to Urban Tolling*', *Constitutional Court Review* 5, 346–365.

Van der Berg, S., 2013. 'Meaningful engagement: Proceduralising socio-economic rights further or infusing administrative law with substance?' *South African Journal of Human Rights* 29(2), 376–398.

Van Zyl, I., 2003. 'Illegal connections threaten lives in over-populated township', *IMIESA* 28(1), 36–38.

Von Schnitzler, A., 2008. 'Citizenship prepaid: Water, calculability, and techno-politics in South Africa', *Journal of Southern African Studies* 34(4), 899–917.

Water Services Act, 108 of 1997.

Williams, L.A., 2010. 'The role of courts in the quantitative implementation of social and economic rights: A comparative study', *Constitutional Court Review* 3, 141–199.

Wilson, S. & Dugard, J., 2011. 'Taking poverty seriously: The South African Constitutional Court and socio-economic rights', *Stellenbosch Law Review* 22(3), 664–682.

Wilson, S. & Dugard, J., 2014. 'Constitutional jurisprudence: The first and second waves'. In: Langford, M., Cousins, B., Dugard, J. & Madlingozi, T. (eds.), *Socio-economic Rights in South Africa: Symbols or Substance?* pp. 35–62. Cambridge, UK: Cambridge University Press.

4 Marginal struggles

Equality, public presence and livelihood

Introduction

Dominant conceptions of urban citizenship are replete with behaviour codes. While typically moral and/or political in origin, these codes intersect with and find expression in various manifestations of power geared towards maintaining order and regulating everyday life in the city. They are created, enforced and reinforced through governance and law, urban management practices, the built environment, and the everyday behaviour of those urban inhabitants who have accepted, internalised or relented to them.[1]

But not everyone can, or wants to, live like model urban citizens. Whether by necessity or by choice, a great many inhabitants depart from urban behaviour codes in their identity or self-expression, their modes of inhabiting and eking out a livelihood in the city, their everyday actions of living, moving around, *being* in the city. In developing-world cities such as Johannesburg, where many features of idealised urban citizenship (engaging in formal employment, residing in formal housing, establishing and maintaining nuclear families, participating self-sufficiently in a consumer-driven economy) are largely unattainable by many inhabitants, there are constant clashes between efforts to enforce hegemonic urban behaviour codes and the myriad forms of being that violate them.[2]

This chapter considers the use of legal rights by marginalised residents of Johannesburg in efforts to resist or transcend their legal, social, economic and spatial sidelining. It looks at the complicity of the law in creating and suppressing social outcasts as well as its potential to protect and re-enfranchise them, in relation to a range of people who, either wholly or in part, fall short of the ideals of 'mainstream' urban citizenship.

Given that many of the behaviour codes of urban citizenship are legally reflected and enforced, many activities by non-conformers are either explicitly illegal or fall outside of the purview or protection of the law. The stigma of illegality overlaps with and reinforces other negative depictions of urban outcasts (for instance, that they are disorderly, dirty or unseemly), hence justifying them being targeted in efforts to maintain or restore law and order to the city. This marginalisation and stigmatisation has definite spatial elements, which often take the form of legally barring, restricting or resisting the extent of marginalised residents' presence in public space.[3] Examples from Johannesburg include regular Metropolitan Police raids and crackdowns on 'illegal' activities, physical alterations of the urban environment (walls, fences, boomgates, street landscaping) aimed at reducing the presence of 'illegals' or 'nuisances', and urban management and bylaw enforcement by private security guards.[4] All of these efforts logically entail a push of 'illegal' activities towards private spaces and, especially in relation to those activities that cannot fully be contained in private space, the concomitant marginalisation and stigmatisation of those public spaces in which non-conformist behaviour still occurs.

So, it comes to pass that marginalised urban inhabitants often find themselves relegated to marginal urban spaces. These tend to be the neglected, dilapidated, desolate and dangerous corners of the city. Such spaces abound across Johannesburg, although in this chapter the focus will mostly be on remaining pockets of decay in the CBD, Hillbrow and the inner-city flatlands. Many of these places have become marginalised precisely because of the presence of marginalised populations or the proliferation of marginalised activities there, whereas others declined for other reasons and subsequently became places towards which marginalised people at once gravitate and get pushed.[5] Moreover, as will be shown below, marginalised groups themselves often actively create marginalised/non-mainstream spaces, in which 'ordinary' rules of civility and behaviour are (at least partly) suspended and replaced with alternative codes of citizenship.[6]

Given the 'illegality' attaching to the day-to-day activities of many marginal individuals, marginal space is often lawless space, where the recognition and assertion of legal rights is either impossible or significantly complicated. From the perspective of marginalised urban inhabitants, this state of 'lawlessness' may well be desirable (in that they often require or depend upon the invisibility, anonymity and/or the flexibility of the 'alternative', extra-legal social structures that prevail in marginal space) but is also dangerous (in that their existence is thereby rendered precarious and unpredictable).[7] Just because 'formal' law and order appears to be suspended in 'informal' and marginal spaces, does not mean that no power structures operate there – '[w]hat typically appears from the outside to be a uniform and monolithic ensemble of equally shared deprivations turns out on closer inspection to be a heterogeneous and finely differentiated assemblage of unequal relationships'.[8] Marginal inhabitants are therefore vulnerable to oppression and exploitation not only by the State and 'mainstream' society, but often also by other, more powerful, marginalised inhabitants.[9]

Yet, the complexities of asserting legal rights in space perceived to be lawless, by persons whose lives are perceived to be (at least partly) illegal, does not mean that marginalised inhabitants are not continuously performing rights. Over and above the constant (extra-legal) assertion of a whole range of rights with and against authorities and each other, marginalised people are performing the right to the city through their very actions which flaunt hegemonic urban behaviour codes. Breaking the law by living lives and making livelihoods in the city is a powerful assertion of urban citizenship in the face of forces seeking to deny it, as is the active creation of marginal urban spaces that support alternative forms of being.[10]

But this is not to say that all such performances of the right to the city are above reproach. While insurgence is often romanticised as unequivocally embodying progressive and transformative, 'alternative' forms of rights assertion, it is also often replete with real power imbalances, oppressive practices and rights violations. Indeed, insurgency often precisely takes the form of denial of or resistance to rights or, as perhaps illustrated most starkly by the sporadic outbursts of xenophobic violence and vigilantism across Johannesburg's marginalised spaces, of actions which themselves violate or disregard the rights of others.[11] Moreover, the creation of spaces and regimes in and through which 'ordinary' behaviour codes and rights are suspended or undermined, may well frustrate ideals of urban integration, mutuality, interdependence and respect for difference.[12]

This chapter, then, looks at rights assertion by marginalised inhabitants of Johannesburg – both legally and by way of the production of space. It starts by taking a closer look at the intersection between the legal and social enforcement of societal behaviour codes and the everyday realities of marginalised lives in Johannesburg, as well as at individual and collective enactments of the right to the city within some of the city's marginalised spaces. Thereafter, it discusses the use of legal rights and litigation, in efforts to resist the effects of marginalisation. Three broad strands of jurisprudence are assessed. The first is equality jurisprudence, with a focus on the subset of equality-based legal challenges pertaining to the rights of non-nationals. Second, I consider a set of decisions located at the intersection of rights to life, personal freedom and dignity, which begins to eke out a right to urban public presence. Third, I discuss judicial decisions vindicating a right to make a livelihood. In conclusion, the chapter takes a step back to reflect upon the potential and limits of legal strategies in efforts to resist legal and social marginalisation.

Marginality, insurgence and the right to the city

Life on/in Johannesburg's margins

> For those who are engaged in a constant struggle to survive, everyday life in the inner city has come to resemble a Darwinian social order permeated with conflict over, and competition for, scarce resources in a hostile environment that offers few opportunities for upward and outward mobility.[13]

Joburg's inner city and surrounding flatlands responded to the crumbling of influx control regulations and the subsequent dawn of the democratic dispensation by inadvertently throwing open their doors to poor and marginalised inhabitants from all over the country and the continent. As formal businesses fled the CBD and surrounds for the predictability and exclusivity of the northern suburbs, where they were joined by middle and upper class workers and residents, the abandoned spaces left in their wake were soon over-filled by those previously excluded from the city. These spaces were new territory to almost everyone (from the outskirts of the city, from rural South Africa and from elsewhere in Africa) who now settled there, and their subsequent daily struggles for survival have therefore coincided with struggles for presence in and control over this territory.[14] As this territory now shrinks due to its re-surrender to the middle- and upper-classes in the course of the CBD's regeneration, these struggles are intensifying.

A particularly fraught focal point of these struggles has been competition between South African-born residents and the many foreign nationals who live in the Johannesburg inner city and its immediate surrounds (including, for instance, the Nigerians and Congolese who settled in Hillbrow and Berea from the early 1990s onwards, as well as more recent waves of Pakistani and Zimbabwean, Ethiopian and Somali arrivals).[15] This competition has often been violent and deadly, as evidenced most palpably when large-scale xenophobic violence erupted across marginalised Johannesburg spaces in 2008, and again (albeit less severely) in early 2015.

Indeed, the perilous existence of undocumented, poor foreign nationals in Joburg's inner city and surrounds, as well as in many of its townships and informal settlements, arguably present the extreme of social marginalisation in the city. This marginalisation is shaped by the law, which draws stark distinctions, first, between 'citizens' and 'non-citizens' and, second, between various categories of 'legal' and 'illegal' foreigners. While documented proof of 'legal' immigration status (usually bestowed only on qualified, middle-class foreigners entering the country through official immigration channels, and on a small group of refugees and asylum seekers) serves as an official threshold for accessing the objects of a wide array of rights in the city and provides a measure of protection against official persecution (to the extent that desperate, fraudulent attempts to obtain documentation, especially in terms of refugee legislation, abound),[16] the effects of ground-level internalisation of these distinctions is that all foreigners in the city are tainted with notions of illegality and non-belonging, regardless of their official immigration status.[17] This, together with the intense economic competition prevailing in Johannesburg's margins, fuels and sustains a particularly violent breed of xenophobia amongst citizens, which endangers the physical safety and significantly diminishes the quality of life of all foreigners in the city.[18]

Notwithstanding that most rights in the Bill of Rights are conferred upon everyone within South African territory and that refugees and asylum seekers further enjoy a range of rights in terms of section 27 of the 1998 Refugees Act, the objects of these rights are, in practice, very difficult to access, especially without official documentation.[19] Bureaucrats in the health and education systems, for instance, are well-known for denying foreigners access to hospitals or schools when they cannot produce official proof of their legality, and are also (sometimes extremely) hostile, even towards those foreigners who can.[20] Undocumented migrants in Joburg therefore tend not to seek health care or other social services from state institutions, whereas services provided by the private sector tend to be beyond their financial means. Instead, many do not access services at all, or do so either in Joburg's (limited and overstrained) non-governmental sector or in its underworld, where care is often of extremely questionable quality.[21]

Proof of legality is further an absolute requirement for entry into formal employment in South Africa, with the result that even skilled foreigners who lack the necessary documentation are relegated to fending for themselves in the city's informal and underground economies.[22] The upshot is that a significant portion of inner-city Joburg's informal traders are foreign-born, while there are also a disproportionate number of foreigners involved in illegal activities, such as the drug trade. Furthermore, it is not possible to open a bank account in South Africa without official identity documentation, which significantly complicates undocumented foreigners' economic activities and renders them vulnerable to crime and extortion.[23]

Apart from fearing authorities because of the possibility of arrest, detention and deportation in terms of immigration legislation, both 'legal' and 'illegal' foreigners in Johannesburg complain of regular harassment, assault and extortion by the police, who are further known for confiscating and/or destroying 'legal' foreigners' identity documentation (hence rendering them effectively 'illegal' for all of the purposes outlined above). Living as a foreigner in Joburg therefore typically involves having to steer clear of the authorities, which further compounds vulnerability to crime and to abuse.[24]

Overall, outside of the middleclass suburbs, foreign lives in Joburg's inner city and townships tend to be hazardous, tentative, informal and fraught with danger.[25] For the most part, it is neither possible for 'illegal'/undocumented (as well as many 'legal') foreigners to assert positive entitlements inherent to rights in a variety of everyday settings, nor for them to avail themselves of the law's protection against (even extreme) rights violations.

This precariousness is shared, albeit to a somewhat lesser extent, by South African residents who also inhabit marginalised space and also live outside of the letter of the law. For instance, Joburg residents who engage in economic activities prohibited by the criminal law (such as sex workers or those involved in the drug trade), many of whom do so out of economic necessity, are similarly situated to 'illegal' foreigners in relation to the authorities, with the police's harassment and assault of sex workers across the city, for instance, being well documented. The result is that those involved in such criminalised activities must also live their lives below the radar, similarly out of reach of the protection of rights and the law. Like foreigners, these 'illegals' are vulnerable to violence and exploitation, and experience difficulties in accessing essential services.[26] This burden is compounded for those who, in addition to being involved in the sex or drug trade, are also foreign.

Then there are those urban residents whose living or working arrangements are not criminal in and of themselves, but are rendered illegal by municipal bylaws which regulate the kinds of activities that may take place in public spaces. For instance, like elsewhere in the world, Johannesburg's population of homeless people are regularly harassed for living their private lives in public, and for contravening municipal bylaws by, for instance, sleeping, urinating, defecating, or 'loitering' in public spaces. Given that homeless people typically do not have access to private spaces in which to perform such acts, their very physical presence in the city is rendered 'illegal', which leads to vulnerabilities similar to those experienced by other 'illegal' inhabitants.[27] A particularly egregious Joburg example pertains to harassment by the Metropolitan Police, who have, for instance, been accused of confiscating homeless people's blankets during late-night wintertime raids, in attempting to drive them off the streets.[28]

The inner city's substantial population of informal traders are similarly positioned in relation to city bylaws, and experience similar problems in relation to law enforcement. Given that unregulated informal trade in the CBD is widely regarded as an instance of blight and decay, various iterations of Johannesburg's bylaws through the last two decades have essentially prohibited informal street trade, except for in a limited number of demarcated areas, where the City would erect infrastructure and allocate stalls for 'licensed' traders, thereby attempting to formalise and regularise informal trade. Street trading without a paid-up licence or outside of designated areas, is 'illegal', and bylaws accordingly bestow authority on the Metropolitan Police to dismantle 'illegal' stalls and to confiscate 'illegally' traded wares.[29] Accordingly, Joburg's informal traders, especially those who operate 'illegally', are regularly subjected to police harassment, with regular reports of the Metropolitan Police physically manhandling traders, 'confiscating' or destroying their goods, and extorting bribes from them.[30]

As with the division between 'legal' and 'illegal' immigrants, the trade bylaws' somewhat artificial distinction between 'legal' and 'illegal' traders serves to tar all informal traders in the city with the brush of 'illegality'. The trade bylaws implementation also introduced significant conflict and competition between 'legal' traders (those who abide bylaws and have duly 'regularised' themselves by obtaining permits and remaining restricted to designated trade areas) on the one hand, and 'illegal' traders on the other, with the former group resenting that the latter are able to trade at a lesser operating cost and in more flexible (and hence business-conducive) locations.[31] There is further significant xenophobic hostility towards foreign traders, who are doubly disadvantaged by the taint of 'illegality' attaching to their persons and their livelihoods.[32]

Another example of residents 'criminalised' both through the enforcement of bylaws and in the popular consciousness is Johannesburg's notorious minibus taxi drivers, who have a long history of urban insurgence, both through their outward presentation and/or driving behaviour (which often contravene traffic and roadworthiness bylaws), and through how they conduct themselves towards passengers, competing forms of public transport and authorities. It is therefore unsurprising that the taxi industry has uneasy links with the city's criminal underworld, that taxis are regularly singled out by official urban management or 'order-restoring' initiatives and that they are disproportionately targeted in everyday traffic law enforcement, during which drivers are typically subjected to similar police harassment and extortion to that suffered by other urban 'illegals'.[33]

Overall, the lives of the inhabitants of Johannesburg's marginalised spaces are clearly shaped not only by their dire socio-economic conditions, but also by the law. By declaring certain forms of being 'illegal', the law relegates urban non-conformers to the physical and figurative margins of society, and largely strips them of the ability to enforce rights. Both through its denial of their realities and through the threat of its punitive power, law drives them into hiding, thereby rendering them invisible to authorities except to the extent that they fail to obscure their non-conformance.[34] This renders them vulnerable to abuse and exploitation not only in the course of law enforcement, but also by other urban residents – 'when some people lack citizen power in relation to other people, the latter benefit from an immunity, an absence of liability'.[35] Given this precarious existence within range of the law's punitive power but outside of the ambit of its protection, struggles over the right to the city by marginalised groups are often struggles for the 'right to have rights'.[36]

Resistance, place-making and the right to the city

Efforts to deny the urban citizenship of marginalised inhabitants by erasing them from 'mainstream' public space are, of course, never entirely successful. Countless acts of resistance against such marginalisation, ranging from active conflict with the law and authorities, to deliberate acts that appropriate and physically alter urban space, and the mundane continuation of everyday life in the face of adversity, are performed daily. Regardless of their legality or their social desirability, all these actions may be viewed as performances of the right to the city, and as challenges to the hegemony of prevailing notions of urban citizenship. [37]

For example, minibus taxi drivers have long resisted official attempts to regularise and co-opt them into mainstream public transport networks (for example, through policies such as the taxi recapitalisation programme and the introduction of the Rea Vaya Rapid Bus Transit system). Actions of resistance have ranged from taxi strikes bringing large sections of the Joburg economy to a halt, to organised disruptions of traffic through road blockades, to blatantly criminal acts of vigilantism such as when rogue taxi drivers opened fire on a Rea Vaya bus shortly after the introduction of the system. Questionable though they may be, these actions, together with taxi drivers' continuous appropriation of Joburg's streets in ways that contravene bylaws and common driving conventions, force authorities and other road users to acknowledge and deal with the fact of their existence.[38]

But not all acts of resistance require such a level of collective action, or such blatant insurgency. The mere performance of marginalised activities (trading, sleeping, soliciting) in public space resists invisibility, thereby staking a claim on public space, inviting conflict and demanding recognition of, and engagement with, a way of life that departs from mainstream behaviour codes.[39] When performed by multiple actors, such everyday actions combine to establish alternative behaviour codes, which enable their performers not only to resist invisibility, but also to function and/or thrive in an otherwise hostile urban environment.[40]

Such collective assertions of the right to the city have the power to alter the urban fabric through the production of spaces that reflect and accommodate the alternative behaviour codes that they embody. Johannesburg is replete with examples of such marginal place-making by members of 'alternative' or side-lined communities. For instance, the formation of distinct immigrant enclaves by groups of foreigners who tend to bear the brunt of Joburgers' xenophobia, provide powerful illustrations of the extent to which such place-making efforts can ameliorate the disadvantage of marginality, can bring about functioning alternative urban behaviour codes and can insist upon a measure of inclusion in the urban fabric.

For example, the so-called 'Ethiopian quarter' on the north-eastern edge of the CBD is increasingly heralded as a textbook example of place-making or urban regeneration 'from below', that confounds mainstream urban planning and management practices.[41] On a number of adjacent city blocks around Jeppe street, Ethiopian migrants (many of them 'legal' refugees or asylum seekers, others not) have established small businesses, first by informally trading clothing and knick-knacks on the street and later formalising by moving into former office buildings on Jeppe street, which they acquired and remodelled into mini-shopping malls housing a conglomerate of small businesses. Other establishments (such as restaurants, supermarkets and coffee shops) followed, more buildings were repurposed, and today the Ethiopian quarter is a bustling retail and wholesale node, specialising in selling cheap (and often counterfeit) clothing and household items imported from China, and serving thousands of customers daily.[42]

Because of their vulnerability to xenophobic violence, as well as to crime, harassment and extortion, the Ethiopian businesspeople have formed their own effective community policing forum, employing private security guards, and they have established stokvel-like communal savings and banking schemes to bypass their difficulties opening 'official' bank accounts without 'legal' documentation.[43] Meanwhile, the organisation of space within the mini-malls mimics that in similar buildings in Addis Ababa, as do the business practices of shop-owners. While remaining vulnerable to regular harassment from authorities because of their precarious 'legality' (given the illegal immigration status of many, the illegality of counterfeit trade and the legion of bylaw infringements occasioned by the organisation and use of space in and around their buildings),[44] the Ethiopian community of Jeppe has managed to establish complex and sophisticated business and social networks, thereby eking out a fairly stable and thriving community life, in the face of poverty, language barriers and xenophobic hostility.

A similar, although more insulated and, accordingly, more marginal, example of ethnic enclave-forming is that of the Somali community in and around 8th Avenue in Mayfair, where former single-storey cluster homes have been transformed into a range of small shops, mini-warehouses and social spaces. The 8th Avenue strip serves as a wholesale base for the many Somali spaza shops in various Joburg townships, and 'houses' an alternative financial and banking 'system' similar in complexity to that operative in the Ethiopian enclave. The enclave further provides safety against xenophobic hostility and violence (to which Somali traders in townships are particularly prone, not least due to their perceived aggressively competitive business practices), fulfils religious needs (with a Mosque on 8th Avenue having been taken over by the community) and serves as a site of social solidarity, whilst reflecting the same class stratifications and social complexities prevailing in Somalia.[45]

Elsewhere, the strong presence of Nigerian immigrants in Hillbrow has led to the suburb for many years being closely associated with all the negative stereotypes attached to this group (such as their perceived involvement in criminal syndicates, pimping and drug trafficking). While there has been some outward claim-staking by Nigerians in Hillbrow's public spaces (notably on Quartz street),[46] Nigerian fortification in Hillbrow has largely taken the form of the 'colonisation' of residential hotels, which have served as the residential and commercial bases for all kinds of Nigerian residents and businessmen, including the notorious drug traders and pimps. In a complex manifestation of marginal place-making, they have shared these buildings with a range of other social outcasts, notably large numbers of sex workers (of various nationalities), drug users, illegal immigrants from elsewhere on the continent, and a fair number of people who are all of the above, all of whom benefit from the relative safety, privacy, anonymity and flexibility provided by these inherently temporary and 'hidden' abodes.[47] While Hillbrow, and especially its Nigerian residents, is the regular focus of law enforcement drives (complete with regular displays of police brutality),[48] with the result that both its Nigerian community and its sex and drug trades have somewhat dwindled in recent years, it remains perhaps the best known example of marginal space in Johannesburg, where official behaviour codes are very much secondary to alternative rules and customs.

Other enclaves that reflect similar coping strategies and alternative behaviour codes to those discussed above, include the Chinatowns in the CBD and Cyrildene, Yeoville's Congolese community and the Pakistani/Bangladeshi conglomeration in Fordsburg.[49] Moreover, some rural South Africans have formed similar enclaves in attempting to cope with life in the city. For instance, rural migrants from KwaZulu Natal have established a strong, insulated community on the southern edges of the CBD, in former mining hostels as well as the abandoned warehouses and adjacent vacant industrial land of Benrose. A traditional leadership-influenced, rural Zulu culture and way of life prevails in these spaces, whereas a particular breed of Zulu masculinity dictates behaviour in the male-dominated hostel spaces.[50] The hostel residents are notorious for insurgence and regularly (violently) resist efforts by the City to formalise and upgrade their living environment. As a counterpoint to the immigrant enclave forming to their north, the hostel community has further been pinpointed as one of the main sources of xenophobic violence against foreigners in the vicinity.

It is clear from this handful of examples that groups of Johannesburg's marginalised inhabitants have reacted to their official 'illegality' and the concomitant denial of their rights by asserting these performatively, often through creating and sustaining alternative networks and governance structures. While exemplary of the right to the city, these performances regularly embody their own networks of inequality and exploitation, and may also, in certain respects, be regarded as undermining ideals of urban coherence, diversity and integration.[51] Yet, whether through asserting and cementing their actors' public presence and visibility, or through creating alternative environments, these performances stand as powerful claims to urban citizenship.

Using legal rights and litigation to resist urban marginality

The above discussion has shown that, despite having legal rights on paper, many of Johannesburg's marginalised inhabitants are effectively prohibited from enforcing them. Given their lack of financial resources and their uncomfortable relationship with the law, it may further be expected that most of these marginalised urban inhabitants will be unlikely to resort to legal challenges in attempts to enforce their constitutional rights. Such challenges will therefore mostly be limited to instances where there is an undisputed legal right at stake, and where some public interest litigation organisation initiates litigation on behalf of the rights-holders. In this subsection, I consider the handful of legal cases that have been decided following attempts to legally enforce different elements of the right to the city, on behalf of marginalised urban residents, in Johannesburg and other South African cities.

Equality, inclusivity and belonging

The right to equality in section 9 of the Constitution (which, in addition to guaranteeing a right to equal treatment, encompasses a prohibition on unfair discrimination) seems to be the most logically implicated constitutional right in instances where persons have been marginalised and/or excluded from the protection of the law, or from the benefits that it bestows.

However, the Constitutional Court's jurisprudence in equality cases signals that the protection of the right will seldom extend to those whose marginalisation flows from their own wilful violation of the law, especially the criminal law. In *President of the Republic of South Africa* v. *Hugo*, the Court dismissed a claim by a male prisoner that the terms of a presidential pardon for certain female prisoners who were also the mothers of minor children discriminated unfairly against similarly situated fathers. In holding that the distinction between men and women in this context did not infringe on the dignity of male prisoners and therefore did not amount to unfair discrimination, several members of the Court emphasised that the 'real harm' suffered by the applicant, i.e. the fact of his imprisonment, was the result of his own criminal activity, thereby signalling that lawbreakers cannot lightly make use of the right to equality to ameliorate the legal consequences of their own wrongdoing.[52]

Similarly, in *Prince* v. *President, Cape Law Society*, courts were unwilling to consider a discrimination challenge against the Cape Law Society's refusal to admit a Rastafarian previously found guilty of possessing and using marijuana, separately from the issue of the criminalisation of the drug. The Constitutional Court ultimately dismissed a freedom-of-religion-based challenge against this criminalisation, with the effect that the claimant's exclusion from the legal profession remained.[53] Then, in *S* v. *Jordan*, a constitutional challenge against the unequal treatment of sex workers and their clients by the 1957 Sexual Offences Act (which criminalised the selling of sex but not its purchase) was dismissed by the majority of the Constitutional Court, while the entire Court further found that sex workers could not rely on rights to dignity and privacy to challenge the criminality of their conduct, since the diminution of these rights was the result of their own, wilful flaunting of the law.[54] Read together, these cases affirm that the protection of the right to equality will seldom extend to those who flaunt society's norms.[55]

The right does however appear to be more helpful in instances where a person's marginalisation relates to some inherent or immutable personal feature or trait, rather than to wilful unlawful conduct. In this respect, the Constitutional Court's jurisprudence pertaining to discrimination against foreign nationals may be of some assistance to marginalised foreigners in Johannesburg. In 1997, the Court held in *Larbi-Odam* v. *Member of the Executive Council, (North-West Province)* that, despite citizenship or nationality not being listed in the interim Constitution as grounds in relation to which unfair discrimination was prohibited, the State could not unfairly exclude permanent residents from employment, since such discrimination diminished individual dignity in a similar manner as discrimination on a prohibited ground, whilst its impact on applicants was similarly severe. The Court thus held that it was unconstitutional for the North-West provincial government to distinguish between citizens and permanent residents in the allocation and renewal of permanent teaching posts.[56]

That the right to equality can protect foreign nationals also in the enjoyment of socio-economic rights was affirmed by the majority of the Constitutional Court in *Khosa and Mahlaule* v. *Minister of Social Development*, where the exclusion of destitute permanent residents of Mozambican origin from eligibility for certain social security grants was found to be unconstitutional, for being in unjustifiable breach of the prohibition on unfair discrimination as well as the right to have access to social security.[57] Described as 'the high-water mark of constitutional jurisprudence on the treatment of foreign nationals living in South Africa' and as 'capturing the constitutional vision of an inclusive society based on dignity, equality and freedom',[58] the *Khoza* decision signalled that distinctions between nationals and permanent residents in relation to legislatively bestowed socio-economic benefits would rarely be tenable.

However, like *Larbi-Odam* before it, *Khoza* was decided specifically in relation to permanent residents, the category of 'legal' foreigners most closely assimilated with South African citizens. Indeed, the judgment explicitly affirmed that its reasoning did not necessarily extend to illegal immigrants (or, indeed, to other categories of legal foreigners), since there might be 'compelling reasons why social benefits should not be made available to all who are in South Africa, irrespective of their immigration status'.[59] Legality thus appears to be a threshold requirement for enforcing the right to equality in South Africa,[60] which means that the right is effectively beyond the reach of Johannesburg's many undocumented foreign inhabitants who, as the discussion above showed, arguably suffer some of its most egregious infringements.

In fact, the Constitutional Court's subsequent judgment in *Union of Refugee Women* v. *Director: Private Security Regulatory Authority* illustrates that there are also limits to the extent to which legal foreigners can avail themselves of the protection of the right to equality. In this case, the Court upheld regulations proclaimed pursuant to the 2001 Private Security Industry Regulation Act, in terms of which only citizens and permanent residents could register themselves (and thereby, legally work) as security guards. One implication of this restriction was that other migrants could not work as 'official' car guards at shopping centres and the like, which is a major form of casual employment for poorer people in South African cities. Dismissing a challenge against this restriction by a group of 'legal' refugees, a majority of the Court found that the Regulations' legitimate purpose of establishing the 'trustworthiness' of security guards was fairly and rationally connected to the restriction, since such trustworthiness was easier to establish in relation to citizens and permanent residents.[61]

Notwithstanding a dissenting opinion that excluding refugees from employment on this basis reinforced harmful stereotypes about them and exacerbated their significant economic vulnerability (which, to the dissenting judges, meant that the regulation discriminated unfairly against refugees),[62] the majority of the Court remained of the opinion that the discrimination was not unfair, not least because refugees could apply for an exemption from the regulations in limited circumstances and could, in any event, eventually overcome the restrictions on their potential employment in the industry by obtaining permanent resident status.[63] Clearly viewing the degree of foreigners' assimilation into mainstream South African society as a legitimate measurement of the extent to which they can avail themselves of constitutional rights, the judgment's departure from the finding in *Larbi-Odam* (which dealt with more middle-class forms of employment) has led Cathi Albertyn to remark that 'it is in access to jobs and resources for the poor that the divisions between "insider" and "outsider" are most keenly felt'.[64] Indeed, the judgment appears to mirror the blurring of lines between poorer 'legal' immigrants and their illegal counterparts on the streets of Johannesburg, and signals that the protection of the right to equality does not extend to marginalisation experienced in the course of competition for resources within marginalised urban space.

Public presence

Since one of the main purposes of law and bylaw enforcement against marginal occupants of urban space is to remove them from public view, it is unsurprising that legal resistance against urban marginalisation often takes the form of asserting a right to be present in public space and to perform marginalised actions there.

That the removal of 'unwanted' persons from the city is unjust has been recognised by South African courts as far back as 1979, when the Natal Provincial Division of the (then) Supreme Court found that it was unlawful for the Durban City Council to order the removal of an unemployable epilepsy sufferer from the city, in terms of apartheid-era legislation authorising such removal of 'idle', unemployed black people from urban areas.[65] Given that the Constitution guarantees a right of freedom of movement, arguably precisely in response to such apartheid-era restrictions on black urban presence, similar blanket legislative or regulatory bans of particular people from cities would most likely never pass constitutional muster.

Yet, municipal bylaws, in Johannesburg as elsewhere, prohibit purposeless 'loitering' in public space, and are regularly used to harass marginalised inhabitants attempting to enact the right to the city. A particularly poignant example of this arose in the aftermath of the 2008 xenophobic violence in Johannesburg, when approximately 3000 inner-city foreign migrants sought refuge in the Central Methodist Church on the corner of Pritchard and Small streets, which has long functioned as a shelter for homeless migrants.[66] With the church's infrastructure simply unable to cope with the sheer number of desperate people seeking refuge there, they spilt over into the immediate vicinity, onto the pavements in front of the Joburg High Court and into the pedestrianised retail artery of the Small Street Mall. Following a legion of complaints from judges at the court and businesses in the vicinity, and legal action from the advocates' chambers adjacent to the church (all concerned with the negative impact of the influx on the urban environment, especially in relation to ablution facilities), the City responded with a Metropolitan Police raid on the church and the arrest and detention of more than 350 foreigners for 'loitering' in the vicinity.[67]

Given significant media coverage of the events, the arrests drew the attention of human rights NGOs, two of which (Section 27 and the Legal Resources Centre) instituted legal proceedings asserting, among other things, that the loitering bylaws in terms of which the arrests were carried out were unconstitutional. A settlement was reached before the case was heard, however, and the migrants were released.[68] While this was an undeniably positive outcome and attested to the power of rights-based litigation to resist the removal of unwanted persons from city space, it is nevertheless lamentable that the arguments on the constitutionality of the bylaws were never heard. The bylaws remain in operation today.

Two decisions of the Cape High Court, pertaining to the presence of urban outcasts in Cape Town's public space, contain important indicators for the outcome of possible similar future challenges in Joburg. In *Victoria & Alfred Waterfront* v. *Police Commissioner, Western Cape*, the Court effectively prohibited the Victoria & Alfred Waterfront (a well-known privately owned and managed retail and entertainment precinct consisting of several shopping complexes, tourist attractions and the outdoor spaces in-between) from barring two homeless persons from begging from customers in the outdoor sections of its premises.

Following well-known Indian jurisprudence in terms of which the right to life includes the right to make a livelihood in public, subject to reasonable regulatory restrictions aimed at upholding the competing rights of others to the same space, the Court found that, in situations such as the present where the right to life (including the right to a livelihood) had to be balanced against property rights, the latter had to give way.[69] It rejected the argument that the Waterfront was entitled to have the beggars removed on the basis that it was legally private property, holding that the Waterfront functioned as public space and was for all intents and purposes a suburb of Cape Town, given its otherwise unhindered accessibility to members of the public and the fact that it contained a number of public services (such as a post office and the embarkation point for boat transport to Robben Island). In light of South Africa's history of excluding black inhabitants from access to urban areas, and in light of the fact that removing beggars from the Waterfront's public spaces would also significantly limit their right to freedom of movement, the Court found that the owners' right to exclude unwanted persons from their property was limited by the Waterfront's public character.[70]

Doubtlessly a significant judicial affirmation of the right to the city and a powerful counterweight to the privatisation of public space,[71] the *V&A Waterfront* judgment nevertheless acknowledges that there are limits to the exercise of the right to public presence. While allowing the beggars to be present at the Waterfront and to beg from customers in the public spaces there, the Court nevertheless interdicted them from 'unlawfully causing harm to visitors and businesses situate[d] at the Victoria & Alfred Waterfront …, in particular, by remaining on the premises of a restaurant after having been instructed by the person in charge to leave those premises' and from 'unlawfully assaulting, intimidating or threatening any employee and/or official of the [Waterfront]'.[72] This is in keeping with the comparative Indian jurisprudence[73] as well as with the recent finding of the Constitutional Court in *South African Transport and Allied Workers Union* v. *Garvas* that it is reasonable and justifiable to limit the exercise of the right to peaceful assembly and protest in public space where such limitation is aimed at protecting the physical integrity, lives and livelihoods of others who make use of the space.[74]

A similarly bold judicial vindication of the right to (public presence in) the city was to follow in *SWEAT* v. *Minister of Safety and Security*, where an NGO representing the interests of street-based sex workers in Cape Town approached the High Court for an interdict against the police, who routinely arrested sex workers on loitering and other bylaw contravention charges, without any intention to charge or prosecute them, only to later release them without charge. The Court found that the only purposes of the arrests were to harass the sex workers and to drive them out of public space. This was held to be a constitutionally unacceptable form of social control, in that it unjustifiably infringed the rights to dignity and to freedom and security of the person.[75] The Court accordingly issued an interdict against the continuation of the practice.

Both the *SWEAT* and *V&A Waterfront* judgments dealt with livelihood-generating practices that are regarded as socially unacceptable and that are outlawed or legally restricted. While there are traces of the development of a right to a livelihood in *V&A Waterfront*, the focus of both judgments is on the respective rights of beggars and sex workers to be present in public space. This meant that neither judgment pronounced on the constitutionality of legal restrictions on beggars or sex workers' particular ways of making a living. Indeed, both judgments appear to accept that such restrictions are legitimate, although both hold that the enforcement of such restrictions may not have the effect of driving people out of public space.

Dignity and (lawful) livelihood

The above discussion showed that the effect of viewing certain people or livelihood practices (such as undocumented foreigners and unlicensed street traders) as 'illegal', is to also taint those similarly situated persons who in fact do comply with the law with the stigma of illegality. 'Legal' members of socially marginalised groups such as non-nationals and informal traders therefore often share the burden of being targeted in law enforcement drives aimed at their 'illegal' counterparts and constantly face the possibility of their rights being scaled back in efforts to address the social 'problems' they are said to represent. Conversely, these 'legal' members of marginalised groups are in a better position to resist their marginalisation and to legally fortify their right to the city. As in the case of the right not to be unfairly discriminated against, the judicial development of a right to an urban livelihood has therefore been confined to the contexts of legally compliant urban inhabitants.

Section 22 of the 1996 Constitution determines that 'every citizen has the right to choose their trade or profession freely', and qualifies this right by adding that 'the practice of a trade, occupation or profession may be regulated by law'. The right is therefore of no assistance to foreign nationals and provides limited ammunition to those, such as informal traders, whose ability to make a livelihood is subjected to significant regulatory restrictions. In cases where marginalised inhabitants have attempted to legally assert a right to a livelihood, courts have therefore supplemented their analysis of section 22 with resort to other constitutional rights, notably the right to dignity.

The parameters of a dignity-based right to a marginal livelihood have crystallised through several legal challenges brought by refugees and asylum seekers against laws and regulations seeking to restrict their ability to work. In *Minister of Home Affairs* v. *Watchenuka*, the Supreme Court of Appeal (SCA) found that it was unconstitutional to completely prohibit refugees and asylum seekers from seeking employment in South Africa. While acknowledging that people's choice of profession may rightly be limited in line with section 22 of the Constitution, the Court held that the right to engage in productive work formed an important part of the right to dignity and that, in cases where work was sought as a means for survival, a prohibition on work was 'not merely a restriction upon the person's capacity for self-fulfilment, but a restriction upon his or her ability to live without positive humiliation and degradation'.[76] Whereas the Court emphasised that restrictions on this element of the right to dignity may be constitutional where they satisfied the requirements set out in the Constitution's general limitations clause, it found that a blanket prohibition on employment of refugees and asylum seekers constituted a material, and unjustifiable, encroachment on the right to dignity and was accordingly not constitutionally tenable.[77]

The Constitutional Court's subsequent judgment in *Union of Refugee Women*, however, did not embroider upon the SCA's notion of a dignity-based right to livelihood and instead considered the question of a right to work solely within the parameters of section 22 of the Constitution. In addition to dismissing the unfair discrimination charge against the legal prohibition on the employment of refugees and asylum seekers in the security industry, a majority of the Court held that the prohibition also did not violate section 22. Moreover, since section 22 allowed for regulatory restrictions on the practice of particular trades, occupations and professions, such restrictions were held not to constitute a diminution of individual dignity to the extent that they would amount to unfair discrimination.[78] While not detracting from *Watchenuka*'s finding that a blanket prohibition on employment of refugees or asylum seekers would be unconstitutional, the *Union of Refugee Women* judgment thus made it clear that legal restrictions on the nature of such employment would nevertheless be in order.

More recently, the SCA again invoked the right to dignity to carve out a minimal entitlement to lawful self-employment from the Constitutional Court's restrictive interpretation of the right to work. In *Somali Association of South Africa* v. *Limpopo Department of Economic Affairs*, organisations of Somali and Ethiopian traders challenged the practice of the Limpopo police to shut down their spaza shops and other businesses in and around Musina. It transpired that, while the Limpopo provincial government initially issued trade permits to Ethiopian and Somali refugees and asylum seekers in the province, it pandered to prevailing xenophobic sentiments among citizens and instructed the police to close down all Ethiopian and Somali establishments, regardless of whether they were in possession of permits. Somalis and Ethiopians were further denied access to the bureaucratic process through which to obtain or renew trade permits.

The SCA found that this practice was unconstitutional. While acknowledging that the practice of a trade may be limited in terms of section 22 of the Constitution, the Court found that the provision did not extinguish a right to seek lawful employment and that, when it comes to survival, the right to dignity entitled those who are unable to secure paid employment to 'advance a case' for the granting of a trade licence in order to ward off starvation, humiliation and degradation. It was therefore neither constitutionally permissible to bar Ethiopian and Somali traders from acquiring trade permits in accordance with the law, nor lawful to shut down businesses for which trade permits had duly been issued.[79]

Given the close links between Somali and Ethiopian traders operating in towns and townships across South Africa and their 'trade headquarters' in Johannesburg's ethnic enclaves, the *Somali Association* judgment is also significant to informal Ethiopian and Somali businesses in Joburg, especially as these traders are increasingly bearing the brunt of xenophobic vigilantism across the city and are facing increasing opposition from South African-born informal traders in the inner city, who are demanding that the Joburg Metropolitan Council givers preference to locals in the granting of informal trade licences.[80]

But Joburg was itself to be the stage for legal resistance against the suppression of licensed informal trade, on a far larger scale than that which sparked the litigation in Musina. In late 2013, the Joburg Metropolitan Council launched 'Operation Clean Sweep', a mayoral initiative to 'clean up' the inner city of undesirable inhabitants and activities. A central part of the operation, which was initially supported by both organised business as well as 'legal' informal traders' organisations in the city, was the removal of all 'illegal' traders from the CBD. Implemented by the Metropolitan Police with all the gusto and brutality for which they had become notorious,[81] the Operation soon spun out of control. Faced with the artificial distinction between legal and illegal traders and with many falsified or fraudulently issued permits, the City proceeded to remove *all* traders, including those with legal permits, from the streets, to confiscate their wares and to prohibit them from returning.

Outraged traders initially negotiated with the City, which undertook to 'verify' the legality of all traders and to allow those who had been duly 'verified' to return to their stalls. But the verification process stalled, and it emerged that the City intended either to relocate or to retract the permits of most 'legal' traders.[82] As the devastating social costs of Operation Clean Sweep (in terms of which a great number of households had suddenly been deprived of their only source of income) mounted, the South African Informal Traders Forum (SAITF) approached the Socio-Economic Rights Institute (SERI) for assistance and, together with the South African National Traders Association (SANTRA) (which, like SAITF, represents mostly 'legal' traders in the inner city), instituted legal proceedings against the City. After an unsuccessful attempt to interdict the City from continuing with the Operation in the Joburg High Court,[83] the traders approached the Constitutional Court, which granted an interim interdict prohibiting the City from interfering with lawful trading by licensed informal traders and ordered that lawful traders could return to their stalls, pending a final decision on the legal merits of Operation Clean Sweep. [84]

In a subsequent judgment providing reasons for this order, the Court affirmed that the City's actions impacted on the traders' rights to dignity (understood as encompassing a right to a livelihood) and freedom of trade, as well as on the basic socio-economic rights of their children.[85] However, its order was not based on a finding that any of these rights had been breached. This is because, since the City's actions were plainly and by its own admission illegal (being in contravention of its own trade bylaws as well as of the relevant provisions of the Businesses Act),[86] it was not necessary for the Court to conduct a constitutional rights inquiry. Instead, it simply affirmed that the 'legal' traders had an 'undisputed right' to occupy their designated trading spots, in terms of the prevailing bylaws.[87] Given that they had no other effective way off asserting this right against the City, whose illegal actions left them destitute, an interdict against the City was regarded as an appropriate remedy.[88]

However, much as the Court lambasted the City for outrightly flouting the law and for its cynical approach to the traders,[89] it appeared to endorse the urban management objectives behind Operation Clean Sweep, going as far as to call these 'laudable'.[90] Its condemnation of the City therefore appeared to be limited to the manner of Clean Sweep's implementation, which was held to be flawed specifically because it meted out the same treatment to both 'legal' and 'illegal' traders. Indeed, the Court stated that 'it is open to the City to use all lawful means to combat illegal trading and other criminal conduct', provided this did not 'cause harm to lawful, if not vulnerable, traders'.[91]

This said, the *SAITF* judgment was certainly 'an unequivocal affirmation of the dignity of street traders in the face of unwarranted and brutal exercises of State power',[92] and quite literally affirmed their right to the city. Both legal and illegal traders returned to the streets of the CBD in the aftermath of the judgment (some on the same day), meaning that the judgment's effect was to derail the implementation of Operation Clean Sweep even beyond its narrow confines.[93]

The judgment also appeared to have positive policy spin-offs for the traders. The City revised its informal trade policy, taking a somewhat more enabling approach to street trade and committing to increasing the amount of designated space for 'legal trade'. However, the policy continued to distinguish between 'legal' and 'illegal' trade and to restrict 'legal' trade to limited spaces within the CBD. It also pledged to rigorously enforce bylaws against illegal traders (albeit this time in strict formal compliance with the letter of the law as well as the terms of the *SAITF* judgment) as well as to enforce immigration laws against traders who were also 'illegal' immigrants.[94]

Meanwhile, much as the judgment appeared to energise SAITF and SANTRA and to increase both their level of organisation and their clout in the eyes of traders, other traders' organisations and City officials, it also appeared to significantly stifle dialogue between them and the City. City Officials, who particularly resent the traders' relationship with SERI (against whom there is significant hostility across all official governance structures in Joburg) are reported to be significantly more circumspect and hostile in their dealings with traders than before. In particular, it appears that the City disbanded its former engagement structures with traders and now negotiates with them only in instances where it is legally obliged to do so, and only when its lawyers are present.[95] The *SAITF* judgment thus seemed to have overly legalised relationships between the City and its marginalised inhabitants, hence stifling the dialogic elements of the right to the city much as it ensconced a right to physical presence in Johannesburg. Reports from the streets, meanwhile, showed that not much had changed in relation to the manner that Metropolitan Police enforced the bylaws. Indeed, there were indications that the *SAITF* judgment had the effect of increasing police officers' hostility towards traders.[96]

This notwithstanding, the *SAITF* case clearly illustrates that the law can be a powerful ally to those marginalised urban inhabitants who are able to operate within its confines. In early 2015, this was underlined by a judgment of the Durban High Court in the matter of *Makwicana* v. *eThekwini Municipality*, which found that, while cities were compelled to regulate informal trade in the interests of public health and safety, bylaws allowing for the impoundment and confiscation of permit-holding traders' goods were unconstitutional, in that they were irrational, and discriminated unfairly against traders on the basis of their race and socio-economic status.[97] The eThekwini municipality was accordingly ordered to pay compensation to a permit-holding informal trader whose wares were unconstitutionally impounded and subsequently disposed of by police.[98] Importantly, the Court also found that future (amended) bylaws had to provide for some form of engagement or dispute resolution mechanism in terms of which disputes between traders and the city over the regulation of informal trade could be resolved.[99]

Reflections

This chapter has shown the centrality of the law in creating marginal lives and identities and in relegating these to marginalised space. By declaring the physical presence or activities of certain urban inhabitants 'illegal', the law at once alienates them from mainstream society, stigmatises them and renders them vulnerable to not only its own punitive power, but also to the lawless actions of others.

This was powerfully illustrated in early 2015, when xenophobic violence once again broke out in Joburg. While authorities' initial response was to deploy the police and the armed forces in ostensible defence of foreigners in the city, this was soon supplemented by raids *on* foreigners (especially in the known immigrant enclaves of Hillbrow, Mayfair and Jeppe), complete with arrests of those without documentation, in an attempt to be seen as upholding the law in the interests of 'law-abiding' citizens.[100]

It further appears that 'illegality' significantly restricts the protective power of legal rights. Much as most constitutional rights theoretically vest in persons regardless of the legality of their actions, legality appears to be a near absolute threshold for the exercise of legal rights, so that 'illegal' persons are typically deprived of the 'right to have rights'.[101]

The human rights jurisprudence emanating from South African courts largely confirms this. Courts appear reluctant to protect the rights of those whose vulnerability is perceived to result from their own violation of the law, and tend to emphasise the legal compliance and social assimilation of those whose rights *are* upheld. Furthermore, where the rights of marginalised inhabitants are protected, such protection tends to take the form of ensuring that authorities abide to the letter of the law in acting against them, except in rare instances where laws themselves are declared unconstitutional. For those who lack the right to have rights, protection or respite as a result of legal rights-assertion mostly occurs incidentally (as when 'illegal' traders disadvantaged by Operation Clean Sweep unintentionally benefited from the successful rights-assertion by their 'legal' counterparts).

The exception to this trend seems to be instances where law enforcement against marginalised persons is explicitly targeted at driving them out of public spaces. Loath to uphold practices recalling apartheid's racist restrictions on entry into cities, courts appear intolerant of efforts to remove people from the city, much as they ostensibly support the regulation of human activity within public space. This suggests that relying on a 'right' to public presence (through invoking the right to dignity in conjunction with, for instance, the right to freedom of movement) works better as a legal resistance strategy against marginalisation than more conventional strategies, such as relying on the prohibition against unfair discrimination. While this does not provide protection against the restriction of lives and livelihoods within public space as long as authorities abide by the law (as illustrated, for instance, by the lack of legal resistance to the City of Johannesburg's 2015 implementation of 'Operation Ke Molao', in terms of which beggars and informal traders were removed from traffic intersections and fined, in strict conformance with road traffic bylaws[102]), it at least enables the right to the city by opening the (physical) space in which to eke out marginalised existences and challenge prevailing urban behaviour codes.

Notes

1 See Gotz and Simone (2003: 134); Murray (2011: 153); Simone (2008: 69–70).
2 See Dinath (2014: 239, 244); Holston (2009: 246); Murray (2011: 153); Simone (2008: 69, 80).
3 See Coggin and Pieterse (2012: 271–272); Waldron (1991: 297–298).
4 See Benit-Gbaffou (2009: 66–68, 74–75); Charlton (2014: 540, 544); Dinath (2014: 232, 243–247); Gotz and Simone (2003: 137–145); Landau (2007: 71); Murray (2008: 7, 16, 25, 155, 208–210, 227; 2011: 153–154, 171, 279–282); Simone 2006: 363; 2008: 69–70). Many 'law abiding' residents are actively complicit in these actions, as will be discussed in Chapter 5.
5 See Benit-Gbaffou (2009: 66–67); Dinath (2014: 238–239); Murray (2011: 150–153, 279–282); Silverman and Zack (2008: 147, 158).
6 See Dinath (2014: 245); Grant and Thompson (2015: 184); Vearey (2010: 40–43).
7 See Dinath (2014: 238; 242–244); Murray (2011: 154–156, 160, 164); Silverman and Zack (2008: 158–159); Simone (2008: 80); Waldron (1991: 297, 315–318); Vearey (2010: 41–46, 49); Zack (2015a: 143–147).
8 Murray (2011: 155). See also Simone (2008: 68–69).
9 Benit-Gbaffou (2009: 68); Meth (2010: 245, 256); Murray (2011: 154–155); Thompson and Grant (2015: 259–260).
10 See Grant and Thompson (2015: 183–186); Holston (2009: 261–262).
11 See Brown (2015: 68–69); Glaser (2015: 139, 141, 143–145, 155); Meth (2010: 241–244, 247–248, 256).
12 See Landau (2007: 71–72); Grant and Thompson (2015: 185).
13 Murray (2011: 150).
14 See Grant and Thompson (2015: 183); Landau (2006a: 126, 130); Murray (2008: 159; 2011: 150–152).
15 It is unsure how many migrants live in Johannesburg, with some estimating that foreigners make up as much as 40 per cent of those who live in the CBD (Grant & Thompson 2015: 182).
16 See Landau (2006a: 65; 2006b: 309, 316, 323); Polzer Ngwato and Jinnah (2014: 392–393); Vearey (2008: 365–366).
17 See Landau (2007: 67); Murray (2011: 153); Polzer Ngwato and Jinnah (2014: 396–397).

18 See Crush and Ramachandran (2015: 31–32); Glaser (2015: 154–155); Grant and Thompson (2015: 182–183); Landau (2007: 64–65); Morris (1998: 1122–1124); Murray (2011: 153–154); Silverman and Zack (2008: 147, 159).
19 See Bloch (2010: 233, 237, 245); Landau (2007: 67); Polzer Ngwato and Jinnah (2014: 392).
20 See Landau (2006a: 132–133; 2006b: 309, 319–320, 323; 2007: 67–68); Murray (2011: 154); Polzer Ngwato and Jinnah (2014: 395–396, 404); Vearey (2008: 365–368).
21 See Vearey (2008: 367–369).
22 See Bloch (2010: 241–242); Landau (2007: 66–67, 70); Morris (1998: 1131); Murray (2011: 154); Vearey (2008: 365).
23 See Landau (2006b: 320); Landau (2007: 67); Willemse (2015: 119); Zack (2015a: 143).
24 See Grant and Thompson (2015: 183, 189); Landau (2006a: 133–134; 2006b: 321; 2007: 68–69); Madsen (2004: 173–174, 179–181, 183); Morris (1998: 1130–1131); Murray (2011: 154, 163); Polzer Ngwato and Jinnah (2014: 396, 403–404); Thompson and Grant (2015: 252); Vearey (2008: 365); Willemse (2015: 126–127); Zack (2015a: 143).
25 See Landau (2006a: 134–135); Murray (2011: 154); Polzer Ngwato and Jinnah (2014: 397); Simone (2008: 76, 78); Zack (2015a: 143–144).
26 See Morris (1999: 261–262); Murray (2011: 164); Richter (2012): The perils of sex work in Johannesburg are considered in more detail in Chapter 6.
27 See Mitchell (2003: 163, 167, 170–172); Waldron (1991: 297–301, 310–318).
28 See generally Charlton (2014: 542–543). On the confiscation of blankets by JMPD, see Nicholson (2014).
29 See for instance City of Johannesburg (2009: 3–6, 10–15, 19–20). While prohibited under apartheid, informal trading in Joburg effectively became legal in the early 1990s, with the passing of the Businesses Act 71 of 1991, s 6A of which allowed for restrictions on such trade by way of municipal bylaws. On the content of the bylaws and the City's attitude towards street traders see, for instance, Dinath (2014: 242–244); Makhetha and Rubin (2014: 532); Murray (2008: 7, 16, 25, 155, 159, 208–210; 2011: 91, 103); Tissington (2009: 5–6, 17–8, 27–29, 33–34); Zack (2015b: 63–66).
30 See Dinath (2014: 243–244); Grant and Thompson (2015: 189); Makhetha and Rubin (2014: 532, 536); Murray (2008: 229, 233); Tissington (2009: 6, 19–20, 39, 55–63).
31 See Benit-Gbaffou (2014: 6, 110–111); Makhetha and Rubin (2014: 536–537).
32 See Grant and Thompson (2015: 183); Makhetha and Rubin (2014: 536–537); Tissington (2009: 54–59).
33 See Murray (2008: 155); Sekhonyane and Dugard (2004: 14–17); Venter (2013: 114–117).
34 See Charlton (2014: 544); Holston (2009: 256); Landau (2007: 71); Vearey (2010: 49, 51); Waldron (1991: 297); Zack (2015a: 147).
35 Holston (2009: 252), see also 260.
36 See Bloch (2010: 237, 245); Murray (2011: 160, 164); Polzer Ngwato and Jinnah (2014: 192–193); Van Marle (2014: 170).
37 See Holston (2009: 261–262).
38 See Coggin and Pieterse (2015: 313); Venter (2013: 114–117).
39 See Charlton (2014: 544); Grant and Thompson (2015: 183–186).
40 See Simone (2008: 68–69); Thompson and Grant (2015: 245).
41 Dinath (2014: 245); Zack (2015a: 132, 147).
42 See Grant and Thompson (2015: 187–189); Le Roux (2014: 498–505); Thompson and Grant (2015: 251–252, 255–256); Zack (2015a: 135–139; 2015b: 68–70).
43 See Grant and Thompson (2015: 189); Thompson and Grant (2015: 255–257); Zack (2015a: 142–143).

44 See Thompson and Grant (2015: 256); Zack (2015a: 141–144, 146).
45 See Grant and Thompson (2015: 190–193); Sadouni (2014: 481–486); Thompson and Grant (2015: 251, 253–254).
46 See Simone (2006: 361–362; 2008: 73).
47 See Gotz and Simone (2003: 132–133); Simone (2008: 75, 81–83); Morris (1999: 90–92, 268–270, 308, 314–319).
48 Morris (1999: 321–322).
49 On coping strategies, behaviour codes and everyday challenges prevailing in Chinatown, see Thompson and Grant (2015: 250, 255–246); Willemse (2015: 119, 126–127). On Fordsburg's Pakistani and Bangladeshi community, see Thompson and Grant (2015: 249, 253–254).
50 See Vearey (2010: 44–49).
51 See Grant and Thompson (2015), contrasting the self-isolation of the Ethiopian and Somali enclaves with the intermingling of immigrants and local South Africans on Yeoville's Rocky street.
52 *President of the Republic of South Africa* v. *Hugo* (1997). See specifically paras 14 (per Goldstone J for the majority), 114 (per O'Regan J, concurring). For discussion, see Pieterse (2008: 404).
53 *Prince* v. *President, Cape Law Society* (2002). See specifically paras 92. 142, where the Court emphasises the appellant's wilful and unrepentant breaking of the law.
54 *S* v. *Jordan* (2002), specifically paras 16. 17. 28 (per Ngcobo J for the majority); 66. 74. 56. 78. 81 (per O'Regan & Sachs JJ, dissenting). The *Jordan* judgment is discussed in more detail in Chapter 6.
55 See Albertyn (2007: 272–273); Pieterse (2008: 403–404, 410–411, 417–418).
56 *Larbi-Odam* v. *Member of the Executive Council, (North-West Province)* (1998), specifically paras 19, 22–25, 30–31, 43–44. See also the earlier similar decision of the Bophuthatswana High Court (in relation to academic staff at tertiary institutions) in *Baloro* v. *University of Bophuthatswana* (1995).
57 *Khosa* v. *Minister of Social Development; Mahlaule* v. *Minister of Social Development* (2004). See specifically paras 42–47, 54, 58–59, 84–55.
58 Albertyn (2008: 183).
59 *Khosa* v. *Minister of Social Development; Mahlaule* v. *Minister of Social Development* (2004: para 58).
60 See Pieterse (2008: 405, 414); Polzer Ngwato and Jinnah (2014: 413).
61 *Union of Refugee Women* v. *Director: Private Security Regulatory Authority* (2007: paras 38–42) (per Kondile AJ for the majority).
62 Ibid., paras 113, 117–118; 122–123 (per Mokgoro and O'Regan JJ, dissenting).
63 Ibid., paras 49–50 (per Kondile J for the majority).
64 Albertyn (2008: 187). See also Pieterse (2008: 405, 414).
65 *In re Dube* (1979).
66 See Murray (2011: 158–159 (on the history of the Central Methodist Church as space of contestation in the Johannesburg CBD), 165–167 (detailing the events described here)).
67 See Consortium for Refugees and Migrants in South Africa (2009: 35); Kulijan (2010: 37–41). The Pitje Chambers litigation and the complaints of other nearby establishments are discussed in Chapter 5.
68 See Kulijan (2010: 41).
69 *Victoria & Alfred Waterfront* v. *Police Commissioner, Western Cape* (2004: 452B), following *Olga Tellis* v. *Bombay Municipal Corporation* (1986: paras 32–33, 49, 51).
70 *Victoria & Alfred Waterfront* v. *Police Commissioner, Western Cape* (2004: 448I-449A, 450B-C-J, 451 E-I).
71 See Coggin and Pieterse (2012: 272–273).
72 *Victoria & Alfred Waterfront* v. *Police Commissioner, Western Cape* (2004: 453A-B).

73 See *Olga Tellis* v. *Bombay Municipal Corporation* (1986: para 43).
74 *South African Transport & Allied Workers Union* v. *Garvas* (2013: paras 67–68, 84). The *Garvas* judgment upheld restrictions imposed on the right to public protest by s 11(2) of the Regulation of Gatherings Act 205 of 1993, in terms of which organisers of a public protest can under certain circumstances be held liable for damages caused to the property or persons of third parties.
75 *SWEAT* v. *Minister of Safety and Security* (2009: paras 6–9, 11–14, 23, 28, 48, 56–57, 60). The *SWEAT* judgment is discussed in greater detail in Chapter 6.
76 *Minister of Home Affairs* v. *Watchenuka* (2004: para 32). See also paras 27, 30.
77 Ibid., paras 27, 29, 33–37, 39.
78 *Union of Refugee Women* v. *Director: Private Security Regulatory Authority* (2007: paras 46–47, 54, 66) (per Kondile AJ for the majority).
79 *Somali Association of South Africa* v. *Limpopo Department of Economic Affairs* (2015: paras 38, 40, 43–46).
80 See Tissington (2009: 54–59).
81 See Beyleveld (2015: 18–19) and authorities cited there; Pieterse (2017); Thompson and Grant (2015: 244); Zack (2015b: 66–68, 71–73).
82 See Benit-Gbaffou (2014: 6); *SAITF* v. *City of Johannesburg* (2014: paras 6–10).
83 For discussion of the High Court's refusal to entertain the matter, see Pieterse (2017).
84 *SAITF* v. *City of Johannesburg* (2014: para 1).
85 Ibid., para 31. See also para 11.
86 Ibid., paras 26–28.
87 Ibid., para 25. Indeed, the Court felt that the City was so obviously in the wrong that it was unlikely that Operation Clean Sweep would ultimately be declared to have been legally permissible in the High Court. Ibid., para 28.
88 Ibid., paras 21, 24, 29–30, 36–37.
89 Ibid., paras 26–28, 33–34, 36.
90 Ibid., para 7. See also para 32.
91 *SAITF* v. *City of Johannesburg* (2014: para 33). See also paras 4–7, as well as Beyleveld (2015: 6, 21); Pieterse (2017).
92 Pieterse (2017: 15).
93 Benit-Gbaffou (2014: 6–7).
94 Benit-Gbaffou (2014: 3–4); Pieterse (2017); Zack (2015b: 67). See also City of Johannesburg (2013: vii, 13).
95 See Benit-Gbaffou (2014: 7–8, 110–114, 194).
96 See Benit-Gbaffou (2014: 79–80); Myambo (2014); Pieterse (2017).
97 *Makwicana* v. *eThekwini Municipality* (2015: paras 72, 75, 92, 100–106, 115–116, 121–125, 135).
98 Ibid., para 149.
99 Ibid., paras 72, 139–144.
100 See Essa and Patel (2015); Nicholson (2015).
101 See Bloch (2010: 233, 245); Landau (2007: 65); Murray (2011: 160).
102 See Webster (2015).

References

Albertyn, C., 2007. 'Substantive equality and transformation in South Africa', *South African Journal of Human Rights* 23(2), 253–276.

Albertyn, C., 2008. 'Beyond citizenship: Human rights and democracy'. In: Hassim, S., Kupe, T. & Worby, E. (eds.), *Go Home or Die Here: Violence, Xenophobia and the Reinvention of Difference in South Africa*, pp. 175–187. Johannesburg: Wits University Press.

Baloro v. *University of Bophuthatswana*, 1995. Decision of the Bophuthatswana Supreme Court, reported as 1995 (4) SA 197 (BSC).

Benit-Gbaffou, C., 2009. 'Who control the streets? Crime, "communities" and the state in post-apartheid Johannesburg'. In: Locatelli, F. & Nugent, P. (eds.), *African Cities: Competing Claims on Urban Space*, pp. 55–79. Leiden, Boston: Brill.

Benit-Gbaffou, C. (ed.), 2014. *A Political Landscape of Street Trader Organisations in Inner City Johannesburg, Post Operation Clean Sweep*. Johannesburg: Centre for Urbanism and Built Environment Studies.

Beyleveld, A., 2015. *Regulating Informal Trade in Johannesburg: The Intersection between the Freedom of Trade and Socio-economic Rights*. Unpublished LLM research report, University of the Witwatersrand, Johannesburg.

Bloch, A., 2010. 'The right to rights? Undocumented migrants from Zimbabwe living in South Africa', *Sociology* 44(2), 233–250.

Brown, J., 2015. *South Africa's Insurgent Citizens: On Dissent and the Possibility of Politics*. Johannesburg: Jacana.

Businesses Act, 71 of 1991.

Charlton, S., 2014. 'Waste pickers/informal recyclers'. In: Harrison, P., Gotz, G., Todes, A., & Wray, C. (eds.), *Changing Space, Changing City: Johannesburg After Apartheid*, pp. 539–545. Johannesburg: Wits University Press.

City of Johannesburg, 2009. *Informal Trading Policy for the City of Johannesburg*.

City of Johannesburg, 2013. *Inner City Transformation Roadmap*.

Coggin, T. & Pieterse, M., 2012. 'Rights and the city: An exploration of the interaction between socio-economic rights and the city', *Urban Forum* 23(3), 257–278.

Coggin, T. & Pieterse, M., 2015. 'A right to transport? Moving towards a rights-based approach to mobility in the city', *South African Journal of Human Rights* 31(3), 294–314.

Consortium for Refugees and Migrants in South Africa, 2009. *Protecting Refugees, Asylum Seekers and Immigrants in South Africa*. Johannesburg: CoRMSA.

Constitution of the Republic of South Africa, 1996 (Act 108 of 1996).

Crush, J. & Ramachandran, S., 2015. 'Doing business with xenophobia'. In: Crush, J., Chikanda, A. & Skinner, C. (eds.), *Mean Streets: Migration, Xenophobia and Informality in South Africa*, pp. 25–59. Cape Town: South African Migration Project.

Dinath, Y., 2014. 'Between fixity and flux: Grappling with transcience and permanence in the inner city'. In Harrison, P., Gotz, G., Todes, A., & Wray, C. (eds.), *Changing Space, Changing City: Johannesburg After Apartheid*, pp. 232–251. Johannesburg: Wits University Press.

Essa, A. & Patel, K., 2015. 'Foreigners targeted in massive police raid in S Africa', aljazeera.com, 28 April 2015, from www.aljazeera.com.

Glaser, D., 2015. 'Uncooperative masses as a problem for substantive and participatory theories of democracy: The cases of "people's power" (1984–6) and the "xenophobia" (2008) in South Africa'. In: Benit-Gbaffou, C. (ed.), *Popular Politics in South African Cities: Unpacking Community Participation*, pp. 139–170. Cape Town: HSRC Press.

Gotz, G. & Simone, A., 2003. 'On belonging and becoming in African cities'. In: Tomlinson, R., Beauregard, R.A., Bremner, L. & Mangcu, X. (eds.), *Emerging Johannesburg: Perspectives on the Postapartheid City*, pp. 123–147. New York, London: Routledge.

Grant, R. & Thompson, D., 2015. 'City on edge: Immigrant businesses and the right to urban space in inner-city Johannesburg', *Urban Geography* 36(2), 181–200.

Holston, J., 2009. 'Insurgent citizenship in an era of global urban peripheries', *City & Society* 21(2), 245–267.

In re Dube, 1979. Decision of the Natal Division of the Supreme Court, reported as 1979 (3) SA 820 (N).

Khosa v. *Minister of Social Development; Mahlaule* v. *Minister of Social Development*, 2004. Decision of the South African Constitutional Court, reported as 2004 (6) SA 505 (CC).

Kulijan, C., 2010. 'Making the invisible visible: A story of the Central Methodist Church', *The Salon* 3(1), 36–44.

Landau, L.B., 2006a. 'Transplants and transients: Idioms of belonging and dislocation in inner-city Johannesburg', *African Studies Review* 49(2), 125–145.

Landau, L.B., 2006b. 'Protection and dignity in Johannesburg: Shortcomings of South Africa's urban refugee policy', *Journal of Refugee Studies* 19(3), 308–327.

Landau, L.B., 2007. 'Discrimination and development? Immigration, urbanisation and sustainable livelihoods in Johannesburg', *Development Southern Africa* 24(1), 61–76.

Larbi-Odam v. *Member of the Executive Council, (North-West Province)*, 1998. Decision of the South African Constitutional Court, reported as 1998 (1) SA 745 (CC).

Le Roux, H., 2014. 'The Ethiopian quarter'. In: Harrison, P., Gotz, G., Todes, A., & Wray, C. (eds.), *Changing Space, Changing City: Johannesburg after Apartheid*, pp. 498–505. Johannesburg: Wits University Press.

Madsen, M.L., 2004. 'Living for home: Policing immorality among undocumented migrants in Johannesburg', *African Studies* 63(2), 173–192.

Makhetha, P. & Rubin, M., 2014. 'Inner-city street traders: Legality and spatial practice'. In: Harrison, P., Gotz, G., Todes, A., & Wray, C. (eds.), *Changing Space, Changing City: Johannesburg after Apartheid*, pp. 532–538. Johannesburg: Wits University Press.

Makwicana v. *eThekwini Municipality*, 2015. Decision of the Durban High Court, reported as 2015 (3) SA 165 (KZD).

Meth, P., 2010. 'Unsettling insurgency: Reflections on women's insurgent practices in South Africa', *Planning Theory & Practice* 11(2), 241–263.

Minister of Home Affairs v. *Watchenuka*, 2004. Decision of the Supreme Court of Appeal, reported as [2004] 1 All SA 21 (SCA).

Mitchell, D., 2003. *The Right to the City: Social Justice and the Fight for Public Space*. New York: Guilford Press.

Morris, A., 1998. '"Our fellow Africans make our lives hell": The lives of Congolese and Nigerians living in Johannesburg', *Ethnic & Racial Studies* 21(6), 1116–1136.

Morris, A., 1999. *Bleakness & Light: Inner-city Transition in Hillbrow, Johannesburg*. Johannesburg: Wits University Press.

Murray, M.J., 2008. *Taming the Disorderly City: The Spatial Landscape of Johannesburg after Apartheid*. Ithaca, London: Cornell University Press.

Murray, M.J., 2011. *City of Extremes: The Spatial Politics of Johannesburg*. Durham, London: Duke University Press.

Myambo, R.R., 2014. 'Joburg's street traders: Swept into a corner', *The Con*, 8 October 2014, from www.theconmag.co.za.

Nicholson, G., 2014. 'Street life: Joburg homeless face cruel, cold, blanket-less nights', *Daily Maverick*, 9 July 2014, from www.dailymaverick.co.za.

Nicholson, G., 2015. 'Freedom day? SANDF conducts Johannesburg stop-and-search-patrols', *Daily Maverick*, 27 April 2015, from www.dailymaverick.co.za.

Olga Tellis v. *Bombay Municipal Corporation*, 1986. Decision of the Indian Supreme Court, reported as 1986 AIR 180 SC.

Pieterse, M., 2008. 'Finding for the applicant? Individual equality plaintiffs and group-based disadvantage', *South African Journal of Human Rights* 24(3), 397–424.

Pieterse, M., 2017. 'Rights, regulation and bureaucratic impact: The impact of human rights litigation on the regulation of informal trade in Johannesburg, South Africa', *Potchefstroom Electronic Law Journal* 20, 1–28.

Polzer Ngwato, T. & Jinnah, Z., 2014. 'Migrants and mobilisation around socio-economic rights'. In: Langford, M., Cousins, B., Dugard, J. & Madlingozi, T. (eds.), *Socio-economic Rights in South Africa: Symbols or Substance?*, pp. 389–420. Cambridge, UK: Cambridge University Press.

President of the Republic of South Africa v. *Hugo*, 1997. Decision of the South African Constitutional Court, reported as 1997 (4) SA 1 (CC).

Prince v. *President, Cape Law Society*, 2002. Decision of the South African Constitutional Court, reported as 2002 (2) SA 794 (CC).

Private Security Industry Regulation Act, 56 of 2001.

Refugees Act, 130 of 1998.

Regulation of Gatherings Act, 205 of 1993.

Richter, M., 2012. 'Johannesburg's "vendors of vice" – from Frenchfontein to Hillbrow: Female sex work, migration and infection control (1868–2012)'. Unpublished paper presented at ACMS Colloquium *Ill People or Sick Cities? Mobility and Access to Health in South African Cities*, 3 October 2012.

S v. *Jordan*, 2002. Decision of the South African Constitutional Court, reported as 2002 (6) SA 642 (CC).

Sadouni, S., 2014. 'Being an immigrant and facing uncertainty in Johannesburg: The case of Somalis'. In Harrison, P., Gotz, G., Todes, A., & Wray, C. (eds.), *Changing Space, Changing City: Johannesburg After Apartheid*, pp. 481–486. Johannesburg: Wits University Press.

Sekhonyane, M. & Dugard, J., 2004. 'A violent legacy: The taxi industry and government at loggerheads', *SA Crime Quarterly* 10(1), 13–18.

Sexual Offenses Act, 23 of 1957.

Silverman, M. & Zack, T., 2008. 'Housing delivery, the urban crisis and xenophobia'. In: Hassim, S., Kupe, T. & Worby, E. (eds.), *Go Home or Die Here: Violence, Xenophobia and the Reinvention of Difference in South Africa*, pp. 147–159. Johannesburg: Wits University Press.

Simone, A., 2006. 'Pirate towns: Reworking social and symbolic infrastructures in Johannesburg and Douala', *Urban Studies* 43(2), 357–370.

Simone, A., 2008. 'People as infrastructure: Intersecting fragments in Johannesburg'. In: Nutall, S. & Mbembe, A. (eds.), *Johannesburg: The Elusive Metropolis*, pp. 68–90. Johannesburg: Wits University Press.

Somali Association of South Africa v. *Limpopo Department of Economic Affairs*, 2015. Decision of the Supreme Court of Appeal, reported as 2015 (1) SA 151 (SCA).

South African Informal Traders Forum v. *City of Johannesburg*, 2014. Decision of the South African Constitutional Court, reported as 2014 (4) SA 371 (CC).

South African Transport and Allied Workers Union v. *Garvas*, 2013. Decision of the Constitutional Court of South Africa, reported as 2013 (1) SA 83 (CC).

SWEAT v. *Minister of Safety and Security*, 2009. Decision by the Western Cape High Court, Cape Town, reported as 2009 (2) SACR 417 (WCC).

Thompson, D. & Grant, R., 2015. 'Enclaves on edge: Strategy and tactics in immigrant business spaces of Johannesburg', *Urban Forum* 26(3), 243–262.

Tissington, K., 2009. *The Business of Survival: Informal Trading in Inner City Johannesburg*. Centre for Applied Legal Studies Research Report, Johannesburg.

Union of Refugee Women v. *Director: Private Security Regulatory Authority*, 2007. Decision of the South African Constitutional Court, reported as 2007 (4) SA 395 (CC).

Van Marle, K., 2014. 'Revisioning space, justice and belonging in the capital city of Pretoria/Tshwane', *De Jure* 47(2), 163–174.

Vearey, J., 2008. 'Migration, access to ART, and survivalist livelihood strategies in Johannesburg', *African Journal of AIDS Research* 7(3), 361–374.

Vearey, J., 2010. 'Hidden spaces and urban health: Exploring the tactics of rural migrants navigating the city of gold', *Urban Forum* 21(1), 37–54.

Venter, C., 2013. 'The lurch towards formalisation: Lessons from the implementation of BRT in Johannesburg, South Africa', *Research in Transportation Economics* 39(1), 114–120.

Victoria & Alfred Waterfront v. *Police Commissioner, Western Cape*, 2004. Decision of the Cape High Court, reported as 2004 (4) SA 444 (C).

Waldron, J., 1991. 'Homelessness and the issue of freedom', *UCLA Law Review* 39(1), 295–323.

Webster, D., 2015. 'Clean sweep of the poor is not constitutional', *Mail & Guardian*, 17 April 2015, from www.mg.co.za.

Willemse, L., 2015. 'The role of economic factors and Guanxi networks in the success of Chinese shops in Johannesburg'. In Crush, J., Chikanda, A. & Skinner, C. (eds.), *Mean Streets: Migration, Xenophobia and Informality in South Africa*, pp. 113–131. Cape Town: South African Migration Project.

Zack, T., 2015a. '"Jeppe" – where low-end globalisation, ethnic entrepreneurialism and the arrival city meet', *Urban Forum* 26(2), 131–150.

Zack, T., 2015b. 'Making an area hot: Interrupting trade in an ethnic enclave in Johannesburg's inner city'. In: Crush, J., Chikanda, A. & Skinner, C. (eds.), *Mean Streets: Migration, Xenophobia and Informality in South Africa*, pp. 60–77. Cape Town: South African Migration Project.

5 Privileged struggles

Property, lifestyle, business and safety

Introduction

Thus far, this book has focused on the rights-based struggles and place-making activities of Johannesburg's poor and marginalised residents. But this presents only part of the picture. As South Africa's economic capital and the wealthiest city on the African continent, Joburg also has a great number of middle and upper class inhabitants. Significantly, the city is home to the lion's share of South Africa's post-apartheid black economic elite, as well as of its ever-growing black middle class. The kind of place that Johannesburg is, is impacted just as much by the daily activities of its privileged residents than by those of the less well-off.

Perhaps predictably, however, most South African urban and human rights scholarship has largely ignored the lives and place-making activities of middle- and upper-class residents, save for problematising their actions, alongside those of the state, where these have impacted perniciously on the lives of the urban poor.[1] This is short-sighted, and not only because rich and middle class residents have lives and rights too. Precisely because of their financial resources, property-ownership, political and social networks, as well as their access to markets, bureaucracies, the justice system and the media, middle- and upper-class urban residents' performances of the right to the city have a significant – arguably disproportionate – impact on the urban form (and thereby, on the daily lives of all other inhabitants of the city). Even if only for this reason, these performances deserve a far greater degree of scrutiny.[2]

My characterisation of middle- and upper-class place-making activities as practices of the right to the city admittedly jars with the left-leaning theoretical origins of the right, and with its conventional focus on vindicating the survival interests of the working class and the urban poor.[3] But denying the application of the right to the city also to those urban residents who are not poor is not only illogical (in that there is little physical difference between the day-to-day activities of poor and better off urban inhabitants when it comes to shaping the urban environment)[4] and incongruous (in that it denies the protective effect of rights and devalues the lived experiences of urban residents solely on the basis of their class), but it also results in a skewed perception of the oeuvre of the city as object of the right – 'no broader claim about urbanity or the city is possible if we do not understand those cohorts of society that happen not to be really poor'.[5]

The realisation of the right to the city as a collective right requires a continuous and unbiased balance between competing interests, which ought to recognise and advance the interdependence that lies at the heart of urban life.[6] Rather than to deny the validity of middle and upper-class expressions of the right to the city, the focus should be on whether the kind of urban space produced through these expressions is conducive to an inclusive, open, diverse and democratic city life, and to a substantively equal urban citizenship. [7] As with the activities of the urban poor, middle- and upper-class expressions of the right to the city which frustrate these ideals may rightly be required to yield to them, albeit only to the extent that this is justifiable in an open and democratic society. But before such justification can be sought, the motivations behind and interests served by these ostensibly anti-social expressions of the right to the city need to be understood.[8]

This chapter, then, pays closer attention to the everyday lives, place-making activities and concerns of Johannesburg's middle- and upper- classes, with a focus, first, on activities in the inner city and, second, on life in the northern suburbs. It details how middle- and upper-class concerns about physical safety, environmental quality, lifestyle, property values and individual identity have manifested spatially, and interrogates the extent to which such spatial manifestations have impacted on urban life and the collective exercise of the right to the city. Thereafter, it considers middle-and upper class residents' reliance upon constitutional rights and the law to further their interests, as well as the extent to which rights and the law have been used to limit or counterbalance these interests.

Spatial practices of Johannesburg's middle- and upper-classes

Capital flight and Johannesburg's socio-economic geography

As detailed in Chapter 1, Joburg's wealthier residents have settled to the north and east of the CBD since the city's early days. As the downtown area's fortunes declined from the 1970s onwards, the character of the northern suburbs increasingly diversified, with an upsurge in commercial and business developments in former predominantly residential areas. This pattern gained momentum from the 1990s onwards, when corporate, middle- and upper-class Johannesburg reacted to South Africa's political transition by increasingly disinvesting from the CBD, to the point where several businesses and property owners abandoned their inner-city holdings and redirected their resources towards developments in the northern suburbs. Middle-class workers and residents soon joined the exodus, leaving a dilapidated and economically depressed CBD in their wake. Whereas the reasons for and processes of the northward relocation have been many, complex and intertwined, middle-class, upper-class and corporate Johannesburg's 'decision' to 'flee' the inner city was clearly a major contributing factor in its spatial deterioration, the after-effects of which continue to pose a challenge to governance and development in the city.

Moreover, this capital flight quite literally recreated the northern suburbs, leading to the large-scale urbanisation of Parktown, Rosebank, Sandton, Randburg, Fourways and the like, to the point where most of these areas today resemble full-blown town centres, rather than suburbs.[9] Sandton is, of course, the extreme example of this, having metamorphosed into Johannesburg's undisputed corporate capital, and boasting high-rise buildings and infrastructure on a scale so staggering that it is today often regarded as a major city in its own right. Spurred both by a desire to recreate a suburban life away from these new corporate nodes and a need to be within their geographical reach, the northern residential suburbs sprawled, seemingly uncontainably, outward. Indeed, alongside informal settlement formation on the outskirts of the former townships, the middle- and upper-class residential expansion to the north has been the main cause of Johannesburg's staggering sprawl, which has brought with it a legion of urban governance challenges.[10]

It is clear, therefore, that much of the geographical make-up of contemporary Johannesburg is due to the settlement patterns of its middle- and upper-class residents, whose activities also predominantly shape commercial and corporate life in the city. Today, many middle- and upper-class Johannesburg residents near-exclusively work, live and play in the northern suburbs, and never or rarely venture into the inner city and surrounds, whereas much of the high-level economic activity in Johannesburg takes place far removed from its CBD.[11] Functioning near-independently from the city of which they form part, the northern suburbs 'have become a national metaphor variously representing white wealth, Eurocentricism, capitalist materialism, cultural elitism, political conservatism, and, in spite of all that, social liberalism'.[12] While not the only wealthy areas in the city, a closer look at life in the northern suburbs thus provides insight into middle- and upper-class Johannesburg's interests and concerns, as well as into the spatial manifestations of these.

Suburban fortification, isolation and privatisation

South Africa's democratic transition caused much trepidation and uncertainty among Johannesburg's wealthier residents, most of whom, at the time, were white, and all of whom, at the time, were unused to (and, in many respects, unprepared for) inter-racial and cross-class cohabitation. Racial and class hostility, fuelled by decades of state and media propaganda, manifested in a fear and distrust of 'otherness', which was exaggerated by the political uncertainties and volatilities of the time.[13]

Two main factors contributed to a sense among these residents that their lives and lifestyles were, quite literally, under threat. The first was a perfectly justified and predictable redirection of local government resources away from Joburg's wealthier areas and towards the severely underdeveloped townships and informal settlements. This inevitably led to some deterioration in the physical environment and in the (high) quality of urban service delivery to which residents of the formerly white suburbs had been accustomed. Perhaps unfairly, the sense amongst privileged residents (whose municipal rates and taxes continued to fund the bulk of public expenditure in the city) was that they had been abandoned by the City, and that the continuing deterioration of their physical environment and quality of life was inevitable.[14]

Second, the end of spatial mobility policing and a similar redistribution of police resources across the city led to crime, formerly restricted to poor areas and townships, also spreading across the northern suburbs and other wealthy areas.[15] While violent crime (which remains particularly brutal and unacceptably frequent across the city) has profoundly affected and traumatised Johannesburg residents of all classes and addresses,[16] and while township residents remain worst affected,[17] residents of the wealthier suburbs felt particularly threatened by its scourge, not least because of the conspicuousness of their wealth. As elsewhere in the city, crime has become the focal point of post-apartheid northern suburb anxieties, and its threat has come to epitomise residents' sense of a lifestyle and identity under siege:

> crime has not only been the experience through which, for many, the transition has been lived, it has also become the imaginary through which it has been interpreted. Feelings of anxiety, impotence, loss, social decay, frustration and anger have been re-ordered through the rubric of crime.[18]

Economically privileged Johannesburg residents' response to the perceived deterioration and danger in their public environment was predictable: they retreated, en masse, to the private realm. Many disinvested, as far as was practicable, from public services, opting instead for private schools, hospitals, transport and, especially, security services – the private security industry has been one of the most rapidly growing in post-apartheid South Africa.[19] More fundamentally and more widespread, however, was a simultaneous retreat from public space – not only did middle- and upper-class residents avoid the inner city and surrounding 'decaying' areas, but they also stopped making use of suburban parks and streets. While there have been notable exceptions to this trend (such as continued use of public space at the Emmarentia dam and Zoo Lake, and a measure of street life in suburbs such as Parkview, Greenside, Melville and Emmarentia), fear of crime has radically altered everyday life in middle-class Joburg suburbia, to the point where children seldom play in the streets, people opt for travel by car rather than walking, and suburban streets are often deserted, especially after dark.[20]

The retreat into private space also manifested spatially, with high walls, (often electrified) security fences, burglar bars, house alarms, automatic gates, and private security guards becoming the order of the day in most suburbs.[21] Moreover, it also colonised public life, with private shopping malls, gymnasiums, entertainment venues and office complexes mushrooming everywhere and becoming the venues in which a whole range of activities, formerly performed in public, now predominantly took place. Inside these places, subtle and not-so-subtle practices of entrance control and behaviour policing served to draw and enforce insider/outsider boundaries and to further isolate the middle-class in artificial bubbles of like-mindedness.[22]

In their built form, these class fortresses often go to great lengths to separate themselves from 'outside' ('degenerated', 'dangerous') Johannesburg and to simulate the kind of lifestyle that had been 'lost' there. In some instances (such as in the case of Nelson Mandela Square in Sandton, an outside square mostly surrounded by a shopping mall, and Melrose Arch, a 'new-urbanism' style development, which literally razed and replaced a sizeable patch of established suburbs, Birnam and Melrose) they evoke upper-class, first-world street life, appearing to the untrained eye as (almost) integrated into the surrounding urban fabric and (almost) accessible to the general public. Yet, they function under close security surveillance and restrict all but the most innocuous and consumerist of 'public' activities.[23] Others, such as Montecasino in Fourways, simulate foreign places and bygone times in kitsch theme-park-like splendour, fortified behind unforgiving perimeter walls and security-controlled entrances.[24] In all of them, entrance is unofficially restricted to paying customers, or to those whose appearance makes them difficult to distinguish from such.

The 'privatisation of public space' represented by these developments, their exclusion of poor and otherwise undesirable residents and their negative effect on the 'outside' urban environment, which continues to disintegrate as resources previously expended there are withdrawn and redirected towards private space, has been widely lamented. Lindsay Bremner, for instance, remarks:

> All of these scenic enclaves ... do the same thing. They hollow out parts of the city and, on the basis of idealised images, construct urban places appealing to the desire, nostalgia or paranoia of people who can pay to be there. None of them have much, if any, connection to the rest of the city or its history. The city is being remade as a collection of juxtaposed fragments. The gritty, complex city, as opposed to its glitzy, idealised counterpart, has highways, crime, suburban sprawl, vacant office space, neglected buildings, congested traffic, poor people, McDonald's. But it has been obscured and upstaged. Simulated glimpses of what cities once were are celebrated as signs of development, while the city they represent, or even copy, decays and disintegrates.[25]

Similar withdrawal, exclusion and simulation is evident in many northern-suburban residential developments in recent years, where the walled off, entry-restricted and security-protected townhouse complex, or, for the better off, residential or ecological 'estates', have become the order of the day. Whereas some of these developments in more established, older suburbs have had the positive spinoff of contributing to their densification (something which established residents have often resisted[26]), their unbridled burgeoning at the outer perimeters of the city have caused significant service delivery and town planning headaches and have been lamented for their contribution to further fragmenting the city, for their 'separate development' mentality and for the stark, class-based exclusion that they embody.[27]

As in the case of some of the shopping centres and office parks discussed above, the interior spaces in (especially some of the more opulent) private residential estates emulate a lifestyle far removed from the Johannesburg outside of their perimeter walls. Many evoke a sense of rurality or small town living, complete with picket fences, golf courses, streams and meticulously landscaped patches of bush or veld. Dainfern in the far north, which goes as far as to incorporate a private school and a post office, is the poster-child for this kind of development, with its 'free', 'open space'd opulence ironically caged in behind an eight feet high perimeter wall, topped with an electrified fence and patrolled by round-the-clock security personnel.[28] Unified by a desire to construct and maintain a sense of order, safety, comfort, familiarity and class homogeneity, these developments literally, and harshly, prohibit entry to those who do not belong, and are not wanted, within.[29]

Giving effect to similar desires in the older, established suburbs, where the streets are public and where there are commercial developments and open public spaces, has been more difficult and more controversial. In several established suburbs, neighbourhood security patrols subtly police the entry and movement of 'non-belonging' residents in addition to 'protecting' residents. In some cases, (such as in Atholl and Glenhazel) these patrols appear rather militarised, hypervigilant and intimidating, and have been accused of infringing on the movement rights and dignity of those whose race or appearance mark them as outsiders.[30]

More concretely and controversially, since the early 1990s, residents in a great many northern suburbs have sought to partially or completely close their suburbs off from the surrounding city, by erecting gates, fences, boom-gates and security access points. Access to these suburbs are then typically monitored and controlled by guards at the entrances. At least initially, these guards tended to record the details of all who entered and to interrogate those who were not clearly residents of the enclosed area.[31] Such gating literally, and brashly, attempts to privatise public space, and has come under heavy fire from both the City, other residents (residing both inside and outside of the gated areas) and even the South African Human Rights Commission (hereinafter 'SAHRC') which investigated and published a report on suburban gating in 2005. The report lambasted the practice as constituting an unjustifiable infringement of rights to freedom of movement, political activity, equality, and dignity,[32] mostly because of the racial and class-based harassment and exclusion of people from public roads and amenities.

In addition to human rights-based criticisms, gating has also been lambasted for its negative effects on the urban environment. In particular, it has significantly complicated movement around the city, with seemingly arbitrary road blockades making suburbs difficult to access and traverse, thereby causing traffic diversions and congestion and complicating access to public amenities.[33] This has led to much frustration and opposition. For instance, in the early 2000s, frustration over restricted access to Hyde Park High School led Sandhurst residents to rebel against the partial gating of their suburb by breaking down erected barriers and fences.[34] Gating has further complicated service delivery by agents of Telkom, Eskom and the Metropolitan Council, and has also been accused of obstructing access by emergency vehicles.[35]

More fundamentally, gating destroys the open and communal elements of city living. As the SAHRC observed:

> the effect and impact of closures materially affects issues of urban mobility and functionality, and militates against the original idea of a city as a place where people could move around freely, engaging in business, social activity and recreation as part of a collective. Given our own history of exclusion and separation we should be extremely careful, even if our motives are otherwise commendable, in embarking on an urban design that works against the notion of a united society. There was considerable evidence that booms and closures do indeed exclude and separate in a manner inconsistent with the idea of an open city.[36]

Gating is clearly simply an extreme manifestation of the widespread suburban desire to be protected against the harsh realities of post-apartheid Johannesburg. All the other forms of withdrawal discussed above can similarly be accused of being exclusionary in their intention and effect, of undermining the communal elements of city living and of thereby contributing to urban fragmentation, social division, alienation, disintegration and a demise of civic responsibility.[37]

Yet, the security threats underlying many of these practices are real, and attempts by residents to fortify themselves against these threats are by no means unique to the northern suburbs. In suburbs where residents have less financial resources at their disposal, attempts at fortification are simply less formidable and less coordinated, and more frequently take the form of 'home security', street patrols or other forms of physical confrontation.[38] Moreover, much of suburban Joburg's inward-looking response to security threats have indirectly been fuelled by the authorities, whose attempts to stretch limited resources have led them to actively encourage those citizens with the resources to do so, to fend for themselves.[39]

Overall, the focus on isolation, alienation, fortification and fear in the northern suburbs easily leads commentators to overlook that these practices have been accompanied by the suburbs' significant densification (which advances many of the positive features of communal urban life) and, importantly, by their racial diversification.[40] In particular, Johannesburg's burgeoning black middle classes' near uniform preference for settling in the northern suburbs, where they have overwhelmingly favoured townhouse developments and gated estates, belies the kneejerk accusations of racism often levelled at northern suburban isolation practices, instead revealing class and access to resources as significant markers of the Johannesburg urban experience.[41]

Indeed, over and above the negative features highlighted here, the northern suburbs contain within them much public life (as, for example, in the commercial 'high streets' of several of the more established northern suburbs), as well as bursts of creativity, vibrant public spaces, and a pleasant, well-functioning environment.[42] Indeed, recent years have seen increasing signs of them relaxing and opening up, as increased population diversity and years of experience of integrated living serve to relieve previous anxieties and as greater Johannesburg, and especially the inner city and surrounds, have become less hostile to middle class sensibilities.

Digging in: corporate, middle- and upper-class interests in the inner city

As alluded to above, the 1990s saw the large-scale abandonment of the Johannesburg CBD by business, as well as by middle- and upper-class consumers, workers and residents. This desertion was, however, never absolute, especially since it was never accompanied by a significant relinquishment or transfer of property rights over inner-city real estate. While much of the CBD was reappropriated by poor inhabitants eking out a living in and among its rapidly decaying infrastructure, corporate and middle-class interests remained vested there, hibernating amidst increasing squalor.

Significantly, a number of mining houses, businesses and three of South Africa's four major banks retained their headquarters in the inner city, providing a measure of desperately needed continuity and stability in its economic life. But the same concerns that inspired the middle- and upper-class flight toward the northern suburbs also had a marked spatial and behavioural impact on those who stayed behind. In particular, a similar retreat from public space soon became evident, with almost all of the corporate powerhouses referred to above isolating and fortifying their buildings from the surrounding city.

The banks, in particular, remodelled their headquarters after northern suburb office parks and shopping malls, constructing bulky fortresses with security-controlled vehicle entrances, raised and covered walkways, and internal leisure and commercial space (to the point of including their own convenience stores, restaurants and hairdressers), so that there would ordinarily be no reason for their employees to leave their buildings during the course of the workday. The somewhat bizarre effect of this was that many white-collar workers who still worked in the CBD daily never actually set foot there, instead spending their entire workdays within the confines of these corporate islands. Severed from the urban environment in this manner, their presence in the inner city thus did little to counter the city's overall social and economic fragmentation.[43]

Given the strong link between middle- and upper-class Johannesburg's retreat from the inner city and the deterioration of both its physical environment and its economic potential, it comes as no surprise that much of the inner city regeneration efforts from the late 1990s onwards have endeavoured to lure better-resourced residents and businesses back to the city. Perhaps predictably, the spatial dynamics of such regeneration has been controversial, specifically for the ways in which it panders to middle-class idiosyncrasies, polices difference and excludes and displaces poorer inner city residents.

In particular, the practice of establishing and maintaining so-called 'city improvement districts' ('CIDs') across the CBD, has been simultaneously lauded and decried. Modelled on a similar approach adopted in pursuit of the regeneration of New York City, CIDs are 'districts' run and maintained by the City in partnership with private sector conglomerates, typically made up of businesses or residents associations active in an area. The private/public partnership in charge of a CID typically takes responsibility for the creation, maintenance and functioning of the public urban environment in a demarcated area, meaning that services such as street cleaning, landscaping, lighting, and security in a CID tend to be privately funded and delivered, while bylaws tend (at least in part) to be privately enforced.[44] In downtown Joburg, CIDs have typically been spearheaded by the remaining corporate entities (such as the mining houses), alongside companies involved in the refurbishment of dilapidated inner city real estate (such as Olitzki Property Holdings) and urban management consultants (notably Urban Genesis).

CIDs have been commended for their appropriation of private resources for the betterment of the public environment, and have changed several formerly dilapidated inner city spaces into vibrant, diverse, cosmopolitan places. By doing this, CIDs (such as, most notably, the partly pedestrianised section of Main street west of Ghandi Square) have been quite successful in their aim of creating space also frequented by middle- and upper-class users of the inner city. As such, they have restored a measure of class diversity to the CBD and have contributed significantly to the sustainability of its urban environment, to its economic functioning and to its ability to (re)attract investment.[45]

Yet, critics of CIDs in Joburg and other South African cities have pointed to subtle instances of spatial policing enforced by private security guards, with certain kinds of behaviour being discouraged, informal trade being outlawed, and 'less desirable' (poorer) inhabitants being discouraged from 'loitering' in privately managed areas. CIDs therefore also display some of the less desirable features of the privatisation of public space, and are viewed by some as spaces of displacement, discrimination and exclusion.[46]

Similar criticisms have been levelled at private-sector led gentrification in the inner city. The bulk of this criticism has been directed at the so-called Maboneng precinct in the south-eastern corner of the CBD, where abandoned (but mostly unoccupied) light-industrial properties have been reappropriated by the Propertuity real estate and development company, to create a gentrified residential, commercial and corporate precinct displaying 'new urbanism' sensibilities and attracting much investment, much urban creativity and a great many cappuccino-sipping hipsters. Representing the first sizeable residential relocation of middle-class Johannesburg back to the inner city, Maboneng is ostensibly aimed at the creation of an open, diverse, creative, multi-racial, cosmopolitan urban community. In many ways the precinct (which is indeed home to an increasing number of young, professional South Africans of different races, origins, occupations and sexualities) has succeeded in this aim, just as it has certainly succeeded in injecting significant economic, social and cultural life into a previously perpetually dilapidated inner-city corner.[47] The creation of the precinct has further been accompanied by a number of community outreach and upliftment initiatives, and recent developments have included a school, the upgrade of existing daycare facilities and leisure activities for inner city children.

Yet, Maboneng continues to bear more than a passing resemblance to Melrose Arch and other new urbanist developments in the northern suburbs. As with these developments and with CIDs, many of its public services are privately provided and its public spaces are privately regulated. Private security guards closely police all movement and activity within the precinct, and have been accused of discouraging the poor black residents of surrounding areas from unnecessarily 'hanging around' in the precinct. Meanwhile, its residential buildings all boast formidable entrance security and all have strict visitation and behaviour rules reminiscent of suburban townhouse complexes. While there are no physical boundaries, the contrast to the surrounding urban fabric (notably commercial Jeppestown directly to its south) is stark, and a sense of superficiality pervades throughout the precinct.[48]

Much as it has therefore been decried as a middle-class colonialisation of the inner city and has doubtlessly occasioned a measure of indirect displacement (as is observed in gentrified areas in cities around the world),[49] Maboneng also represents a rebellion against the isolation and alienation of life in the northern suburbs and increasingly seems to be bringing a measure of mutuality and diversity into inner city Johannesburg.[50] As such, it is a fitting representative of urban regeneration efforts across the city more generally, in that it sees a middle class gradually reintegrating with the city and community it once fled – re-appropriating, yes, but also reinvesting, diversifying and beginning to reach across class divides. Much as many of its residents' middle-class concerns remain, and continue to be spatially expressed in problematic ways which jar with ideals of urban integration, Maboneng, like the CIDs that it resembles, holds within it the promise of a Johannesburg citizenry coexisting across class and benefiting from a diverse, economically viable and sustainable urban environment.

Middle- and upper-class rights and responsibilities in the courts

Like Johannesburg's poorer residents, its middle- and upper-class inhabitants have regularly expressed frustration at the City's lack of responsiveness to their concerns. Indeed, many of the spatial practices discussed in the previous section have been a direct reaction to this perceived lack of concern. While middle- and upper-class residents often engage City authorities through the appropriate administrative channels and through the ward councillor system, with a far greater deal of success than their poorer counterparts, they have also often resorted to the legal process where this engagement has proved fruitless.

Deficiencies in official structures for participatory local governance has exacerbated this tendency, with the result that lawsuits aimed at asserting residents' property and environmental rights against the City or other private entities (notably property developers) have become commonplace.[51] It has thus come to pass that courts are often called upon to mediate disputes over the extent of rights and responsibilities that arise in the course of day-to-day urban management and through competing performances of the right to the city.

Respecting and protecting existing rights

In terms of section 7(2) of the 1996 Constitution, the State must respect, protect, promote and fulfil all the rights in the Bill of Rights. Since economically privileged residents tend generally to have vested rights in property, secured access to urban services and enjoyment of an urban environment that is conducive to meeting their needs, they tend to resort to rights-based litigation in attempts to assert, secure or protect these against infringement by others. This means that many of the cases involving their interests have centred on defensive attempts to enforce the obligations to respect and protect the rights in question. Unlike the positive obligation to fulfil rights, these obligations are well developed in South African constitutional law and also find expression in many rules of common law, in the fields of delict, contract and property law.[52]

Unsurprisingly, therefore, the jurisprudence of the Constitutional Court has signalled that existing rights to property, housing and services enjoy strong constitutional protection, even as they need to be balanced against the rights of others who may be less fortunate. In *Jaftha* v. *Schoeman*, the Court found that its usual 'reasonableness approach' to adjudicating socio-economic rights matters did not apply to the obligation to respect housing rights, meaning that infringements of existing access to socio-economic rights would only be constitutionally permissible where they satisfied the more exact requirements set out in the Constitution's general limitations clause.[53] Then, in *Law Society of South Africa* v. *Minister of Transport*, the Court found, in the context of health care services for persons rendered paraplegic or quadriplegic by motor vehicle accidents, that the obligation to respect existing access to services implied that unjustifiable reductions in access to private services would be unconstitutional in circumstances where public services were not of sufficient standard and quality.[54]

As for the obligation to protect fundamental rights, a series of judgments pertaining to infringements of physical integrity rights vindicated the interests of all persons to be protected from violent crime. After two judgments where the State was held vicariously liable for the failure of police officers to protect women from sexual assault (as a direct consequence of its obligation to protect the right to be free from public and private violence alongside the rights to life, dignity and freedom and security of the person),[55] the Constitutional Court effectively held in *Rail Commuters Action Group* v. *Transnet t/a Metrorail* that service providers also bore a constitutional (and statutory) obligation to ensure the physical safety of users of urban public services.[56] The combined effect of these judgments is that all residents of Johannesburg can, in principle, hold the City liable for failing to protect them from crime, both in their homes and in public.

Then, in *Modderklip*, the SCA found that the obligation to protect persons against infringements of their rights by others, as developed in the personal security cases, applied also to property rights. The Court found that the landowner had to be compensated for loss of enjoyment of its property, since the State failed to help it to assert its property rights against unlawful occupiers and wrongly expected it to bear the public burden of providing access to housing to those in need.[57] On appeal, the Constitutional Court found that it was unnecessary to decide on the extent to which private property owners could be bound by homeless people's right to have access to adequate housing, but affirmed that the State should not expect private property owners to bear unreasonable burdens imposed by the rights of others and that the State also had to ensure the reasonable exercise of the right to property.[58] It therefore confirmed the order of damages.

The string of inner city housing and eviction cases discussed in Chapter 2 showed similar appreciation for the rights of property owners, much as the Court attempted throughout to ensure that their exercise of these rights did not impact unreasonably on poor building occupiers in the Joburg CBD. In *Blue Moonlight*, for instance, the Court found that Blue Moonlight could not be expected to indefinitely provide free housing, and thus ultimately allowed for the occupiers of its building to be evicted, although it did hold that such eviction would only be just and equitable if the City provided alternative temporary accommodation to the occupiers, whereas the owner had to exercise a 'degree of patience' while the City attempted to orchestrate this.[59] Similarly, in *Maphango*, the Court acknowledged the building owner's desire to profit from its investment through redevelopment, much as it took care to ensure that the rental dispute was resolved fairly and through the proper procedural channels.[60]

As in *Modderklip*, in both these cases the Court protected owners' property rights alongside occupiers' housing rights, to the effect that it ultimately protected property developers' 'right' to dictate the shape and form of the inner city, through enabling them to remake inner city buildings in ways that serve their commercial interests.[61] While the Court expected property owners to delay the exercise of their rights where this was necessary in the interests of protecting the habitation rights of less fortunate urban dwellers, it nevertheless viewed the fate of building occupiers as mostly being the concern of the State and, over and above the duty of patience elaborated in *Blue Moonlight*, was unwilling to impose onerous obligations on better-off residents to contribute to the establishment of an inclusive inner city housing market.[62]

Obligations of citizenship and urban services

Much of middle- and upper-class Joburg residents' uncomfortable relationship with City authorities stems from disputes about service delivery. As alluded to above, the sense among privileged residents since 1994 has been that, as far as service delivery is concerned, they are constantly required to pay more, for less. In recent years, this sense has been strengthened by bureaucratic inefficiencies in relation to billing for services.

Of course, things started off on a bad foot – when the Johannesburg Transitional Metropolitan Council was established in 1994, northern suburbs ratepayers (who formerly fell under a separate Sandton municipality) rebelled against their amalgamation with the broader city and the cross-subsidisation of poorer districts by income derived from their municipal rates payments, by staging a large-scale rates boycott, which is widely cited as a major contributing factor to Joburg's late 1990s fiscal crisis. The boycott was accompanied by legal action, with ratepayers' groups mounting a slew of administrative law challenges to the amalgamation, as well as to the structure through which rates and taxes were levied and their income expended by the Council.

The matter reached the Constitutional Court (in the form of a challenge based on the right to just administrative action enshrined in section 24 of the interim Constitution) where the various objections to the implementation of the cross-subsidisation were ultimately dismissed. In a laborious and technically complex judgment, the 10-member bench in *Fedsure Life Assurance* v. *Greater Johannesburg Transitional Metropolitan Council* found itself evenly divided on whether the Council was levying rates in a procedurally just manner, which meant that the judgment of the lower court, which dismissed the challenge and upheld the rates structure, prevailed. Of the various judgments handed down in the matter, only that of Kriegler J tackled the issue of cross-subsidisation head on. Judge Kriegler emphatically dismissed the suggestions that the City was not empowered to levy and expend taxes in a manner that amounted to cross-subsidisation, stating:

> the genesis, the very reason for the creation of metropolitan areas, was to promote, facilitate and expedite the eradication of the inequalities of the past. A single city without a single tax-base achieves little. A single tax-base without the power to prioritise and direct expenditure is equally ineffective. In order to fulfill its essential purpose, a metropolitan council needs to be able to re-allocate budgetary benefits. One would therefore not readily conclude that the drafters of the interim Constitution, the LGTA and the three proclamations built a transitional vehicle but didn't give it an engine.[63]

Together with the contemporaneous judgment in *Pretoria City Council* v. *Walker* (in which, as will be recalled, the Constitutional Court held that it did not amount to unfair discrimination to levy different service charges in formerly advantaged and disadvantaged areas of Pretoria where this was aimed at overcoming the historical legacy of uneven service provision, and emphasised that there was no disadvantage in privileged residents being required to pay for the high-quality services that they consumed, regardless of billing and credit control practices in poor areas),[64] *Fedsure* sent a strong message to northern suburb residents that resistance to the appropriation of their resources in addressing historical inequalities in service provision across the city would be futile. It thereby brought an end to attempts to ensure that wealthy residents' tax contributions remained largely to be spent on themselves.

Fedsure and *Walker* further set the stage for the Constitutional Court's approach towards service consumption by wealthier urban residents. In judgments such as *Mnkontwana* (where the Court held that it was not unconstitutional to require home owners to ensure that all service charges levied against a property had been paid before the property could be transferred, not least because this accorded with home owners' 'civic responsibility'),[65] *Rademan* (where the Court effectively found that a suburban resident was not entitled to refuse payment for services in protest against what she perceived as poor service delivery)[66] and *National Treasury* v. *Opposition to Urban Tolling Alliance* (where the Court found that no rights in the Bill of Rights were implicated by levying electronic tolls on users of Gauteng's highways, not least because '99% of the burden of tolling will be borne by more affluent road users'[67]), the Court again indicated that wealthier residents could legitimately be expected to bear a greater share of the cost burden of service delivery across the city.

As in the inner-city housing cases, it seems from the Constitutional Court's treatment of privileged consumers in these judgments that the Court is attempting to inculcate in them a sense of communitarian social citizenship, where they not only pay their dues, but also stand back in appropriate circumstances to allow for the realisation of the rights of others who are less fortunate. Yet, over and above legitimising a measure of cross-subsidisation and underlining the importance of payment for services consumed at the rates levied, the jurisprudence in this area has not really hindered or altered service consumption patterns by wealthier residents in any meaningful way.[68]

Struggles over urban shape, form and life

The case law discussed thus far reflects a particular conception of the relationship between middle- and upper-class residents and the City. The State is required to protect inhabitants from threats to their person and to their living environment, and must enable them to exercise their environmental and property rights within a context of urban interdependence. Residents, on the other hand, are required to contribute resources to the urban 'project' by paying both taxes and service charges, and must allow the State some leeway in accomplishing its objectives, even where this requires them to exercise some patience or restraint. In return, they are, for the most part, left alone to lead their lives in the manner they prefer.

Things get complicated, however, when there is a direct clash between this preferred way of life and the objectives of the City, or between the coexisting objectives of different inhabitants. In Joburg, these clashes have often centred on residents' attempts to assert their environmental and property rights against the City or against other 'outside' agents attempting to transform their environment.

As will be clear from the discussions below, not all these attempts have been equally conducive to realising ideals of urban interdependence. The challenge for courts and other adjudicative fora in these matters has therefore been to articulate and uphold a conception of the 'common good' which can guide the balance of competing rights, while also taking into account the rights of those not directly embroiled in the dispute.

The standoff over suburban gating

In many ways, the attempts by residents of certain northern suburbs to isolate their neighbourhoods from (and fortify them against) the surrounding city, through the erection of fences and boom-gates across public roads, presents the quintessential conflict between private property and security rights, on the one hand, and the common good on the other. As discussed above, these 'gating' practices have come under fire for their negative impact on the urban environment and individual freedom of movement, as well as for the pernicious racial and class dimensions inherent in their attempts to discourage 'outsiders' from entering 'restricted' areas.

As instances of gating increased towards the end of the 1990s, the Gauteng provincial government passed legislation in principle authorising the practice, albeit subject to local government regulation.[69] The sense in government appeared to be that gating was a 'necessary evil' to be tolerated, since it created jobs, enhanced security and prevented wealthy suburbanites from leaving the city (or, indeed, the country) together with the rates-income on which cities so heavily depend.[70] The legislation thus enabled gating, while leaving the day-to-day management of its negative effects to cities.

Whereas the northern substructure of the transitional metropolitan council (formerly the independent Sandton municipality) gave permission to a large number of applications for gating in terms of the legislation, the 'unified' Joburg Metropolitan Council has, unsurprisingly, been opposed to gating since its formation. Accusing citizens of a racist 'laager mentality' that undermines ideals of urban integration and harmonious coexistence, the City's initial policy on security closures attempted to dissuade gating, by imposing strict and bureaucratically cumbersome requirements on proposed security closures, and the City denied permission for security closures more often than it granted it. However, residents had the law on their side and organised to collectively oppose the City. A number of actual or threatened lawsuits either forced the City to grant permission for closures, or prevented it from tearing them down. At the same time, many residents' associations simply went ahead and erected barriers without the necessary permission.[71]

The City turned towards the SAHRC, whose 2005 report (which found that gating infringed a number of constitutional rights by restricting free movement across public space, requiring persons to furnish personal particulars as preconditions for entry into restricted areas and adversely targeting black pedestrians in enforcing entry controls)[72] was a watershed in the struggle and led to a de facto moratorium on further gating across the city.[73] But, by the end of the decade, residents' organisations had renewed their pressure on the city to enable gating in terms of the prevailing law, leading the City once more to refine and revise its policy on security closures.

In terms of its 2014 Security Access Restriction Policy, the City grants permission for security road closures only upon detailed motivation by residents, who must demonstrate that closures are necessary for security purposes and that measures less restrictive of individual freedoms have failed. Applications for closures must contain detailed traffic impact studies, must explicitly be supported by at least two thirds of the residents in a proposed enclosed area and can be granted only after consideration of the views of residents, the public, city officials and any businesses or amenities inside or affected by a proposed closure.[74] Where permission is granted, moreover, the policy prescribes that access points to suburbs must provide 24 hour, unrestricted pedestrian access, that no one may be searched or required to furnish personal particulars as a condition of entry and that unobstructed access must be granted to emergency vehicles, employees of the City or other branches of government, as well as the police, Telkom and Eskom.[75]

While the ongoing standoff over suburban gating on the one hand provides a cautionary example of the manner in which organised residents' associations can use the law in attempts to frustrate attempts by the City to advance rights for the broader urban population, it also shows how the City, too, can rely on the rights of its inhabitants in order to resist private place-making activities that frustrate constitutional ideals. Today, an uneasy truce appears to prevail. Many road enclosures remain and continue to complicate movement across the northern suburbs, but their exclusionary impact has significantly been softened through regulation. Overall, the balance between the safety and security rights of suburban residents, on the one hand, and those of freedom of movement, equality and dignity of non-residents on the other, remains precarious. Yet, the discussion here attests that, while residents' property and security rights must be taken seriously, they are by no means absolute.

Residential property rights

Defending boom gates and fences is not the only way in which wealthier Johannesburg residents have sought to secure their way of life. In fact, their resort to law in defence of their financial interests and property rights has often taken the form of attempting to prevent others (be that the City, non-residents or property developers with spatial visions different from their own) from altering the shape, form and feel of their suburbs.

In this respect, densification tends to be the main bugbear of those living in the established inner suburbs, who regularly lobby the Council for stricter enforcement of building regulations, zoning bylaws and the like, so as to protect the suburban character of their neighbourhoods (and thereby, so the logic goes, to keep the danger and decay of urbanisation at bay). Residents' associations in suburbs such as Rosebank, Sandton, Hyde Park and Craighall regularly use these laws and regulations to oppose new commercial and high-density developments in their suburbs, both at council level and in the courts, to the point where it has been reported that many property developers prefer to engage with residents' associations directly in attempts to secure permission to build.[76]

Courts have, through the years, upheld several bylaw-, building regulation- and neighbour law-based challenges by residents against place-making actions by developers or other residents that impact negatively on the exercise of suburban property rights. For instance, in *Walele* v. *City of Cape Town*, the majority of the Constitutional Court overturned the granting of building permission by the City of Cape Town to a property owner in Woodstock for erecting a block of flats, since the relevant officials did not properly apply their mind to the potential negative effect that the construction would have on the value of neighbouring properties.[77] More recently, in *Aboobaker* v. *Serengeti Rise Body Corporate*, the Durban High Court overturned the granting of building permission for a suburban apartment block, and ordered its partial demolition so as that it complies with height requirements posed by zoning bylaws. Emphasising that neighbouring homeowners were acting in legitimate defence of 'their rights pertaining to their homes and their right to live in these homes in peace and harmony',[78] the Court found that they were insufficiently consulted in the course of a rezoning application for the property, which rendered the Metropolitan Council's decision to grant the rezoning and accompanying building permission invalid.[79]

But the more noteworthy court struggles over suburban property owners' rights in Johannesburg have been on the outskirts of the city, where suburbanites' main adversary has been the development of informal settlements or low-cost housing projects on vacant land adjacent to middle- or upper-class neighbourhoods.[80] In the pre-constitutional era, such developments were kept at bay through apartheid spatial planning practices, and were in any event fairly easily resisted through reliance on common-law doctrines aimed at protecting property rights, such as the law pertaining to trespass and nuisance. But such assertion of property rights was to become significantly more complex in the constitutional dispensation.

This was illustrated shortly before the coming into operation of the interim Constitution, when the (then) Appellate Division of the Supreme Court handed down judgment in *Diepsloot Residents' and Landowners' Association* v. *Administrator, Transvaal*. The judgment essentially dismissed common law challenges by property owners on Johannesburg's north-western outskirts, against the proclamation of Diepsloot township. While acknowledging that the establishment of the township would be accompanied by the forming of informal settlements, which would impact on the exercise of property rights by nearby residents (for instance, due to the nuisance caused by smoke from fires, increased pollution and crime, and a reduction in property values), the Court found that the Administrator of Transvaal acted reasonably and within his statutory power in proclaiming the township. [81] Its reasons for this finding included that a homeless community had to be accommodated *somewhere* in the vicinity of where they had already settled informally, that the Administrator had duly applied his mind to the various interests impacted by the decision (ranging from the existing residents' interest in maintaining their class homogeneity to the acute socio-economic needs of the newcomers), and that the burden to be borne by the more privileged residents as a result of the decision was a 'consequence of the necessary reconstruction of our society'.[82]

Subsequent to the 1996 Constitution's explicit entrenchment of housing rights, a similar dispute in Kyalami, then a cluster of opulent small holdings on the far northern fringes of the Johannesburg metropolitan area, made it all the way to the Constitutional Court in 2001. Early the previous year, heavy rains caused floods all over the city. In Alexandra, the Jukskei River burst its banks, washing away some 300 informal houses and necessitating the evacuation of several others. Flood victims were initially housed in tents on open, state-owned land in Marlboro, although the Gauteng Provincial Government soon intervened by constructing a transit camp consisting of some 200 houses on state-owned land adjacent to Leeuwkop Prison, not far from Kyalami. Kyalami residents were not consulted and, upon learning of the establishment of the camp, instituted legal proceedings in order to prevent its construction.[83]

Relying on several provisions of the 1998 National Environmental Management Act and bolstered by the constitutional right to a healthy environment conducive to well-being, the Kyalami residents' objections to the construction of the transit camp boiled down to the fact that it would 'affect the character of their neighbourhood and reduce the value of their properties'.[84] While acknowledging that these interests were valid and grounded in constitutional rights, the Court held that they had to be balanced against the competing constitutional right to have access to adequate housing which, in this case, corresponded to 'the interests of the flood victims to be accommodated at a place reasonably close to the place where they had previously been living and the interests of other homeless communities in search of land on which to settle'.[85] In fact, the Court felt that the flood victims should have been joined as parties to the dispute, given that their constitutional rights were so central to it.[86]

The Court proceeded to find that the relevant principles in the National Environmental Management Act had to be understood in light of the State's constitutional obligation to progressively realise the right of access to adequate housing.[87] Given this, as well as the fact that the State was the owner of the land on which the camp was being constructed (meaning that it had property rights of its own, to be weighed against those of the Kyalami residents) and the temporary nature of the camp, the Court concluded that the balance of competing interests favoured its construction. It therefore dismissed the Kyalami residents' objections.

The *Kyalami Ridge* judgment shows how the constitutional ensconcement of socio-economic rights serves as a counterweight to the otherwise unfettered exercise of established, negative rights by more affluent sectors of society. By affirming that the State's constitutional obligations towards poorer residents must be taken into account when deciding disputes between government and better-off citizens, *Kyalami Ridge* at once legitimises and lends credibility to state attempts at redistribution and spatial transformation and ensures that the interests of (often unrepresented) poorer inhabitants are afforded due weight in the proportionality inquiry into the limitation of rights of the better off.[88]

This was affirmed some years later, by a judgment of the Cape High Court in *Stock* v. *Minister of Housing*, which allowed the construction of temporary housing for people displaced by Cape Town's N2 Gateway Housing project on land near the Cape Town airport, despite objections by nearby land owners who had wrongly not been consulted before the development commenced, and whose plans to develop light industrial facilities on their properties were effectively thwarted by the development (since it would be difficult to attract investors to a project adjacent to low-cost housing). While acknowledging that the City of Cape Town did not follow the correct legal process in developing the temporary housing, and while upholding the applicants' right to property by requiring that structures that encroached on their land be immediately removed, the Court relied on *Kyalami Ridge* to find that, given the importance of the N2 Gateway project for spatial justice in Cape Town, and given the importance of the constitutional right of access to adequate housing, the development could nevertheless go ahead.[89]

The clear message sent by judgments such as *Diepsloot* and *Kyalami Ridge* notwithstanding, similar disputes would significantly delay or disrupt the construction of several low-cost housing projects over the following years. For instance, the construction of the mixed income Cosmo City mega-development northwest of Johannesburg was delayed for several years, due to being embroiled in litigation by residents of surrounding high income areas, who invoked every law, bylaw and right in the book, in an (ultimately unsuccessful) attempt to protect their property values and living environment from the 'threat' of being located near a mixed income area.[90]

Overall, it appears that courts are aware of the danger of middle-class capture of rights, and are taking care to decide disputes over the impact of developments on the residential environment, regardless of their scale, with reference to the public good and the constitutional rights of urban inhabitants of different classes. While quick to insist that proper processes are followed when it comes to changing the urban fabric (with a particular focus on whether residents were properly consulted and engaged in the course of these processes), courts have shown that middle-class property rights no longer unceremoniously trump competing habitation concerns. While this does not mean that middle-class interests will always pander to those of less well-off groups, it does appear that they have a larger chance of being vindicated where they can be shown to coincide with ideals of democracy and substantive equality.

This is perhaps best illustrated by the judgment of the Western Cape High Court in *Sea Front for All* v. *MEC, Environmental and Development Planning, Western Cape*. The case concerned resistance by a neighbourhood organisation and property owners to the granting of building permission for the construction of a hotel in Cape Town's Sea Point, which would have entailed the effective privatisation of a significant part of the Sea Point pavilion and promenade, one of the city's most popular urban public spaces. Using the environmental right in the Constitution as its point of departure, the Court contemplated the importance of the public space (including the fact that it was widely used by Capetonians of all races and classes) for infusing urban Cape Town life with social equality and democracy. It also considered whether the construction of the hotel would be beneficial to Sea Point, taking into account that, while the area was formerly dilapidated, it had significantly revived in recent years, so that it could no longer be said that a hotel development was necessary to regenerate the area. Overall, the Court found that the MEC (Member of the Executive Council) for development planning did not take these factors into account, and therefore did not properly apply her mind, when approving the development. The Court accordingly remitted the decision to her for reconsideration.[91]

Commercial property rights

Corporate entities' attempts to protect their business interests and those of their (middle class) customers by insulating their commercial space from 'unwanted' outsiders provide another clear example of the defensive use of rights and the law. In a handful of reported judgments, South African courts have struggled to balance these commercial interests against performances of the right to the city which threaten them. These disputes need to be understood in the context of the struggle for control over public space and, particularly, of the tensions inherent in the privatisation of such space.

In *Fourways Mall* v. *South African Commercial Catering and Allied Workers Union*, the owners of the Fourways Mall in the north of Johannesburg, which is for all intents and purposes a private space (much as members of the public are invited to shop there), sought an interdict against striking workers of the Edgars clothing chain, who had been disrupting activities in the mall during their strike. An interim interdict, prohibiting the workers from coming within 500 metres of, or obstructing, the shopping mall's entrances, harming customers' vehicles and harassing the mall's employees, tenants and customers, was granted.[92] In deciding whether to convert the temporary interdict into a final order, the Joburg High Court found that the applicants had 'a fundamental, as well as constitutional, right to ply their trade and enjoy their property to the full' and that 'the law will not tolerate the frightening off of custom by labour troubles, reprisals, fear of unpleasantness et cetera'.[93] However, since it did not have sufficient evidence before it to establish whether these rights were indeed still being infringed by the striking workers, the Court referred the matter for hearing of oral evidence.[94]

In *Victoria & Alfred Waterfront* v. *Police Commissioner, Western Cape*, the Cape High Court indicated that it would be somewhat less vociferous in vindicating private commercial and property rights in space that was only partly private in character. As will be recalled from the discussion in Chapter 4, the Court was not amenable to banning beggars from the Waterfront, which it regarded as being 'for all practical purposes a suburb of Cape Town'.[95] While thus upholding the beggars' rights to life (interpreted as encompassing a right to a livelihood), dignity and freedom of movement by refusing to ban them from the area, the Court also recognised that their conduct threatened the Waterfront's owners' 'clear right to protect their custom and business interests ... from unlawful interference', and that the owners had 'a sufficient interest in having the physical integrity of their employees protected'.[96] In an attempt to resolve the dispute 'in a manner which permits the rights of both parties to be vindicated to the greatest extent possible',[97] the Court therefore issued an order interdicting the beggars from assaulting, harming or threatening any of the Waterfront's visitors, employees and businesses, and requiring them to leave the premises of individual restaurants after being instructed by those in charge to do so, at risk of criminal sanction.[98]

Another Cape High Court judgment, in *Intercape Ferreira Mainliner* v. *Minister of Home Affairs*, ordered the closure of a refugee reception office by the Department of Home Affairs, because its operation (which involved large crowds and queues outside the office, and caused much noise, litter, traffic congestion and similar nuisances) impacted negatively on neighbouring businesses' ability to use their premises. While acknowledging the social utility of the refugee reception office, the Court found that this was insufficient to outweigh the general negative impact that the office had on the business activities in the immediate vicinity.[99]

The Joburg High Court was faced with striking a similar balance between commercial and property rights, on the one hand, and refugees' rights to life and dignity, on the other, in the High Court precinct in Pritchard Street, in the aftermath of the xenophobic violence in Joburg in mid-2008. As discussed in Chapter 4, the violence caused a great many foreign residents of the inner city to seek sanctuary at the Central Methodist Church in the CBD. The church was overfull, and many of the refugees congregated in the surrounding streets. The urban infrastructure was battling to cope, and the large numbers of effectively homeless people in the street had an impact on commerce in the area, with business owners in the adjacent Small Street Mall going as far as to club together to erect a palisade fence between the church and their shopping arcade.[100]

Also particularly heavily affected was Pitje Chambers, an inner city chamber of advocates in the building next to the church, whose tenants could not access their parking lot due to destitute foreigners sleeping on the ramps, and whose advocates and their clients were said to be severely inconvenienced by scores of people washing and urinating in the street, as well as by the stench and sight of temporary portable toilets that the City had installed next to the church. Pitje Chambers tried to engage the City to deal with the attendant public health bylaw violations by accommodating the refugees elsewhere and, when their efforts proved fruitless, instituted legal proceedings demanding the enforcement of loitering and public health bylaws. Judges from the High Court (situated less than one city block away) voiced similar complaints in a letter to the City, and the City capitulated, reaching a settlement with Pitje in terms of which it would relocate a majority of the refugees, remove the portable toilets and take a range of steps (including stepping up street cleaning and refuse removal in the area) to correct infringement of the public health bylaws.[101]

While the Pitje Chambers matter accordingly never went to trial, its outcome shows the power of environmental rights in resolving conflicts over shared public urban space. Viewed together with the *Fourways Mall*, *Intercape* and *V&A Waterfront* decisions, the settlement in Pitje Chambers appears to affirm that the 'right' to a business-conducive environment is at least considered to be at a par with the residents' 'right' to urban presence. In the context of the debate over the privatisation of public space, this suggests that, while courts will not tolerate attempts to outright exclude inhabitants from public spaces, they are nevertheless prepared to uphold restrictions on individual behaviour where such restrictions serve the public good, which is interpreted as encompassing not only the rights of poor and marginalised urban dwellers, but also of better-off residents and commercial enterprises.

Reflections

The discussion above illustrates how struggles over control of space in post-apartheid Johannesburg have at once been intensified and skewed by real concerns over environmental deterioration, safety and security. Middle- and upper-class residents' intertwined desires for safety, predictability and control over personal space have often been expressed physically, through attempts to control public spaces. These attempts have ranged from the creation of new, privately controlled, communal spaces to the partial privatisation of erstwhile public spaces. As with the instances of marginal enclave forming discussed in Chapter 4, these practices have enabled a group of persons with common concerns to advance and assert their version of the good life in an environment that is (at least perceived to be) hostile to their unique needs and concerns. As such, these practices amount to performances of the right to the city, which need to be viewed in conjunction with, and balanced against, competing performances of the right by others.

While it is true that many of the spatial practices discussed here indicate a retreat from civic engagement and are inimical to the creation of an urban environment that embraces difference and enables a diversity of fulfilling human interactions,[102] this chapter has also illustrated that many of their underlying concerns are real, pressing and understandable. Moreover, dysfunctional public participation structures, a lack of resources and (however rightly) skewed public priorities have meant that suburban residents have in many respects been left to fend for themselves (and indeed, have often been officially encouraged to do so).[103] In particular, the State's failure to control violent crime in the city has profoundly impacted all facets of Johannesburg life and underlies many of the antisocial practices described here. While this chapter has focused on middle- and upper-class suburban responses to safety and security threats, it needs to be emphasised that similar antisocial tendencies of fortification and civic disengagement are common across all classes, neighbourhoods and population groups in the city.[104]

Due to the amount of financial resources at their disposal, their greater capacity to assert themselves in interactions with City authorities and the general predisposition of common law and negative rights discourse to their interests, the middle- and upper-classes generally have easy access to the justice system and are generally well placed to enforce their rights against both city authorities and other urban inhabitants. Much as poorer and more vulnerable residents often indirectly benefit from the protection of the rights granted or affirmed through these processes, there are real concerns that urban rights-discourse may get captured by middle and upper class issues and concerns. This may serve to sideline the interests of the poor and to resist public efforts at redistribution and transformation, especially in environments such as the city where different class interests are in constant tension.[105]

Indeed, the judicialisation of disputes over urban shape and form means that control over processes that shape the urban environment is increasingly wrestled from city authorities and everyday actors, and vested instead with lawyers and courts, who are required to take decisions that impact on the broader urban environment within the confines of individual disputes that are inevitably coloured by the middle- and upper-class interests that sparked them.[106]

However, most of the judgments discussed in this chapter illustrate that the inclusion of justiciable socio-economic rights in the South African Constitution has had an important counterbalancing effect, and has enabled courts to temper the otherwise counter-transformative effects of middle- and upper-class-led litigation by enabling them to explicitly balance the interests of individual litigants against those of other inhabitants of the city, especially against the socio-economic rights of the city's poorer and marginalised inhabitants.[107]

Along these lines, courts have dismissed attempts by middle- and upper-class residents to resist the appropriation of resources generated through their taxes and service charges towards the public good (as in *Fedsure* and *Opposition to Urban Tolling Alliance*), have required middle- and upper-class property rights to yield to the emergency housing needs of destitute, poorer residents (as in *Kyalami Ridge* and *Stock*) and have limited the powers of urban property owners to exclude 'unwanted' members of different classes from urban public space under their control (as in *V&A Waterfront* and the ongoing dispute over suburban gating).

At the same time, courts have required public authorities to take steps to protect the freedom and security rights of all residents and have taken seriously the rights of middle- and upper-class residents to thrive in an urban environment that is conducive to the satisfaction of their needs. Judgments such as *V&A Waterfront*, *Sea Front for All* and the settlement in the Pitje Chambers case suggest a balancing of competing demands on urban space and an enabling approach to conflicting, simultaneous performances of the right to the city, even as this sometimes requires that such performances have to be limited in favour of the public good.

Notes

1 See Mabin (2014: 409); Visser (2013: 85, 88).
2 See Visser (2013: 76, 86–88).
3 For criticism of using the right to the city to describe middle-class interests, see Walsh (2013: 400–403).
4 On the theoretical ease with which right-to-the-city thinking can be extended to place-making activities across class, see Layard (2010: 439); Purcell (2002: 103–104, 106).
5 Visser (2013: 88).
6 See Purcell (2002: 102).
7 See Frug (1996: 1051–1053); Landman (2006: 64, 70); Layard (2010: 436, 438–440); Pindell (2006: 438, 441).
8 See Visser (2013: 86–88).
9 See Murray (2014: 180, 182).
10 See Murray (2011: 175).
11 See Czegledy (2003: 38).
12 Czegledy (2003: 29–30).
13 See Bremner (2004a: 458–460); Van der Walt (2007: 221–222).
14 See Benit-Gbaffou (2009: 57); Murray (2011: 189–191); Visser (2013: 86).
15 See Benit-Gbaffou (2008a: 1941; 2009: 58); Bremner (2004a: 461).
16 See Beall *et al.* (2002: 176–177); Bremner (2004a: 461, 464). For analysis of recent national crime figures in this context, see Dirsuweit (2014: 546–548).
17 See Beall *et al.* (2002: 177).
18 Bremner (2004a: 461). See also Ballard (2004); Benit-Gbaffou (2009: 62).
19 See Benit-Gbaffou (2008a: 1934; 2009: 56); Bremner (2004a: 465–466); Le Roux (2006: 38); Visser (2013: 86).
20 See Beall *et al.* (2002: 179–180); Benit-Gbaffou (2008a: 1934); Czegledy (2003: 35; 2004: 82).
21 See Beall *et al.* (2002: 180); Bremner (2004a: 464–465); Czegledy 2003: 36; 2004: 83–84); Murray (2011: 273).
22 See Beall *et al.* (2002: 180); Bremner (2004b: 62–63); Czegledy (2004: 85); Dirsuweit (2014: 549); Murray (2011: 215; 2014: 186).
23 On Melrose Arch, see Bremner (2004b: 121–124); Landman and Badenhorst (2014: 222); Le Roux (2006: 36).
24 On Montecasino, see Bremner (2004b: 129–130).
25 Bremner (2004b: 132–134). See also ibid., 135; Dirsuweit (2014: 549); Landman and Badenhorst (2014: 217); Murray (2011: 215–216; 2014: 191).
26 See Benit-Gbaffou (2008b: 6–8); Murray (2011: 189–191; 2014: 184).
27 See Beall *et al.* (2002: 181–183, 195); Czegledy (2004: 85); Landman (2006: 62–63); Murray (2011: 175, 183–184, 210–211, 314–316; 2014: 181, 186–187).
28 See Bremner (2004b: 130–132); Czegledy (2004: 86); Landman and Badenhorst (2014: 220–222); Lemanski *et al.* (2008: 145–146); Murray (2011: 285–289, 294–302). On Dainfern specifically, see Murray (2011: 303–314).
29 See Landman (2006: 62, 64); Landman and Badenhorst (2014: 215–217); Lemanski *et al.* (2008: 134–136, 143–147, 150, 155); Le Roux (2006: 37–38); Murray (2011: 210, 289; 2014: 181, 186–189).
30 See Benit-Gbaffou (2006: 309–310); Benit-Gbaffou (2008a: 1937–1939; 2008c: 94–95, 98; 2009: 56, 66); Murray (2011: 273–276).
31 On the nature and extent of road closures across the city, see Benit-Gbaffou (2008a: 1935–1937); Landman (2006: 58–60); Lemanski *et al.* (2008: 149); Murray (2011: 192, 203).
32 SAHRC (2005). For similar academic arguments, see Landman and Badenhorst (2014: 219). The effects of the SAHRC report are discussed below.

33 See Benit-Gbaffou (2008a: 1935); Czegledy (2004: 86); Landman and Badenhorst (2014: 224); Lemanski *et al.* (2008: 151); SAHRC (2005: 5, 22–23).
34 See Benit-Gbaffou (2008a: 1935).
35 See Landman (2006: 61); SAHRC (2005: 13).
36 SAHRC (2005: 5). See also Benit-Gbaffou (2009: 69); Lemanski *et al.* (2008: 134–136, 148–151, 155); Le Roux (2006: 49); Van der Walt (2007: 221–222).
37 See Benit-Gbaffou (2008a: 1947); Bremner (2004b: 135); Dirsuweit (2014: 548–549); Landman (2006: 64, 70); Layard (2010: 415–416, 428, 436, 439); Le Roux (2006: 37–38); SAHRC (2005: 4, 26); Van der Walt (2007: 221–222).
38 See Benit-Gbaffou (2006: 302–309, 320; 2009: 70); Czegledy (2004: 82); Le Roux (2006: 27).
39 See Benit-Gbaffou (2006: 310–312, 320; 2008a: 1934, 1938–1939, 1947–1948; 2008c: 94–95).
40 See Beal *et al.* (2002: 175); Mabin (2014: 409–413).
41 See Beall *et al.* (2002: 182–183, 195); Benit-Gbaffou (2006: 306–307); Lemanski *et al.* (2008: 149); Mabin (2014: 409, 412–413).
42 See Mabin (2014: 410–412).
43 For detailed discussion of these inner city corporate enclaves, see Bremner (2004b: 54–58); Murray (2011: 217–238); Van der Walt (2007: 223).
44 On the central features of CIDs in Johannesburg, see Benit-Gbaffou (2008a: 1940); Murray (2011: 240–241, 260–267); Peyroux (2006: 9–11).
45 See Murray (2011: 241); Peyroux (2006: 10–11, 13); Van der Walt (2007: 223).
46 See Miraftab (2007: 617–621); Murray (2011: 242–243); Peyroux (2006: 12); Van der Walt (2007: 231); Walsh (2013: 406).
47 See Nevin (2014: 188–190, 194–195).
48 See Nevin (2014: 188, 191–194, 196–197).
49 See Nevin (2014: 194); Walsh (2013: 400–406).
50 See Nevin (2014: 194–195, 198); Walsh (2013: 400, 403). On the benefits of middle class reintegration in the city more broadly, see Van der Walt (2007: 223).
51 See Benit-Gbaffou (2008b: 7–8, 11–13); Murray (2011: 189–192).
52 See Liebenberg (2011: 38, 40–41).
53 *Jaftha* v. *Schoeman* (2005).
54 *Law Society of South Africa* v. *Minister of Transport* (2011).
55 See *Carmichele* v. *Minister of Safety & Security* (2001: paras 44–45, 57, 60, 62, 81–83); *K* v. *Minister of Safety & Security* (2005: paras 18, 51–53).
56 See *Rail Commuters Action Group* v. *Transnet t/a Metrorail* (2005: paras 66, 69–72, 82–84, 88, 111). The case arose from actions for damages against Transnet after several commuters were violently attacked while travelling on passenger trains in Cape Town. Transnet denied that it was obliged to protect commuters from violence, arguing that such a duty rested exclusively on the police. The Court rejected this argument and held that Transnet indeed bore such an obligation.
57 *Modder East Squatters* v. *Modderklip Boerdery; President of the RSA* v. *Modderklip Boerdery* (2004: paras 27–28, 31, 52).
58 *President of the RSA* v. *Modderklip Boerdery* (2005: paras 26, 45, 51, 68). See discussion in Chapter 2.
59 *City of Johannesburg Metropolitan Municipality* v. *Blue Moonlight Properties* (2012: paras 3, 34, 97, 100).
60 *Maphango* v. *Aengus Lifestyle Properties* (2012: paras 60, 126–129). See discussion in Chapter 2.
61 See also *Hatting* v. *Juta* (2013), where the Court sided with an owner of a farm on the outskirts of Stellenbosch, by finding that it would be just and equitable to limit the right of a lawful occupier of a farm cottage to be accompanied by her family, where the owner wanted to make different use of the part of the cottage where her family members were staying and acted reasonably towards them.

62 For opposing views on this judicial stance see Kruger (2014: 330, 339–340, 348–352) and Strydom and Viljoen (2014: 1207–1208, 1211, 1217–1219).
63 *Fedsure Life Assurance* v. *Greater Johannesburg Transitional Metropolitan Council* (1999: 148). The Court further situates its deliberations in the context of addressing historical inequalities. Ibid., paras 1, 121–123, 132. The cross-subsidisation 'scheme' is set out at ibid., paras 13–14.
64 See *Pretoria City Council* v. *Walker* (1998: paras 53, 56, 62–63, 65, 94, 96, 103, 105, 107, 110, 123, 127), as well as discussion in Chapter 3.
65 See *Mnkontwana* v. *Nelson Mandela Metropolitan Municipality* (2005: paras 38, 40, 42, 53, 73) as well as discussion in Chapter 3.
66 See *Rademan* v. *Moqhaka Local Municipality* (2013: paras 40–45), as well as discussion in Chapter 3.
67 *National Treasury* v. *Opposition to Urban Tolling Alliance* (2012: para 62). See also paras 47, 67–68, as well as discussion in Chapter 3.
68 The Court's judgment in *Mazibuko* v. *City of Johannesburg* (2010) has for instance been criticised for not interrogating wasteful consumption of water in Johannesburg's wealthier northern suburbs, whilst regarding the imposition of pre-paid meters in Soweto as being partly justified by concerns over water conservation. See Dugard (2008: 604); Pieterse (2014: 191).
69 See Gauteng Rationalisation of Local Government Affairs Act (1998: ss 43–48).
70 See Landman (2006: 62); Lemanski *et al.* (2008: 150); Le Roux (2006: 44–45).
71 See Benit-Gbaffou (2008a: 1935–1939, 1947–1948; 2009: 71); Lemanski *et al.* (2008: 146, 153–155); Le Roux (2006: 45–47).
72 SAHRC (2005: 33).
73 See Benit-Gbaffou (2008a: 1937; 2009: 69–70).
74 City of Johannesburg (2014: clauses 4–6).
75 City of Johannesburg (2014: clauses 7.2.1, 7.1.6–7.1.7, 7.1.9).
76 See Benit-Gbaffou 2008b: 6–8; Murray 2011: 189–191.
77 *Walele* v. *City of Cape Town* (2008).
78 *Aboobaker* v. *Serengeti Rise Body Corporate* (2015: para 11).
79 Ibid., paras 13–14, 26.
80 See generally Ballard (2004).
81 *Diepsloot Residents' & Landowners' Association* v. *Administrator, Transvaal* (1994: 351F-I, 353H-J, 354I-J).
82 Ibid., 353H. See also 344J-345B, 353G-J, 354F-J. For discussion, see Coggin (2016: 445–446).
83 These facts are set out in detail in the Constitutional Court's judgment in *Minister of Public Works* v. *Kyalami Ridge Environmental Association* (2001: paras 2–8).
84 Ibid., para 93. See also para 103.
85 Ibid., paras 103, 106–107.
86 Ibid., paras 18–19, 29–32. The Court however did not insist on such joinder as its judgment did not negatively affect the flood victims' rights.
87 Ibid., para 68.
88 See Coggin (2016: 447–448); Pieterse (2007: 3, 9–10, 20).
89 *Stock* v. *Minister of Housing* (2007: 16E-G, 18B-J, 19E-20C).
90 See Murray (2011: 197–203).
91 *Sea Front for All* v. *MEC, Environmental and Development Planning, Western Cape* (2011: paras 12–13, 31, 40–44, 67; 71–75).
92 *Fourways Mall* v. *South African Commercial Catering and Allied Workers Union* (1999: 755B-G).
93 Ibid., 756G-H.
94 Ibid., 760F-761F. The judgment is similar (though somewhat more sensitive to the rights of protestors) to the pre-constitutional judgment of the same court in *Deneys Reitz* v. *South African Commercial, Catering and Allied Workers Union* (1991),

which found (at 696F) that 'the right to peace of mind free from another making a nuisance of himself can be an adequate basis for legal protection' and granted an interdict preventing protestors from interfering with the applicant's (a firm of attorneys then based in the CBD) business activities. For comparison between the *Deneys Reitz* and *Fourways Mall* judgments see Van der Walt (2007: 231–232).

95 *Victoria & Alfred Waterfront* v. *Police Commissioner, Western Cape* (2004: 449A). See also 448I-449A, 450H-I, 451D-G.

96 Ibid., at 452E-F.

97 Ibid., at 452B.

98 Ibid., at 452I-453D.

99 *Intercape Ferreira Mainliner* v. *Minister of Home Affairs* (2010: 35–38, 53, 57, 147, 165–168, 186–187). For discussion of the *Intercape* judgment in light of the right to the city see Coggin (2016: 449–451).

100 Kulijan (2010: 41).

101 See Consortium for Refugees and Migrants in South Africa (2009: 35); Kulijan (2010: 40).

102 See Frug (1996: 1051; 1074); Landman (2006: 64, 70); Lemanski *et al.* (2008: 134–135, 150–155); Layard (2010: 415–416, 436–440); Le Roux (2006: 36, 49).

103 See Benit-Gbaffou (2008a: 1938–1939; 1947–1948; 2009: 57–58, 77); Visser (2013: 86).

104 See Beall *et al.* (2002: 175–177); Benit-Gbaffou (2009: 55, 70); Czegledy (2004: 82); Le Roux (2007: 27).

105 See Liebenberg (2011: 46; 56–57); Pieterse (2007: 1); West (2001: 1904, 1906–1907, 1912).

106 See Benit-Gbaffou (2008b: 8).

107 On this effect of socio-economic rights more broadly, see Pieterse (2007: 3, 20).

References

Aboobaker v. *Serengeti Rise Body Corporate*, 2015. Decision of the Durban High Court, reported as 2015 [3] All SA 538 (KZD).

Ballard, R., 2004. 'Middle class neighbourhoods or "African kraals"? The impact of informal settlements and vagrants on post-apartheid white identity', *Urban Forum* 15(1), 48–73.

Beall, J., Crankshaw, O. & Parnell, S., 2002. *Uniting a Divided City: Governance and Social Exclusion in Johannesburg*. London: Earthscan.

Benit-Gbaffou, C., 2006. 'Police-community partnerships and responses to crime: Lessons from Yeoville and Observatory, Johannesburg', *Urban Forum* 17(4), 301–326.

Benit-Gbaffou, C., 2008a. 'Unbundled security services and urban fragmentation in post-apartheid Johannesburg', *Geoforum* 39(6), 1933–1950.

Benit-Gbaffou, C., 2008b. 'Are practices of local participation sidelining the institutional participatory channels? Reflections from Johannesburg', *Transformation: Critical Perspectives on Southern Africa* 66(1), 1–33.

Benit-Gbaffou, C., 2008c. 'Community policing and disputed norms for local social control in post-apartheid Johannesburg', *Journal of Southern African Studies* 34(1), 93–109.

Benit-Gbaffou, C., 2009. 'Who control the streets? Crime, "communities" and the state in post-apartheid Johannesburg'. In: Locatelli, F. & Nugent, P. (eds.), *African Cities: Competing Claims on Urban Space*, pp. 55–79. Leiden, Boston: Brill.

Bremner, L., 2004a. 'Bounded spaces: Demographic anxieties in post-apartheid Johannesburg', *Social Identities* 10(4), 455–468.

Bremner, L., 2004b. *Johannesburg: One City Colliding Worlds*. Johannesburg: STE Publishers.

Carmichele v. *Minister of Safety and Security*, 2001. Decision of the South African Constitutional Court, reported as 2001 (4) SA 938 (CC).

City of Johannesburg, 2014. *Security Access Restriction Policy*.

City of Johannesburg Metropolitan Municipality v. *Blue Moonlight Properties*, 2012. Decision by the South African Constitutional Court, reported as 2012 (2) SA 104 (CC).

Coggin, T., 2016. 'Redressing spatial apartheid: The law of nuisance and the transformative role of social utility and the right to the city', *South African Law Journal* 133(2), 434–451.

Consortium for Refugees and Migrants in South Africa, 2009. *Protecting Refugees, Asylum Seekers and Immigrants in South Africa*. Johannesburg: CoRMSA.

Constitution of the Republic of South Africa, 1996 (Act 108 of 1996).

Czegledy, A.P., 2003. 'Villas of the Highveld: A cultural perspective on Johannesburg and its "northern suburbs"'. In: Tomlinson, R., Beauregard, R.A., Bremner, L. & Mangcu, X. (eds.), *Emerging Johannesburg: Perspectives on the Postapartheid City*, pp. 21–42. New York, London: Routledge.

Czegledy, A.P., 2004. 'Getting around town: Transportation and the built environment in post-apartheid South Africa', *City & Society* 16(2), 63–92.

Deneys Reitz v. *South African Commercial, Catering and Allied Workers Union*, 1991. Decision of the Witwatersrand Supreme Court, reported as 1991 (2) SA 685 (W).

Diepsloot Residents' and Landowners' Association v. *Administrator, Transvaal*. Decision of the Appellate Division of the Supreme Court, reported as 1994 (3) SA 336 (AD).

Dirsuweit, T., 2014. 'The fear of others: Responses to crime and urban transformation in Johannesburg'. In: Harrison, P., Gotz, G., Todes, A., & Wray, C. (eds.), *Changing Space, Changing City: Johannesburg after Apartheid*, pp. 546–552. Johannesburg: Wits University Press.

Dugard, J., 2008. 'Rights, regulation and resistance: The Phiri water campaign', *South African Journal of Human Rights* 24(3), 593–611.

Fedsure Life Assurance et al. v. *Greater Johannesburg Transitional Metropolitan Council*, 1999. Decision of the South African Constitutional Court, reported as 1999 (1) SA 374 (CC).

Fourways Mall v. *South African Commercial Catering and Allied Workers Union*, 1999. Decision of the Witwatersrand High Court, reported as 1999 (3) SA 752 (W).

Frug, J., 1996. 'The geography of community', *Stanford Law Review* 48(5), 1047–1108.

Gauteng Rationalisation of Local Government Affairs Act, 10 of 1998.

Hatting v. *Juta*, 2013. Decision by the South African Constitutional Court, reported as 2013 (3) SA 275 (CC).

Intercape Ferreira Mainliner v. *Minister of Home Affairs*, 2010. Decision of the Cape High Court, reported as 2010 (5) SA 367 (WCC).

Jaftha v. *Schoeman; Van Rooyen* v. *Stolz*, 2005. Decision of the South African Constitutional Court, reported as 2005 (2) SA 140 (CC).

K v. *Minister of Safety and Security*, 2005. Decision of the South African Constitutional Court, reported as 2005 (6) SA 419 (CC).

Kruger, M., 2014. 'Arbitrary deprivations of property: An argument for the payment of compensation by the State in certain cases of unlawful occupation'. *South African Law Journal* 131(2), 328–364.

Kulijan, C., 2010. 'Making the invisible visible: A story of the Central Methodist Church', *The Salon* 3(1), 36–44.

Landman, K., 2006. 'Private space – "private citizen": What kind of cities are we creating?' *Southern African Public Law* 21(1), 51–71.

Landman, K. & Badenhorst, W., 2014. 'Gated communities and spatial transformation in greater Johannesburg'. In: Harrison, P., Gotz, G., Todes, A., & Wray, C. (eds.), *Changing Space, Changing City: Johannesburg after Apartheid*, pp. 215–229. Johannesburg: Wits University Press.

Law Society of South Africa v. *Minister of Transport*, 2011. Decision of the South African Constitutional Court, reported as 2011 (1) SA 400 (CC).

Layard, A., 2010. 'Shopping in the public realm: A law of place', *Journal of Law & Society* 37(3), 412–441.

Lemanski, C., Landman, K. & Durington, M., 2008. 'Divergent and similar experiences of "gating" in South Africa: Johannesburg, Durban and Cape Town', *Urban Forum* 19(2), 133–158.

Le Roux, W., 2006. 'Planning law, crime control and the spatial dynamics of post-apartheid street democracy', *Southern African Public Law* 21(1), 25–50.

Liebenberg, S., 2011. '*Grootboom* and the seduction of the negative/positive duties dichotomy', *Southern African Public Law* 26(1), 37–59.

Mabin, A., 2014. 'In the forest of transformation: Johannesburg's northern suburbs'. In: Harrison, P., Gotz, G., Todes, A., & Wray, C. (eds.), *Changing Space, Changing City: Johannesburg after Apartheid*, pp. 395–417. Johannesburg: Wits University Press.

Maphango v. *Aengus Lifestyle Properties*, 2012. Decision of the South African Constitutional Court, reported as 2012 (5) BCLR 449 (CC).

Mazibuko v. *City of Johannesburg*, 2010. Decision of the South African Constitutional Court, reported as 2010 (4) SA 1 (CC).

Minister of Public Works v. *Kyalami Ridge Environmental Association*, 2001. Decision of the South African Constitutional Court, reported as 2001 (3) SA 1151 (CC).

Miraftab, F., 2007. 'Governing post apartheid spatiality: Implementing City Improvement Districts in Cape Town', *Antipode* 39(4), 602–626.

Mkontwana v. *Nelson Mandela Metropolitan Municipality*, 2005. Decision of the South African Constitutional Court, reported as 2005 (1) SA 530 (CC).

Modder East Squatters v. *Modderklip Boerdery; President of the RSA* v. *Modderklip Boerdery*, 2004. Decision of the Supreme Court of Appeal, reported as 2004 (8) BCLR 821 (SCA).

Murray, M.J., 2011. *City of Extremes: The Spatial Politics of Johannesburg*. Durham, London: Duke University Press.

Murray, M.J., 2014. 'City of layers: The making and shaping of affluent Johannesburg after apartheid'. In: Haferburg, C. & Huchzermeyer, M. (eds.), *Urban Governance in Post-Apartheid Cities: Modes of Engagement in South Africa's Metropoles*, pp. 179–196. Pietermaritzburg: UKZN Press.

National Treasury v. *Opposition to Urban Tolling Alliance*, 2012. Decision of the South African Constitutional Court, reported as 2012 (6) SA 223 (CC).

Nevin, A., 2014. 'Instant mutuality: The development of Maboneng in inner-city Johannesburg', *Anthropology Southern Africa* 37(3), 187–201.

Peyroux, E., 2006. 'City Improvement Districts (CIDs) in Johannesburg: Assessing the political and socio-spatial implications of private-led urban regeneration', *Trialog* 89(1), 9–14.

Pieterse, M., 2007. 'The legitimizing/insulating effect of socio-economic rights', *Canadian Journal of Law & Society* 22(1), 1–20.

Pieterse, M., 2014. 'The right to the city and the urban environment: Re-imagining section 24 of the 1996 Constitution', *Southern African Public Law* 29(1), 175–193.

Pindell, N., 2006. 'Finding a right to the city: Exploring property and community in Brazil and in the United States', *Vanderbilt Journal of Transnational Law* 39(2), 435–480.

President of the Republic of South Africa v. *Modderklip Boerdery*, 2005. Decision of the South African Constitutional Court, reported as 2005 (5) SA 3 (CC).

Pretoria City Council v. *Walker*, 1998. Decision of the South African Constitutional Court, reported as 1998 (2) SA 363 (CC).

Purcell, M., 2002. 'Excavating Lefebvre: The right to the city and its urban politics of the inhabitant', *GeoJournal* 58, 99–108.

Rademan v. *Moqhaka Local Municipality*, 2013. Decision of the South African Constitutional Court, reported as 2013 (4) SA 225 (CC).

Rail Commuters Action Group v. *Transnet t/a Metrorail*, 2005. Decision of the South African Constitutional Court, reported as 2005 (2) SA 359 (CC).

Sea Front for All v. *MEC, Environmental and Development Planning, Western Cape*, 2011. Decision of the Cape High Court, reported as 2011 (3) SA 55 (WCC).

South African Human Rights Commission, 2005. *Report on the Issue of Road Closures, Security Booms and Related Matters*.

Stock v. *Minister of Housing*, 2007. Decision of the Cape High Court, reported as 2007 (2) SA 9 (C).

Strydom, J. & Viljoen, S., 2014. 'Unlawful occupation of inner-city buildings: A constitutional analysis of the rights and obligations involved', *Potchefstroom Electronic Law Journal* 17(4), 1207–1261.

Van der Walt, J., 2007. 'Johannesburg: A tale of two cases'. In: Philippopoulos-Mihalopoulos, A. (ed.), *Law and the City*, pp. 221–236. Oxford, New York: Routledge.

Victoria & Alfred Waterfront v. *Police Commissioner, Western Cape*, 2004. Decision of the Cape High Court, reported as 2004 (4) SA 444 (C).

Visser, G., 2013. 'Looking beyond the urban poor in South Africa: The new terra incognita for urban geography?' *Canadian Journal of African Studies* 47(1), 75–93.

Walele v. *City of Cape Town*, 2008. Decision of the South African Constitutional Court, reported as 2008 (6) SA 129 (CC).

Walsh, S., 2013. '"We won't move": The suburbs take back the center in urban Johannesburg', *City* 17(3), 400–408.

West, R., 2001. 'Rights, capabilities, and the good society', *Fordham Law Review* 69(5), 1901–1932.

6 Struggles over autonomy, equality and identity

Sex, gender and sexuality

Introduction

While writings on the right to the city typically focus on class struggles, the right is about more than economic survival – it is also about the individual freedom to live openly in the city, about tolerance, respect for difference and diversity. Right-to-the-city theorists therefore acknowledge that their work also applies to the production of urban space and the resistance of marginalisation in relation to more personal aspects of individual identities, such as gender, race and sexual orientation.[1]

In this chapter, the focus is on legal, social and spatial struggles for sexual liberation in Johannesburg. Like all the world's big cities, Joburg presents a variety of spaces and opportunities for sexual expression and exploration, and accordingly draws people of all sexual persuasions, predilections and peculiarities.[2] Within morally conservative South Africa it has, since its naissance, had a reputation for sexual permissiveness, open-mindedness, promiscuity and immorality, as a result of which it has always been both a prime showcase of sexuality and sexual diversity, as well as a key site for State attempts to control and suppress these.[3]

Spatially, Johannesburg's continued reflection of a legacy of racial and class-based segregation dovetails with its history of sexual repression to result in a very divergent geography of sexual liberation, suppression and resistance. Moreover, the close overlap between societal norms, conventions and power structures around sexuality and those around gender mean that studying performances of sexual autonomy across Johannesburg also shows up significant limitations in women's enjoyment of the right to the city.

Below, I briefly exposit some of the theory on the inter-linkages between rights, the city, gender and sexual citizenship, and contextualise the legal regulation of sexuality in South Africa. I then trace the history of different struggles for sexual visibility, presence and acceptance in Johannesburg's courts, streets, buildings and bedrooms. I focus first on sex work, canvassing its history in Joburg, the legal and public struggles for its legalisation and for the protection of sex workers' rights, and the interaction between the spatial practices of sex work and these rights-based struggles. Thereafter, I trace the history of LGBTI life, spaces and activism in Johannesburg, assess the impact of the Constitutional Court's widely celebrated sexual orientation rights jurisprudence on these, and contemplate the links between legal rights strategies and the divergent experiences of sexual freedom across the city. Gender is then highlighted as a common feature in the preceding discussions, and the chapter considers the restriction and policing of female sexuality in Johannesburg, as well as some public manifestations of resistance thereto, before reflecting upon the limits of rights-based adjudication on the advancement of sexual citizenship more broadly.

Rights, sex, sexuality and the city[4]

> Far from being a neutral backdrop against which sexual relations are played out, [the city] is an active agent in the making of sexualities, promoting some and repressing others.[5]

Societal norms and values are reflected and enforced through the legal regulation, the physical configuration and the social use of urban spaces. This is also the case for values and rules around sexuality, with the law, the built environment and social behaviour codes all conspiring to regulate public (and, to a lesser extent, private) forms of sexual expression. Indeed, alongside the requirement that only consenting adults ought to be having sex, the distinction between private and public spaces is a central tenet of sexual citizenship in most societies, with law and morality typically dictating that people should only be having sex in private, usually understood to mean the privacy of the home.[6]

This notion rests on several questionable assumptions (for instance, that all people have unencumbered access to home space, that such space always affords the privacy for unhindered sexual expression and that it is conducive to the equal exercise of sexual autonomy),[7] and is not consistently enforced. In all societies, certain sexual practices, relationships and identities are frowned upon, discouraged or outlawed even when they are confined to the private sphere. At the same time, some forms of sexual expression are sometimes allowed to spill over into the public realm, or are tolerated when they do, whereas others are not. Society's sexual mores (complete with its inborn preferences and prejudices) can thus often be gauged by its spatial treatment of different forms of sex.[8]

In South Africa, as in many places elsewhere, these sexual mores are overwhelmingly morally conservative, patriarchal and heteronormative. The particularly morally conservative breed of Afrikaner Christianity, which was the driving force behind the laws and policies of the apartheid state, abhorred all forms of non-procreative, non-monogamous and extramarital sex, with special scorn reserved for homosexuality, transactional sex and sex between people of different races. While considerably relaxed after the demise of apartheid, this 'official' morality continues to hold sway among large segments of the population, due in no small part to the considerable influence that religion has exercised across all racial and cultural groups, ever since the days of missionaries.[9] Legally, it continues to be reflected by various provisions of criminal law, public health law and municipal bylaws, including those upholding the ostensible 'sexlessness' of public space.

Much of the legal regulation of sexuality in South Africa takes place in terms of still-operative provisions of the 1957 Sexual Offenses Act, renamed from its more descriptive earlier moniker, the 'Immorality Act' 5 of 1927.[10] Previously, the Act criminalised interracial sex and sex between men (regardless of whether this took place in public or in private), although these provisions have since been repealed.[11] Its currently operative provisions remain centred on an extremely narrow and comically antiquated concept of 'unlawful carnal intercourse' (defined as 'carnal intercourse otherwise than between husband and wife') and, while aimed more broadly, complement the common law in outlawing most forms of sex in public. For instance, public copulation, masturbation, nudity and cruising are all criminalised as 'public indecency' in terms of the Act, whereas a different Act proscribes the public visibility of pornography.[12] Sex work is outlawed as 'unlawful carnal intercourse for reward' by section 20(1)(A)(a), while the Act's prohibition of brothel keeping (and accompanying definition of 'brothel' as 'any house or place kept or used for purposes of prostitution or for persons to visit for the purpose of having unlawful carnal intercourse or for any other lewd or indecent purpose') is wide enough to apply to all manner of private, yet publicly visible establishments where people have sex or display sexuality, such as sex clubs, strip clubs and porn theatres.

In Johannesburg, as elsewhere in the country, these criminal law provisions are supplemented by a range of municipal bylaws aimed at maintaining and ordering public space. Nuisance bylaws, liquor and drug laws and public health laws are all used in different ways against sexual establishments such as those listed above, whereas Joburg police, like their counterparts elsewhere, prefer to use nuisance and loitering bylaws, rather than the relevant provisions of the Sexual Offenses Act (which come with a cumbersome burden of proof), to combat street sex work, as is elaborated below.

Over and above the law, the desire to cleanse public spaces (especially in middle-class residential areas) of sex is often reiterated by urban planners, managers and regenerators, who tend to depict publicly visible sexuality (reflected, for instance, by premises operating as sex shops or strip clubs) as blight to be eradicated with the help of bylaw enforcement, zoning laws and the like.[13] The general public, too, assist in the social policing of sexuality, by voicing their opposition to the sexualisation of public space through a range of channels (complaints to authorities, local newspapers, community meetings and so forth) and by themselves policing public space through a variety of measures ranging from admonishment and ridicule to physical violence. As a result, as with other forms of socially scorned behaviour discussed in Chapter 4, the marginalisation of nonconformist sexual behaviour is often mirrored spatially, and sexualised city spaces tend to be dilapidated, neglected and dangerous.

Beyond widespread moral distaste for public copulation, it transpires that the opposition is not so much against the sexualisation of public space, but rather against the public display of sexuality in ways that depart from prevailing heteronormative and patriarchal social codes. The result is a 'mainstream' public environment that, by the looks of it, is devoid of sex but, upon closer inspection, reveals itself to be riddled with subtle endorsements of heteronormative and patriarchal sexuality.[14] For instance, sexual imagery abounds on magazine covers and advertising billboards, but is near-exclusively heterosexual and coupled and adheres closely to gendered scripts (whereby female sexuality, in particular, is either depicted as homely and nurturing or is predictably objectified for the heterosexual male gaze). Meanwhile, visible personal public displays of sexuality (through, for instance, dress) or of sexualised affection between people (kissing, hand-holding, touching and so forth) abound, but are overwhelmingly heteronormative and conventional.[15]

Overall, law and society's efforts to keep sex confined to private space and thereby to 'de-sexualise' public space serves to entrench and reinforce heteronormativity. Sexual liberation struggles thus revolve around rights to be present as non-heteronormative sexual creatures in public space as frequently as they comprise the right to freely engage in private sexual activity. For this reason, the right to the city presents a useful theoretical lens through which to understand such sexual liberation struggles – through physical acts of claiming and appropriating public space, and asserting public presence, subversive sexualities physically challenge the hegemony of heteronormativity.[16]

This happens in various ways, including through overt public displays of non-heteronormative sexuality, public sex, the creation of commercial sex spaces (such as saunas, swingers clubs and sex clubs) or of alternative domestic realities (for example, in single sex mining hostels across South Africa), as well as through collective political occupations of public spaces at, for instance, gay pride marches, or protests by groups of sex workers or HIV positive persons.[17] In some cities, the production of sexual space occurs at such a scale as to encompass entire city areas, such as in the case of gay 'ghettos' and red light districts.[18]

All these assertions of a right to the (sexual) city also occur, to a greater or lesser extent, in Johannesburg. In most cases, the heteronormative mainstream has pushed back, either through law enforcement, urban management, social sanction or physical violence. In the course of these struggles, constitutional rights have entered the fray respectively as tools to resist heteronormative and patriarchal oppression and thereby to remake Joburg's public sexual face, or as means of balancing the interests of mainstream society against those of its non-conformist members. The results, as will appear below, have been mixed and uneven.

Sex work in Johannesburg

Female, street-based sex work has been claimed to be the epitome of 'dangerous', 'unacceptable' and 'immoral' excesses of female sexuality, and so its legal and spatial treatment reveals a lot about society's treatment of women as sexual creatures.[19] South Africa, and Johannesburg in particular, are no exceptions. While there have been male sex workers, as well as a legion of home- or establishment-based sex workers of different genders in Joburg since its early days, it is the stereotypical image of the female street prostitute that immediately comes to mind when sex work is discussed.

Sex work and related forms of transactional sex happens across all walks of life, and in a variety of different contexts in Johannesburg and elsewhere. However, debates about the legal status of sex work tend to centre on the activities of the 'most vulnerable' female sex workers, those that are poor, foreign, drug-addicted, trafficked, abused, or any combination of these. As the spatial reflection of social vulnerability would have it, these tend to be the sex workers that ply their trade directly on the streets, rather than in safer and less detectable off-street spaces such as brothels, massage parlours, taverns, hotels and suburban apartments.[20] While perhaps a misleading sample of sex work in Johannesburg, the lives of such vulnerable sex workers and their interactions with the law and with city space present a useful lens for the study of gender vulnerability in the city more broadly. In particular, it '… draws attention to the many and complex ways in which the state, commercial interests, and society as a whole, are complicit in upholding the conditions which underpin women's sexual exploitation'.[21]

The pre-constitutional era

In the early 'mining camp' years, Joburg's working population was overwhelmingly young, single and male, and sex workers (many relocating from the then-starting-to-wane Kimberley and others from as far as Eastern Europe), who made up a substantial portion of the total women in the city, capitalised on this obvious market.[22] While the laws of the Zuid Afrikaansche Republiek prohibited prostitution, powerful business interests in Joburg's booming sex trade meant that these were not enforced by local authorities.[23] By the mid-1890s, a red light district known as 'Frenchfontein' (situated in a roughly square area between Anderson, Kruis, Bree and Sauer streets in today's Marshalltown) contained a high concentration of bars and more than a dozen brothels.[24]

An official clampdown on prostitution only occurred after the South African war at the turn of the century, and then mainly because of concerns over inter-racial sex between black mineworkers and white sex workers, which led to the passing of the first of South Africa's many pieces of race-obsessed 'immorality' legislation, and culminated in the forced shutdown of most Frenchfontein brothels in 1906.[25] In the years and decades that followed, Joburg's sex work industry became less organised and more street based, while the politics of its prohibition remained entangled in the government obsession to eradicate sex across the colour bar (which fairly quickly shifted in emphasis from a fear of black clients 'abusing' white sex workers to one of black prostitutes 'corrupting' white men).[26] Meanwhile, anti sex work legislation and law enforcement mostly focused on female prostitution (subsequent to the unmasking of a Joburg rent boy ring in the 1930s, immorality legislation instead targeted male prostitution under the blanket crime of homosexuality),[27] and almost exclusively targeted sex workers, rather than their clients.[28]

Hillbrow's transition in to a skyscraper-filled hub of bohemian cosmopolitanism from the 1960s onwards led to the relocation of much of Joburg's adult entertainment and sex work industry there. By the 1970s, Hillbrow was also at the forefront of the collapse of group areas regulation, and became the city's unofficial red-light district, as well as the focal point of societal moral panic and of the crumbling apartheid state's efforts to quash both commercial and interracial sex.[29] It retains its close association with sex work, moral decay and 'illegal' migration to this day.

A somewhat relaxed nationwide morality, as well as an increasing sense of apartheid's impending demise, led to increased calls for the legalisation of sex work, which remained a frequent topic of discussion in the press (and, albeit less frequently, in politics) from the mid-1970s onwards.[30] Meanwhile, Sandton's rise as a commercial and business hub in the mid-1980s saw increased indoor, and relatively upmarket, sex-for-sale businesses operating under various monikers from commercial and residential premises there, whereas street sex work remained predominantly CBD- and Hillbrow-based. Indeed, as Hillbrow slid down its path of urban decline towards the end of the 1980s, its residential hotels became near synonymous with sex work as well as with Joburg's drug trade, and they largely remain so to this day.[31]

Hillbrow's decline continued into and throughout the 1990s, to a point where many of its buildings were reduced to slums and its streets were considered particularly unsafe. Its sex workers, kept out of safer and more respectable suburbs by community and police efforts to contain nuisance and blight, plied their trade in dangerous and unhealthy conditions, vulnerable to abuse by clients, criminals and the police.[32] As in red light districts around the world, the city had contained its 'fallen' women within its least safe and least savoury space, thereby both reflecting and exacerbating their vulnerability.[33] Yet the women, together with their pimps and other marginalised residents, stubbornly eked out an existence on Hillbrow's streets and in its hotels, so that a tough subculture of survival prevailed amid the decay.

Sex worker activism from the mid-1990s onwards

The demise of apartheid and its associated moral repression, together with the enactment of the interim and final Constitutions with their Bills of Rights entrenching rights to equality, dignity, privacy and freedom and security of the person, brought about a marked moral enlightenment, and increased sexual openness and tolerance in South Africa from the mid-1990s onwards. Interracial sex had been decriminalised in the late 1980s, and possession of pornography, homosexuality and polygamous customary marriages were legalised in the aftermath of the Constitution's enactment and of the first decisions of the Constitutional Court.[34] Sex work (including, for the first time, male sex work and other forms of transactional sex such as the casual sex-for-reward exchanges that had become commonplace in the taverns of Soweto and other formerly black townships[35]) was increasingly 'normalised' and acknowledged in the popular press, and calls for its legalisation were increasingly articulated in rights-based terms.[36]

Spurred on by this, sex workers' rights organisations began to form, and to rally around the rights ensconced in the Constitution. These were led by the Sex Workers Education and Advocacy Taskforce (SWEAT), a Cape-Town based organisation formed in the early 1990s and formally institutionalised in 1996.[37] SWEAT continues to lead South Africa's sex workers' rights campaigns, with the result that these have a distinct Cape-Town flavour and represent Joburg sex workers only incidentally. In Joburg, sex workers' interests were for the most part advanced by women's and sexual health organisations (such as Wits University's Hillbrow-based Rural Health Research Unit), until SWEAT supported the establishment of the (somewhat less vocal) Sisonke sex worker movement, based in Hillbrow, in 2002.[38]

In response to the Constitution and its accompanying air of moral permissiveness, the Gauteng Department of Safety and Security decided to decriminalise sex work in 1996, ostensibly in a drive to 'free up' police resources to enable a focus on 'more serious' crimes. Other provincial departments, as well as local governments in Joburg, Pretoria and Ekurhuleni, were supportive of this move, and the Gauteng cabinet approved decriminalisation in 1997. However, a moral public and press backlash (decrying, among other things, the 'un-African-ness' of sex work) followed, as did disapproval and opposition from national government, which was quick to point out that the legislative competence to decriminalise sex work rested with it, rather than with Gauteng. Nationally, the ANC decided to postpone deliberation on decriminalisation until after the 1999 elections, by which time the momentum had seemingly passed. The legislative initiative accordingly waned, although the South African Law Reform Commission would launch a tardy (and still incomplete) investigation into the matter at around the same time.[39]

Partly because of the sense that there were more serious crimes to combat, and partly because the Constitution with its heightened standards of criminal justice and proof made successfully enforcing the sex work provisions of the Sexual Offenses Act near impossible, the police indeed de-prioritised the criminal prosecution of sex workers.[40] Instead, such policing of sex work as still took place was almost exclusively in terms of municipal bylaws that prohibited loitering, public indecency and nuisance, and usually in response to complaints from suburban residents that prostitutes were disturbing their peace or otherwise spoiling their environment.[41] This means that only street prostitution effectively remains targeted, so that those sex workers who can afford to work indoors (as many throughout Joburg do) generally escape police harassment. The harassment to which street sex workers are subjected is, however, significant and often includes different levels of sexual assault.

In the constitutional era, therefore, the prohibition on sex work has effectively become exclusively about maintaining the heteronormativity of public space. Collectively and individually, sex workers thus struggle not only for the legal benefits of decriminalisation, but also for the right to be present in public.

A judicial setback: S *v.* Jordan

As the Law Reform Commission continued with its inquiry into the continued criminalisation of sex work, SWEAT and other women's rights organisations engaged in a variety of law reform initiatives. These were, however, disrupted when an unrelated challenge to the constitutionality of the criminalisation of sex work was brought before the Pretoria High Court in 2001, leaving the anti-criminalisation lobby scrambling to join the litigation and to provide contextual evidence.[42]

S v. *Jordan* primarily involved a challenge, by a Pretoria brothel madam and some of her employees (who were arrested after an undercover policeman received a 'pelvic massage' on the premises), against the criminalisation of sex for reward in terms of section 20(1)(aA) of the Sexual Offenses Act, as well as some related challenges to the Act's brothel-keeping provisions. It was alleged that section 20(1)(aA) unjustifiably infringed the constitutional rights to dignity, privacy and occupational freedom, and also the right to equality, in that it targeted only sex workers (who were mostly women) and not also their (predominantly male) clients. The Pretoria High Court agreed and declared the provision unconstitutional, upon which the State appealed to the Constitutional Court.

The Constitutional Court handed down its judgment in the matter in March of 2002. Surprisingly, it found that the challenged provisions were not unconstitutional. The Court unanimously dismissed the challenges based on the rights to dignity, privacy and occupational freedom, and was divided on the issue of the right to equality, with the majority of the Court holding that the provision did not discriminate unfairly on the basis of gender.

In a short and peculiarly formalistic majority judgment, Ngcobo J rejected the argument that to criminalise sex workers but not their clients amounted to gender discrimination, since section 20(1)(aA) was phrased gender-neutrally.[43] The minority judgment by Sachs and O'Regan JJ, meanwhile, did regard the distinction as amounting to unfair discrimination because of its reflection of problematic, gendered stereotypes of acceptable male and female sexuality (which the judges bemoaned in some detail), but suggested that this could be remedied by also criminalising clients.[44]

Both judgments clearly regarded prostitution as morally wrong and thus viewed the legislative choice to criminalise it as justifiable in an open and democratic society. This was evident especially from their treatment of the challenges based on the rights to privacy and dignity. The majority judgment held that the right to privacy did not entitle people to commit crimes in public and that, in any event, commercial sex lay at the periphery of privacy rather than at its constitutionally protected 'inner core'.[45] The minority echoed this, stating that commercial sex 'involves the most intimate of activity taking place in the most impersonal and public of realms' and that its criminal prohibition would therefore not 'ordinarily encroach upon intimate or meaningful human relationships'.[46] They further reasoned that commercial sex's 'indiscriminate and loveless' character removed it from the realm of constitutionally protected privacy, stating that:

> By making her sexual services available for hire to strangers in the marketplace, the sex worker empties the sex act of much of its private and intimate character. She is not nurturing relationships or taking life-affirming decisions about birth, marriage or family, she is making money.... We accordingly conclude that her expectations of privacy are relatively attenuated. Although the commercial value of her trade does not eliminate her claims to privacy, it does reduce them in a great degree.[47]

All the judges thus agreed that any infringement of the right to privacy was both reasonable and justifiable. As to the right to dignity, both judgments were in agreement that sex workers were themselves to blame for any diminution of their dignity arising from criminalisation because, in the words of the minority, 'the very work that [sex workers] undertake devalues the respect that the Constitution regards as inherent in the human body'.[48]

Jordan was received extremely negatively. Sex workers marched to the Union Buildings in Pretoria to communicate their disdain of the judgment.[49] Virtually every aspect of the judgment has been severely criticised in the press, by sex work advocates, feminists, members of civil society and academics, mostly for the way in which it upheld a conservative, outdated and somewhat twee societal morality. Scholars have bemoaned the majority judgment's formalism and its ignorance of the strongly gendered context of sex work, the conservatism underlying the finding that the protection of the right to dignity is forfeited by immoral, 'undignified' sexual behaviour, as well as the deeply gendered, blandly heteronormative and severely moralistic notion of domesticity underlying the Court's conception of 'acceptable' private sex, which rejects loveless, impersonal and pleasure-seeking sex, and values female sexuality only when it is de-eroticised, safe, nurturing, self-sacrificial and aimed towards procreation and maintenance of the nuclear family.[50]

Certainly, *Jordan* dealt a significant blow to the building movement for the decriminalisation of sex work. It understandably demotivated sex work advocates and appeared to derail the South African Law Reform Commission's policy reform process, which was delayed, ostensibly to make sense of the judgment and its impact on the legal landscape.

More significantly, the legislature's reaction to the judgment was somewhat predictable and disappointing. Understanding the minority judgment to imply that the distinction between sex worker and client was the only potentially constitutionally problematic aspect of the current legal approach to sex work, Parliament introduced a provision into the Sexual Offenses Amendment Act which also made it a crime to purchase sex.[51] While this indeed allowed for more even-handed prosecution of all participants in the crime of sex work,[52] the effect of the amendment was to exacerbate the vulnerability of sex workers, by driving sex work even further underground (in order for clients to escape prosecution or police blackmail). Geographically, this meant that street-based sex work moved into more secluded spaces, whereas off–street transactions were more likely to take place in spaces more directly under the control of clients. Given the problematic gender power dynamics underlying sex work, both of these posed more danger for sex workers.[53]

After Jordan*: sex work and sex worker advocacy in the 2000s*

Sex worker advocacy took some time to recover from the setback of *Jordan*. The South African Law Reform Commission published an issue paper on adult sex work in 2002, around the time of the *Jordan* judgment, but then only followed it up with a Discussion Paper in 2009. Content-wise, the Discussion Paper was disappointingly non-committal. It presented a detailed overview of the law currently applicable to sex work and canvassed arguments for and against its regulation, but did not commit to any particular policy position. Instead, it postulated a range of options for law reform and future regulation of sex work, including decriminalisation, regulation, partial criminalisation (of pimps, brothel keepers, traffickers and perhaps clients, but not of sex workers) and continued criminalisation.[54] Public comment was invited by a closing date in June 2009. At the time of writing, the Commission was yet to issue its final report.[55]

A significant window for activism and law reform presented itself when South Africa was announced as host country for the 2010 soccer World Cup. Popular perception was that there would be an increase in demand for sex work during the event. Reacting to this, the Durban Metropolitan Council mooted the possibility of establishing temporary red light districts, where a blind eye would be turned to sex work for the duration of the World Cup. Johannesburg and other metropolitan governments were supportive of the suggestion, which also curried favour with the National Police Commissioner, who went as far as to publicly call for the temporary decriminalisation of sex work, to enable the police to focus on more pressing issues of safety and security during the event.[56]

Cynical and unconcerned with sex workers themselves as these proposals were, they reinvigorated sex work organisations, who rallied to enhance their profile and to campaign for more lasting reforms. Unfortunately, their efforts were countered by a massive, press-driven moral panic about the social ills that would ostensibly accompany greater tolerance for sex work during the World Cup. Exaggerated and near-hysterical reports of a deluge of sex workers upon South African cities, with accompanying increases in illegal migration, child prostitution, human trafficking, drug-related crimes and – social ill of ills – nuisance, loitering and littering by sex workers in public space, abounded.[57] While none of these fears eventually materialised, the manufactured moral hysteria was sufficient to counter the drive for legalisation and, once again, nothing came of mooted reforms. Indeed, as it turned out, sex workers bore the brunt of the various pre-World Cup urban 'clean-up' initiatives, aimed at removing blight from tourist view.[58]

Meanwhile, on the positive side, two significant legal victories around the same time undid some of the damage done by *Jordan* and reinvigorated the rights-based struggle for the recognition of sex work. In the first, *Kylie* v. *CCMA*, a sex worker sued the management of the Cape Town massage parlour where she was working for having unfairly dismissed her. The Commission for Conciliation, Mediation and Arbitration (CCMA) refused to entertain the matter, holding that it could not deliberate on matters flowing from employment contracts which were, by their nature, illegal and hence unenforceable. This view was confirmed by the Labour Court but, surprisingly, overturned by the Labour Appeal Court.

While at pains to emphasise that the legalisation of sex work was within the exclusive purview of Parliament and that its judgment could thus not be read as condoning sex work, the Court held that the illegality of sex work did not mean that sex workers were stripped of constitutional and statutory rights. Noting that sex workers are particularly vulnerable to exploitation by their employers, the Court regarded their protection against unfair labour practices as being of particular importance in the context. It found that, the illegality of her work notwithstanding, Kylie was to be considered a rights-bearer under the Constitution and labour legislation, and could therefore potentially avail herself of relevant labour-law remedies. The Court proceeded to overturn the CCMA's refusal of jurisdiction and found that it should go ahead and deliberate the matter.[59]

While obviously limited in its impact, the *Kylie* judgment is significant because it counters the discourse, prevalent in *Jordan*, that sex workers forfeit their constitutional rights because of the nature of their work. It thereby empowers sex workers to assert their rights *in their capacity as sex workers*, which goes a long way towards enhancing their visibility.

Even more significant was *SWEAT* v. *Minister of Safety and Security*, where SWEAT challenged the constitutionality of a prevalent Cape Town police practice, whereby police would routinely arrest and detain street-based sex workers on loitering and nuisance bylaw contraventions, without any intention to charge or prosecute them, only to later release them without charge. This kind of conduct has also been complained of in Johannesburg and elsewhere in the country.[60] SWEAT protested outside the courtroom for most of the trial.

The Cape High Court declared the arrests unconstitutional, finding that they infringed the rights to dignity and to freedom and security of the person. This, according to the Court, was because the police's conduct was intended solely to harass the sex workers, in an attempt to drive them out of public space. It stated:

> The pattern of police conduct described hereinbefore is directed at outdoor sex workers, a particularly vulnerable segment of our society. They are rounded up, arrested, detained and, virtually without fail, thereafter discharged without being prosecuted for any offence. I agree with the contention of the applicant, that what the police are therefore targeting, is not the illegality of sex work per se, but rather the public manifestations of it. The arrests of the sex workers therefore amount to a form of social control. This clearly infringes on sex workers' rights to dignity and freedom.[61]

The police were therefore interdicted from continuing with the practice.

What is especially powerful in the *SWEAT* judgment is the manner in which the Court vindicates sex workers' right to the city. The Court's understanding of the rights to dignity and freedom in relation to their spatial dimensions, as well as its depiction of the arrests as an unjustifiable form of control of public space, strikes specifically at the interaction between legal and spatial marginalisation and goes a long way towards establishing the right of a marginalised sexual minority to be present in public space.[62]

Both *SWEAT* and *Kylie* were decided in Cape Town, and relate specifically to the context of sex work there. Obviously, their impact would also be mostly felt in Cape Town. Yet, sex workers in Joburg and elsewhere are also able to benefit from and leverage these victories. Meanwhile, the struggle for greater recognition and presence of sex workers continues around the country, as the legal victories above have, alas, not added much momentum to official law reform processes.

In post-World Cup Joburg, the day-to-day practice of sex work continues much as before. In recent years, there have been annual collective appropriations of city space in the form of inner-city sex worker protest marches on International Sex Workers' Day[63] but, apart from that, activism has been sparse. Most hope seemingly remains focused on the Law Reform Commission process, although there is clearly ample reason to be sceptical over its potential for meaningful change.

The continued criminal prohibition of sex work is testament to society's continued commitment to ostracise its sexual non-conformers. Moreover, as will be explored below, it is no coincidence that this ostracising has been particularly gendered. Not only does criminalisation disproportionately stigmatise and spatially marginalise female sex workers, it also significantly limits their socio-economic survival options in a city that cannot otherwise readily economically sustain them.[64] While the Joburg sex trade is certainly as healthy as it has been before, acknowledgement of its presence and its importance in the economy and everyday life of the city still appears to be a long way off.

LGBTI rights struggles in Johannesburg[65]

Sexuality is fluid and multifaceted, and its expression varies significantly across South African cultures and subcultures, and also within Johannesburg. Whereas it is therefore certainly not possible to speak of a uniform LGBTI identity or experience in Joburg or in South Africa, LGBTI Joburgers are nevertheless similarly situated in relation to the law and to societal morality which, across all South African cultures, remains deeply homophobic.

Due to the pervasiveness of homophobia, the perceived sexual permissiveness of urban areas draws LGBTI persons to cities, especially to those cities with a reputation for sexual openness and possibilities of alternative sexual lifestyles.[66] In South Africa, this has been especially true of Joburg, Pretoria, Durban and Cape Town, all of which boast sizeable, 'out', queer 'communities'. Compared with these cities' 'communities' of sex workers, the 'out' LGBTI population is more diverse in terms of race, gender and class and, in particular, appears outwardly to contain a greater proportion of upper and middle-class persons.

This may mean that LGBTI persons have more social clout and better access to law and related resources, and may therefore be in a better position to mobilise around rights than is the case with sex workers. Joburg's experience of LGBTI rights struggles, both in the courts and on the streets, thus presents an interesting comparison with the struggles concerning sex work discussed above.

The pre-constitutional era

While sex between men was illegal in South Africa, under different legislative and common-law iterations, from the late nineteenth century onwards, Johannesburg had a discernible (predominantly white) gay and lesbian community and an (albeit fairly underground) gay 'scene' from as early as the 1930s,[67] whereas an institutionalised culture of same-sex sex and relationships between black men living in the city's mining hostels has been documented from as early as the 1920s.[68]

The public face of homosexuality in the city, and the focal point of moral and legal opposition thereto, was however overwhelmingly white and male – partly because the State at the time had a more direct and pressing interest in maintaining the hegemony of white, heterosexual male superiority,[69] but also because a combination of gender, racial and class privilege allowed white men to be unapologetically public about their sexual difference. Whereas the lesbian scene of 1940s to 1960s' Joburg has been described as 'clique-y', suburban and private,[70] and while black queers of both genders in the outlying townships were typically not 'out' in the 'Western' sense,[71] and were in any event excluded from the inner city 'scene' by racist laws and spatial policing, white gay men more blatantly appropriated inner city space. Several gay-focused bars and clubs, and a number of well-known cruising spots, developed around the Joburg CBD, Park Station and Joubert Park.[72]

Opposition to homosexuality gained traction following a moral panic after a gay, Joburg-based rent-boy ring was 'exposed' in the late 1930s. Gay venues in the CBD were regularly raided by police under the guise of enforcing liquor and drug laws, while the public indecency provisions of the 1957 Immorality Act were often used to justify police harassment of men suspected of cruising for sex. This state-led suppression of publicly expressed homosexuality also created space for 'private' victimisation of gay men, and incidences of inner-city gay-bashing became frequent. Paradoxically, gay appropriation of inner city space intensified, with several sex-focused 'health clubs' and bathhouses opening around the inner city, Joubert Park and Hillbrow.[73]

The grey area of (illegal) public sex taking place in legally private space, was thrust into the public consciousness in early 1966, when Johannesburg police raided a large, private, all male sex party at a house in the wealthy suburb of Forest Town, arresting several men on public indecency charges. Amid ensuing moral panic, police vowed to crack down on homosexuality, but were hampered by the fact that the public vice that they were targeting mostly took place in private places.[74]

To assist, Parliament amended the Immorality Act by inserting the rather bizarre section 20A, which criminalised acts between men that 'stimulate sexual passion or … give sexual gratification' at a 'party', defined as any occasion with more than two people present.[75] The impracticalities of enforcing the provision would make for amusing case-law, such as the decision of the Joburg Supreme Court in *S* v. *C*, which considered whether a 'party' came into being when a policeman entered a private cubicle in an inner city Joburg sauna, causing the two men inside to jump apart.[76]

The Forest Town raids also led to the first instance of collective political action by LGBTI persons in South Africa, with the 'Homosexual Law Reform Fund' established to fund the defence of those arrested at the party and later branching out to lobby for decriminalisation of same-sex activity.[77] Forest Town further sparked a lively debate about the acceptability of homosexuality, in the letter columns of several South African newspapers, with a surprising amount of support for gay rights being voiced amidst the opposition.[78]

The intensification of the struggle against apartheid from the late 1970s onwards also politicised urban gay life. While initial gay rights organisations were exclusively white, male and politically conservative,[79] the Joburg based 'Gays and Lesbians of the Witwatersrand' (GLOW) was formed in the mid-1980s under the leadership of Simon Nkoli (a well-known, black struggle activist), and brought to Joburg's LGBTI community a previously unheard of level of multiracialism, as well as of political and spatial activism.[80] GLOW pertinently organised Joburg's (and the African continent's) first lesbian and gay Pride march in October of 1990, appropriating inner city space in a protest march calling for the decriminalisation of homosexuality, the recognition of same-sex relationships and the inclusion of a prohibition on discrimination on the basis of sexuality in a future Bill of Rights.[81] This latter demand was also the focal point for subsequent Pride marches, as well as for sustained political lobbying campaigns. These bore fruit, and the equality clause in the 1993 interim Constitution explicitly prohibited discrimination on the ground of sexual orientation.[82]

In 1994, GLOW was incorporated into the broader National Coalition for Gay and Lesbian Equality (NCGLE), formed to ensure that the anti-discrimination provision in the final Constitution retained the prohibition on discrimination based on sexuality. It pursued this goal less publicly, however, because its leaders felt that it was important for LGBTI activism to present a discreet, professional and unthreatening face.[83] This tactic was successful, and the 1996 Constitution continued to protect LGBTI persons from discrimination.

The LGBTI legal rights campaign

Bolstered by constitutional protection, the NCGLE launched a meticulously strategised litigation campaign targeting the criminalisation of sex between men and the legal non-recognition of same-sex relationships. In 1998, it brought and won a high-profile challenge against various laws (including the post-Forest Town 'party law') that criminalised sex between men, with the Constitutional

Court unanimously finding in *National Coalition of Gay and Lesbian Equality* v. *Minister of Justice* that all these prohibitions were unconstitutional, for unjustifiably breaching the rights to equality, privacy, dignity and freedom and security of the person.

The *National Coalition* judgment has been widely lauded for its permissive and fluid understanding of sexual orientation, its condemnation of different manifestations of societal heteronormativity and its explicit championing of the value of difference in relation to sexual orientation.[84] On the other hand, some commentators have remarked that the Court's understanding of sex in *National Coalition* was nevertheless rather conventional and heteronormative, in the sense that the Court appeared to affirm only sex that occurred in private, between (implicitly monogamous) loving couples.[85]

After *National Coalition*, the campaign's focus shifted to the recognition and affirmation of same-sex relationships. While the Coalition would splinter over the next few years,[86] its strategy endured, with a string of High Court and Constitutional Court judgments declaring that it was unconstitutional to exclude partners of permanent same-sex relationships from statutory, relationship-based benefits (such as spousal citizenship rights under immigration legislation, pension benefits, medical aid membership and joint adoption).[87] These cases culminated in *Minister of Home Affairs* v. *Fourie*[88] (brought jointly by the Equality Project, the main remnant of the NCGLE), where the Constitutional Court instructed Parliament to devise inclusive marriage legislation, failing which the Court would nullify the common-law definition of marriage, as well as its statutory manifestations, since these discriminated unfairly on the basis of sexual orientation by restricting marriage to heterosexual couples. Parliament complied, and the right to enter into legally binding marriages was extended to same-sex couples by the 2006 Civil Union Act.

Much as this was a momentous victory and was taken up widely across Johannesburg (with figures showing that most same-sex marriages in South Africa had been conducted in cities in Gauteng[89]), commentators have remarked that the rights won in *Fourie* and the relationship-based cases that preceded it, were practically claimable predominantly by a white and middle-class subset of 'out' gays and lesbians. Conversely, these rights seemed to make little difference to the lives of black and less unequivocally gay/lesbian identified queers (for whom marrying and forming families with someone of the same sex was seldom a realistic or acceptable personal, social or cultural option), or to poorer LGBTI persons (who in any event lacked the means to, for instance, join pension funds and medical aid schemes).[90]

It has further been pointed out that the relationship-based sexual orientation jurisprudence of the Constitutional Court has largely reinforced heteronormative social values, by extending recognition to same sex relationships 'only to the extent (and, arguably, on the condition) that they mirror idealised heterosexual marriage relationships in their monogamy, coupledom [and] domesticity'.[91] This is arguably directly traceable to the deliberate litigation strategy behind this jurisprudence, with the NCGLE and its successors having taken great care to front their legal challenges with plaintiffs who conformed to the tenets of heteronormative morality in as many ways as possible (with most of the cases mentioned here brought by monogamous, middleclass, white, lesbian, suburban couples), and to consistently present sexual orientation as harmless, inborn and immutable.[92]

While the judgments discussed here and the Civil Union Act have therefore certainly removed legal impediments to publicly identifying as gay or lesbian and have established legal equality between same-sex and opposite sex relationships, they appear to have done little to destabilise the heteronormative tenets of public citizenship, public rights and public space. As elsewhere, it would therefore seem that LGBTI legal struggles in South Africa have, over and above securing a more LGBTI-friendly legislative framework, achieved little other than to secure the inclusion of LGBTI persons in existing heteronormative societal structures, without in any meaningful way altering or disrupting these.[93]

Performing non-heterosexuality in the constitutional era

Much as the constitutional victories discussed above allowed unprecedented space for LGBTI South Africans of all walks of life to be more out and open about their sexualities,[94] and thus led to greater queer visibility across Johannesburg, they also appeared to depoliticise queer life, whilst showing up the divide between those who could effectively make use of their newly-won legal rights and those who could not.

Joburg's class-based spatial reconfiguration in the mid-1990s also changed the geography of LGBTI social life across the city. White and middle-class LGBTI Joburgers joined their heterosexual compatriots in the exodus to the north, with the result that the gay 'scene' dispersed across the northern suburbs, where it gradually became (somewhat) more racially integrated. It also became less unequivocally queer, with exclusively LGBTI-targeted venues increasingly making place for 'gay-friendly' establishments catering to a clientele of mixed sexual orientations.[95] To the extent that a discernible LGBTI culture existed in the northern suburbs today, it was a rather brash, consumerist and exclusionary one, 'geared primarily towards a young, white, well-resourced, gay, male audience, while continuously alienating poor, female and black queers, as well as those whose sexual identities were more complex or less mainstream'.[96]

Indeed, middle-class white gay Joburgers, being sufficiently empowered to exercise their recently-won rights, appeared increasingly to distance themselves not only from the notion of a dissident, anti-heteronormative gay 'community', but also from the issues that continued to be faced by black and poorer LGBTIs.[97] A particularly poignant illustration of this has been the depoliticisation, geographic shift and racial stratification of Joburg Pride parades. A far cry from the acutely politicised sites of conflict and confrontation of their 1990s inner-city heyday, Pride parades basically degenerated into tame, assimilated and heavily commercialised northern suburb social events. Reconceptualised as an unthreatening 'celebration' of queer culture, the parades have mostly involved a mobile costume party moving across Rosebank or Sandton, followed by entry-fee charging parties in the vicinity. While still evoking the right to the city in their flamboyant queering of otherwise drably heteronormative public space,[98] the marches have lost most of their political currency, and have rightly been accused of deliberately sidelining and alienating poorer and black queers (who have, in protest, started more political but less attended 'splinter-prides' in the inner city and Soweto).[99]

Meanwhile, more subversive and overtly sexualised displays of anti-heteronormative sexuality continue to be vociferously subjugated across Johannesburg, both by the State and by residents. While no longer actively persecuting homosexuals, City officials and the police remain disproportionately occupied with discouraging homosexual uses of space, especially for sex. Gay clubs, saunas and cruising spaces are regularly (and disproportionately) scrutinised for compliance with municipal bylaws and national drug laws.[100] For instance, in the late 1990s, a smidgeon of gay clubs in lower Rosebank were shut down following residents' complaints of bylaw contraventions, whereafter the gay 'scene' shifted to Braamfontein, with the 'Heartlands' district becoming as close to a gay 'ghetto' as Joburg has ever managed. However, this area, too, was soon stamped out through ardent bylaw enforcement.[101]

Furthermore, gay bashing, ranging from insults to physical and sexual assault in a variety of public and private spaces, remains rife, even in the more gay-friendly northern suburbs. Men cruising for sex in public (such as in the parks surrounding Zoo Lake or the Emmarentia dam) or leaving well-known gay venues are still sporadically assaulted, as are men who publicly appear in drag.[102] The concomitant dangers of private space is illustrated by an intriguing spate of seemingly connected murders of eight suburban Joburg gay men, all of whom had been killed in their homes after they had electronically arranged to hook up for sex, from 2010 onwards. As rumours of a serial killer gained momentum and credibility, LGBTI organisations urged men not to invite strangers into their homes, but rather to hook up in semi-public spaces such as saunas or sex clubs.[103]

But the perils of gay male life in the northern suburbs pale in comparison to those in the townships and informal settlements, where LGBTI persons are not only on average far more economically vulnerable, but are also subjected to far more hostile socio-cultural and spatial environments. 'Out' LGBTI persons in township spaces were a rare occurrence prior to the constitutional era and remain somewhat of an anomaly (albeit certainly more common) after 1994. Whereas their increased visibility (also reflected by a smidgeon of small LGBTI taverns and other social spaces) is credited for a slow spread of tolerance, it has also been the catalyst for particularly acute resistance, with township anti-gay violence being known as particularly violent and, often, deadly.[104]

Black lesbians, especially, are regularly subjected to extreme (indeed, often fatal) homophobic violence, both in public and in the home environment. High-profile incidences of public brutalisation in recent years have included the 2012 assault of a woman, who was kissing her girlfriend goodbye, by Carlton Centre security guards, the gang-rape of two lesbians in Braamfontein following the 2000 Gay Pride march, and a number of so-called 'corrective rapes' and murders across townships and informal settlements, epitomised by the brutal rape and killing of 'out' national soccer player Eudy Simelane in an East Rand township in 2008.[105]

Overall, the constitutional entrenchment and judicial vindication of LGBTI rights has certainly enabled greater queer visibility and led to increased tolerance towards LGBTI persons across the city, which has significantly simplified the day-to-day lives of a great many LGBTI Joburgers. Yet, for those whose lives depart from the model of homosexuality sculpted by the legal activism and litigation, as well as for those who do not live in the northern suburbs and are not cushioned from homophobia by middle-class status and conformance to heteronormative societal standards, things remain complicated. Indeed, outside of the shopping malls and entertainment-oriented 'high streets' of the northern suburbs, and the tolerant 'hipster enclaves' of Braamfontein and Maboneng,[106] Joburg queers often remain intimidated into concealing or underplaying their sexuality, by residents and officials alike.[107]

Gender, sex and the city: female sexuality in Johannesburg

Gender norms around sexuality show up as a main determinant of the legal, spatial and social suppression of sexual autonomy in both the previous subsections. The discussion on sex work showed how female, street-based sex workers are routinely vilified, persecuted and assaulted for being the personification of inappropriate (and inappropriately public) female sexuality, and how they accordingly tend to be relegated to the dangerous and marginalised spaces of the city. The section on LGBTI Joburg further showed that, while gay and gender non-conforming men do risk physical and sexual violence, it is lesbian Joburgers, especially in marginal spaces, whose lives are most at risk from the violent policing of societal norms on sexual orientation. In both cases, the trigger appears to be the outward, public display of non-conformance with patriarchal gender norms through, for instance, dress, physical presentation and/or sexual behaviour.

But it is not only extreme cases of female non-conformance that attracts scorn, harassment and violence. All women are expected to conduct themselves 'appropriately' as sexual creatures in public space and, depending on the manner of their diversions from gendered norms, get typecast and subjected to similar treatment as prostitutes and/or lesbians when they do not.[108] In Johannesburg, as in many other cities, the extreme manifestation of this is that all women risk sexual harassment, or assault, simply by being present in public space without male company, especially at night, when streets are popularly regarded as being unsafe and inappropriate spaces for unaccompanied women. Indeed, women who do fall victim to sexual violence in deserted city space, or at night, or while unaccompanied, are often overtly blamed for having brought their assault upon themselves, by 'foolishly', 'naively' or 'irresponsibly' having flaunted the 'common sense' 'rule' of confining themselves to home space and venturing out only in male company.[109]

This is, of course, not to say that home space provides a haven from sexual assault or gendered violence. Much as women are socialised to fear public space, statistics everywhere show unequivocally that domestic violence remains the main threat to their bodily and sexual autonomy.[110] Indeed, both domestic violence and 'public' sexual assault (and rape) figures in South Africa are among the highest in the world, while Johannesburg has the statistically backed reputation of being the most violent, and sexually violent, city in the country.

In Johannesburg, thus, many women's daily private and public lives are acutely coloured by gendered violence. This is especially so in marginalised space, where the feminisation of poverty, other forms of vulnerability and the 'lawlessness' prevailing in the margins combine in particularly pernicious webs of oppression.[111] In its public dimensions, this violence directly and acutely limits the most fundamental aspect of women's right to the city – the right to be present there.[112]

Of course, law protects women against sexual violence and harassment by criminalising both, but is notoriously ineffective in this regard. This is at least in part because the social and legal norms of public sexuality create and sustain many of the vulnerabilities described here.

Litigation, too, has had limited effect in this respect. Two well-known Constitutional Court judgments have laudably vindicated women's right to bodily integrity, by holding the State liable for the police's failures to protect women against sexual violence. In *Carmichele* v. *Minister of Safety and Security*, where the claimant asked for police protection against a man who was harassing her, and was subsequently brutally attacked by him after such protection was not forthcoming, the Court ordered for the principles of the common law of delict to be developed in a manner that would enable the claimant to successfully claim damages against the State.[113] A similar development was ordered in *K* v. *Minister of Safety and Security*, where the State was held liable when two policemen raped the claimant after offering her a lift late at night because for her to walk home would have been 'unsafe' (despite this crime having been committed outside of the normal scope of their work).[114] But, as Nicole Fritz observes, both these judgments conceived of women primarily as potential victims of sexual violation in need of (patriarchal) protection, rather than as autonomous sexual agents.[115]

As such, the judgments failed to disrupt the general heteronormative and patriarchal way within which female sexuality is generally framed, especially when they are read with the Court's effective endorsement of gendered standards of public sexuality in *Jordan*. The general heteronormativity of the Constitutional Court's LGBTI jurisprudence has also not created much space for men and women to conduct themselves differently in their private sex lives. Indeed, when read with the Constitutional Court's much maligned judgment in *Volks* v. *Robinson*, where the Court refused to extend some of the material benefits of marriage to the survivors of long-term, heterosexual cohabitation relationships (justified by reference to the 'free choice' to enter into marriage and the 'special', protection-worthy consortium that comes into being as a result of exercising that choice),[116] the pull very much remains towards conventional social structures for sexual expression, complete with their problematic notions of privacy, hetero-normative coupledom and procreation-focused, subservient expressions of female sexuality.[117]

When it comes to gendered norms about sexuality, thus, constitutional rights jurisprudence appears not to have pushed South African society much further towards greater sexual openness. It has been left to women themselves to exploit the increased open-mindedness of contemporary South African urban life to flaunt gendered norms and thereby to carve out greater sexual liberty. For the most part, though, this has occurred through individual behaviour rather than through sexual place-making and, unlike in the case of male homosexuality, most (conventional or other) expressions of female sexuality remain confined to private space.

In recent years, though, there have been some collective assertions of female sexual autonomy through the temporary appropriation of city space, specifically in relation to gendered standards of dress. In early 2007, there was an outcry in the Johannesburg and national press when a woman was sexually assaulted at the Noord Street taxi rank, ostensibly simply for having worn a miniskirt. (Male) taxi drivers stripped her naked, poured alcohol over her and paraded her in front of a cheering public, averring that her attire insulted African culture. In response to the incident, significant numbers of women joined the victim in marching to the taxi rank wearing miniskirts, asserting their right to wear what they like in the city.[118]

A more organised expression of resistance to patriarchal standards of appropriate public behaviour has been the annual Joburg 'Slutwalk', which has taken place in the northern suburbs since 2011. An internationally observed day of anti-rape protest, Slutwalk originated in Toronto in 2011, when women took to the streets in all kinds of sexually provocative and other forms of dress, after a police officer made a public speech at an anti-crime rally during which he said that women should 'avoid dressing like sluts' if they wanted to be safe against sexual crimes. His words lent the title to 'Slutwalks' around the world, during which women claim the right to be present in public in whichever clothes they please.[119]

Controversial precisely for the manner in which it departs from other anti-rape protests by the flaunting of female sexuality and sexual agency (both through provocative dress and through its use of the derogatory term 'slut' as its rallying cry),[120] it is possible to view 'Slutwalk' as an assertion of the right to the city, a right to be publically present as female, sexual creatures without sanction, regardless of whether such sanction is legally ordained or abhorred. As such, beyond the issue of rape, Slutwalk has the potential to be about broader issues of sexual liberation and autonomy.[121]

Unfortunately, this potential has been somewhat diminished by Slutwalk's narrow focus on rape and, in Joburg, by its choice of route – like recent Pride marches, Slutwalk traverses northern suburb streets, which have typically not been sites of struggle for sexual presence and autonomy. The event also seems to be losing traction – while the initial 2011 Joburg Slutwalk was a great success, participation and media coverage have dwindled in subsequent years.

Overall, while Johannesburg is a freer place for women than it used to be, it most certainly does not embody equal sexual liberty. Indeed, as the limits of female sexual liberation continue to be perceived through the struggles of its extreme proponents (such as sex workers and township lesbians), most everyday struggles for sexual autonomy by the majority of gender-conforming Joburg women remain obscured.

Reflections

This chapter has shown that struggles for acceptance, presence and equal citizenship by sexual non-conformers in Johannesburg may be understood as struggles for a right to the city, mirroring struggles based on nationality, race, class or socio-economic status. Indeed, such forms of exclusion often dovetail squarely with sexual exclusion, as attested by the much divergent experiences of Joburg queers and sex workers of different races, addresses and financial status.

In this regard, law, once again, presents itself as a double-edged sword. On the one hand, it has (in South Africa, much as elsewhere) always been one of the prime tools for the policing and repression of sex and sexuality. On the other, legal rights have provided potentially powerful tools with which to resist such policing and repression. In a particularly morally conservative country with a long history of lamentable and ridiculous state transgressions into private sex lives, the post-1994 constitutional rights era presents a moral watershed of sexual permissiveness and tolerance, with which society has, in many ways, struggled to keep up.

The 1996 Constitution with its guarantee of equality based on sex, gender and sexuality, alongside its protection of bodily autonomy, privacy and freedom of expression, has undoubtedly lent momentum to struggles for sexual visibility, sexual liberty and sexual citizenship in heteronormative and patriarchal Johannesburg. All of Joburg's sexual minority residents have, to a greater or lesser extent, rallied around constitutional rights and have invoked these rights through the legal process, in efforts to create greater space for sexual freedom and diversity in the city. In all the cases discussed here, rights-based activism and litigation has enhanced the visibility and voice of sexual non-conformers[122] and thereby disrupted the moral and sexual hegemony of South African public life.

However, as attested by the race and class 'face' of the LGBTI jurisprudence, as well as by the volume of this jurisprudence compared with that on sex work and other gender-based dimensions of sexual liberty, this has been easier and more successful for those sub-groups within the sexually marginalised population who are in a socio-economic position to access the justice system. These have also typically been the sexual non-conformers who were better placed to avail themselves of the benefits of legal victories and who could cushion themselves against the harsher elements of social backlashes thereto.[123]

Moreover, a closer look at the legal jurisprudence on sexual autonomy and equality reveals that there are definite limits to invoking the law in attempting to advance sexual freedom. It is clear that the presence of constitutional rights and the outcome of constitutional litigation processes have significantly softened the oppressiveness of laws governing sexual conduct, thereby significantly enhancing sexual liberty.[124] But a number of antiquated, moralistic and oppressive legal provisions remain, for which there seem little justification other than upholding the outdated moral conventions of a heteronormative and patriarchal society. The failure of constitutional adjudication to bring an end to this situation is perhaps predictable, but nevertheless lamentable.

However, the limits of constitutional adjudication in this context involve more than the danger of occasional morally conservative kneejerk judgments. An analysis of the sexual orientation and gender judgments of the Constitutional Court shows that *Jordan* is not as out of step with the Court's ordinary sexual mores as would appear at first glance. Indeed, the Court's jurisprudence reveals that it tends to affirm only those sexual relationships and practices that broadly reverberate with heteronormative societal morality. In particular, the Court has been unwilling to affirm the sexual choices of women where these take them away from conventional expressions of sexuality in a nurturing, nuclear family-orientated, private environment.[125]

Whereas the power of the Court's inclusive judgments on sexual orientation is not to be underestimated, it is only *National Coalition* that really comes close to living up to the ideal of sexual difference. That judgment indeed showcases the potential of rights to disrupt and challenge societal understandings of appropriate sexual behaviour, much as it also falls somewhat short of subverting the private/public divide that continues to inhibit sexual difference. The most direct and forceful legal disruption of that divide thus far has come in *SWEAT*, which signals that liberty-based challenges to the public pervasiveness of heteronormativity, which centre on the right of public presence rather than the acceptability of sexual conduct as such, perhaps stand a better chance of success.

Notes

1 See Coggin and Pieterse (2012: 259–261, 271–272); Fernandes (2007: 208); Purcell (2002: 106).
2 See Hubbard (2012: xii–xiv, 11, 30, 33); Young (1990: 238).
3 See Murray (2008: 2–3); Reid and Dirsurweit (2002: 99); Richter (2012: 2, 11).
4 The theory in this subsection is more thoroughly canvassed in Pieterse (2015a: 483–487, 494–497).
5 Hubbard (2012: xiv–xv, 6, 30).
6 See, for instance, Berlant and Warner (1998: 551–552); Castiglia (2002: 155); Cossman (2002: 485, 500); Hubbard (2012: 51, 55, 64, 156–161); Nalbantoglu (2000: 211); Robson (2007: 414, 417).
7 On the perniciousness of these assumptions in various contexts, see Berlant and Warner (1998: 553); Hubbard (2012: 81–84); Meth (2003: 318–321); Mitchell (2003: 135–137, 170–172); Nalbantoglu (2000: 214); Pantazis (2002: 309–310); Robson (2007: 417); Waldron (1991: 300–306, 310–315).

8 See Bell (1995: 140); Cossman (2002: 502); Hubbard (2001: 52–53, 64–65; 2012: 73–74); Kirby (2008: 79, 91); Richardson (2000: 105–107); Robson (2007: 427); Sanders (2009: 518, 520).

9 See Boudin and Richter (2009: 183–184); De Vos (2008: 256); Martens (2007); Richter (2012: 6–7).

10 Most of the Act has been repealed by the Criminal Law (Sexual Offences and Related Matters) Amendment Act 2007, which also codifies various common-law sex crimes and constitutes the operative law on 'conventional' sex crimes such as rape, sexual assault, child abuse and the like. My focus here is exclusively on 'victimless', adult, consensual sex crimes as well as on sexual offences that are deemed such specifically (and only) because they take place in public. These are all criminalised either in terms of the 1957 Act or under common law.

11 The prohibition on sex across the colour bar was lifted by the Immorality and Prohibition of Mixed Marriages Amendment Act, 1985. The provisions that criminalised sex between men became inoperative upon being declared unconstitutional by the Constitutional Court in 1998.

12 Sexual Offenses Act 1957: s 19(2) (it is an offence to openly and publicly 'exhibit' oneself in 'indecent dress or manner'), s 20(1)(A)(b) (it is an offence to commit an 'act of indecency' in public). Section 24 of the Films and Publications Act 1996 allows pornography to be displayed only in/on 'adult premises' with restricted access, where images are not visible from outside.

13 See Berlant and Warner (1998: 551–552); Hubbard (2002: 357–358; 2004: 1688–1689, 1695–1699; 2012: 51, 55, 156, 161); Papayanis (2000: 342, 348–352); Prior *et al.* (2012: 1840, 1845).

14 See Berlant and Warner (1998: 553, 562–563); Castiglia (2002: 155, 160–161); Cossman (2002: 484, 486); De Vos (2008: 259); Du Plessis (2006: 34); Hubbard (2012: 24–29, 115–116); Johnson (2002: 319–320); Pantazis (2002: 305); Robson (2007: 427); Sanders (2009: 518).

15 See De Vos (2008: 257–258); Du Plessis (2006: 26); Johnson (2002: 320–322, 328); Hubbard (2001: 55–57; 2012: 24, 73–74, 105); Pantazis (2002: 305–307, 311, 316); Reid and Dirsuweit (2002: 100). On the gender dimensions of this, see further Hubbard (2012: 132, 134); Hassim (2009: 458–459).

16 See Berlant and Warner (1998: 551–552, 562–563); Castiglia (2002: 155–158); Hubbard (2001: 51–52, 61–62, 66–68; 2004: 1696–1697; 2012: 91–92, 116–117); Johnson (2007: 529–531); Kirby (2008: 79, 82, 91); Mitchell (2003: 35); Pantazis (2002: 305, 314–316); Papayanis (2000: 350–352); Reid and Dirsuweit (2002: 99); Richardson (2000 106, 121); Weeks (1998: 36–39).

17 See, for instance, Bell (1995: 141, 148); Hubbard (2001: 61; 2012: 107, 110–117); Hubbard and Sanders (2003: 83); Johnson (2002: 329, 387; 2007: 535–538); Pantazis (2002: 305); Papayanis (2000: 348–352); Prior *et al.* (2012: 1839, 1848); Sonnekus (2007: 46–48).

18 On gay 'villages'/'ghettos', see Hubbard (2012: 20); Pantazis (2002: 307); Prior *et al.* (2012: 1839); Rink (2008: 208–210); Sonnekus (2007: 46–47, 50–52). On red light districts, see Hubbard and Sanders (2003: 80, 87).

19 Fritz (2004: 232, 237–239); Hubbard (2012: 35–36); Hubbard and Sanders (2003: 75).

20 See, specifically in relation to sex work in Johannesburg, Boudin and Richter (2009: 191); Stadler and Delaney (2006: 455).

21 Bonthuys (2012: 16). See also Hubbard and Sanders (2003: 75, 79, 82–83).

22 Richter (2012: 6); Van Onselen (1982: 110).

23 Van Onselen (1982: 136–137); Wojcicki (2003: 92). See also Gaum (2003: 326).

24 See Richter (2012: 6); Van Onselen (1982: 12–46).

25 Richter (2012: 7–8); Van Onselen (1982: 160–161).

26 For discussion on the legal and practical overlaps between the prohibitions on sex work and interracial sex, see Boudin and Richter (2009: 182–184).

27 Du Pisani (2012: 183–184). See also Gaum (2003: 326).
28 Gaum (2003: 328–329).
29 See Morris (1999: 258–263); Richter (2012: 11); Wojcicki (2003: 93).
30 See discussion by Wojcicki (2003: 93–95).
31 On the continuing close association between Hillbrow's commercial hotels and the sex trade, see Leggett (2002: 19–22); Morris (1999: 259–260); Richter (2008: 328; 2012: 11–12); Stadler and Delaney (2006: 451–455); South African Law Reform Commission (hereinafter 'SALRC') (2009: 49).
32 See Bonthuys (2012: 6); Hubbard and Sanders (2003: 78); SALRC (2009: 58). On the dangerous conditions of sex work in Hillbrow and the forms of police and other abuse most often complained of by Hillbrow-based sex workers, see Fick (2006: 13); Richter (2008: 325, 328–329); Stadler and Delaney (2006: 455); Vearey *et al.* (2011: 229, 232); Vetten and Dladla (2000: 70–74).
33 On spatial marginalisation and danger in red light districts, see Hubbard (2012: 61); Hubbard and Sanders (2003: 75, 79–83).
34 Interracial sex was effectively legalised by the Immorality and Prohibition of Mixed Marriages Amendment Act, 1985. The Constitutional Court found that the statutory ban on possessing pornography was unconstitutional in *Case & Curtis* v. *Minister of Safety & Security* (1996), after which Apartheid-era censorship legislation was replaced by the more permissive Films and Publications Act, 1996. The criminalisation of sodomy was found unconstitutional in *National Coalition of Gay & Lesbian Equality* v. *Minister of Justice* (1999), as will be discussed below. Potentially polygamous customary marriages were recognised by the Recognition of Customary Marriages Act, 1998.
35 On these forms of transactional sex, which participants typically do not regard as sex work, see Boudin and Richter (2009: 188–190); Richter (2008: 324).
36 Richter (2012: 10); Wojcicki (2003: 85–87, 96–99).
37 SWEAT (n.d.). See also Wojcicki (2003: 95–96).
38 SWEAT (n.d.).
39 Wojcicki (2003: 85–91). See also Richter (2008: 323, 325).
40 Richter (2008: 323, 325); Wojcicki (2003: 85–91).
41 See Bonthuys (2012: 14); Fick (2006: 13–14); Richter and Massawe (2010: 24); SALRC (2009: 58–59, 61).
42 See Albertyn (2005: 227–228).
43 *S* v. *Jordan* (2002: paras 9–14).
44 Ibid., paras 60, 64–65, 68–69.
45 Ibid., paras 28–29.
46 Ibid., para 81.
47 Ibid., para 83. See also paras 78, 94.
48 Ibid., para 74. See also paras 16, 66, 75.
49 Gaum (2003: 336).
50 See, for instance, Albertyn (2005: 228, 233; 2007: 269–270); Bonthuys (2006: 392, 400–403); Boudin and Richter (2009: 191–192, 194); Fritz (2004: 230–236, 245); Meyerson (2004: 145–154); Pieterse (2008: 417, 422); Robson (2007: 424).
51 Criminal Law (Sexual Offenses and Related Matters) Amendment Act (2007: s 11).
52 See SALRC (2009: 17, 61).
53 See Boudin and Richter (2009: 194).
54 See SALRC (2009: 12–14).
55 For criticism of the tardy and protracted Law Reform Commission process, see Richter (2008: 325–326); Richter and Massawe (2010: 28).
56 See Bonthuys (2012: 7); Richter (2008: 323).
57 The various dimensions of this moral panic are analysed in detail by Bonthuys (2012). See specifically Bonthuys (2012: 15–16).
58 Richter and Massawe (2010: 22).

59 *Kylie* v. *CCMA* (2010). See specifically paras 26, 39, 41–44, 54.
60 See SALRC (2009: 62–63).
61 *SWEAT* v. *Minister of Safety & Security* (2009: para 57). See also paras 6–9, 11–14, 23, 28, 48, 56 as well as discussion by Bonthuys (2012: 18).
62 See Pieterse (2015a: 497).
63 For press on such marches in recent years, see, for instance, Olifant (2013); Mngoma (2014).
64 Richter (2008: 324).
65 This subsection presents a revised and updated summary of Pieterse (2015b).
66 Hubbard (2012: xii–xiv, 11, 30, 33).
67 Du Pisani (2012: 184, 187–188).
68 See, for instance, Moodie (2001); Du Pisani (2012: 189); Tucker (2010: 110–112).
69 On the manner in which Apartheid South Africa 'looked the other way' from black displays of homosexuality, see Livermon (2012: 303).
70 Gevisser (1994: 19).
71 The sense of an 'out', queer identity was relatively unknown in 'traditional', rural, black South Africa, which rejected homosexuality as a lifestyle but accommodated same-sex practices and relationships in different guises. This approach to homosexuality was initially also prevalent in Joburg's townships, see Tucker (2010: 111). For more on African conceptions of homosexuality (which remain more fluid and more accommodating of different shades of bisexuality than their 'Western' counterparts), see Bonthuys (2007: 533–537); Livermon (2012: 306–314).
72 Gevisser (1994: 18–19, 22–23, 26).
73 See Du Pisani (2012: 183–184, 189–190); Galli and Rafael (1994: 134–139).
74 See Du Pisani (2012: 191) as well as the sensationalist press articles cited in Pieterse (2015b: 102).
75 For discussion of s 20A, see Cameron (1993: 455); De Vos (1996: 279); Robson (2007: 417).
76 *S* v. *C* (1987). The Court found that this did not constitute a party. See also Cameron (1993: 455).
77 Du Pisani (2012: 191, 197).
78 Du Pisani (2012: 207–209).
79 For instance, the (exclusively white and male) Gay Association of South Africa (GASA) was expelled from the International Gay and Lesbian Alliance in the mid-1980s for failing to publicly condemn apartheid. See De Vos (2007: 435); Dirsuweit (2006: 329).
80 See De Vos (2007: 435); De Waal and Manion (2006: 7).
81 See De Waal and Manion (2006: 7–8, 15); Gevisser and Reid (1994: 278–280).
82 See De Waal and Manion (2006: 7); De Vos (2007: 436–439); Gevisser and Reid (1994: 279).
83 De Vos (2007: 441–443); Dirsuweit (2006: 329–330); Oswin (2007: 652–653).
84 See Albertyn (2007: 271); De Vos (2004: 185–186; 2008: 261–265); Pantazis (1999: 188–191).
85 See De Vos (2008: 259); Fritz (2004: 233–234); Pantazis (2002: 313); Pieterse (2015a: 489). This calls to mind the argument that using the right to privacy to secure protection for gay rights leads to an 'exception-based' jurisprudence of tolerance for depravity, so long as this is kept from public view (see Cameron 1993: 464). These arguments were acknowledged by the Court (*National Coalition of Gay & Lesbian Equality* v. *Minister of Justice* 1999: paras 29–30), which accordingly treated the infringement of the right to privacy as incidental to the breach of the guarantee of non-discrimination (see Pantazis 1999: 189).
86 On the demise of the NCGLE see Oswin (2007: 660–661).
87 See *National Coalition of Gay & Lesbian Equality* v. *Minister of Home Affairs* (2000) (spousal benefits for foreign partners of same sex relationships); *Langemaat*

v. *Minister of Safety & Security* (1998) (medical aid benefits); *Satchwell* v. *President of the RSA* (2002) (judges' pension benefits); *Du Toit* v. *Minister of Welfare and Population Development* (2003) (joint parental rights through adoption); *J* v. *Director General, Department of Home Affairs* (2003) (joint parental rights over children conceived through artificial insemination).

88 *Minister of Home Affairs* v. *Fourie; Lesbian & Gay Equality Project* v. *Minister of Home Affairs* (2006).

89 De Vos (2007: 463).

90 See Bonthuys (2007: 535); De Vos (2007: 453, 464–465); Livermon (2012: 302). Take-up of the opportunities provided by the Act has been slow among black queers in townships, for instance, whereas research among Muslims in Mayfair showed that LGBTI and heterosexual community members alike were uncomfortable with the 'flaunting' of gay sexuality inherent in the notion of a civil union (see Bonthuys & Erlank 2011: 283, 292–293).

91 Pieterse (2015b: 104). See also Albertyn (2007: 271–273); De Vos (2004: 196–192; 2008: 260, 266–271); Pieterse (2015a: 491); Robson (2007: 420, 431).

92 See De Vos (2007: 439–445, 451–453, 457); Pieterse (2008: 415–416; 2015b: 104). Indeed, the NCGLE and its successors have often been accused of being elitist and undemocratic, and of only paying lip service to the issues of poorer and black LGBTI persons (Oswin 2007: 653–654).

93 See De Vos (2007: 464–465); De Vos (2008: 259); Oswin (2007: 656, 665); Pieterse (2015a: 490–493, 498); Willse and Spade (2004: 311–320, 324–325). For similar conclusions on to queer citizenship elsewhere, see Castiglia (2002: 160–161); Cossman (2002: 484, 486); Hubbard (2012: 115).

94 Bonthuys and Erlank (2011: 283); Tucker (2010: 112–113).

95 See Pieterse (2015b: 105–106) and authorities cited there.

96 Pieterse (2015b: 106). See also De Waal and Manion (2006: 115); Dirsuweit (2006: 332–340).

97 See Oswin (2007: 662).

98 De Waal and Manion (2006: 6, 9); Gevisser and Reid (1994: 281–282); Pieterse (2015b: 107).

99 On the decline of and ructions in the Pride 'movement', including a recollection of physical scuffles during the 2012 parade, which led to the splintering off of the so-called 'People's Pride', see Pieterse (2015b: 107–109) and authorities there cited. See also Davis (2012); De Waal and Manion (2006: 7–9); Dirsuweit (2006: 340–341); Gevisser and Reid (1994: 278–281); Nel and Judge (2008: 25).

100 See Pieterse (2015b: 106) and authorities cited there.

101 De Waal (2008: 220); Harrison (2005: 59).

102 See Breen and Nel (2011: 46); Dirsuweit (2006: 325–326, 331); Reid and Dirsuweit (2002: 103, 108–111); Nel and Judge (2008: 24, 26); Shackleford (2013).

103 See OUT (2012); Germaner (2012). Online hook-up services and phone applications such as Grindr have, as elsewhere, significantly 're-privatised' the Joburg casual sex scene (see Pieterse 2015a: 496).

104 See Livermon (2012: 300–301); Tucker (2010: 116–117).

105 See Breen and Nel (2011: 36); Dirsuweit (2006: 325); Naidoo and Karels (2012: 236–259); Pieterse (2015b: 106–107) and authorities cited there; Reid and Dirsuweit (2002: 105–108, 115–116).

106 On Maboneng as a space where (especially young and black) queers can be unashamedly 'out', see Nevin (2014: 194–195).

107 Livermon (2012: 302); Nel and Judge (2008: 27).

108 See Fritz (2004: 237–239); Goebel (2015: 130); Hassim (2009: 458–459); Hubbard (2012: 36, 61); Pieterse (2015b: 101); Sanders (2009: 519).

109 Hubbard (2012: 132–134); Valentine (1989: 385–386). On Joburg women's experiences of this, see Vetten and Dladla (2000: 70–72).

110 See Erwin *et al.* (2014: 318); Valentine (1989: 386; 1992: 22–24).
111 See Erwin *et al.* (2014: 314); Goebel (2015: 55–56, 71–73, 188, 190).
112 Goebel (2015: 187).
113 *Carmichele* v. *Minister of Safety & Security* (2001).
114 *K* v. *Minister of Safety & Security* (2005).
115 Fritz (2004: 230).
116 *Volks* v. *Robinson* (2005) see specifically paras 62, 68 (per Skweyiya J for the majority); 91–93 (per Ngcobo J, concurring separately).
117 See Albertyn (2005: 233); De Vos (2004: 204); Pieterse (2014: 377–378); Robson (2007: 426).
118 See Hassim (2009: 458); Kwenaite and Van Heerden (2011: 142).
119 On the origins of Slutwalk, see Tuerkheimer (2014: 1458–1459).
120 See Borah and Nandi (2012: 415); Tuerkheimer (2014: 1467, 1471–1473, 1481).
121 Borah and Nandi (2012: 419).
122 Albertyn (2007: 275).
123 See Weeks (1998: 45).
124 For instance, even prior to the Civil Union Act, there have been some 18 legislative amendments eliminating discrimination against LGBTI persons (see Oswin 2007: 650–651).
125 See Albertyn (2005: 233; 2007: 254, 274); Bonthuys (2008: 34–35).

References

Albertyn, C., 2005. 'Defending and securing rights through law: Feminism, law and the courts in South Africa', *Politikon* 32(2), 217–237.

Albertyn, C., 2007. 'Substantive equality and transformation in South Africa', *South African Journal of Human Rights* 23(2), 253–276.

Bell, D., 1995. 'Pleasure and danger: The paradoxical spaces of sexual citizenship', *Political Geography* 14(2), 139–153.

Berlant, L. & Warner, M., 1998. 'Sex in public', *Critical Inquiry* 24(2), 547–566.

Bonthuys, E., 2006. 'Women's sexuality in the South African Constitutional Court', *Feminist Legal Studies* 14(3), 391–406.

Bonthuys, E., 2007. 'Race and Gender in the Civil Union Act', *South African Journal of Human Rights* 23(3), 526–542.

Bonthuys, E., 2008. 'Institutional openness and resistance to feminist arguments: The example of the South African Constitutional Court', *Canadian Journal of Women & the Law* 20(1), 1–36.

Bonthuys, E., 2012. 'The 2010 Football World Cup and the regulation of sex work in South Africa', *Journal of Southern African Studies* 38(1), 11–29.

Bonthuys, E. & Erlank, N., 2011. 'Attitudes to same-sex marriage in South African Muslim communities – An exploratory study'. In: Jones, J., Grear, A., Fenton, R.A. & Stevenson, K. (eds.), *Gender, Sexualities and the Law*, pp. 283–296. Oxford, New York: Routledge.

Borah, R. & Nandi, S., 2012. 'Reclaiming the feminist politics of "slutwalk"', *International Feminist Journal of Politics* 14(3), 415–421.

Boudin, C. & Richter, M., 2009. 'Adult, consensual sex work in South Africa – the cautionary message of criminal law and sexual morality', *South African Journal of Human Rights* 25(2), 179–197.

Breen, D. & Nel, J.A., 2011. 'South Africa – A home for all?' *South African Crime Quarterly* 38(12), 33–43.

Cameron, E., 1993. 'Sexual orientation and the Constitution: A test case for human rights', *South African Law Journal* 110(4), 450–472.

Carmichele v. *Minister of Safety and Security*, 2001. Decision of the South African Constitutional Court, reported as 2001 (4) SA 938 (CC).

Case and Curtis v. *Minister of Safety and Security*, 1996. Decision of the South African Constitutional Court, reported as 1996 (3) SA 617 (CC).

Castiglia, C., 2002. 'Sex panics, sex publics, sex memories', *boundary* 2, 149–175.

Civil Union Act, 17 of 2006.

Coggin, T. & Pieterse, M., 2012. 'Rights and the city: An exploration of the interaction between socio-economic rights and the city', *Urban Forum* 23(3), 257–278.

Constitution of the Republic of South Africa, 1996 (Act 108 of 1996).

Cossman, B., 2002. 'Sexing citizenship, privatizing sex', *Citizenship Studies* 6, 483–506.

Criminal Law (Sexual Offenses and Related Matters) Amendment Act, 32 of 2007.

Davis, R., 2012. 'Joburg Pride: A tale of two cities', *Daily Maverick*, 9 October 2012, from www.dailymaverick.co.za.

De Vos, P., 1996. 'On the legal construction of gay and lesbian identity and South Africa's transitional Constitution', *South African Journal of Human Rights* 12(2), 265–290.

De Vos, P., 2004. 'Same-sex sexual desire and the re-imagining of the South African family', *South African Journal of Human Rights* 20(2), 179–206.

De Vos, P., 2007. 'The "inevitability" of same-sex marriage in South Africa's post-Apartheid state', *South African Journal of Human Rights* 23(3), 432–465.

De Vos, P., 2008. 'From heteronormativity to full sexual citizenship?: Equality and sexual freedom in Laurie Ackermann's constitutional jurisprudence'. In: Barnard-Naude A.J., Cornell, D. & Du Bois, F. (eds.), *Dignity, Freedom and the Post-Apartheid Legal Order: The Critical Jurisprudence of Laurie Ackermann*, pp. 254–272. Cape Town: Juta.

De Waal, S., 2008. 'Gay Joburg'. In: Brodie, N. (ed.), *The Joburg Book*, pp. 219–220. Johannesburg: Pan Macmillan & Sharp.

De Waal, S. & Manion, A., 2006. 'Introduction'. In De Waal, S. & Manion, A. (eds.), *Pride: Protest and Celebration*, pp. 6–10. Johannesburg: Fanele.

Dirsuweit, T., 2006. 'The problem of identities: The lesbian, gay, bisexual, transgender and intersex social movement in South Africa'. In: Ballard, R., Habib, A. & Valodia, I. (eds.), *Voices of Protest: Social Movements in Post-Apartheid South Africa*, pp. 325–347. Pietermaritzburg: UKZN Press.

Du Pisani, K., 2012. 'Shifting sexual morality? Changing views on homosexuality in Afrikaner society during the 1960s', *Historia* 57(2), 182–221.

Du Plessis, R., 2006. 'Exhibiting the expulsion of transgression'. In: Van Marle, K. (ed.), *Sex Gender Becoming: Post-Apartheid Reflections*, pp. 19–40. Pretoria: PULP.

Du Toit v. *Minister of Welfare and Population Development*, 2003. Decision of the South African Constitutional Court, reported as 2003 (2) SA 198 (CC).

Erwin, K., Bass, O. & Houghton, J., 2014. 'Women and urban governance: The disjuncture between policy and everyday experiences in intimate spaces'. In: Haferburg, C. & Huchzermeyer, M. (eds.), *Urban Governance in Post-Apartheid Cities: Modes of Engagement in South Africa's Metropoles*, pp. 313–326. Pietermaritzburg: UKZN Press.

Fernandes, E., 2007. 'Constructing the "right to the city" in Brazil', *Social & Legal Studies* 16(2), 201–219

Fick, N., 2006. 'Sex workers speak out: Policing and the sex industry', *South African Crime Quarterly* 15(1), 13–18.

Films and Publications Act, 65 of 1996.

Fritz, N., 2004. 'Crossing *Jordan*: Constitutional space for (un)civil sex', *South African Journal of Human Rights* 20(2), 230–248.

Galli, P. & Rafael, L., 1994. 'Johannesburg's "health clubs": Places of erotic languor or prison-houses of desire?' In: Gevisser, M. & Cameron, E. (eds.), *Defiant Desire: Gay and Lesbian Lives in South Africa*, pp. 134–139. Johannesburg: Ravan Press.

Gaum, L., 2003. 'Turning tricks: A brief history of the regulation and prohibition of prostitution in South Africa', *Stellenbosch Law Review* 14(3), 319–336.

Germaner, S., 2012. 'Gauteng's gay serial murder mystery', *IOL News*, 6 March 2012, from www.iol.co.za.

Gevisser, M., 1994. 'A different fight for freedom: A history of South African lesbian and gay organisation from the 1950s to 1990s'. In: Gevisser, M. & Cameron, E. (eds.), *Defiant Desire: Gay and Lesbian Lives in South Africa*, pp. 14–29. Johannesburg: Ravan Press.

Gevisser, M. & Reid, G., 1994. 'Pride or protest? Drag queens, comrades and the lesbian and gay pride march'. In: Gevisser, M. & Cameron, E. (eds.), *Defiant Desire: Gay and Lesbian Lives in South Africa*, pp. 278–283. Johannesburg: Ravan Press.

Goebel, A., 2015. *On Their Own: Women, Urbanization and the Right to the City in South Africa*. Montreal: McGill-Queens University Press.

Harrison, P., 2005. *South Africa's Top Sites: Gay and Lesbian*. Cape Town: New Africa Books.

Hassim, S., 2009. 'After Apartheid: Consensus, contention, and gender in South Africa's public sphere', *International Journal of Politics, Culture & Society* 22(4), 453–464.

Hubbard, P., 2001. 'Sex zones: Intimacy, citizenship and public space', *Sexualities* 4(1), 51–71.

Hubbard, P., 2002. 'Maintaining family values? Cleansing the streets of sex advertising', *Area* 34(4), 353–360.

Hubbard, P., 2004. 'Cleansing the metropolis: Sex work and the politics of zero tolerance', *Urban Studies* 41(9), 1687–1702.

Hubbard, P., 2012. *Cities and Sexualities*. Oxford: Routledge.

Hubbard, P. & Sanders, T., 2003. 'Making space for sex work: Female street prostitution and the production of urban space', *International Journal of Urban & Regional Research* 27(1), 75–89.

Immorality Act, 5 of 1927.

Immorality and Prohibition of Mixed Marriages Amendment Act, 72 of 1985.

J v. *Director General, Department of Home Affairs*, 2003. Decision of the South African Constitutional Court, reported as 2003 (5) SA 621 (CC).

Johnson, C., 2002. 'Heteronormative citizenship and the politics of passing', *Sexualities* 5(3), 317–336.

Johnson, P., 2007. 'Ordinary folk and cottaging: Law, morality and public sex', *Journal of Law & Society* 34(4), 520–543.

K v. *Minister of Safety and Security*, 2005. Decision of the South African Constitutional Court, reported as 2005 (6) SA 419 (CC).

Kirby, A., 2008. 'The production of private space and its implications for urban social relations', *Political Geography* 27(1), 74–95.

Kwenaite, S. & Van Heerden, A., 2011. 'Dress and violence: Women should avoid dressing like "sluts" to avoid getting raped', *South African Journal of Art History* 26(1), 141–155.

Kylie v. *CCMA*, 2010. Decision of the Labour Appeal Court, reported as 2010 (4) SA 383 (LAC).

Langemaat v. *Minister of Safety & Security*, 1998. Decision of the Pretoria High Court, reported as 1998 (3) SA 312 (T).

Leggett, T., 2002. 'A den of iniquity? Inside Hillbrow's residential hotels', *South African Crime Quarterly* 2(11), 19–22.

Livermon, X., 2012. 'Queer(y)ing freedom: Black queer visibilities in postapartheid South Africa', *GLQ: A Journal of Lesbian and Gay Studies* 18(2–3), 297–323.

Martens, J., 2007. 'Citizenship, "civilization" and the creation of South Africa's Immorality Act, 1927' *South African Historical Journal* 59(1), 223–241.

Meth, P., 2003. 'Rethinking the "domus" in domestic violence: Homelessness, space and domestic violence in South Africa', *Geoforum* 34(3), 317–327.

Meyerson, D., 2004. 'Does the Constitutional Court of South Africa take rights seriously? The case of *S* v. *Jordan*', *Acta Juridica* 138–154.

Minister of Home Affairs v. *Fourie; Lesbian and Gay Equality Project* v. *Minister of Home Affairs*, 2006. Decision of the South African Constitutional Court, reported as 2006 (1) SA 524 (CC).

Mitchell, D., 2003. *The Right to the City: Social Justice and the Fight for Public Space*. New York: Guilford Press.

Mngoma, N., 2014. 'Sex workers demand equal rights', *Daily News*, 7 March 2014, from www.iol.co.za.

Moodie, T.D., 2001. 'Black migrant mine labourers and the vicissitudes of male desire'. In: Morell, R. (ed.), *Changing Men in Southern Africa*, pp. 297–316. Pietermaritzburg: University of Natal Press.

Morris, A., 1999. *Bleakness & Light: Inner-city Transition in Hillbrow, Johannesburg*. Johannesburg: Wits University Press.

Murray, M.J., 2008. *Taming the Disorderly City: The Spatial Landscape of Johannesburg After Apartheid*. Ithaca, London: Cornell University Press.

Naidoo, K. & Karels, M., 2012. 'Hate crimes against black lesbian South Africans: Where race, sexual orientation and gender collide', *Obiter* 33(2), 236–259.

Nalbantoglu, G.B., 2000. 'Fantasies of domesti(city)', *Urban Forum* 1(2), 211–223.

National Coalition of Gay & Lesbian Equality v. *Minister of Home Affairs*, 2000. Decision of the South African Constitutional Court, reported as 2000 (2) SA 1 (CC).

National Coalition of Gay & Lesbian Equality v. *Minister of Justice*, 1999. Decision of the South African Constitutional Court, reported as 1999 (1) SA 6 (CC).

Nel, J.A. & Judge, M., 2008. 'Exploring homophobic victimisation in Gauteng, South Africa: Issues, impacts and responses', *Acta Criminologica* 21(3), 19–36.

Nevin, A., 2014. 'Instant mutuality: The development of Maboneng in inner-city Johannesburg', *Anthropology Southern Africa* 37(3), 187–201.

Olifant, K., 2013. 'Prostitutes protest against cop brutality', *The Star*, 8 March 2013, from www.iol.co.za/the-star.

Oswin, N., 2007. 'Producing homonormativity in neoliberal South Africa: Recognition, redistribution and the equality project', *Signs* 32(3), 649–669.

OUT, 2012. *Gay, Bisexual and Men Who Have Sex with Men Urged to Remain Cautious and Safe*, 27 January 2012, from http://men2men.co.za/mobile-home/32-gay-bisexual-and-men-who-have-sex-with-men-urged-to-remain-cautious-and-safe.

Pantazis, A., 1999. 'How to decriminalise gay sex', *South African Journal of Human Rights* 15(1), 188–192.

Pantazis, A., 2002. 'Home and the world: Lesbian and gay places in the law'. *South African Law Journal* 119(2), 305–316.

Papayanis, M.A., 2000. 'Sex and the revanchist city: Zoning out pornography in New York', *Environment & Planning D: Society & Space* 18(3), 341–353.

Pieterse, M., 2008. 'Finding for the applicant? Individual equality plaintiffs and group-based disadvantage', *South African Journal of Human Rights* 24(3), 397–424.

Pieterse, M., 2014. 'May real men cry in court? Masculinity, equality and the South African Constitutional Court', *Journal of Southern African Studies* 40(2), 361–379.

Pieterse, M., 2015a. 'Law, rights, space and sexual citizenship in South Africa', *Social Dynamics* 41(3), 482–501.

Pieterse, M., 2015b. 'Perverts, outlaws and dissidents: (Homo)sexual citizenship and urban space in Johannesburg', *Urban Forum* 26(2), 97–112.

Prior, J., Boydell, S. & Hubbard, P., 2012. 'Nocturnal rights to the city: Property, propriety and sex premises in inner Sydney', *Urban Studies* 49(8), 1837–1852.

Purcell, M., 2002. 'Excavating Lefebvre: The right to the city and its urban politics of the inhabitant', *GeoJournal* 58, 99–108.

Recognition of Customary Marriages Act, 120 of 1998.

Reid, G. & Dirsuweit, T., 2002. 'Understanding systemic violence: Homophobic attacks in Johannesburg and its surrounds', *Urban Forum* 13(3), 99–126.

Richardson, D., 2000. 'Constructing sexual citizenship: Theorizing sexual rights', *Critical Social Policy* 20(1), 105–135.

Richter, M., 2008. 'Sex work, reform initiatives and HIV/AIDS in inner-city Johannesburg', *African Journal of AIDS Research* 7(3), 323–333.

Richter, M., 2012. 'Johannesburg's "vendors of vice" – from Frenchfontein to Hillbrow: Female sex work, migration and infection control (1868–2012)'. Unpublished paper presented at ACMS Colloquium *Ill People or Sick Cities? Mobility and Access to Health in South African Cities*, 3 October 2012.

Richter, M. & Massawe, D., 2010. 'Did South Africa's soccer bonanza bring relief to sex workers in South Africa? The 2010 FIFA World Cup and the impact on sex work', *Agenda* 24(1), 21–30.

Rink, B.M., 2008. 'Community as utopia: reflections on De Waterkant', *Urban Forum* 19(2), 205–220.

Robson, R., 2007. 'Sexual democracy', *South African Journal of Human Rights* 23(3), 409–431.

S v. *C*, 1987. Decision of the Witwatersrand Supreme Court, reported as 1987 (2) SA 76 (W).

S v. *Jordan*, 2002. Decision of the South African Constitutional Court, reported as 2002 (6) SA 642 (CC).

Sanders, T., 2009. 'Controlling the "anti-sexual" city: Sexual citizenship and the disciplining of female street sex workers', *Criminology & Criminal Justice* 9(4), 507–525.

Satchwell v. *President of the RSA*, 2002. Decision of the South African Constitutional Court, reported as 2002 (6) SA 1 (CC).

Sexual Offenses Act, 23 of 1957.

Shackleford, G., 2013. 'Alleged gay-bashing in Rosebank', *Rosebank Killarney Gazette*, 11 September 2013, from www.rosebank killarneygazette.co.za.

Sonnekus, T., 2007. 'The queering of space: Investigating spatial manifestations of homosexuality in De Waterkant, Cape Town', *De Arte* 75(1), 42–57.

South African Law Reform Commission, 2009. *Sexual Offenses: Adult Prostitution*, Project 107, Discussion Paper 0001/2009.

Stadler, J. & Delaney, S., 2006. 'The "healthy brothel": The context of clinical services for sex workers in Hillbrow, South Africa', *Culture, Health & Sexuality* 8(5), 451–464.

SWEAT, n.d. *Our History*, from www.sweat.org.za/index.php/about-sweat/history.

SWEAT v. *Minister of Safety and Security*, 2009. Decision by the Western Cape High Court, Cape Town, reported as 2009 (2) SACR 417 (WCC).

Tucker, A., 2010. 'Shifting boundaries of sexual identities in Cape Town: The appropriation and malleability of "gay" in township spaces', *Urban Forum* 21(2), 107–122.

Tuerkheimer, D., 2014. 'Slutwalking in the shadow of the law', *Minnesota Law Review* 98(4), 1453–1511.

Valentine, G., 1989. 'The geography of women's fear', *Area* 21(4), 385–390.

Valentine, G., 1992. 'Images of danger: Women's sources of information about the spatial distribution of male violence', *Area* 24(1), 22–29.

Van Onselen, C., 1982. *New Babylon, New Nineveh: Everyday Life on the Witwatersrand 1886–1914*. Johannesburg, Cape Town: Jonathan Ball Publishers.

Vearey, J., Oliveira, E., Madzimure, T. & Ntini, B., 2011. 'Working the city: Experiences of migrant women in inner-city Johannesburg', *Southern Africa Gender & Media Diversity Journal* 9(4), 228–233.

Vetten, L. & Dladla, J., 2000. 'Women's fear and survival in inner-city Johannesburg', *Agenda* 16(4), 70–75.

Volks v. *Robinson*, 2005. Decision of the South African Constitutional Court, reported as 2005 (5) BCLR 446 (CC).

Waldron, J., 1991 'Homelessness and the issue of freedom', *UCLA Law Review* 39(1), 295–323.

Weeks, J., 1998. 'The sexual citizen', *Theory, Culture & Society* 15(1), 35–52.

Willse, C. & Spade, D., 2004. 'Freedom in a regulatory state?: *Lawrence*, marriage and biopolitics', *Wildener Law Review* 11, 309–329.

Wojcicki, J.M., 2003. 'The movement to decriminalize sex work in Gauteng Province, South Africa 1994–2002', *African Studies Review* 46(1), 83–109.

Young, I.M., 1990. *Justice and the Politics of Difference*. Princeton: Princeton University Press.

7 The right to Joburg?

Introduction

Throughout, this book has described the conflation, and sometimes juxtaposition, of everyday exercises of the right to the city and the invocation of legal rights through litigation. It has shown that the right to the city coexists uncomfortably with legal rights, sometimes supplementing, translating and animating them, while at other times detracting, diverting from, and diluting their operation.

In Chapter 1, I pointed out that the right to the city extends significantly beyond conventional understandings of legal rights – that it is far more unstable, insurgent, relational and place-bound. Indeed, it appears that many features of legal rights could be inimical to, even restrictive of, the right to the city. Legal rights are invoked discretely, hierarchically, atomistically and consistently, within a fixed procedural and substantive theoretical framework that does not easily respond to everyday contingencies. While recognising individual agency, legal rights also often underplay and subvert it, ascribing in the first instance to a notion of the common good to which individual interests contribute and to which, in appropriate circumstances, they must yield. Moreover, legal rights belong to everyone in equal measure, not only to the poor and the working classes, and must often be balanced and reconciled in ways that require some interests to give way to others. From this it follows that, unlike the right to the city which is limited only by the agency of those who enact it, legal rights can and must be limited far more regularly, not only in respect for the rights of others but also in deference to the common good.[1]

Moreover, unlike the right to the city, legal rights accept and serve to promote the legitimacy of the State and its institutions, while assuming and requiring respect for and adherence to the outcome of democratic processes, as well as commitment to the rule of law. Indeed, they are at their core mere restrictions on and preferred channels for state power, and are invested in maintaining social stability, peaceful coexistence and the efficient functioning of the State. Unlike urban citizenship located solely in the physical fact of inhabitance, which underpins the right to the city, legal rights therefore typically hinge on a far more restrained notion of citizenship, one committed to the maintenance of societal structures and the pursuit of a democratic consensus.[2]

While ostensibly restrictive of human agency, these features of legal rights are arguably some of their greatest strengths. Whereas insurgency, spontaneity and an unbridled right to the city are easy and tempting to romanticise, history has shown all too sharply that 'the people unleashed can act in undemocratic and unjust ways'.[3] One only has to point at contemporary instances of destructive protests, xenophobic and homophobic violence, violent crime and vigilantism across Johannesburg to appreciate that a free-for-all right to the city will not necessarily produce space or structure relations in ways that can credibly be termed just or conducive to human flourishing.[4] Legal rights, like their fellow stalwarts of liberal democracy, exist as much to curb the potentially destructive excesses of an unbridled right to the city as they do to enable its more noble aspirations.[5]

This is of course not to say that all societal rules and conventions, and all ostensibly shared definitions and pursuits of the common good, are unproblematic. This book has engaged several instances where dominant legal and social codes of 'proper' citizenship have harshly been inscribed with hierarchical, racialist, middle-class, neoliberal and heteronormative values which, if left unchecked, operate to exclude and oppress a great many. But given the democratic vision of an open, tolerant, inclusive, substantively equal and free society espoused, for instance, by the South African Constitution, legal rights are often invoked to challenge and disrupt the hegemony of such values and to overthrow their legal and social imposition. Indeed, while accepting the near inevitability of the State, markets and other social forces that undeniably shape modern-day urban life, legal rights have unequivocally shown themselves to be well-suited to the balancing of competing interests, the maintenance of law and order and the pursuit of communal aspirations in a fair, open and transparent manner. Through the power of law, legal rights and the processes that vindicate them can shape space – physically, politically, socially and in the imagination – in ways that promote dignity, tolerance, participation, diversity and human flourishing.[6] These are also, albeit in different contexts and to differing extents, the end goals of the right to the city.

Accordingly, much of the discussion in this book has centred on the instances of confluence between the right to the city and legal rights. While it has never explicitly been invoked before a court, interests associated with the right to the city have inevitably come to be embroiled in the increasing amount of legal rights disputes originating from struggles over access to, appropriation of and participation in urban life and space. For the most part, courts called upon to decide these disputes have intuitively given effect to various components of the right to the city, much as they have balanced these against other, competing components and have, at times, limited their realisation.[7]

In fact, the right to the city draws attention to many features of the exercise, enforcement and enjoyment of legal rights that human rights scholars often overlook or underplay. It highlights the interdependence, participatory nature and relationality of legal rights, their context-specificity and their contingency. Crucially, it concretely links rights to space and to place.[8] In urban areas, this means that the context of rights' invocation is rendered concrete and that the common good associated with their continuous balancing becomes infused with concern for the production and maintenance of physical urban space that is inclusive, participatory, conducive to individual and communal health and well-being, enabling of individual agency and capability and, most importantly, sustainable.[9]

In the remainder of this final chapter, then, I consider the extent to which these lessons have become embedded in South African urban rights jurisprudence and on how this jurisprudence has shaped everyday life and struggles for justice in Johannesburg. I start by looking at the extent to which the granting of constitutional rights has shaped the legal and regulatory environment governing South African cities and consider the institutional spaces, within this environment, for participation and deliberation over the shape, form and functioning of the city. This discussion culminates in weighing up the advantages and disadvantages of courts as such deliberative spaces. This is followed by an evaluation of South African courts' adjudicatory approaches to the resolution of disputes over urban space, where the focus is predominantly on the way in which such disputes are resolved under the Constitutional Court's approach to deciding socio-economic rights claims. I then turn to consider the impact of court judgments on governance in the City of Johannesburg, as well as on individual litigants, social movements and the everyday lives of other actors in the city. Thereafter, I reflect on the notion of urban citizenship emerging from South African urban rights litigation. The concluding section then steps back to situate rights-based litigation alongside other forms of participation in the city.

Rights, space, dialogue and contestation

There can be no doubt that the enactment of the 1993 and 1996 Constitutions radically altered the legal landscape around competing claims over urban space and urban resources. The mere legislative fact of granting enforceable rights pertaining to a range of goods, services and actions that were not formerly conceived of as being the objects of legally sanctioned entitlements, had the effect of clothing the actions associated with the physical performance of those rights in a measure of legitimacy and political significance that they had formerly lacked. Suddenly, these actions could not be outlawed, suppressed, regulated or denied without constitutionally acceptable justification and had to be accommodated, even enabled, in the legal, political and everyday spheres.[10]

The law had to respond to this transformed constitutional landscape by creating and enforcing normative and institutional frameworks for the enforcement, enablement and realisation of the newly granted rights and, importantly, also for their balancing and limitation. A large-scale overhaul of the South African statute books thus followed the constitutional enactments. The last of apartheid's restrictive laws and regulations limiting movement and access to public and private spaces were repealed, managerialist and authoritarian municipal governance frameworks were replaced with rights-conscious, participatory and development-orientated local government legislation, and the Promotion of

Administrative Justice and Access to Information Acts tilted the balance in interfaces between the citizenry and the bureaucracy towards openness, fairness and transparency. Legislation and regulations pertaining to essential service delivery acknowledged and structured rights to access survival requirements, whereas a plethora of housing-related legislation and policy documents had the effect of completely overthrowing the exclusionary and ownership-centred logic of South African property law[11] to also acknowledge and give effect to claims of habitation. Elsewhere, legislation aiming to give effect to different aspects of the right to equality outlawed discrimination in public and private life and served to enhance individual liberty, autonomy and capacity for hitherto marginalised and excluded sections of the population.

While shortcomings remain, especially in relation to vindicating the rights of marginalised inhabitants (Chapter 4 has, for instance, shown that foreign migrants still mostly lack legal rights, whereas the pernicious impact of the continued criminalisation of sex work on the lives of sex workers was discussed in Chapter 6), and while the sudden alteration of the legal landscape had some negative spatial effects (such as the over-occupation of the suddenly unregulated Johannesburg CBD and the sudden spike in violent crime across the city), this transformation of the legislative and policy landscape has considerably enhanced citizens' freedoms and capabilities and has significantly empowered them, not only in relation to the State, but also in relation to each other.[12] In this respect, rights not only have the effect of restricting government regulation, but often require it, precisely to ensure that relatively more powerful inhabitants do not exercise their rights in ways that exclude or oppress others.[13] As perhaps most pointedly illustrated by the eviction disputes related in Chapter 2 and by Chapter 5's discussion of struggles over the exercise of conflicting rights to freedom of movement and personal security in the northern suburbs, a rights-based legal and policy environment requires the explicit balancing and accommodation of competing interests, often resulting in far greater accommodation of the interests of comparatively weaker inhabitants than would have been the case in its absence.

In addition to altering the rules of engagement between citizens and state, the legal instruments ushered in to give effect to constitutional rights also established various institutional spaces for the resolving of tensions between competing rights or for the assertion of rights against state or private power. These include constitutionally created bodies such as the South African Human Rights Commission and the Public Protector, statutory dispute resolution bodies such as the Rental Housing Tribunal and statutory structures feeding directly into local government and the democratic process, such as municipal ward committees. While South Africans have for the most part disappointingly underutilised these deliberative institutional structures,[14] the discussions in previous chapters have also illustrated their growing impact on the mediation of struggles over urban space and resources.

But it is the justiciability of constitutional rights that has arguably been their most empowering feature and that has turned South African courts into perhaps the most influential institutional actors in struggles over the right to the city. This book has told how a growing number of interest groups have resorted to the courts in attempts to protect or enforce a diverse array of rights against the actions of either local government, business or fellow urban dwellers. The formality of legal processes and the measures of finality and authority inherent in their outcomes have made litigation an especially attractive resort for all who attempt to assert their urban rights (entwined, as they are, with their asserters' own visions for the city and for how it should fulfil their interests or needs) with some measure of force.[15]

There can be little doubt that the effect of this increasing resort to litigation, at least as far as it has structured the rules of city life and of the mediation of competing claims to the right to the city, has been significant. Residents from all walks of life have found themselves empowered to resist the many ways in which government or market forces have attempted to restructure or regulate their lives in the city, and have used litigation (or threats of litigation) to insist that processes which shape urban life or the urban form are at the very least responsive to their interests. In particular, this legalisation of the right to the city has served to enhance the (otherwise muted, sidelined or ignored) voice of the poor in conversations about how the shape, form and functioning of the city determine their fate, and has protected and asserted their basic fundamental rights against many forms of unjustly wielded public and private power.[16] Litigation has also clearly enhanced the popular and legal legitimacy of poor and marginalised city dwellers' interests and has ensured that these interests are included, and taken seriously, in a whole range of urban agendas and debates in which they would otherwise arguably have featured far less prominently.[17]

Crucially, the outcome of litigation or related legal processes that asserted the rights of the urban poor has also often included concrete, tangible benefits – access to water and/or electricity, the provision of temporary housing or the right to remain in an occupied building, the granting of access to a space in which to make a livelihood, and so forth. However indirectly they happen to have resulted from it, these rewards of litigation (which, as has been shown, sometimes followed even from the outcome of cases that have on the face of it been lost), concretely attest to the power of rights to make a physical difference in the lives of their beneficiaries.[18]

A related effect has been that litigation has altered the physical form of the city and its many spaces – the removal of barriers, the construction or conversion of low-cost housing, buildings remaining undeveloped or being appropriated for purposes other than that intended by their owners or the state, the establishment and continuation of informal settlements or informal markets, and the like. Of course, wealthier and more powerful residents and commercial entities have regularly used the law to similar effect, with the cityscape telling the tales of developments approved, halted or resisted, boomgates erected, buildings renovated and areas gentrified. Certainly, granting Johannesburg's inhabitants rights and the means to enforce them has altered both the city and their ways of life in it, in myriad direct and indirect ways.

But has this always been for the good? A glaring problem with a preference for litigation as a way of asserting a right to the city is that it is an avenue that is only affordable and accessible to, and navigable by, a precious few. These are, first, corporations and well-resourced or well-connected residents (and residents' associations) who can repeatedly afford lawyers and litigation costs and, second, a small number of NGOs representing a narrow band of interests on behalf of (only some) of the city's poorer and excluded residents.[19] In both cases, the city is opened up for interest group capture, with the limited, often acutely class-coloured, agendas of better resourced citizens, or those of grant-funded NGOs emphasising some of the interests of the vulnerable groups that they represent over competing interests or the interests of others who are equally vulnerable, coming to dominate the political agenda and to frame judicial engagement with the city.[20]

The result is judgments that, both in their message and their socio-spatial effects, at best only benefit a small group of beneficiaries (as with building occupation judgments only vindicating the right to housing of building occupiers as opposed to those of rough sleepers and other homeless persons, or with sexual orientation rights being vindicated in ways that assist only middle-class, suburban LGBT persons) or that, at worst, directly or indirectly undermine the rights of unpopular, unconnected, unrepresented or un-representable parties.[21] This significantly negative potential impact of litigation is exacerbated when, as appears to have been the case, a preference for litigation by well-resourced or connected entities serves to further sideline, straitjacket, circumvent or otherwise deflate the other, more broadly accessible and potentially more constructive, democratic structures or avenues for engagement.

Linked to this, the fact that judges are typically limited to deciding issues as they are framed by the (often only two) parties before them in a particular matter combines with the individualist, piecemeal and adversarial nature of the legal process, and with its typical win-or-lose, all-or-nothing-type outcomes, to produce results, backed by all the finality and coercive power of the law, that inevitably reflect and express preference for only some of the many interconnected interests at stake in a right-to-the-city dispute.[22] Together with court judgments' tendency to reflect mainstream (often middle-class, heteronormative and state-deferential) values and their built-in preference for notions of lawfulness, stability, efficient regulation, cooperation with authorities and so on, these features of the litigation process further run the risk of closing off extra-legal avenues for enacting the right to the city, and of further alienating or sidelining the interests of those (such as 'illegal' migrants, 'illegal' traders or sex workers) whose modes of enactment are, by necessity or by choice, not generally in line with the expectations of the law.[23]

Of course, courts offer more constructive and socially acceptable ways for balancing competing claims for the right to the city than, for instance, vigilantism, vandalism or deliberately destructive protests.[24] They also offer an opportunity for citizens to engage with authorities over their right to the city as equals, are less susceptible to manipulation or undue influence than other deliberative spaces, and have the advantage of requiring bureaucratic responsiveness and the yielding of state or capital powers to their reasoned solutions.[25] But their general lack of accessibility to the very people who might resort to less constructive forms of engagement means that their potential to resolve the more explosive urban conflicts will remain limited. It is accordingly imperative that the legal process be rendered more accessible than is currently the case and that it supplements, invigorates and sustains, rather than circumvents, more broadly participatory, democratic channels for joint city-making.

Judges, meanwhile, need to take care to tailor their findings in ways that avoid interest-group capture, finality and closure, that encourage dialogue and that preserve the space for contestation and (re)negotiation over the meaning of the right to the city as well as over its object – the city's shape and form.[26] Judgments must further take care to preserve the fluidity of urban rights and to allow for their contingent, context-bound and participatory actualisation and negotiation by all urban inhabitants outside of the courtroom. Provided they become more accessible and that their officers heed these cautions, courts could be able to balance competing rights to the city in ways that advance communal interests, long-term goals and overarching constitutional objectives.

Judicial vindication of rights to the city

This book has covered many instances of urban inhabitants employing rights-based litigation strategies in attempts to protect or advance their interests, to satisfy their needs, or to produce urban space that enables their livelihoods and their versions of the good life.

As Chapter 5 has detailed, comparatively wealthier and more powerful residents, who already exercise significant control over 'their' portions of urban space, tend to use rights defensively. This is in keeping with the general tendency of powerful social actors around the world to employ so-called 'negative liberties' (rights to exclude others from property, to privacy, freedom of commerce, freedom of association and so forth) and the negative obligations engendered by socio-economic rights (for instance, to respect and refrain from interfering with existing access to urban services) to maintain the legal and social status quo, to insulate themselves from danger, hardship or redistributive claims, and to exclude persons who may disrupt their lives from 'their' space.[27] Accordingly, we have seen Johannesburg's wealthier residents employing the right to freedom and security of the person and the right to privacy alongside procedural rights (such as the right to administrative justice) and the environmental right in attempts to safeguard 'their' spaces from outside interference, to resist developments that threaten their vision of the good life and to secure their lifestyles against the perils of living in a violent, deeply unequal, society.

Chapter 5 has also shown that courts' responses to these attempts have been somewhat mixed and uneven. While aware of the danger of middle-class capture of rights and the potential exclusionary repercussions of overzealous enforcement of privacy, autonomy, environmental and safety interests, courts have also been unwilling to underplay or jettison these interests, especially in light of seemingly inadequate state protection. This is not least because decisions in cases concerning wealthier residents also shape the law's protection of the similar interests of residents with less resources to 'privately' safeguard their own rights. Case law discussed in Chapters 4 and 5 thus show courts trying to eke out entitlements to public presence and shared public and residential space in the face of inimical actions by relatively powerful social actors, while at the same time remaining respectful of commercial, environmental and autonomy interests. Indeed, some have argued that many of the cases take the worthiness of these interests for granted and do not sufficiently interrogate whether the manner in which they are being safeguarded always serves the public interest.[28]

What seems missing in cases of this nature is an overarching judicial approach that properly captures the interplay between communal and individual interests, especially when it comes to the construction of an urban environment conducive to both individual and collective flourishing. To this end, I have suggested elsewhere that the relative lack of judicial engagement with the environmental right in section 24 of the Constitution in an urban context, especially in relation to obligations to ensure sustainable development and inter- and intragenerational equity, presents a missed opportunity in the development of an urban jurisprudence that adequately balances the tensions that arise in this context.[29] The *Sea Front for All* decision, for instance, illustrates how judicial understanding of the nature of public space, its connection to the city and the extent to which it can foster and nurture democracy, social cohesion and the virtues of heterogeneous living, can enrich courts' conception of the public good and can thereby enhance achievement of a collective right to the city, across boundaries of class.

On the other side of the spectrum, the city's most vulnerable residents often rely on the twin rights to equality and dignity to gain a foothold in the city. Chapter 4 detailed various instances where marginalised residents (such as undocumented migrants and informal traders) relied on these rights in attempting to assert a right to presence in the city, a right to make a livelihood and a right to protection against victimisation and exploitation. This dovetails with the discussion in Chapter 6 of struggles over sexual identity rights which, while more obviously transcending boundaries of race and class, also essentially boil down to an insistence on inclusion, accommodation and tolerance by outgroups falling foul of hegemonic urban behaviour codes.

In all of these cases, the discussion has highlighted limits to the protection flowing from current judicial approaches to the right to equality which, arguably due to its employment of a particularly value-laden notion of human dignity in the inquiries after unfair discrimination and exclusion, appears often to deny protection and relief to those who are regarded as co-constructors of their own marginalisation, by virtue of living their lives and/or making their livelihoods illegally, or of failing to conform to conventional societal norms and morals.[30] Indeed, outsiders tend to succeed in equality cases far more often when they are middle-class, or at least display a significant degree of assimilation to middle-class values. In both Chapters 4 and 6, this has been shown to result in a situation where, even where equality challenges have been won, their benefits tended to befall only those 'outsiders' who, due to their class or the extent of their assimilation, have been in a position to exploit them, whereas the most vulnerable members of the groups in question (such as poor black lesbians in the townships, sex workers, and undocumented migrants in the inner city) have remained almost wholly outside of the protective ambit of the law. Chapter 6 further showed how this has served in particular to exacerbate marginalised women's vulnerability to violence and thereby to restrict the performance of the right to the city by women more generally.[31]

On a more positive note, it also seems from Chapters 4 and 6 that the rights to equality and dignity are more likely to provide protection to vulnerable groups when used in conjunction with the right to freedom and security of the person, to found a right to presence in public space. While the jurisprudence on such a 'right' is but in its infancy, cases such as *SWEAT* and *V&A Waterfront* suggest that it could be a potentially useful springboard for a more inclusive equality jurisprudence, and point to potentially fruitful linkages between judicial rights-vindication and the physical enactment of the right to the city.

But it is the Constitutional Court's socio-economic rights jurisprudence in relation to urban service provision and the right to have access to adequate housing that has drawn most academic commentary, and also on the extent to which it enables a more equal and spatially just city. The long line of high-profile housing cases discussed in Chapter 2 together with the string of service provision decisions considered in Chapter 3 are further arguably the most illustrative of the Court's construction of a notion of urban citizenship and most directly relatable to conventional understandings of the right to the city.

In deciding these cases, the Constitutional Court has quite unequivocally indicated that it does not view itself as a primary formulator or driver of socio-economic policy and instead prefers to oversee and direct the manner in which the 'democratic' branches of state exercise their power in giving effect to the rights of access to housing, health care services, food, water, education and social security.[32] The result has been the development of a range of adjudicatory approaches to socio-economic rights characterised, first, by their conceptual sparsity and reluctance to define the extent of citizens' entitlements inherent in the rights in question;[33] second, by their significant deference to the State's vision of social and spatial justice as well as to its policy priorities;[34] third, for their remedial flexibility and their focus on preserving for the state a margin of discretion in how it accommodates and implements the findings of the Court;[35] and, fourth, for channelling citizens and state towards alternative participatory, dialogic and democratic spaces for dispute resolution.[36]

Three of these adjudicatory approaches have dominated the cases discussed in Chapters 2 and 3. The first has been the Constitutional Court's well-known 'reasonableness' approach, first developed in *Grootboom* and thereafter employed in a number of high-profile socio-economic rights cases, most notably in *Mazibuko*, where the Court found that the City of Johannesburg's approach to water delivery and cost-recovery in Soweto was not unreasonable. Long derided in much of the socio-economic rights literature for its abstract and procedural nature, and for failing to clearly articulate substantive entitlements inherent to socio-economic rights,[37] the application of the reasonableness approach in *Mazibuko* was further lambasted for being overly deferent to the City's understanding of its service delivery mandate and the associated policy challenges.[38]

Indeed, the *Mazibuko* Court found that it was 'ordinarily ... institutionally inappropriate for a court to determine precisely what the achievement of a particular social and economic right entails and what steps government should take to ensure the progressive realisation of the right',[39] not least because what socio-economic rights demand would 'vary over time and context',[40] so that an authoritative judicial determination of its content would ossify the right and straitjacket the legislature and executive, who were in any event, by virtue of their expertise and their democratic accountability, far better placed to make these determinations within the various physical contexts of delivery.[41] Instead, the appropriate role for courts was said to be to require government to take steps to progressively realise socio-economic rights and then to evaluate its chosen legislative and policy vehicles for doing so for reasonableness,[42] i.e. for balance, inclusivity, flexibility, responsiveness to emergency needs and so forth.

While the criticism that the reasonableness approach responds inadequately to the concrete needs and struggles of claimants need to be taken seriously (not least because, if it is indeed experienced as such, claimants will seek other, potentially extra-legal avenues to meet these needs and wage these struggles),[43] several experts have pointed out that its context-sensitive nature, openness and flexibility does render it far more responsive, dialogic and dynamic than a more top-down judicial determination and enforcement of the content of a right.[44] In fact, these features of the reasonableness approach may go a long way to ameliorate the tensions between judicial rights-vindication and the right to the city, which is arguably inimical to closure, fixedness and top-down definition.[45]

The second adjudicatory approach, emerging from evictions jurisprudence (notably *PE Municipality*, *Olivia Road* and *Joe Slovo*), is the Constitutional Court's reading of reasonableness together with the constitutional guarantee against eviction, with the effect that evictions that might result in homelessness are generally to be allowed only in circumstances where there has been meaningful engagement between the potential evictees and the City. Arguably the clearest indication of the Court's preference for democratic, dialogic and context-specific solutions for urban habitation disputes over firm, interpretation-based pronouncements on what socio-economic rights require, the employ of 'meaningful engagement' as both a constitutional requirement and (in appropriate circumstances) a remedy in eviction cases has generally been welcomed by commentators, not least for its clear dialogic and democracy-enhancing potential, which resonates well with the participatory elements of the right to the city.[46] However, some have warned that meaningful engagement, too, appears to be unmoored in a substantive understanding of the City's obligations in eviction cases and, accordingly, runs the risk of amounting to little other than a conceptually thin, ad hoc dispute resolution process.[47]

Third, the Constitutional Court's employ of a 'public law right' to procedural fairness in service delivery, rooted in the developmental responsibilities of local government, as developed in *Joseph* (though not since further elaborated), betrays a similar preference for procedural review and participation within predetermined democratic frameworks. While generally welcomed for its potential to foster responsive urban service delivery and participatory urban citizenship, it is perhaps too early to say whether the remedial potential of this 'public law right' will extend beyond that of reasonableness and meaningful engagement.[48]

Perhaps the defining, unifying feature of these adjudicatory approaches, at least as they have been employed in right-to-the-city-type disputes, has been the way in which the Constitutional Court has diverted the actual determination of rights and obligations, as well as the resolution of disputes, to outside deliberative processes and structures, either ones that already existed (as in the case of the Rental Housing Tribunal to which it channelled the dispute in *Maphango*) or ones which it created anew (as with meaningful engagement, which became institutionalised within local government processes subsequent to the *Olivia Road* judgment). The institutional deference inherent in reasonableness appears to be similarly geared towards strengthening democratic channels, as the Court itself remarked in *Mazibuko*:

> The purpose of litigation concerning the positive obligations imposed by social and economic rights should be to hold the democratic arms of government to account through litigation. In so doing, litigation of this sort fosters a form of participatory democracy that holds government accountable and requires it to account between elections over specific aspects of government policy.[49]

While generally appreciative of the Court's efforts to strengthen participatory democracy, several commentators have been critical of the manner in which the Court avoids some of the issues before it and diverts their resolution elsewhere instead. Stuart Wilson and Jackie Dugard, for instance, have argued that, as with communities' resort to violent protests, litigants approach the Court precisely because they have found democratic structures to be unresponsive, and that it is therefore incongruous for the Court to simply bat their real disputes away. They have accordingly implored the Constitutional Court to abandon its participatory-democracy focus in socio-economic rights cases in favour of a more directly engaging approach, which both substantively interprets rights, and remedies breaches thereof in a way that appropriately affirms the needs and real-life experiences underlying the litigation.[50]

I generally support arguments for a greater connection between the Constitutional Court's adjudicatory approach to housing and service delivery cases and the needs of Johannesburg's residents, especially the more vulnerable among them. But the conclusions drawn in previous chapters of this book lead me to disagree with the suggestion that the Court is misguided to focus its energies on the creation and strengthening of deliberative democratic spaces for the resolution of disputes over the right to the city.

In this regard, I am strongly persuaded by Katharine Young's analysis of the Constitutional Court's adjudicatory approaches, which disputes the conclusion that the Court is avoiding the polycentric issues before it in socio-economic rights cases. Young argues instead that the Court has carefully crafted for itself a catalytic role, shifting strategically between different modes of review (sometimes being deferential or minimalist, sometimes experimentalist, sometimes managerialist) depending on what it is that the Court perceives to be required in order to resolve disputes in a manner that is both fair to the parties and respectful of a broader commitment to constitutional democracy:

> The Court is variously active or passive, ambitious or modest, involved or restrained. In all counts, it is not the embrace or avoidance of substance that separates the decisions … [but] the pragmatic sense of catalysing the resolution to the problem at hand: in this case [of housing disputes], of the Court requiring other actors – the legislature, bureaucracy, City, landlords, eviction companies, occupiers, and social movements to work together to realise the right to housing.[51]

Depending on its assessment of the legitimacy and urgency of the interests at stake and of the overall reasonableness of government's response thereto, Young argues, the Court thus aims in the first instance to 'lower the political energy that is required in order to change the way in which government responds to the protection of economic and social rights'.[52]

Assuming that Young is correct to characterise the Court's approach as such, there are several reasons, aside from the obvious counter-majoritarian tensions inherent in judicial review and the need to respect the separation of powers, why this catalytic model of judicial review in socio-economic rights cases (together with the shifting but definite extent of judicial deference towards democratic channels and spaces that it implies) may be more appropriate in right-to-the-city-type disputes than an approach involving the more normative and direct engagement with and determination of the issues before the Court.

The first group of reasons relate to the aggrieved litigants. While Wilson and Dugard are no doubt correct that litigants and violent protestors are often persons who have been sidelined or failed by democratic channels, processes and structures, their criticism underplays the extent to which marginalised residents ordinarily *do* participate constructively in the affairs of the city – regardless of their sense of alienation, research shows that residents continue to participate through a range of actions, from peaceful, 'legitimate' protests to more institutionalised and formal actions, such as attending ward committee meetings and voting.[53] There is further the uncomfortable fact that both litigants and violent protestors are sometimes deliberately acting *undemocratically* by seeking to bypass, circumvent or overthrow the outcomes of democratic and deliberative processes (as happened for instance in *Maphango*, where applicants attempted to circumvent the Rental Housing Tribunal in favour of a determination by the Constitutional Court), and that they are sometimes aggrieved precisely because the outcome of more broadly representative democratic processes was, or would likely be, against them (as was possibly the case in *Mazibuko*, where the APF resisted the installation of prepaid water meters in Phiri despite evidence that the majority of the community appeared to accept them).[54]

Given that litigation inevitably only centres on the interests of some of the (potentially great many) people who would be affected by the outcome of a dispute (and that courts therefore risk inadvertently sidelining compelling competing interests), and that the avenue of litigation is only realistically accessible to a precious few (those who are themselves well-resourced or well-connected, or those whose views and plight happen to correspond to the political objectives of a well-resourced social movement or NGO), it is probably wise for the Court to insist that matters ultimately be resolved by far more representative and accessible bodies, while reserving for itself the role of ensuring that such bodies resolve the issues in a constitutionally acceptable manner:

> If city politics is to be democratic and not dominated by the point of view of one group, it must be a politics that takes account of and provides voice for the different groups that dwell together in the city without forming a community.[55]

Second, the dynamic and volatile nature of life in the city means that contingent, ad-hoc and context specific decisions are far more likely to be in line with the right to the city, and far more likely to accommodate or allow for different and competing modes of self-realisation of rights, than the judicial process. Indeed, a judicial determination of issues may well close off a range of (both legitimate and less than legitimate) everyday performative channels for the satisfaction of needs. As *Mazibuko* all too clearly illustrates, it is naive to believe that matters will always be decided in favour of applicants on all points, which means that judicial determination of the content of rights and of the correctness of state efforts to limit them may well have the effect of restricting the agency of marginalised urban dwellers, of vindicating the interests of more powerful urban players or of legitimising state efforts to limit rights. It is accordingly often in the interests of (especially more vulnerable) urban residents that aspects of everyday struggle are left to play out beyond the purview of the law.

Third, on a more abstract level, it is important not to lose sight of the fact that there are myriad competing and, in principle, equally legitimate views on the content and meaning of rights, as well as myriad competing and, in principle, equally legitimate visions for the shape, form and functioning of the city. Opinions differ legitimately, for instance, on whether the right to have access to adequate housing should encompass an entitlement to a free choice of housing or settlement location, or on the extent to which rights to urban service provision should be limited by a civic obligation to pay for services consumed. Similarly, people disagree over the extent to which space in the inner city of Johannesburg should be given over to informal trade or to low cost housing, over which mechanisms of water and electricity delivery are appropriate for different communities, over what degree of control suburban residents should be allowed over entry of others to their properties or neighbourhoods, and so forth.[56] While it is no doubt so that courts must insist on constitutionally compatible outcomes for processes aiming to solve or mediate between such competing views, representative democratic processes are infinitely better at accommodating and balancing the divergent visions and views in different contexts and at different times, than are courts.[57]

Fourth, on the assumption that we accept the democratic legitimacy of local government, as well as the general terms of a social contract under which government is both obliged and granted the authority to pursue the common good and to respect, protect, promote and fulfil the rights of all inhabitants, the oppositional logic of litigation far too easily paints local governments as monolithic entities bent on the pursuit of neoliberal objectives and opposed to the realisation of the rights of vulnerable inhabitants.[58] This not only underplays various tensions and contradictions within the state, but also assumes that it more often than not acts in bad faith.

I would wager that, as with most other South African cities, a study of Johannesburg's policy documents, as well as of its officials' stated positions on a whole range of matters, and of its everyday urban management practices across the board, often (though admittedly not always) points to the opposite conclusion – that we are dealing with an immensely complex 'entity' which, for all its contradictions, capacity challenges and occasional misguidedness, is generally committed to building a city that reflects and enables the constitutional vision of an equal, tolerant, diverse and prosperous society.[59] The *Mazibuko* Court went as far as to explicitly acknowledge this:

> the applicants took issue with the sheer quantity of information placed before the courts by the City and Johannesburg Water in particular. It is true that the volume of material was substantial, but none of it was irrelevant. Reading it made plain that this was a government agency that has approached the challenges it faces with an impressive seriousness of purpose and commitment to improving the lives of the residents of the City in a sustainable fashion. Unsurprisingly, given the scale and complexity of the challenge, the policy was not perfect. But that is not the constitutional standard.[60]

While partly agreeing with criticism that courts far too easily accept local government's versions of the facts in urban rights disputes (arguably a result not so much of bias as of the operation of longstanding evidentiary rules),[61] and while also acknowledging criticism that judges tend to be overly sympathetic to the urban management challenges that face the state (as opposed to the daily survival challenges facing many urban residents),[62] I would wager that understanding and appreciating these challenges is crucial to a fair, workable and sustainable determination of urban disputes. As will be shown in the following subsection, a more hands-off judicial approach to such disputes and, especially, a significant degree of remedial flexibility, appears to be key if the objectives are for the reception and internalisation of judgments at all levels of the state bureaucracy and for everyday rights-conducive governance.[63]

In this respect, Katharine Young has wagered that the Constitutional Court's catalytic approach to socio-economic rights adjudication is intuitively similar to Kent Roach and Geoff Budlender's suggested paradigm for the exercise of remedial discretion in socio-economic rights matters, and also when it comes to interpreting rights and to evaluating whether government has complied with the obligations imposed by them.[64] Roach and Budlender argued that the extent to which courts should insist upon a particular course of remedial action, and the extent to which they should proceed to supervise compliance with their orders, do and should depend on the reasons for government's infringement of a particular right in particular circumstances. They proceeded to contend that different margins of governmental discretion and judicial oversight inherent in court orders vindicating socio-economic rights would be appropriate in relation to governmental agencies that are intransigent or opposed to rights, on the one hand, and for governmental agencies that are in favour of rights but are unaware of their full implications, or which lack capacity or resources to fully give effect to these, on the other.[65] It may well be argued that the Constitutional Court's catalytic and democratic-process-focused approach does exactly this in relation to the definition and implementation of rights more generally, while at the same time insisting on a baseline of constitutional compliance, accountability and justifiability.

Certainly, regardless of the wisdom of not engaging in a more elaborate and purposive interpretation of socio-economic rights, and of affording local government significant discretion in the manner in which it complies with them, the Constitutional Court's socio-economic rights jurisprudence appears to have succeeded in its objective of 'exact[ing] a detailed accounting from government and, in doing so, impact[ing] beneficially on the policy-making process'.[66] This is evident not only from the manner in which the City of Johannesburg altered both the content of its policies and the manner of their implementation in ways significantly more attuned to the rights of residents in matters such as *Mazibuko* and *Olivia Road*, but also from the rights-conducive laws and policies drafted and implemented in attempted compliance with cases such as those in *SAITF*, *Olivia Road* and *Grootboom*.[67]

The impact of rights-based litigation in Johannesburg

The analysis above has shown a judiciary which, despite generally preferring a hands-off, democracy-enhancing approach to most kinds of urban rights disputes, nevertheless intervenes more directly when seized by a matter in which residents' immediate interests are unacceptably being compromised. The obvious next question, then, is whether and under what circumstances judicial intervention has assisted in producing a more just, inclusive and prosperous city.

Research on the impact of human rights litigation often understandably focuses mainly on whether individual litigants obtained the reinforcement or benefits they had sought from the courts, and on whether there had been any legal or policy changes that can directly be related back to the outcome of a case or series of cases. The systemic, medium- and long-term impact of legal processes and judgments on the political, social and physical environment around a legal process is obviously more diffuse, subtler and more difficult to gauge, not least since it is less likely to be ascribable solely to any particular instance or pattern of litigation.

While trends in this regard are changing, most rights-based litigation is still brought by or on behalf of citizens against some branch of the State – in our case, against urban local government. An obvious starting point for an investigation into the broader impact of litigation in any particular area is thus a look at the manner in which the relevant branch of the State has responded thereto, both in the course of particular matters and in their aftermaths.

International studies on the bureaucratic and policy impact of legal processes have shown that government agencies' response to litigation depends on a range of factors, both internal and external to the agency in question. Internally it depends, first, on the political climate within the agency and, second, on its capacity to respond to or comply with legal processes against it. The internal political climate in a State agency is influenced by, for instance, the policy vision of the agency, the extent of uniformity and commitment to this vision within the organisation, the degree of internal agreement over how the vision is best achieved, the extent to which this vision is being threatened or its implementation is being bedevilled by the litigation, and officials' view of the opposing litigating parties and their purpose. These factors will have an impact both on the conduct of an agency in the course of a legal process (determining whether the agency is willing to accede to demands or to reach a settlement, influencing the extent to which it willingly participates in the process, and so forth) and on its 'political will' to internalise and comply with an outcome against it (which includes carrying out the policy and practical directives in a judgment).[68] In this regard, it is important to keep in mind that state agencies are not monolithic and do not always act uniformly, predictably or consistently.[69]

Capacity, meanwhile, refers to the agency's human, financial and technological resources, and to the strength, responsiveness, resilience and flexibility of its systems and their underlying policy frameworks. Capacity to comply with a court judgment is impacted not only by the extent of an agency's resources and skills, but also by the extent of the pressures under which it operates, the number of competing demands on its skills and resources, the feasibility, cost and effects of compliance, and so forth.[70] Capacity-issues interact with political factors to determine whether, to what extent and how fast an agency responds to a judgment, how exactly it carries out court orders, whether, to what extent and how soon policy frameworks are altered in response to judicial findings and to what degree changes to policy are internalised and operationalised within an organisation.

External factors that cause pressure on bureaucracies to respond (or not to respond) to court judgments or other outcomes of legal processes, or that influence the manner in which they respond, include the conduct, approach and motivations of the opposing litigating parties (including the nature of their demands, their litigiousness, the constructiveness of their interactions with the bureaucracy, their openness to compromise and how realistic or feasible it would be for the agency to accede to the demands); the number, level of organisation, capacity, resourcefulness, political inclination and clout of social movements around an issue; the nature of competing demands (as well as the strength and multitude of organisations or social movements rallying around such demands); the leaning of the press and other media; public sentiment and so forth.[71]

Interestingly, the factors listed here appear to predict bureaucratic response to litigation and court judgments somewhat better than the content of the judgments or the actual outcome of the processes themselves – for instance, sometimes unsuccessful litigation, or threats of litigation, against a state agency may have a more favourable outcome for the parties or for the persons on whose behalf litigation was waged, than a successful challenge backed up by the force of a court order.[72]

As alluded to in Chapter 1, the City of Johannesburg is a vast and complex bureaucratic entity that most certainly contains various internal political struggles and contradictions, while facing significant resource and capacity constraints. While it contains some notable gaps (notably around the intricacies of low cost housing provision) the City's policy vision is generally sophisticated, focused and progressive. It prioritises people-centred development, the overcoming of the spatial fragmentation and injustices of its apartheid design and the realisation of a vibrant, economically successful, resilient and sustainable city for all, through inner-city regeneration, densification, transport-orientated development and various citizen-empowerment initiatives.[73] However, Chapter 1 has shown that there are various internal agencies and political groupings in the city with differing approaches when it comes to the manner of implementation of this policy vision. As has appeared throughout this book, some of these approaches have been (sometimes by far) more rights-friendly and community-minded than others. There have been significant internal tensions, for instance, over the approach to be followed in the regulation of informal trade in the CBD, with significant numbers of officials opposing Operation Clean Sweep and supporting the *SAITF* litigation. There are also reportedly significant internal differences, for instance, over evictions from hijacked or dilapidated inner city buildings and over implementation of security bylaws in relation to gating practices in the northern suburbs.

Capacity-wise, Johannesburg, while better off than many other South African municipalities, does take strain from a general skills shortage in the public sector and from scarcity of resources. Much as the City raises impressive amounts of its own revenue and has a reputation for strong financial systems and good fiscal governance, it remains dependent on budget allocations from national and provincial governments for carrying out many of its responsibilities, especially in relation to housing provision. It is generally accepted that such resource allocations in South Africa have been disproportionately small when compared with the extent of the developmental responsibilities of local government.[74]

Externally, while few residents or organisations generally oppose the City's policy vision on most issues, there is perceptible levels of general discontent over its urban management, especially in relation to erratic or inefficient service delivery processes (much as these are often due to the actions or performance of entities other than the City, such as trade unions, Eskom or Rand Water) and in relation to billing and credit control practices. Wealthier residents are well-organised and regularly resort to actual or threatened litigation to resolve their problems in this regard, or to resist urban developments to which they are opposed. In poorer townships and informal settlements, on the other hand, discontent regularly manifests itself in the form of service delivery protests displaying different levels of hostility and destructiveness. The City is thus quick to be alerted to instances where its policies, or their implementation, are failing to find favour with residents.

In addition, civil society in Johannesburg is strong and many of South Africa's urban social movements have their origins and their nucleus here. The APF, for instance, was Johannesburg-based and many of its notable activities, including its resort to legal process in *Mazibuko*, have taken place here. Other recent Joburg-based social movements discussed in this book have included the Landless Peoples' Movement and the Soweto Electricity Crisis Committee.

As alluded to earlier, Johannesburg is also the office base and the focus of the work of several NGOs interested in urban social justice issues. Most significantly, Joburg is home to the Socio-Economic Rights Institute (SERI), which has been behind almost all the inner-city housing litigation discussed in Chapter 2, has participated in some of the service delivery cases discussed in Chapter 3 and also represented inner city traders in the *SAITF* case. The City's relationship with SERI is reportedly very acrimonious and hostile, with neither party, for the most part, willing to engage the other outside of the legal process.[75] Other human rights organisations active in the city and sometimes resorting to the litigation include the Legal Resources Centre, the Centre for Applied Legal Studies, Section 27 and Lawyers for Human Rights (who often represent the interests of undocumented migrants in the City and rendered them assistance around the time of the Pitje Chambers litigation).

Together, these social movements and civil society organisations form a formidable pressure group in favour of rights-conducive urban development, especially in the inner city, and have lent significant clout to the demands of the inner city's marginalised residents, such as informal traders, building occupiers and undocumented migrants. But conversely, in the same CBD, the City also faces pressure from coalitions of businesses, developers and property owners, the Johannesburg Heritage Foundation and so forth, all of which typically exert pressure to accelerate urban regeneration in favour of a business and middle-class-friendly urban environment.

All these factors and pressures considered, it is perhaps unsurprising that the City's compliance with the judgments discussed in this book has been uneven.

On the one hand, the City has very often responded progressively to the pressures of litigation and has altered its policies in response to rights-based legal challenges, often with tangible, rights-conducive effects. *Mazibuko*, where the City introduced an entitlement to extra free water for indigent residents during the course of the litigation, and kept adjusting its policies in response to the litigation (to the point where the Constitutional Court ultimately dismissed the challenges against it), is the prime example of this.[76] There have also been positive policy responses in the wake of judgments such as *Olivia Road* (which is credited for spurring the City towards increasing its inner-city low cost housing stock and for dedicating bureaucratic energy towards meaningful engagement processes)[77] and *SAITF* (which has led to the adoption of a revised inner city trade policy). On the other hand, hardened responses by officials to applicants (or similarly situated residents) subsequent to litigation, and a reduced willingness to engage with them outside of the legal process, has been reported in the wake of both of the latter cases.

In particular, activists, commentators and even the Joburg High Court have bemoaned the City's slow, incomplete, haphazard and foot-dragging responses to the housing judgments discussed in Chapter 2.[78] The City seems to have been especially unable or unwilling to absorb the impact of *Blue Moonlight* which, as will be recalled, required it to provide emergency temporary housing to persons evicted from inner-city buildings by 'private' building owners. While (eventually) complying with the order in relation to the specific applicants, the City has consistently indicated that, going forward, it simply lacks the resources for full compliance with this order on a city-wide scale.

Indeed, *Blue Moonlight* appears to have left the City spinning, with human rights organisations threateningly watching its every move in relation to every inner city eviction, evictees becoming less compromising in their demands for well-located, near-permanent 'temporary', low-cost, City-provided accommodation that adequately serves their needs (going as far as to legally challenge the rules and conditions prevailing at those temporary housing facilities that do exist) and, on the other hand, building owners and developers getting increasingly impatient with the city's slow assistance in effecting evictions, to the point of themselves turning to the courts and the Public Protector for assistance. On the streets, meanwhile, the City has reportedly often ignored evictions taking place unless threatened with legal action, and it is sometimes accused of deliberately making conditions in temporary housing facilities uncomfortable for residents, so as to encourage them to leave the facilities and fend for themselves.[79]

While it is probably true that much of this seemingly bumbling and cynical response is ascribable to lack of political will within the City,[80] this lack of political will must arguably be understood not so much as opposition to assisting poor residents in fulfilling their housing needs, but rather as opposition to the extent to which unbridled compliance with the demands of inner-city building occupiers would derail the City's achievement of its compelling long-term policy objectives in relation to the inner city environment. It also has to be appreciated that, rightly or wrongly, the *Blue Moonlight* judgment (which, recall, held that the City ought to have budgeted for emergency housing and could not rely on the Provincial government's unwillingness to supplement its funds in this regard as an excuse for non-compliance) had left the City in a real resource bind, at least in the short term.[81] Moreover, the discursive space around the question of inner city regeneration and evictions has arguably become so politicised, hostile and litigious that officials feel powerless to take concrete steps in *any* direction, lest they be hauled before a court.

While this does not absolve the City of its obligations, it would therefore seem that a dead end is approaching, unless a more constructive way of engaging the city around inner city homelessness can be found. It appears unlikely that the City will respond constructively to demands around inner city habitation in the current hostile environment where it feels itself constantly to be on the back foot – 'citizen action that relies exclusively on an oppositional logic or a political stance of perpetual resistance is unlikely to achieve reforms in the mundane functioning of the State'.[82] In this regard, the Constitutional Court's indicated preference for engagement and participatory solutions provides one obvious way forward.

But the extent to which authorities comply with judgments is only one of the ways in which the judgments shape the political, social and physical spaces into which they are received. Over and above the perhaps counterproductive way in which rights-based litigation in Joburg has pitched NGOs and social movements against the City, assessments of the litigation's impact on these bodies have generally been optimistic. Even where cases have been lost (as, for instance, in *Mazibuko*), movements have used them as ways to expose, politicise and raise the profile of everyday urban injustices, and it appears that litigation has lent significant credibility and legitimacy to their plights.[83] While there has been some predictable deflation of movements following the conclusion of litigation processes, litigation has also often served (at least initially) to energise them and to raise their profile.[84] As discussed above, this then has had the effect of raising the sensitivity and enhancing the responsiveness of the City and of other significant urban players to their plight, and has ultimately arguably led to greater accommodation of their perspectives.

Of course, perhaps the ultimate assessment of the impact of litigation is whether it has made any difference to everyday lives in the city, in particular those of the people by whom, or on whose behalf, cases were brought.[85] Much as the cases discussed in this book have certainly not solved all the problems faced by those struggling for survival or otherwise attempting to realise their right to the city across Johannesburg, there can be little doubt that their impact has been significant.

This is so perhaps most glaringly in relation to the beneficiaries of the inner-city housing jurisprudence who, but for the consistent and dogged intervention of public interest organisations, would have found themselves evicted onto the streets. Over time, the housing rights jurisprudence discussed in Chapter 2 has imposed a legal framework upon the City, in terms of which such evictions may not occur without at least some form of alternative accommodation being provided.[86] Chapter 2 has further shown that, as a direct result of the litigation, the voices of inner city building occupiers have immeasurably been amplified in discussions over their accommodation in the city. Of course, litigation has not always been able to stave off evictions, and has not solved the general problems associated with a lack of affordable housing across the city. Indeed, it has been remarked that the effect of successful litigation in this context has often been to simply shift state resources from one group of vulnerable, homeless residents to another.[87] But there can be little doubt over its general empowering effects, its (albeit reluctant and far from perfect) bureaucratic impact and the extent to which it has lent legitimacy to the habitation claims of people who previously had little public sympathy.[88]

On the service delivery front, *Mazibuko* shows that the empowering effects and policy spinoffs of litigation are not necessarily always limited to its success or to the actual terms of judgments. Not only did the City significantly alter its policy in a manner far more sensitive to the needs of poor township residents as a direct response to the legal challenge, with the result that indigent households could access a greater amount of free water, but the issue of prepaid water meters in Soweto was so heavily politicised by the litigation, that further meters were not installed in Phiri for quite some time. Many residents, meanwhile, felt empowered by the initial victory in the High Court to rip out their meters, showing how legal strategies can sometimes enable or amplify insurgent performances of the right to the city.[89]

However, it would also seem from *Mazibuko* and other isolated service delivery cases that single cases seldom bring lasting relief. Rather, as the housing jurisprudence again illustrates most convincingly, a direct consequence of the piecemeal and guarded approach of courts to socio-economic rights litigation has been that more fundamental changes to governance and to the legal framework come about only over time, in response to a consistent and coordinated litigation strategy over many matters and in many related contexts.[90] This again raises the question of access to justice, and points to more readily and regularly accessible participatory channels as more likely engines of change. But this is not to say that even single cases are of no use – all judgments alter the possibilities of the law and of the city, and they interact and build on each other over time, to bring about remedial frameworks, opportunities for collective action and spaces for individual performances of rights in ways that were not previously imagined.[91]

Urban constitutional citizenship

Perhaps law's most pervasive power is how it invisibly structures lives and relationships and how it constructs parameters for different aspects of citizenship. Much of the discussion in this book has been around dimensions of urban citizenship for inhabitants of Johannesburg. Essentially, all struggles over urban inhabitance, appropriation and participation are struggles over citizenship and its spoils – who can claim rights to the city, who gets to shape its contours, who get to participate in its form, who get to live freely in it.

According to section 3 of the 1996 Constitution, 'there is a common South African citizenship' and 'all citizens are equally entitled to the rights, privileges and benefits of citizenship, and equally subject to the duties and responsibilities of citizenship'. Certainly, the Bill of Rights' bestowal of justiciable rights equally on 'everyone' in South African territory, regardless of their standing in society, has driven home the equality of the rights of citizenship. Indeed, the defining characteristic of citizenship in post-apartheid South Africa is that it is a rights-bearing one. Being the bearers of rights is empowering to citizens who can, as the many cases discussed in this book attest, force both governmental agencies as well as powerful private actors to engage with them on the content of their rights and obligations, within the structure of the legal process.[92] Justiciable rights are therefore an important equalising force within constitutional citizenship – when legally asserted, deliberations over rights' inherent entitlements and obligations take place on an equal footing, and all actors are equally bound by the outcomes of such deliberations.[93]

But this means that the manner in which courts decide disputes over the content and implications of constitutional rights becomes determinative of the spoils and burdens of citizenship itself. Sachs J recognised this in *Joe Slovo*:

> [t]his case compels us to deal in a realistic way with what it means to be a South African living in a constitutional democracy. It concerns the responsibilities of government to secure the ample benefits of citizenship promised for all by the Constitution. It expands the concept of citizenship beyond traditional notions of electoral rights and claims for diplomatic protection, to include the full substantive benefits and entitlements envisaged by the Constitution for all the people who live in the country and to whom it belongs. At the same time it focuses on the reciprocal duty of citizens to be active, participatory and responsible and to make their own individual and collective contributions towards the realisation of the benefits and entitlements they claim for themselves, not to speak of the well-being of the community as a whole.[94]

Many of the judicial decisions discussed in this book illustrate how the legal determination and vindication of rights can enhance urban citizenship. Several decisions have affirmed equal entitlement to the benefits of citizenship even for those who, for various reasons, are generally regarded as marginalised outsiders. Decisions such as *SWEAT* and *V&A Waterfront* have driven home that urban citizenship, at its most basic level, must accommodate difference by allowing everyone to be present in the public spaces of the city to exercise and dispute their rights. Flowing from this entitlement to urban presence, Courts have vindicated rights to inhabit the city (*Olivia Road*, *Blue Moonlight*), to appropriate its spaces while making a living (*SAITF)* and to be consulted, engaged and heard when these activities are required to be limited or interfered with (*Olivia Road*, *Joseph*).

However, the book has also shown that this has more often been the case where citizens have themselves behaved in accordance with societal behaviour codes (especially where these codes are embedded in the law), and have shown themselves to be both willing and able to carry out the obligations associated with urban citizenship. Citizens who conduct themselves 'illegally' or 'irresponsibly', or who opt for asserting their visions for the city antisocially, or through self-help rather than structured deliberation (as in the case, for instance, of violent protests,[95] unauthorised road closures, 'unlawful' street trade and so forth) have typically encountered little sympathy from courts, with decisions such as *SATAWU* v. *Garvas*, *SAITF*, *Olivia Road* and *Mazibuko* quick to endorse and uphold the law's restriction of 'illegal' or 'antisocial' activities.

Apart from being problematic where the law or societal behaviour codes in question reflect values that are themselves racialist, sexist, classist or heterosexist (which, as several of the chapters of this book has pointed out, is not uncommonly the case), myself and others have warned that, especially when it comes to cases concerning service delivery, courts' understandable tendency to reward law-abidingness may sometimes have the unintended effect of endorsing a neo-liberal leaning, consumerist notion of citizenship, that rests upon the willingness and the ability to pay for life in the city and everything that it entails.[96] Cases such as *Mazibuko*, *Joseph*, *Mkontwana* and *Rademan* perhaps too readily assume that paying one's way in the city should be a logical threshold for entering into deliberation over the content of rights. While denying the costs of housing, services and social life would be naive and counterproductive, there arguably remains work to be done in tailoring a rights-based jurisprudence that distributes and enforces the financial burdens of urban citizenship realistically and even-handedly.

But this is not to say that the right to the city and ideals of urban social justice are adequately served by a free-for-all, lawless pursuit of self-interest. Urban living is communal, reciprocal and interdependent, and often requires as much compromise and restraint from citizens as it does from the state. For Iris Marion Young, for instance,

> city life is a vast, even infinite, economic network of production, distribution, transportation, exchange, communication, service provision, and amusement. City dwellers depend on the mediation of thousands of other people and vast organizational resources in order to accomplish their individual ends. City dwellers are thus together, bound to one another, in what should be and sometimes is a single polity. Their being together entails some common problems and common interests, but they do not create a community of shared final ends, of mutual identification and reciprocity.[97]

The atomistic nature of legal rights often complicates the articulation and upholding of a common good. Where this common good itself remains contested, malleable and in flux, as is the case with life in the city, its pursuit arguably lies in agreement over basic rules of engagement and a commitment to its shared definition and redefinition.

The Constitutional Court's urban rights jurisprudence has arguably shown remarkable awareness of this. Much as the Court has required of the State to engage its citizens and to respect, protect and accommodate their individual visions of the good life, it has also acknowledged and emphasised residents' agency and has required of them, too, to deliberate, engage and compromise in order to respect and enable the rights of others.[98] This relational, dialogic and deliberative understanding of constitutional urban citizenship, as institutionalised through the Court's preference for deliberative solutions to rights conflicts, its guardedness against the ossification of urban citizenship through top-down rights-definition and its commitment to the establishment and strengthening of more accessible, even-handed public fora for continued deliberation, is strongly welcomed.

The jurisprudence discussed in this book, then, reveals that urban constitutional citizens are in the first instance participants – through actions that create space and structure relationships, but also through adherence to deliberated ground rules, through compromise and cooperation and through a commitment to mediation and dialogue.[99] The strengthening and increased utilisation of a whole range of deliberative institutional spaces in Johannesburg and other South African cities must therefore be a clear collective priority.[100]

Conclusion

As I write this, Johannesburg, as always, finds itself at multiple crossroads. A dramatic, largely unanticipated change of local government after what appears to have been a stay-away protest by ANC supporters during the local government elections of August 2016, has thrown Joburg's everyday governance and its policy direction open for renewed contestation, and has ridiculed the widely-held belief that South Africans do not make use of conventional channels of political participation to assert their convictions. This political sea change comes at the same time as intensified environmental challenges (notably, a serious and resolute drought) and a significant national tightening of a whole range of economic belts, meaning that renewed debates over the city's future will take place in an environment of increasingly acute resource scarcity. It also remains an environment of social tension and conflict, with the last two years having seen violent student and service delivery protests, a perceived resurgence in violent crime and renewed xenophobic hostility, all displaying a perhaps unprecedented nervous energy.

This book has shown how justiciable legal rights have found their way into Johannesburg civil society and everyday life, and has studied the manner in which courts have given effect to constitutional rights in the city. As such, it has been a study of the judicialisation of everyday politics and has revealed the need not only for broadened access to the justice system, but also for the broadening and strengthening of a whole range of alternative civic channels for democratic participation. Perhaps most significantly, it has underlined the interplay between struggles for the right to the city and struggles for the meaning of legal rights, affirming Michael McCann's assertion that 'legal norms and rights rarely persist uncontested, but are subject to constant battles over official enforcement, extension to different relational contexts, and substantive reformulation by variously situated citizens'.[101] Rights and the law will undeniably play a leading part in renewed struggles over Johannesburg's future shape and form, and will also (perhaps increasingly) animate the everyday lives of its residents. It is hoped that this book has contributed, even if only slightly, to understanding the challenges and opportunities that this poses for governance and everyday life in the city.

As for Joburg, it undeniably remains a city of poverty and struggle, of social, economic and spatial inequality and strife, where the right to the city remains subverted daily by a whole array of structural forces. But it is also a city that has, in the course of the last few years, undeniably become far more integrated, more open and accessible and consequently more vibrant than perhaps ever before.[102] Moreover, it is slowly becoming a city in which a range of citizens participate more actively, through official channels but also through public presence and action.[103] Certainly, it remains the ultimate petri-dish for transformation in post-apartheid South Africa and, as such, remains a city to be watched.

Notes

1 On these and related tensions between legal rights and the right to the city, see Coggin and Pieterse (2012: 274–275); Pieterse (2014a: 193); Purcell (2002: 106).
2 See Coggin and Pieterse (2012: 275); Pieterse (2014b: 163); Purcell (2002: 102); Von Schnitzler (2008: 906, 913–914).
3 Glaser (2015: 139).
4 See Brown (2015: 68–69); Glaser (2015: 141, 143–145, 157).
5 See Glaser (2015: 159–160).
6 On these and related virtues of legal rights and the legal process in this context see Coggin and Pieterse (2012: 274); Liebenberg (2015a: 448, 466).
7 See Coggin and Pieterse (2012: 274–275).
8 See Purcell (2002: 101).
9 See for instance Charlton (2010: 2); Liebenberg (2015a: 466); Pieterse (2014a: 178–181).
10 See Langford *et al.* (2014: 435); McCann (1994: 65, 89–90, 138).
11 See Wilson (2009) and discussion in Chapter 2.
12 On this tendency of legal rights generally see McCann (1994: 297).
13 See Pieterse (2007a: 17–18); West (2001: 1904–1907).
14 See Benit-Gbaffou (2008); Parnell and Pieterse (2010: 158).
15 For similar arguments, see Smith and Rubin (2015: 249–251).
16 See Bilchitz (2015: 103–105); Holston (2009: 252); Liebenberg (2006: 20); Rosa (2011: 548–549).
17 See Brown (2015: 126); Dugard and Langford (2011: 55–57); Langford *et al.* (2014: 435); Liebenberg (2006: 20); Madlingozi (2014: 112); Ray (2014: 177); Rosa (2011: 549).
18 See also Dugard and Langford (2011: 58); Langford *et al.* (2014: 432).
19 See Bilchitz (2015: 108–109); Gloppen (2005: 158–159, 165); Liebenberg (2015b: 418); Wilson (2011: 130).
20 On such dangers inherent to liberal rights discourse more generally see West (2001: 1904–1915).
21 See Sinwell (2010: 167).
22 See Coggin and Pieterse (2012: 274); Parnell and Pieterse (2010: 158); Pieterse (2014a: 193); West (2001 1912–1913).

23 See Gloppen (2005: 155–156); Liebenberg (2015a: 470); Sinwell (2010: 167–168); Von Schnitzler (2008: 916).
24 See Brown (2015: 64–66, 126); Parnell and Pieterse (2010: 158).
25 See Bilchitz (2015: 105, 107–108); Dixon (2007: 402–406); Smith and Rubin (2015: 274–275). For further advantages of courts as deciders of polycentric socio-economic disputes see Pieterse (2004: 395).
26 See Coggin and Pieterse (2012: 275–276); Dixon (2007: 399–402); Gloppen (2005: 159–160); Liebenberg (2006: 30; 2015a: 466, 468); Ray (2014: 177).
27 On this 'antisocial' use of liberal rights, see Pieterse (2007a: 1, 7–8); West (2001: 1904–1907; 1912–1915).
28 See Strydom and Viljoen (2014: 1207–1209, 1211, 1217–1219, 1236–1237).
29 See Pieterse (2014a: 181–187, 191–193).
30 For detailed criticism of these features of the Constitutional Court's equality jurisprudence see for instance Albertyn (2007: 271–273); De Vos (2008: 259); Pieterse (2008: 405, 410–418).
31 On the gendered implications of the Constitutional Court's approach to the right to equality see for instance Albertyn (2007: 254, 274); Bonthuys (2008: 34–35).
32 See Bilchitz (2015: 105–107); Liebenberg (2015a: 454); Ray (2014: 174–175); Steinberg (2006: 269); Wilson *et al.* (2015: 477).
33 See Brand (2003: 43–50); Liebenberg (2010: 173–174; 2015b: 415); Pieterse (2007b: 810–811); Ray (2014: 174); Wilson (2011: 128–129); Wilson and Dugard (2011: 669, 672); Wilson *et al.* (2015: 502).
34 See Brand (2011: 624–630); Liebenberg (2015a: 455); Ray (2014: 176).
35 See Roach and Budlender (2005); Liebenberg (2010: 434–438); Woolman (2013: 269–270).
36 See Brand (2011: 623–624, 635–636); Gloppen (2005: 156); Liebenberg (2015a: 466–467); Ray (2014: 178); Rosa (2011: 553); Van der Berg (2013: 396–397); Young (2010: 387, 412).
37 See for instance Brand (2011: 43–50); Liebenberg (2010: 173, 176–77; 2015b: 415); Pieterse (2007b: 810–812); also discussion in Chapter 1.
38 See Coggin and Pieterse (2012: 275); Liebenberg (2010: 470–480; 2015a: 455); Ray (2014: 183, 194–195); Roithmayr (2010: 328); Smith and Rubin (2015: 274–275); Williams (2010: 189–195); Wilson and Dugard (2011: 674–679).
39 *Mazibuko* v. *City of Johannesburg* (2010: para 61).
40 Ibid., para 60.
41 Ibid., para 61. See also paras 60; 66; Liebenberg (2015a: 455); Ray (2014: 175).
42 *Mazibuko* v. *City of Johannesburg* (2010: paras 50, 57–59, 67).
43 See Liebenberg (2010: 173, 176–177); Pieterse (2007b: 803–804); Wilson and Dugard (2011: 665, 670–671).
44 See Dixon (2007: 409–410); Liebenberg (2006: 30; 2010: 174); Pieterse (2014c: 85); Steinberg (2006: 272, 275); Young (2010: 390).
45 See Coggin and Pieterse (2012: 274–276).
46 See Brand (2011: 635–636); Liebenberg (2015a: 467–468); Pieterse (2014b: 169–170); Ray (2014: 178–179); Smith and Rubin (2015: 270); Van der Berg (2013: 377, 380, 383, 385–386, 392–393); Wilson (2011: 149); Woolman (2013: 326–327, 440–441, 462); Young (2010: 399–401).
47 See Liebenberg (2010: 422–423; 2015a: 468–469); Ray (2014: 186); Van der Berg (2013: 377, 380–381); Wilson *et al.* (2015: 502–503).
48 See Bilchitz (2010: 56–58); Pieterse (2012: 362–363).
49 *Mazibuko* v. *City of Johannesburg* (2010: para 160). See also para 161.
50 Wilson and Dugard (2011: 665, 670–672). See also Brand (2011: 623–625, 628–633); Brown (2015: 135); Dugard (2014: 273); Liebenberg (2015b: 418); Ray (2014: 177, 181, 193, 201–208); Wilson (2011: 128–130).
51 Young (2014: 239). See also pp. 235–238 as well as Young (2010: 387–412).

52 Young (2010: 412). See also Ray (2014: 176–177); Smith and Rubin (2015: 251); Van der Berg (2013: 382); Woolman (2013: 269, 271).

53 See Benit-Gbaffou (2008: 6–8); Brown (2015: 18–19); Goebel (2015: 156–157); Matlala and Benit-Gbaffou (2015: 45–46).

54 See Smith and Rubin (2015: 261); Von Schnitzler (2008: 904, 913–914). Another example from Johannesburg is the Thembelihle 'service delivery' protests alluded to in Chapter 3, note 46, which were at least partly fanned by the fact that the disgruntled citizens' preferred candidate in the 2011 local government elections lost by a significant margin. See Brown (2015: 99–100).

55 Young (1990: 227).

56 See Charlton (2010: 2–3; 2014: 188–189); Pieterse (2014a: 190).

57 Also argued by Steinberg (2006: 272, 275). See further Dixon (2007: 400–402, 411–414); Van der Berg (2013: 380).

58 See Parnell and Pieterse (2010: 157).

59 Ray (2014: 177) warns against assuming this too readily.

60 *Mazibuko* v. *City of Johannesburg* (2010: para 164). See also para 168, as well as Ray (2014: 188).

61 See Brand (2014: 196–198); Van Marle and De Villiers (2013: 144); Wilson (2006: 559–561).

62 See Wilson *et al.* (2015: 500).

63 See also Parnell and Pieterse (2010: 157–158).

64 See Young (2010: 416–417).

65 Roach and Budlender (2005: 327, 333, 346–351). See also Dixon (2007: 400–414).

66 *Mazibuko* v. *City of Johannesburg* (2010: para 163).

67 See Langford *et al.* (2014: 433); Ray (2014: 177–178, 190–191); Smith and Rubin (2015: 267–268); Wilson (2009: 271–272, 275, 282, 288–289).

68 See Canon (2004: 80, 85, 91–92, 95); Pieterse and Van Donk (2002: 196–97); Pieterse (2014c: 86).

69 See Parnell and Pieterse (2010: 157); Pieterse and Van Donk (2002: 196–197).

70 See Pieterse (2014c: 86); Pieterse and Van Donk (2002: 207).

71 See Canon (2004: 96); Parnell and Pieterse (2010: 157–158); Pieterse (2014c: 86–87); Pieterse and Van Donk (2002: 209–210, 219); Sunkin (2004: 48–51).

72 See McCann (1994: 138); Sunkin (2004: 51–53).

73 See for instance City of Johannesburg (2007; 2009; 2011; 2013a; 2013b; 2016).

74 See Pieterse (2014b: 162) and authorities there cited.

75 See for instance Benit-Gbaffou (2014: 7–8, 110–114, 194); Charlton (2014: 189).

76 See discussion in Chapter 3 as well as Dugard and Langford (2011: 58).

77 See Langford *et al.* (2014: 432–433); Wilson (2011: 149).

78 See *Hlope* v. *City of Johannesburg* (2013) as well as discussion in Chapter 2.

79 See Dugard (2014: 274, 279), as well as discussion in Chapter 2.

80 As argued for instance by Wilson *et al.* (2015: 484).

81 See in this regard Pieterse (2014b: 173–174).

82 Parnell and Pieterse (2010: 158).

83 See Brown (2015: 125–126); Dugard and Langford (2011: 55–57); Langford *et al.* (2014: 427, 429); Madlingozi (2014: 112).

84 See Brown (2015: 135); Langford *et al.* (2014: 436); Smith and Rubin (2015: 273–274). On the general impact of legal processes on movements at different levels, see McCann (1994: 82–84).

85 See Gloppen (2005: 163).

86 See generally Wilson (2009; 2011).

87 See Sinwell (2010: 167–168).

88 On this latter effect, see Wilson (2011: 143–144).

89 See Dugard and Langford (2011: 55–58); Madlingozi (2014: 112–113); Langford *et al.* (2014: 435).

90 See Wilson (2011: 130–131).
91 Langford *et al.* (2014: 440).
92 See Brown (2015: 128); McCann (1994: 89–90); Smith and Rubin (2015: 270).
93 See Brown (2015: 139–140).
94 *Residents of Joe Slovo Community, Western Cape* v. *Thubelisha Homes* (2010: para 408). See also Pieterse (2012: 374–375).
95 On authorities' depiction of protest as an instance of 'bad' citizenship, see Brown (2015: 74). See also Roithmayr (2010: 327) (arguing that a commitment to the legal process in resolving citizenship disputes ties the hands of social movements and activists and restricts many of the most effective modes of engagement at their disposal).
96 See Bilchitz (2010: 57–59); Dugard and Langford (2011: 51–52); Pieterse (2012: 375–377; 2014b: 152); Von Schnitzler (2008: 916).
97 Young (1990: 238).
98 See Bilchitz (2010: 59, 62, 66–69, 73–77); Woolman (2013: 271).
99 See Bilchitz (2010: 63–64); Woolman (2013: 271).
100 See also Mbazira (2013: 275).
101 McCann (1994: 304).
102 For various indicators in this respect see City of Johannesburg (2016: 1–2, 5–6). See further Van der Walt (2007: 223).
103 See also Goebel (2015: 154).

References

Albertyn, C., 2007. 'Substantive equality and transformation in South Africa', *South African Journal of Human Rights* 23(2), 253–276.

Benit-Gbaffou, C., 2008. 'Are practices of local participation sidelining the institutional participatory channels? Reflections from Johannesburg', *Transformation: Critical Perspectives on Southern Africa* 66(1), 1–33.

Benit-Gbaffou, C. (ed.), 2014. *A Political Landscape of Street Trader Organisations in Inner City Johannesburg, Post Operation Clean Sweep*. Johannesburg: Centre for Urbanism and Built Environment Studies.

Bilchitz, D., 2010. 'Citizenship and community: Exploring the right to receive basic municipal services in *Joseph*', *Constitutional Court Review* 3, 45–78.

Bilchitz, D., 2015. 'Are socio-economic rights a form of political rights?' *South African Journal of Human Rights* 31(1), 86–111.

Bonthuys, E., 2008. 'Institutional openness and resistance to feminist arguments: The example of the South African Constitutional Court', *Canadian Journal of Women & the Law* 20(1), 1–36.

Brand, D., 2003. 'The proceduralisation of South African socio-economic rights jurisprudence, or "what are socio-economic rights for?"'. In: Botha, H., Van der Walt, A. & Van der Walt, J. (eds.), *Rights and Democracy in a Transformative Constitution*, pp. 33–56. Stellenbosch: SUN Press.

Brand, D., 2011. 'Judicial deference and democracy in socio-economic rights cases in South Africa', *Stellenbosch Law Review* 22(3), 614–638.

Brand, D., 2014. 'Law and the city: Keeping the poor on the margins', *De Jure* 47(2), 189–201.

Brown, J., 2015. *South Africa's Insurgent Citizens: On Dissent and the Possibility of Politics*. Johannesburg: Jacana.

Canon, B.C., 2004. 'Studying bureaucratic implementation of judicial policies in the United States: Conceptual and methodological approaches'. In: Hertogh, M.

& Halliday, S. (eds.), *Judicial Review and Bureaucratic Impact: International and Interdisciplinary Perspectives*, pp. 76–100. Cambridge, UK: Cambridge University Press.

Charlton, S., 2010. 'Inclusion through housing: Limitations and alternatives in Johannesburg', *Urban Forum* 21(1), 1–20.

Charlton, S., 2014. 'Public housing in Johannesburg'. In: Harrison, P., Gotz, G., Todes, A., & Wray, C. (eds.), *Changing Space, Changing City: Johannesburg After Apartheid*, pp. 176–193. Wits University Press: Johannesburg.

City of Johannesburg, 2007. *Inner City Regeneration Charter.*

City of Johannesburg, 2009. *Informal Trading Policy for the City of Johannesburg.*

City of Johannesburg, 2011. *Joburg Growth and Development Strategy 2040.*

City of Johannesburg, 2013a. *Corridors of Freedom: Restitching our City to Create a New Future.*

City of Johannesburg, 2013b. *Inner City Transformation Roadmap.*

City of Johannesburg, 2016. *State of the City Address 2016 Delivered by the Executive Mayor, Cllr Mpho Parks Tau.*

City of Johannesburg Metropolitan Municipality v. *Blue Moonlight Properties*, 2012. Decision by the South African Constitutional Court, reported as 2012 (2) SA 104 (CC).

Coggin, T. & Pieterse, M., 2012. 'Rights and the city: An exploration of the interaction between socio-economic rights and the city', *Urban Forum* 23(3), 257–278.

De Vos, P., 2008. 'From heteronormativity to full sexual citizenship?: Equality and sexual freedom in Laurie Ackermann's constitutional jurisprudence'. In: Barnard-Naude A.J., Cornell, D. & Du Bois, F. (eds.), *Dignity, Freedom and the Post-Apartheid Legal Order: The Critical Jurisprudence of Laurie Ackermann*, pp. 254–272. Cape Town: Juta.

Dixon, R., 2007. 'Creating dialogue about socio-economic rights: Strong-form versus weak-form judicial review revisited', *International Journal of Constitutional Law* 5(3), 391–418.

Dugard, J., 2014. 'Beyond *Blue Moonlight*: The implications of judicial avoidance in relation to the provision of alternative housing', *Constitutional Court Review* 5, 265–279.

Dugard, J. & Langford, M., 2011. 'Art or science? Synthesising lessons from public interest litigation and the dangers of legal determinism', *South African Journal of Human Rights* 27(1), 39–64.

Glaser, D., 2015. 'Uncooperative masses as a problem for substantive and participatory theories of democracy: The cases of "people's power" (1984–6) and the "xenophobia" (2008) in South Africa'. In: Benit-Gbaffou, C. (ed.), *Popular Politics in South African Cities: Unpacking Community Participation*, pp. 139–170. Cape Town: HSRC Press.

Gloppen, S., 2005. 'Social rights litigation as transformation: South African perspectives'. In: Jones, P. & Stokke, K. (eds.), *Democratizing Development: The Politics of Socio-economic Rights in South Africa*, pp. 153–180. Leiden: Martinus Nijhoff.

Goebel, A., 2015. *On Their Own: Women, Urbanization and the Right to the City in South Africa.* Montreal: McGill-Queens University Press.

Government of the RSA v. *Grootboom*, 2001. Decision of the South African Constitutional Court, reported as 2001 (1) SA 46 (CC).

Hlope v. *City of Johannesburg*. Decision by the South Gauteng High Court, reported as 2013 (4) SA 212 (GSJ).

Holston, J., 2009. 'Insurgent citizenship in an era of global urban peripheries', *City & Society* 21(2), 245–267.

Joseph v. *City of Johannesburg*, 2010. Decision of the South African Constitutional Court, reported as 2010 (4) SA 55 (CC).

Langford, M., Dugard, J., Madlingozi, T. & Cousins, B., 2014. 'Concluding perspectives'. In: Langford, M., Cousins, B., Dugard, J. & Madlingozi, T. (eds.), *Socio-economic Rights in South Africa: Symbols or Substance?*, pp. 421–458. Cambridge, UK: Cambridge University Press.

Liebenberg, S., 2006. 'Needs, rights and transformation: Adjudicating social rights', *Stellenbosch Law Review* 17(1), 5–36.

Liebenberg, S., 2010. *Socio-economic Rights Adjudication under a Transformative Constitution.* Cape Town: Juta.

Liebenberg, S., 2015a. 'Social rights and transformation in South Africa: Three frames', *South African Journal of Human Rights* 31(3), 446–471.

Liebenberg, S., 2015b. 'Toward an equality-promoting interpretation of socio-economic rights in South Africa: Insights from the egalitarian liberal tradition', *South African Law Journal* 132(2), 411–437.

Madlingozi, T., 2014. 'Post-apartheid social movements and legal mobilisation'. In: Langford, M., Cousins, B., Dugard, J. & Madlingozi, T. (eds.), *Socio-economic Rights in South Africa: Symbols or Substance?*, pp. 92–130. Cambridge, UK: Cambridge University Press.

Maphango v. *Aengus Lifestyle Properties*, 2012. Decision of the South African Constitutional Court, reported as 2012 (5) BCLR 449 (CC).

Matlala, B. & Benit-Gbaffou, C., 2015. 'Against ourselves – local activists and the management of contradictory political loyalties: The case of Phiri, Johannesburg'. In: Benit-Gbaffou, C. (ed.), *Popular Politics in South African Cities: Unpacking Community Participation*, pp. 42–69. Cape Town: HSRC Press.

Mazibuko v. *City of Johannesburg*, 2010. Decision of the South African Constitutional Court, reported as 2010 (4) SA 1 (CC).

Mbazira, C., 2013. 'Service delivery protests, struggle for rights and the failure of local democracy in South Africa and Uganda: Parallels and divergences', *South African Journal of Human Rights* 29(2), 251–275.

McCann, M.W., 1994. *Rights at Work: Pay Equity Reform and the Politics of Legal Mobilization.* Chicago, London: University of Chicago Press.

Mkontwana v. *Nelson Mandela Metropolitan Municipality*, 2005. Decision of the South African Constitutional Court, reported as 2005 (1) SA 530 (CC).

Occupiers of 51 Olivia Road, Berea Township v. *City of Johannesburg*, 2008. Decision of the South African Constitutional Court, reported as 2008 (3) SA 208 (CC).

Parnell, S. & Pieterse, E., 2010. 'The "right to the city": Institutional imperatives of a developmental state', *International Journal of Urban & Regional Research* 34(1), 146–163.

Pieterse, E. & Van Donk, M., 2002. 'Incomplete ruptures: The political economy of realising socio-economic rights in South Africa', *Law, Democracy & Development* 6(2), 193–229.

Pieterse, M., 2004. 'Coming to terms with judicial enforcement of socio-economic rights', *South African Journal of Human Rights* 20(3), 383–417.

Pieterse, M., 2007a. 'The legitimizing/insulating effect of socio-economic rights', *Canadian Journal of Law & Society* 22(1), 1–20.

Pieterse, M., 2007b. 'Eating socio-economic rights: The usefulness of rights talk in alleviating social hardship revisited', *Human Rights Quarterly* 29(3), 796–822.

Pieterse, M., 2008. 'Finding for the applicant? Individual equality plaintiffs and group-based disadvantage', *South African Journal of Human Rights* 24(3), 397–424.

Pieterse, M., 2012. 'Procedural relief, constitutional citizenship and socio-economic rights as legitimate expectations', *South African Journal of Human Rights*, 28(3), 359–379.

Pieterse, M., 2014a. 'The right to the city and the urban environment: Re-imagining section 24 of the 1996 Constitution', *South African Public Law* 29(1), 175–193.

Pieterse, M., 2014b. 'Development, the right to the city and the legal and constitutional responsibilities of local government in South Africa', *South African Law Journal* 131(1), 149–177.

Pieterse, M., 2014c. *Can Rights Cure? The Impact of Human Rights Litigation on South Africa's Health System*. Pretoria: PULP.

Port Elizabeth Municipality v. *Various Occupiers*, 2004. Decision of the South African Constitutional Court, reported as 2005 (1) SA 217 (CC).

Purcell, M., 2002. 'Excavating Lefebvre: The right to the city and its urban politics of the inhabitant', *GeoJournal* 58, 99–108.

Rademan v. *Moqhaka Local Municipality*, 2013. Decision of the South African Constitutional Court, reported as 2013 (4) SA 225 (CC).

Ray, B., 2014. 'Evictions, aspirations and avoidance', *Constitutional Court Review* 5, 173–232.

Residents of Joe Slovo Community, Western Cape v. *Thubelisha Homes*, 2010. Decision of the South African Constitutional Court, reported as 2010 (3) SA 454 (CC).

Roach, K. & Budlender, G., 2005. 'Mandatory relief and supervisory jurisdiction: When is it appropriate, just and equitable?' *South African Law Journal* 122(2), 325–351.

Roithmayr, D., 2010. 'Lessons from *Mazibuko*: Persistent inequality and the commons', *Constitutional Court Review* 3, 317–346.

Rosa, S., 2011. 'Transformative constitutionalism in a democratic developmental state', *Stellenbosch Law Review* 22(3), 542–565.

Sea Front for All v. *MEC, Environmental and Development Planning, Western Cape*, 2011. Decision of the Cape High Court, reported as 2011 (3) SA 55 (WCC).

Sinwell, L., 2010. 'The Wynberg concerned residents' disempowering court victory', *Urban Forum* 21(2), 153–169.

Smith, L. & Rubin, M., 2015. 'Beyond invented and invited spaces of participation: The Phiri and Olivia Road court cases and their outcome'. In: Benit-Gbaffou, C. (ed.), *Popular Politics in South African Cities: Unpacking Community Participation*, pp. 248–281. Cape Town: HSRC Press.

South African Informal Traders Forum v. *City of Johannesburg*, 2014. Decision of the South African Constitutional Court, reported as 2014 (4) SA 371 (CC).

South African Transport and Allied Workers Union v. *Garvas*, 2013. Decision of the Constitutional Court of South Africa, reported as 2013 (1) SA 83 (CC).

Steinberg, C., 2006. 'Can reasonableness protect the poor? A review of South Africa's socio-economic rights jurisprudence', *South African Law Journal* 123(2), 264–284.

Strydom, J. & Viljoen, S., 2014. 'Unlawful occupation of inner-city buildings: A constitutional analysis of the rights and obligations involved', *Potchefstroom Electronic Law Journal* 17(4), 1207–1261.

Sunkin, M., 2004. 'Conceptual issues in researching the impact of judicial review on government bureaucracies'. In: Hertogh, M. & Halliday, S. (eds.), *Judicial Review and Bureaucratic Impact: International and Interdisciplinary Perspectives*, pp. 43–75. Cambridge: Cambridge University Press.

SWEAT v. *Minister of Safety and Security*, 2009. Decision by the Western Cape High Court, Cape Town, reported as 2009 (2) SACR 417 (WCC).

Van der Berg, S., 2013. 'Meaningful engagement: Proceduralising socio-economic rights further or infusing administrative law with substance?', *South African Journal of Human Rights* 29(2), 376–398.

Van der Walt, J., 2007. 'Johannesburg: A tale of two cases'. In: Philippopoulos-Mihalopoulos, A. (ed.), *Law and the City*, pp. 221–236. Oxford, New York: Routledge.

Van Marle, K. & De Villiers, I., 2013. 'Law and resistance in the city of Pretoria: Space, history and the everyday', *Australian Feminist Law Journal* 38(1), 129–145.

Victoria & Alfred Waterfront v. *Police Commissioner, Western Cape*, 2004. Decision of the Cape High Court, reported as 2004 (4) SA 444 (C).

Von Schnitzler, A., 2008. 'Citizenship prepaid: Water, calculability, and techno-politics in South Africa', *Journal of Southern African Studies* 34(4), 899–917.

West, R., 2001. 'Rights, capabilities, and the good society', *Fordham Law Review* 69(5), 1901–1932.

Williams, L.A., 2010. 'The role of courts in the quantitative implementation of social and economic rights: A comparative study'. *Constitutional Court Review* 3, 141–199.

Wilson, S., 2006. 'Judicial enforcement of the right to protection from arbitrary eviction: Lessons from Mandelaville', *South African Journal of Human Rights* 2(4), 535–562.

Wilson, S., 2009. 'Breaking the tie: Evictions from private land, homelessness and a new normality'. *South African Law Journal* 126(2), 270–290.

Wilson, S., 2011. 'Litigating housing rights in Johannesburg's inner city: 2004–2008', *South African Journal of Human Rights* 27(1), 127–151.

Wilson, S. & Dugard, J., 2011. 'Taking poverty seriously: The South African Constitutional Court and socio-economic rights', *Stellenbosch Law Review* 22(3), 664–682.

Wilson, S., Dugard, J. & Clark, M., 2015. 'Conflict management in an era of urbanisation: 20 years of housing rights jurisprudence in the South African Constitutional Court', *South African Journal of Human Rights* 31(3), 472–503.

Woolman, S., 2013. *The Selfless Constitution: Experimentalism and Flourishing as Foundations of South Africa's Basic Law*. Cape Town: Juta.

Young, I.M., 1990. *Justice and the Politics of Difference*. Princeton: Princeton University Press.

Young, K.G., 2010. 'A typology of economic and social rights adjudication: Exploring the catalytic function of judicial review', *International Journal of Constitutional Law* 8(3), 385–420.

Young, K.G., 2014. 'The avoidance of substance in constitutional rights', *Constitutional Court Review* 5, 233–243.

Index

For Product Safety Concerns and Information please contact our EU
representative GPSR@taylorandfrancis.com
Taylor & Francis Verlag GmbH, Kaufingerstraße 24, 80331 München, Germany

www.ingramcontent.com/pod-product-compliance
Ingram Content Group UK Ltd.
Pitfield, Milton Keynes, MK11 3LW, UK
UKHW011002180926
475701UK00004B/513

* 9 7 8 0 3 6 7 8 8 8 6 5 7 *